MW00701005

PRAISE FOR SARA AHMED

PRAISE FOR *WHAT'S THE USE?*

"In this close reading of *use*, Sara Ahmed leads the reader from object to object at a pace that moves with the deliberateness of a philosopher and the grace of a literary scholar. With this and other books, Ahmed has established herself as one of the most important feminist thinkers in the world."—ROSEMARIE GARLAND-THOMSON, author of *Staring: How We Look*

"A well-written, engaging text. Highly recommended. All readership levels."—C. R. McCALL, *Choice*

"As with many of Ahmed's writings, *What's the Use?*, with feminist solidarity radiating from its pages filled with her characteristic rhetorical and language-repurposing writing, will allow readers to question and contest their lived realities and surroundings. . . . Ahmed leaves another landmark impression on intersectional feminist thinking, praxis, and pedagogy, and develops new modes for examining the co-constitution of spaces, bodies, and social relations that will animate feminist and queer geographical study."—JAMES D. TODD, *Gender, Place and Culture*

"Ahmed sought to write a text that intervenes in the everyday, that elevates a threadbare backpack to a place of unbound theoretical play. And she has done so. . . . Accessible and innovative, *What's the Use?* will be of serious interest to activists, artists, and academics working at the intersections of queer and critical race studies."—CAITLIN MACKENZIE, *QED*

PRAISE FOR *LIVING A FEMINIST LIFE*

"From the moment I received Sara Ahmed's new work, *Living a Feminist Life*, I couldn't put it down. It's such a brilliant, witty, visionary new way to think about feminist theory. Everyone should read this book. It offers amazing new ways of knowing and talking about feminist theory and practice. And, it is also delightful, funny, and as the song says, 'your love has lifted me higher.' Ahmed lifts us higher."—BELL HOOKS

"Beautifully written and persuasively argued, *Living a Feminist Life* is not just an instant classic, but an essential read for intersectional feminists."—ANN A. HAMILTON, *Bitch*

"Anyone at odds with this world—and we all ought to be—owes it to themselves, and to the goal of a better tomorrow, to read this book."—MARIAM RAHMANI, *Los Angeles Review of Books*

"*Living a Feminist Life* is perhaps the most accessible and important of Ahmed's works to date. . . . [A] quite dazzlingly lively, angry and urgent call to arms. . . . In short, everybody should read Ahmed's book precisely because not everybody will."—EMMA REES, *Times Higher Education*

"Fans of bell hooks and Audre Lorde will find Ahmed's frequent homages and references familiar and assuring in a work that goes far beyond Betty Friedan's *The Feminine Mystique*, capturing the intersection so critical in modern feminism."
—ABBY HARGREAVES, *Library Journal*

"*Living a Feminist Life* offers something halfway between the immediacy and punch of the blog and the multi-layered considerations of a scholarly essay; the result is one of the most politically engaged, complex and personal books on gender politics we have seen in a while."—BIDISHA, *Times Literary Supplement*

"*Living a Feminist Life* hopes we can survive doing feminist theory, and energizes us to do so."—CLARE CROFT, *Feminist Theory*

"Undeniably, Ahmed's book is a highly crafted work, both scholarly and lyrically, that builds upon itself and delivers concrete, adaptable conclusions; it is a gorgeous argument, crackling with kind wit and an invitation to the community of feminist killjoys."—THEODOSIA HENNEY, *Lambda Literary Review*

"Ahmed gifts us words that we may have difficulty finding for ourselves. . . . [R]eading her book provides a tentative vision for a feminist ethics for radical politics that is applicable far beyond what is traditionally considered the domain of feminism."—MAHVISH AHMAD, *New Inquiry*

PRAISE FOR *ON BEING INCLUDED*

"Just when you think everything that could possibly be said about diversity in higher education has been said, Sara Ahmed comes along with this startlingly original, deeply engaging ethnography of diversity work. *On Being Included* is an insightful, smart reflection on the embodied, profoundly political phenomenology of doing and performing diversity in predominantly white institutions. As Ahmed queers even the most mundane formulations of diversity, she creates one eureka moment after another. I could not put this book down. It is a must-read for everyone committed to antiracist, feminist work as key to institutional transformation in higher education."—CHANDRA TALPADE MOHANTY, author of *Feminism without Borders: Decolonizing Theory, Practicing Solidarity*

"This book offers a grounded and open exploration of what it means to 'do' diversity, to 'be' diverse. It challenges the reader, both in style and in content, to reconsider relations of power that stick to the multiple practices, meanings, and understandings of diversity, and to reconsider how we engage, reproduce, and disrupt these relations."—JULIANE COLLARD AND CAROLYN PROUSE, *Gender, Place and Culture*

PRAISE FOR *WILLFUL SUBJECTS*

"Like her other works known for their originality, sharpness, and reach, Ahmed offers here a vibrant, surprising, and philosophically rich analysis of cultural politics, drawing on feminist, queer, and antiracist uses of willing and willfulness to explain forms of sustained and adamant social disagreement as a constitutive part of any radical ethics and politics worth its name."—JUDITH BUTLER, Maxine Elliot Professor of Comparative Literature, University of California, Berkeley

"Ahmed's insights, as always, are both intellectually fertile and provocative; *Willful Subjects* will not disappoint."—MARGRIT SHILDRICK, *Signs*

"There is no one else writing in contemporary cultural theory who is able to take hold of a single concept with such a firm and sure grasp and follow it along an idiosyncratic path in such surprising and illuminating ways."—GAYLE SALAMON, author of *Assuming a Body: Transgender and Rhetorics of Materiality*

PRAISE FOR *THE PROMISE OF HAPPINESS*

"Ahmed's language is a joy, and her work on each case study is filled with insight and rigor as she doggedly traces the social networks of dominance concealed and congealed around happiness. . . . *The Promise of Happiness* is an important intervention in affect studies that crucially approaches one of the major assumptions guiding social life: the assumption that we need to be happy."—SEAN GRATTAN, *Social Text*

"*The Promise of Happiness* bridges philosophy and cultural studies, phenomenology and feminist thought—providing a fresh and incisive approach to some of the most urgent contemporary feminist issues. Ahmed navigates this bridge with a voice both clear and warm to convey ideas that are as complex as they are intimate and accessible. Her treatment of affect as a phenomenological project provides feminist theorists a way out of mind-body divides without reverting to essentialisms, enabling Ahmed to attend to intersectional and global power relations with acuity and originality."—AIMEE CARRILLO ROWE, *Signs*

PRAISE FOR *QUEER PHENOMENOLOGY*

"Ahmed's most valuable contribution in *Queer Phenomenology* is her reorienting of the language of queer theory. The phenomenological understanding of orientation and its attendant geometric metaphors usefully reframes queer discourse, showing disorientation as a moment not of desperation but of radical possibility, of getting it twisted in a productive and revolutionary way."—ZACHARY LAMM, GLQ

"In this dazzling new book, Sara Ahmed has begun a much needed dialogue between queer studies and phenomenology. Focusing on the directionality, spatiality, and inclination of desires in time and space, Ahmed explains the straightness of heterosexuality and the digressions made by those queer desires that incline away from the norm, and, in her chapter on racialization, she puts the orient back into orientation. Ahmed's book has no telos, no moral purpose for queer life, but what it brings to the table instead is an original and inspiring meditation on the necessarily disorienting, disconcerting, and disjointed experience of queerness."—JACK HALBERSTAM, author of *Female Masculinity*

COMPLAINT!

COMP
SARA

LAINT!

AHMED

Duke University Press
Durham and London 2021

© 2021 Duke University Press
All rights reserved

Designed by Aimee C. Harrison
Typeset in Minion Pro and ITC Franklin Gothic
by Westchester Publishing Services

Library of Congress Cataloging-in-Publication Data
Names: Ahmed, Sara, [date] author.
Title: Complaint! / Sara Ahmed.
Description: Durham : Duke University Press, 2021. | Includes
bibliographical references and index.
Identifiers: LCCN 2021012492 (print)
LCCN 2021012493 (ebook)
ISBN 9781478015093 (hardcover)
ISBN 9781478017714 (paperback)
ISBN 9781478022336 (ebook)
Subjects: LCSH: Sexual harassment in universities and colleges. |
Sexual harassment in universities and colleges—Prevention. | Sexual
harassment in education. | Bullying in the workplace. | Harassment. |
Abuse of administrative power. | Corporate culture—Moral and
ethical aspects. | BISAC: SOCIAL SCIENCE / Women's Studies |
EDUCATION / Higher
Classification: LCC LC212.86 .A364 2021 (print) | LCC LC212.86
(ebook) | DDC 371.7/86—dc23
LC record available at https://lccn.loc.gov/2021012492
LC ebook record available at https://lccn.loc.gov/2021012493

Cover art: Rachel Whiteread, *Double-Doors II (A + B)*, 2006/2007.
Plasticized plaster with interior aluminum framework; two panels:
A (white): 78¹¹⁄₁₆ × 32¹¹⁄₁₆ × 7½ inches (200 × 83 × 19 cm); B (light
gray glazed): 78 × 30¹¹⁄₁₆ × 4¹¹⁄₁₆ inches (198 × 78 × 12 cm). © Rachel
Whiteread; courtesy of the artist, Luhring Augustine, New York,
and Gagosian Gallery.

CONTENTS

ACKNOWLEDGMENTS

To go through a complaint can be a difficult experience not just for those who make them but for those who share lives with those who make them. My love and appreciation to everyone who helped me get through the work of complaint, and to research that work, including my partner, Sarah Franklin; our companions Poppy and Bluebell; and friends, colleagues, and co-complainers, especially Rumana Begum, Sirma Bilge, Fiona Nicoll, Heidi Mirza, and Elaine Swan. Thanks to Audre Lorde, whose work keeps inspiring me to turn toward what is difficult. To everyone who helped me with this research by providing offices, lending ears, or giving a home to my words—that's you, Duke University Press—I am truly grateful.

To our complaint collective, Alice Corble, Heidi Hasbrouck, Chryssa Sdrolia, Tiffany Page, Leila Whitley, and others: thank you for the work you began and the work you enabled. This book comes out of our many dialogues and is shaped by our shared struggles. And thank you for your moving and profound "collective conclusions."

My thanks and appreciation to everyone who shared their experiences of complaint with me, whether by giving oral or written testimonies or through informal communications. What you have given us, the description, the insight, the wisdom, is precious. It has been a privilege to bring your words to the world.

I completed this book during the coronavirus pandemic, a time that has brought home the abject cruelty and harshness of inequalities. It is also a time that has taught us that, when necessary, we can organize worlds in other ways. It should not take a global pandemic to learn that lesson. It is my hope this book can contribute to discussions of how to open universities up, to dismantle existing structures, to build alternative futures.

To make the kinds of complaints I discuss in this book, complaints that name and identify abuses of power, that confront hierarchies and inequalities, is very risky. My thanks to all who have risked so much and given so much by complaining for a more just and equal world. This book is for you.

Acknowledgments

HEARING COMPLAINT

To be heard as complaining is not to be heard. To hear someone as complaining is an effective way of dismissing someone. You do not have to listen to the content of what she is saying if she is *just* complaining or *always* complaining. Consider how many self-help books teach you how not to complain or how to stop complaining. Titles are telling: *No Complaints: How to Stop Sabotaging Your Own Joy*; *A Complaint Free World: How to Stop Complaining and Start Enjoying the Life You Always Wanted*; *Stop Complaining: Adjust Your Mind-Set and Live a Happier Life*. Instructions to stop complaining are messages about complaint. The message received: to complain is not only to be negative; it is to be stuck on being negative. To complain is how you would stop yourself from being happy, to stop others from being happy too, complaint as a killjoy genre.

Who is heard as complaining? A hearing can be a judgment. A hearing can be a history. We can turn to the archives of Black feminism to hear how that judgment has a history. In one instance, Lorene Cary (1991), a working-class African American woman, is writing about her mother: "I always saw it coming. Some white department-store manager would look at my mother and see no more than a modestly dressed young black woman making a tiresome complaint. He'd use that tone of voice they used when they had *important* work elsewhere. Uh-oh. Then he'd dismiss her with his eyes. I'd feel her body stiffen next to me and I'd know that he'd set her off" (58). Cary "always saw it coming." She has come to know her mother's reactions; she can feel them as they happen. Earlier she describes how her mother had "studied" the "rich white people" she'd worked for, as her mother's mother had done before, and how Cary "studied" her mother (57). To study her mother is to learn what sets her off, the "rich white people," store managers, employers, who dismiss her as a "modestly dressed young black woman making a tiresome complaint." Cary can hear and see it herself: the "tone of voice they used," how he would "dismiss her with his eyes." She can also hear her mother hear it, see her mother see it. Cary shows how Black feminist knowledge can be passed down as intimacy with bodily reactions.

To be heard as making a tiresome complaint is to be heard as being tiresome, as distracting somebody from doing "*important* work elsewhere." In that moment, it is history we hear, a history of how Black women are heard as just complaining, history as going on, history as going on about it. This story is not just about how her mother as a Black woman is heard as making "a tiresome complaint." It is a story of how her mother reacts, how her body stiffens; how she is set off. Her mother refuses the message: this is not important, you are not important, what is important is elsewhere. Those deemed tiresome complainers have something to teach us about complaint, to teach us about the politics of how some are received, to teach us what it takes to refuse a message about who is important, what is important.

What it takes, who it takes. I found Cary's memoir because it was referenced in Patricia Hill Collins's ([1990] 2000) classic text *Black Feminist Thought*. Collins draws upon Cary's description to show how emergent Black women went about "surviving the everyday disrespect and outright assaults that accompany controlling images" (96). Citation too can be hearing. We depend upon what others can hear. Collins could hear what Cary's mother could hear because of what Cary could hear her mother hear. Collins uses that hearing to show what Black women know about "controlling images" in the strategies they develop to survive them.

A complaint: how you show what you know. Later in the text, Collins evokes the figure of the complainer. With reference to the problem of color blindness, how racism is often reproduced by not being seen, she observes, "Black women who make claims of discrimination and who demand that policies and procedures may not be as fair as they seem can more easily be dismissed as complainers who want special, unearned favors" (279). Racism as such can be dismissed as a complaint.

There is history to *that* dismissal. A history can be made up of many instances. In another instance, Amrit Wilson ([1976] 2000) discusses a report written by Hamida Kazi in the feminist magazine *Spare Rib* in

1976.[1] The story is about an Asian woman who is assaulted by her husband. Wilson offers a subtle account of how such stories are framed by the media and delivered to a wider public. She writes, "When such stories are reported they are used to show how Asians are 'uncivilised,' and that they should be setting their community in order instead of complaining about racism" (188). This is a rather light use of the word *complaining*; it might not seem worth singling it out. Uses can be light when words are heavy. *Complaining, complaint, complainer*: we can be weighed down by words as well as judgments. We learn from a single sentence that to speak about racism is to be heard not only as complaining but as complaining about the wrong thing, to make racism a complaint as how some avoid addressing problems in their own community. Racism becomes that tiresome complaint, how some tire themselves out or tire others out, stopping themselves from doing what they should be doing ("setting their community in order").

The judgment of complaint can also be an order: to stop complaining as a demand to set things right. Wilson shows that a story used for racist purposes (evidence of Asians being "uncivilized") can be the same story used to dismiss racism as complaint. Racism is often enacted by the dismissal of racism as complaint. Stories about violence against Asian women are instrumentalized to demand allegiance to a national project. Allegiance would be enacted by being willing to locate the problem of violence in your community rather than in the nation; the latter violence we often summarize as racism. You can become a complainer because of where you locate the problem. To become a complainer is to become the location of a problem. Wilson, by hearing how Asian women activists are "answering back," to reference the title of her piece, teaches us how some are willing to become complainers, to locate a problem, to become the location of a problem.

A FEMINIST EAR

It was important to me to open this book with how complaints are not heard or how we are not heard when we are heard as complaining. My aim in the book is to counter this history by giving complaint a hearing, by giving room to complaint, by listening to complaint. A history can become routine; a history can be how those who complain are dismissed, rendered incredible. I think of my method in this project as being about hearing, lending my ear or becoming a feminist ear. I first introduced the idea of a feminist ear in my book *Living a Feminist Life* (2017). I was describing a scene from the feminist film *A Question of Silence* (directed by Marleen Gorris, 1982). In the scene, a secretary is seated at a table. She makes a suggestion. The men at the table say nothing. It is as if she has not said anything. A man at the table then makes the same suggestion. They rush to congratulate him on his good idea.

She sits there silently. A question of silence: she can hear how she was not heard; she knows how and why she is passed over. She is just a secretary; she is the only woman seated at a table of men: she is not supposed to have ideas of her own; she is supposed to write down their ideas.[2] To hear with a feminist ear is to hear who is not heard, how we are not heard. If we are taught to tune out some people, then a feminist ear is an achievement. We become attuned to those who are tuned out, and we can be those, which means becoming attuned to ourselves can also be an achievement. We learn from who is not heard about who is deemed important or who is doing "important work," to return to the sharpness of Cary's Black feminist insights. We learn how only some ideas are heard if they are deemed to come from the right people; right can be white. What would you say or do if you were the one being passed over? What would you say or do if your ideas were heard as originating with another person? Would you complain? Would you say something, express something? The question of complaint is intimately bound up with the question of hearing, of how we express ourselves given what or who is passed over.

To hear complaint is to become attuned to the different forms of its expression. We can pause here and consider the different meanings of complaint. A complaint can be an expression of grief, pain, or dissatisfaction, something that is a cause of a protest or outcry, a bodily ailment, or a formal allegation.[3] In researching complaint, I began with the latter sense of complaint. But as I will show throughout this book, the latter sense of complaint as formal allegation brings up other, more affective and embodied senses. It was a feminist ear that led me here; it was what I could hear in complaint or from complaint that led me to the project. I was inspired to do this project after taking part in a series of inquiries into sexual harassment and sexual misconduct that had been prompted by a collective complaint lodged by students. Another way of saying this: the project was inspired by students. If my task in this book is to hear complaints, to listen to them, to work through them and with them, the book is a continuation of a task I began with students.

Where we hear complaint matters; when we hear complaint matters. I still remember the day I first heard from the students who had put forward a collective complaint. The students had requested a meeting. I was asked to attend as a feminist academic from a different department. The students had requested this meeting because an inquiry into sexual harassment that had taken place over the summer of that year did not find sufficient evidence, or evidence that took the right form, to take their complaint further. The students I met that day had already formed a collective to write a complaint. I learned from them how and why they had formed that collective. You too will have an opportunity to learn from and about their collective in chapter 7 of this book. I also learned there had been a number of earlier inquiries prompted by earlier complaints. I have since found out how common this is: when you are involved in a complaint, you come to hear about earlier complaints. You come to hear about what you did not know about.

I attended the meeting with the students with another academic. Before the meeting, I wrote to her to say that it had been "stressed" to me that "the institutional will is such that any formal letters of complaint will have immediate consequences." If I passed on this stress before the meeting, the students taught me to question it. By insisting that the students individually make formal written complaints, the university was asking them to give up their anonymity, to make themselves even more vulnerable than they had already made themselves. The following day I wrote to the colleague with whom I attended the meeting that if the position was that we needed formal written complaints by individuals to reopen the inquiry, then "strategically" we might need to try to "get that evidence." But we also agreed that we needed to push for a change of position. We realized our task ought not to be to persuade the students to make formal written complaints but to persuade the university to hear the complaints that had already been made.

We wrote a report giving a full account of what the students had shared with us. We quoted a legal expert who had confirmed that formal written statements should not be necessary to establish "the balance of probability" that harassment has happened, which was all that was needed, by law, to establish. We concluded the report by stating that those who have been harassed "should not be made responsible for redressing it." Listening to the students, we had realized just how much work, time, and energy they had already given to identifying and documenting the problem. As I will explore throughout this book, making a complaint is never completed by a single action: it often requires you do more and more work. It is exhausting, especially given that what you complain about is already exhausting.

The report we wrote up after the meeting led to further communications between academics and administrators, to the reopening of the inquiry, and then to further inquiries. We can identify a problem in this sequence of events. For the students' complaint to be heard, or for the complaint to be heard with a stronger commitment to action, it had to be written up by academics. Complaints, it seems, go further the extent to which those positioned higher up in an organization express them or give support to them. The path of a complaint, where a complaint goes, how far it goes, teaches us something about how institutions work, what I call in part I of this book *institutional mechanics*. It should *not* be the case that support from those who are more established is necessary for a complaint to be heard. But when this is the case, that support can be vital to stop a complaint process from being stalled.

To work on a complaint is often to work out how a complaint is stalled. It was given how the process had stalled that we agreed on a compromise: students could make complaints anonymously. When the requirements for the form of complaint were loosened, more students came forward to testify in the inquiries. There was nothing automatic about this process; complaints did not rush out like water from a tap that had been unblocked. It still took a conscious and collective effort by students to make complaints that would be, in their terms, "legible to the university."[4] It is not only that a complaint is not completed by a single action; you often have to keep making the same complaints in different ways before they will be heard or in order for them to be heard. Many of the students who testified in these inquiries shared their stories with me. Those stories remain their stories. I do not share their stories in this book. But I have written *Complaint!* with their stories in mind. I hear their stories alongside those I have collected for this book. To become a feminist ear is to hear complaints together.

A feminist ear can be understood as an institutional tactic. To hear complaints, you have to dismantle the barriers that stop us from hearing complaints, and by barriers, I am referring to institutional barriers, the walls, the doors that render so much of what is said, what is done, invisible and inaudible. If you have to dismantle barriers to hear complaints, hearing complaints can make you more aware of those barriers. In other words, hearing complaints can also be how you learn *how* complaints are not heard.

It takes work to hear complaints because it takes work for others to reach you. Becoming a feminist ear meant not only hearing the students' complaints; it meant sharing the work. It meant becoming part of their collective. Their collective became *ours*. I think of that *ours* as the promise of feminism, *ours* not as a possession but as an invitation, an opening, a combining of forces. We worked together to confront the institution more directly about its role in enabling and reproducing a culture of harassment. The harder it is to get through, the more you have to do. The more we tried to confront the problem of sexual harassment as an institutional problem, the more we refused to accept weak statements about what the university was committed to doing, the more we questioned how they were changing policies without communicating with anyone why we needed to change policies (chapter 1), the more resistance we encountered.

Complaint: a path of more resistance. The institution becomes what you come up against. At times it felt like we were getting somewhere. At other times the wall came down and we realized that however far they were going to go, they were not going to go far enough. We could not even get public acknowledgment from the administration that there had been any inquiries. It was as if they had never happened. To hear complaint can be to hear that silence: what is not being said, what is not being done, what is not being dealt with. It was during one of those times, walls coming down, the sound of silence can be walls coming down, that I decided I wanted to conduct research on other people's experience of complaint. My own experience of working with students on these inquiries led me to this project. So much of what you do, the labor, the struggle, happens behind closed doors: no one knows about it; no one has to know about it. My desire to do this research came from a sense of frustration, the feeling of doing so much not to get very far. *Frustration can be a feminist record*. My desire to do this research also came from my own conviction that if you ask those who complain about their experiences of complaint, you will learn so much about institutions and about power: *complaint as feminist pedagogy*.[5] Yes, frustration can be a feminist record. Another way of putting this: *Watch out, we have the data*.

The knowledge we acquire from being in a situation can sometimes require we leave a situation. What I learned about institutions from supporting a complaint led me to leave; at the time it did not feel like a choice but like what I had to do. I think back to that room where I first heard from the students. When you are involved in a complaint, you are still at work; you are still doing your work. I would keep entering that room, the same room in which we had that meeting. It was my department's meeting room, a much-used room. We would have other meetings in that room, academic meetings, papers shuffling, papers and persons being rearranged. It was the same room, but it might as well have been a different room; perhaps it was a different room. It was filled with memories, occupied by a history that felt as tangible as the walls. What you hear in the room comes to fill that room. I could not just turn up at the same old meetings, doing the same old things.

COLLECTING COMPLAINTS

I decided to undertake this research on complaint before I resigned, but I did not begin the research until over a year after.[6] That I resigned changed the nature of the research as well as how I could do it. I shared that I resigned in a post on my blog on May 30, 2016. My resignation was widely reported in the national media less than two weeks later. While I found the exposure difficult, I was moved and inspired by how many people got in touch with me to express their solidarity, rage, and care. I received messages from many different people telling me what happened to them when they had complained. I heard from others who had left their posts and professions as a result of a complaint. One story coming out can lead to more stories coming out. I realized something from what came out: by resigning from my post, I had made myself more accessible as a feminist ear. Having become a feminist ear within my own institution, I could turn my ear outward, toward others working in other institutions. I think it was because I resigned in protest about the failure of the institution to hear complaints that people entrusted me with their stories of complaint. It remains my responsibility to earn that trust.

Given that my own resignation put me in a better position to collect other people's stories of complaint, I am not just telling the story; I am part of the story. In *Living a Feminist Life* (2017), I described my resignation as a snap, a feminist snap. "Snap" can be what you say when you make the same connection. A snap can also be the sound of something breaking. So often a complaint is understood as snapping a bond, breaking ties, connections, to a university, to a department, to a project, to a colleague. One of the reasons some people do not hear about a complaint or are not willing to hear about a complaint is because of how it would threaten a bond they have to a university, a department, a project, or a colleague. Snap: when a break becomes a connection.

Also snap: how we hear what each other can hear. A feminist ear can thus be a research method as well as an institutional tactic. I could write this book because of how many people shared with me their experiences of making complaints. I could write this book because of who I came to hear. My task is to hear *about* complaints *from* those who have made them. The data comes primarily from communications with academics and students who have made or considered making formal complaints at universities (or comparable educational institutes) about unequal or unjust working conditions or abuses of power such as harassment and bullying.[7] This book is a collection of their complaints. Of course, there are other complaints, other kinds of complaints, and thus other stories to tell about complaint. In order to hear the complaints that I collect *here*, I cannot hear *all* complaints.

How did I come to collect these stories? Most people who participated in this research got in touch with me through my website or blog.[8] Not everyone who got in touch with me went on to tell me their story. Sometimes getting in touch can be telling enough. People gave different reasons for getting in touch. Some said they wanted to help or to help out. One student emailed, "I write because I went through a years-long complaints procedure that I would like to share with you if you are still in this phase of your project and/or if it might be helpful in your work." Another wrote, "Thank you so much for doing this study. In order to help out, I want to share my own experience in submitting a formal complaint to my university's reporting office after being sexually harassed by another student." Some people got in touch with me because they felt I would or could hear them. One student wrote, "And so do bear with me as I write this to you. I know you'll get it. You'll get me, and what's happened and where one might go from here." Another student wrote, "I am writing because I need a feminist ear. Perhaps you can use this complaint in your work." To become a feminist ear is to indicate you are willing to receive complaints. An academic wrote, "I want the story to go somewhere (apart from round and round in my head) which is why I am contacting you." It can be hard when our stories of complaint go round and round in our heads. It can feel like a lot of movement without getting very far. Telling someone the story of complaint can be how the story goes somewhere. To become a feminist ear is to give complaints somewhere to go.

The project gathered momentum as I began to share stories of complaint in posts, lectures, and seminars. The more you share, the more you hear. I think some people offered to tell me their stories of complaint because they could connect their own experiences with the stories I had already shared. To share a story of complaint can be to make a connection. To share a story of complaint can be to add to a collection. A postgraduate researcher wrote to me, "I am happy to share my experience for your study if you are still collecting narratives." To collect can mean to go to a place and to bring something or somebody back. To collect can also mean to bring something together from different places or periods of time. To receive complaints, to hear them, is thus also to collect them; to go there is to go back; to bring something back is to bring us together.

That most of the people whose experiences I share in this book got in touch with me has shaped the tone and texture of this work. Those who contacted me often had to pay a high price for the complaints they made; in fact, this is why some people contacted me. One former professor wrote, "I took an off-the-record grievance pay-out (not massive) and a much-reduced pension to get out of academia two years ago after an unremitting fifteen years of sexist (and disablist) bullying. I would be willing to participate in your study if you can guarantee complete confidentiality. I had to sign a gagging clause when I got my grievance pay-out, which—as I'm sure you are aware—is how universities typically try to cover up the sexism that is rampant within them." She needed me to keep her complaint confidential because of what the institution had covered up through the use of a gag clause, or an NDA (nondisclosure agreement). To cover up a complaint is to cover over what the complaint was about, in this instance, sexist and ableist bullying, the "sexism that is rampant" within universities.

You are more likely to share a story of complaint if you have been stopped from sharing that story. Another academic wrote, "I would be happy to talk about my experience of being pushed into an NDA." Many people who contacted me did so because of what they were pushed into or how they were pushed out. In other words, much of the data in this book came out of complaints that led people into direct confrontations with institutions (and by "institutions" I would include the people employed by institutions, peers and colleagues as well as administrators and managers). We do not need to assume that complaints about unequal working conditions or abuses of power necessarily lead to such confrontations to learn from those that do.

There is so much to confront in these stories. I conducted interviews with forty students, academics, researchers, and administrators who had been involved in some way in a formal complaint process, including those who did not take their complaints forward, who started the process only to withdraw from it.[9] The interviews for the project were conducted over a twenty-month period between June 2017 and January 2019. I spoke to many more people than I had originally planned. I could have spoken to many more people than I did. It was hard not to keep speaking to those who asked to speak to me, but I knew I needed to stop if I was to have any chance of doing justice to the material I had collected.[10] In addition to interviews, I received eighteen written statements. I have over the past years communicated informally with hundreds of other people by email, by phone, or in person. Some of these communications have also made their way into the book.[11] In this book I also draw on my own experiences of going through a formal complaint process. When you spend three years trying to get complaints through the system, you end up with a lot of data.

Most of the interviews were conducted by Skype. This decision was in part pragmatic: I did not have funding for this project to enable me to travel across the country. In fact, I did not apply for funding. Given that one of my main concerns was to explore how complaints can lead to confrontations with institutions in which they are made, it seemed appropriate for the project to be conducted outside the influence of institutions to the extent that was possible.[12] I want to add here that working as an independent scholar without access to institutional resources, I did not experience this situation as a lack, or only as a lack, but as an opportunity to conduct a project on my own terms and in my own way. Decisions made for pragmatic reasons, because of not having access to space, funds, or resources, often ended up being the right decisions from a research point of view as well as an ethical point of view. Let me give an example. I had asked for and was given permission to record all of these interviews.[13] I did the transcription myself as I did not have the means to employ someone else. This transcription was a time-consuming process. But I am so glad I transcribed the interviews myself as I learned so much from listening slowly and carefully to each person's words. I needed my time to be consumed; there was so much to take in. I needed to be immersed in the material.

Although most interviews were conducted by Skype, I did speak to some interviewees in person either by using their offices or rooms at the university at which they worked or by borrowing offices from friends or colleagues. In one case, I interviewed two women who were no longer based at a university in a city in which I did not know anyone who had an office I could use. We ended up meeting in a large café. Although we found a corner that was relatively private, you could hear the hustle and bustle around us, the clattering of plates, sounds of laughter; clattering, chattering. Being there together made a difference; hearing life go on can be a reminder that life goes on. In the middle of our conversation, a very intense and difficult conversation, a ladybird (or *ladybug*) landed on the table. One woman said, "Oh, look, it's a ladybird." You can hear our murmurs of appreciation on the recording; *How cute, How sweet.* Then I said, "Oh no, it's fallen on its back." Then the other woman I was interviewing said, "A person I know was recently bitten by a ladybird." I replied, "They bite? They do not look like a creature that bites." We laughed. The ladybird returned to our table at certain moments, and each time we remarked upon it with affection. I was reminded listening to the recording of their testimony how distractions can be necessary, also precious, so I am sharing the distraction with you. We can lighten the load by lightening the mood. I also learned from my in-person interviews how the room in which we conducted the interview became a talking point. I interviewed an academic in an office belonging to a colleague. When she talked about what happened to her many years ago, how she had been assaulted by a lecturer in his office, she compared the windows and doors of that office to the windows and doors of the office we were in.[14] What surrounds us in the present can become a reference point, helping us to describe something that happened in the past. I will return to how the past returns.

Most of the people I spoke to on Skype were at home. I was listening at home. That too mattered. My dog, Poppy, for instance, came into view a few times, and thus into the dialogue, rather like that ladybird, a friendly landing and a helpful distraction in the middle of the intensity of a conversation. But this question was never far from my mind: What does it mean to be at home when you tell the story? People have different relationships to home. I knew that; I sensed that. There were advantages to being at home. One time a person stopped the interview to take a break, and I realized how helpful it was for her to be able to leave the conversation quickly and easily because we were not in the same space. I will return to how I made use of her break in due course. But there are also difficulties in sharing these stories while being at home that are not unrelated to the difficulties of making a complaint. I will explore throughout the book that however much complaints happen behind closed doors, for those who make complaints it can be hard to close the door on them; complaints can follow you home.[15]

On a few occasions I spoke to people by Skype when they were at work. One time I began a conversation with someone when she was on a bus. It was a bit difficult to hear each other over the noise of the bus, so we stopped and started again when she got to work. She rang me back when she was in a room, a seminar room. And she started telling me about a very difficult meeting that took place, to use her words, "in this exact room." Being "in this exact room," the same room, it matters. You end up telling the story of complaint in the same place you made the complaint.

How we hear stories of complaint matters. How to describe what I was hearing? When I first imagined the project, I thought I would conduct semistructured interviews using similar sorts of questions that I had prepared for my earlier study of diversity. I remember arriving for my first interview with the first person who had contacted me. I had my prepared questions typed out neatly. This was an in-person interview and it was conducted at the university where she was now based. I realized very quickly, in the first minutes of that first interview, that the questions I had prepared were not going to work. Complaints tend to be too messy even for a loose series of questions. From the second interview onward, I asked people just one opening and very general question: I asked them to share the experiences that led them to consider making a complaint as well as their experiences of making a complaint if that is what they went on to make. I wanted the stories to come out, fall out, in whatever order they did. We then had time for a dialogue, a to-and-fro that was possible because I too had an experience of complaint.

Over time I came to think of the spoken words less as an interview and more as testimony.[16] A testimony can refer to an oral or written statement given in a court of law. The purpose of a testimony in such a setting is to provide evidence; testimony is used to establish what happened, the facts of the matter or the truth. Testimony is also what is required to identify an injustice, a harm, or a wrong. Shoshana Felman (1992, 3) describes "the process of testimony" as "bearing witness to a crisis or trauma." The accounts given to me had the mood of testimony, solemn statements about a crisis or trauma. Making a complaint is often necessary because of a crisis or trauma. The complaint often becomes part of the crisis or trauma. A complaint testimonial can teach us the nonexteriority of complaint to its object. In making a complaint you have already been called upon to testify, to give evidence. To testify to a complaint is to testify to testimony, or to what Felman calls "the process of testimony." To testify to complaint is a *double testimony*.[17] You are testifying to an experience of testifying although you are also testifying to more than that experience.

Testimony was thus in the accounts as well as being how they took form. And what has been so important to the process of receiving these statements as testimony is receiving them together. To hear these accounts as testimony is to hear how they combine to allow us to bear witness to an experience, to show what they reveal, to bring out what is usually hidden, given how complaints are made confidential. I too was called upon to bear witness. And that I was called upon to bear witness is to point to the many ethical dilemmas of conducting research on complaint. To testify to a complaint, to what happened that led you to complain, to what happened when you complained, is almost always to testify to a traumatic experience. I was never not conscious of this. I was aware throughout that enabling people to share painful experiences was risky and complicated. How would it affect the person testifying? Where would sharing the story leave them? How would it affect me, given that my own experience of complaint was so entangled with the trauma of having had to leave my post?[18] And what responsibility did I have to those who shared an experience of complaint not only as a researcher but as a fellow human being? Ethics requires keeping the question of ethics alive.

Most of the people I spoke to were speaking about past experiences. To speak about a past trauma can be to make that trauma present. One postdoctoral researcher began her testimony by saying, "What I remember is how it felt." A memory can be of a feeling; a memory can be a feeling. In remembering, we make the past present; we make present. [19] The past can enter the room in and with that feeling. I had, I have, an immense responsibility in creating a time and space that felt as safe as possible for each person I spoke to. It did not always feel right; I did not always get it right. An effort can be what matters, and that effort was shared. I think of the dialogues that followed each testimony as how we shared that effort by sharing reflections on what it does, how it feels to go through complaint. Going through complaint can heighten your sense of responsibility as it can heighten your sense of fragility; you are aware of how hard it can be, also how important it can be—what is hard is close to what is important—to share such shattering experiences.

Being shattered is not always a place from which we can speak. I did not talk to everyone who asked to talk to me. In some instances, people asked to talk to me in the middle of a complaint process. Mostly I explained why this would not be a good idea and offered to be in touch more informally instead. In one case I decided not to receive a testimony from someone who wanted to speak to me because I felt she needed the kind of support I could not give. I was conscious of what I could not provide: therapy or practical guidance. It was clear to me the limits of what I could do. I was an ear. That was my task. That was the point, to receive. But of course, even if reception was the point, it was not the end point. I was being called upon not only to receive stories but to share them. It was very important, then, that if complaints were given to me, I send them back out in a different form than the form in which they were given but in a way that was true to how they were given. I did not want people to share their complaints with me only for me to sit on them. I did not want to become a filing cabinet. We have too many of them already.[20]

Testimonies were given to me so that I could pass them on to you, readers, audiences, complainers. I had to find a way to pass them on in confidence. So much of the material I share in this book is confidential—many of those with whom I have communicated would fear the consequences for their lives and careers if they were recognizable from the data, whether or not they signed confidentiality or nondisclosure agreements. This book offers fragments from many different testimonies. A fragment is a sharp piece of something.[21] Each quote is a sharp piece of illumination. A complaint can be shattering; like that broken jug, we can be left in pieces. In the book I pick up these pieces not to create the illusion of some unbroken thing, but so that we can learn from the sharpness of each piece, how they fit together.

A fragment of a story, a fragment as a story. How do we tell such stories? So many of those I spoke to spoke about what it meant to share their story. It can be hard to know where to begin. It can be hard to know where to begin a story of complaint because it is hard to know when a complaint begins. Let me share the opening words from a testimony offered by a senior researcher who made a complaint about bullying and harassment:

> It is always so complex and so difficult and so upsetting still; even just knowing where to start is. And it's funny, even just starting I can feel emotion coming out, and all I want to do is I want to start crying. And I am also going to have to present a good front, professional and correct, and know I just can't let it affect me, and I am going to have to talk about this as something that is detached. And I think why I am putting so much effort into presenting something that is so much part of me.

Emotion comes out in telling the story; emotion makes it hard to tell the story. You make an effort to present something because it has become part of you, because it matters to you, to what you can do, who you can be, but how it matters makes it hard to present.

How do you pull yourself together to share an experience if an experience is of breaking apart? You talk about why you need to pull yourself together; you talk about how you pull yourself together. There are moments still, of falling apart, when something gets under your skin. The senior researcher described receiving the results of an independent investigation:

The conclusion of their report was that I participated actively in the conflict and that I monopolized the work. This word *monopolized*: I had so much rage and anger. Not only did they abandon me, but they made it my fault for monopolizing the work. And this is it: this thing, I have it inside me in my head all the time: I monopolized, monopolized, monopolized. The word stops me from doing anything, from writing something, writing a text, writing an article. What am I doing: am I monopolizing things again; how dare I even enjoy what I do now, who do I think I am, I am nothing, I am worthless, my work might be good but I am not, and I have completely internalized this in a way that is very, very, very damaging.

How we feel in a situation can be how we learn about a situation. We learn from what gets under our skin. The word *monopolized* gets under her skin; when it sticks to her, she becomes stuck, unable to write, to do her work. Words carry a charge; you can end up being made to feel that you are the problem, that the problem is you.

Words can chip at your sense of self, of your own worth. Words can carry the weight of injustices; they can transmit a history. To internalize such a history can be damaging, "very, very, very damaging." The words we use to tell the story of complaint can be the same words that get under our skin, words like *monopolized*. A Black feminist student told me that the word that got to her was *unreasonable*. There were many words that could have stuck; she was conscious they perceived her as an angry Black woman, but it was that word that got under her skin, leading her to question herself: "I am constantly questioning am I being unreasonable?" Even if the word does not fit, it can make you question whether you fit.

We can share the experience of words getting under our skin, even if the words that do that or go there are different words. An Indigenous academic who described the racism she encountered from white settler colleagues described a word used by the chair of her department: "My chair constantly uses this word, in many things that she speaks about but in particular in my annual review and other meetings, she uses this word often, *inappropriate*, her qualifier, at my interactions. It causes me to put this big lens upon myself, how I am inappropriate, what does that mean, what does she see, how is that being defined?" You can hear how you are being heard in the repetition of the word *inappropriate*. And that hearing can be a lens on how you view yourself, you can feel inappropriate, or ask yourself, "Am I being inappropriate?" or you can ask, "What does it mean to be so?" How is she defining that word? How is she defining you? In listening to those who make complaints, I am listening to how different words can get under our skin: *monopolized, unreasonable, inappropriate.*

To acquire a feminist ear is to become attuned to the sharpness of such words, how they point, to whom they point. To be heard as complaining is often to become attuned to sound, to how we sound, how we are heard as sounding, to how words sound, stories too. Many of those I spoke with conveyed a concern about how long they were taking to tell the story; I knew this because of how often people apologized for the length of time they were taking. I kept saying, "Take your time. Take the time you need to tell me what you need to tell me." Many of those I spoke with told me that they had to keep abbreviating, to keep shortening the story, because the story was always going to require more time than we could take given how much time it would take to tell the story.[22] One person used the expression "to cut a long story short" seven times in her account; there is much cutting, so much shortening, so much consciousness of length, of time, energy too.

Another person described how she went through multiple complaints by going through them with me. You make or have multiple complaints if you encounter multiple situations you need to complain about. But even if you know this, that the multiplicity is a measure of what you come up against, you can be conscious about how it sounds, how you sound: "I'd changed quite a lot between the first time and this time. I know I sound like the people who had fifteen car crashes: then this happened, then this happened. It gets to the point, I have never told this story before, like the whole story, because I know I sound like that person and I don't trust the space to sound like that person." The whole story can be a story of crashing through. There is crashing in the story, wave after wave that I can hear, that transmit something, something difficult, painful, traumatic. We might need a space to tell that story, the whole story, the story of a complaint, a space that is safe because we know how it can sound, how we can sound; you can feel that you are the car crash, a complaint as how you are crashing through life. The word *complaint* too can sound like a crash, a collision, the loud sound of something breaking into pieces. The word *complaint* derives from Old French, *complaindre*, "to lament," an expression of sorrow and grief. *Lament* is from Latin, *lamentum*, "wailing, moaning; weeping." *Complaint* seems to catch how those who challenge power become sites of negation: to complain is to become a container of negative affect, a leaky container, speaking out as spilling over.[23] We can hear something because of its intensity. The exclamation point in the title of *Complaint!* is a way of showing what I am hearing, how a complaint is heard as intensity, an emphasis, a sharp point, a sore point, a raising of the voice, a shrieking, a shattering.[24]

Negation is quite a sensation. The word *complaint* shares the same root as the word *plague*, "to strike, to lament by beating the breast."[25] Complaint can be sick speech. A body can be what is stricken. If in the book I approach the communications shared with me, oral and written, as testimonies, I also approach complaint as testimony in other ways, complaint as how we give expression to something. If a body can express a complaint, a body can be a complaint testimony. The word *express* comes from *press*; to express is to press out. I learn from the sense evolution of the word *expression*. It came to mean "to put into words" or "to speak one's mind" via the intermediary sense of how clay "under pressure takes the form of an image."[26] Expression can be the shape something takes in being pressed out. My approach to the material collected in this book is to attend to its shape, to listen to what is pressed out, what spills, what seeps, what weeps. In *Complaint!* I hear spillage as speech.

If attending to spillage can be a method, spillage can be a connection between works. I think of Alexis Pauline Gumbs's (2016) *Spill: Scenes of Black Feminist Fugitivity*, her ode to the work and wisdom of Hortense Spillers. Gumbs attends to Spillers's words with love and care, to what spills, to words that spill, to liquid that spills out from a container, to being somebody who spills things. Spillage can be a breaking, of a container, a narrative, a turning of phrases so that "doors opened and everyone came through" (xii). Spillage can be, then, the slow labor of getting out of something. A story too can be what spills, which is to say, a story can be the work of getting the story out.

COMPLAINT BIOGRAPHIES

From fragments I have already shared, you will be able to hear that to tell the story of a complaint is to reflect on what it means and how it feels to tell that story, to bring into the present time an experience that is shattering. The data is experiential. The data is theoretical. Those I am speaking with are theorizing as they are speaking to me, reflecting upon their experience. It is a profound commitment of mine to show this: making a complaint within an institution often requires reflecting upon it. Reflection can happen in the same time, the same place, as action. To make a complaint can be to experience a profound change in one's situation. That you complain is how you come to experience so much that you would not otherwise experience.

Complaint does not tend to be experienced as something that is or can be kept apart. We learn from the story of a complaint how complaint can be a way of apprehending what is around you: so much appears if you make or try to make a complaint that would not otherwise appear. This is why, in chapter 1, I describe complaint as a *phenomenology of the institution*. One lecturer talked about her experience of complaint as being able to see something: "It's like you put glasses on, and now you can see it." She emphasized that having seen the world through the lens of complaint, you cannot unsee that world: "It's a bit like if you complain you get extra vision. It is suddenly like you can see in extra violet. And you can't go back." You can't go back to the person you were before the complaint; you can't unsee what you have come to see through complaint. Putting glasses on, being able to see what is going on, to see more, is also to see what you did not see before. Complaint can also give you a capacity to explain what is happening. As she describes, "The feeling of being able to name what is happening to you is very powerful." In complaining about what is happening, you become equipped to explain what is happening. That equipment given to you by complaint, being able to name, to explain, can be "very powerful."

Making a complaint can change your sense of self, what you can do, who you can be. She likened becoming a complainer to being "the problem child": "In getting to that point, the complainer, you never shed it, it is like the problem child: having done it, you cannot go back." A complaint becomes part of you, part of who you become, that problem child, you can't shed it; you can't shed her, having done it, made it, that complaint, "you cannot go back." Perhaps it is a promise: having become a complainer, you cannot unbecome a complainer. Promises don't always feel promising. That a complaint can take over your life, become your life, even become you, can be what makes complaint so exhausting.[27] When making a complaint changes your sense of self, it changes your sense of the world.

Telling the story of a complaint can feel like telling a life story. It wasn't long into the research, in the middle of my fifth interview, that I began thinking of formal complaints as part of a much longer and more complicated story, a story of a person, a story of an institution, a story of relationships between persons and institutions. I was talking to a woman of color academic. She began with an informal complaint she made about racism and sexism in the department in which she worked. But then she talked about more: she talked about the experiences you are likely to have as a woman of color in a white patriarchal institution, all those incidents that happen, keep happening. In the middle of the interview, she asked to stop for a break. I kept the tape on and began talking into it. I talked about what I could hear in what she had been saying. It was then I first used the term *complaint biography*. If the term was mine, the inspiration for it came from her. I had begun my project on complaint by thinking of complaints as having their own biography. I had thought of myself as following complaints around, the way I had followed diversity around (Ahmed 2012). I was interested in how complaints were put together, as documents, as files, where they were sent, where they end up.

I am still interested in these questions. I will show throughout the book how complaint files matter to the complainer as records of what you have done, where you have been. But by *complaint biography* I meant something quite different. The term *complaint biography* helps us to think of the life of a complaint in relation to the life of a person or group of people. A complaint biography is not simply what happens to a complaint, a story of how a complaint comes about, where it goes, what it does, how things end up; that is, it is not simply about the institutional life (and death) of a complaint. To think of a complaint biography is to recognize that a complaint, in being lodged somewhere, starts somewhere else. A complaint might be the start of something—so much happens after a complaint is lodged, because it has been lodged—but it is never the starting point. And then what happens when you make a formal complaint (or don't make a formal complaint) affects what you might subsequently do. Some people decide not to make a complaint because of their past experiences of having made a complaint and not getting anywhere. Some people decide to make a complaint because they regretted a decision they had made not to complain before. Where a complaint goes, or what happens to a complaint, can affect whether we make them.

Decisions matter. The need to decide whether to complain is often experienced as a crisis. It is not clear what to do or what is the right thing to do. It might be you are uncertain whether what happened merits a complaint. That uncertainty is part of the story. Or it might be that you are certain what happened merits a complaint, but you are not certain that complaint is the right course of action. You might not trust the process; you might not trust the institution. A complaint biography would include those times we decide not to make complaints, not to say something or not to do something, despite an experience or because of an experience. A complaint can mean being prepared to talk about difficult and painful experiences, often over and over again, including to those with whom you have not built up a relationship of trust and those who represent an organization that is implicated in some way in what you are complaining about. The decision whether to complain is usually made in the company of others; you will most likely receive advice, suggestions, and guidance from peers as well as friends, whether welcomed or not.[28] You might decide not to complain because you cannot deal with the consequences of complaint that have been made vivid to you through warnings. You might not feel confident that your complaint will be taken seriously when your complaint is about not being taken seriously.

Those of us doing feminist work or diversity work will have our own complaint biographies. How would you give your own complaint biography? I invite each of you to ask yourselves this question as you read the stories I have collected in this book. Approaching complaint biographically is also a way of picking up on the question of how we are heard when we are heard as complaining as well as who is heard as complaining. You might be heard as making a complaint even though you don't think of yourself as making a complaint; perhaps you are asking for a more inclusive syllabus or perhaps you are asking for an accessible room. Or you might think of yourself as making a complaint—perhaps you are complaining about sexist or racist jokes—and be laughed off, as if you don't really mean it. You might even submit a formal complaint, but your action is not received as a complaint; perhaps you don't use the right form, or perhaps you don't send the form to the right person, which means that a formal complaint process is not triggered. I learned quickly that when complaint is narrowed as genre, to complain as the requirement to fill in certain forms, in a certain way, at a certain time, many problems are not recorded. To keep the focus of the project on formal complaints would have been to narrow it too much, to miss too much.[29]

Even what is narrowed at the level of form is not always contained. We learn from listening to those who do make formal complaints how hard it is to contain a complaint: a complaint becomes almost what you are *in*, a zone, a space, an environment. The formal process, the motions—sometimes complaint can feel like going through the motions—is time-consuming enough. But being in a complaint can also mean dealing with more than that, more than the motions necessary for the formal process. The difficulty of containing complaint includes the difficulty of leaving complaint behind. One student said of her experience, "It never leaves you." This book comes out of complaint; it comes out of what does not leave. It comes from talking to those whose lives became deeply entangled with the complaints they had or the complaints they made, whether formally or not.

I have told you the story of the book. I have told you about the stories in the book. It is also important for me to share how I understand this book as participating in a wider sharing of stories. The #MeToo movement, at least the one inspired by the Twitter hashtag, began after I had already started the research on complaint. As a political campaign the Me Too movement began much earlier, in 2006, organized by the Black feminist activist Tarana Burke as a "space for supporting and amplifying the voices of survivors of sexual abuse, assault and exploitation."[30] Many of those I spoke to after #MeToo went viral referred to it: sometimes as a source of inspiration for their own decision to speak to me; sometimes as what heightened their sense of vulnerability, as a reminder of the trauma and pain of complaint; sometimes as a way of reflecting on the status of their own complaint as a story. One senior researcher asked of her own testimony, "It is just another story. Another #MeToo?" It makes sense that #MeToo would become not only a reference point but a question, a question of what telling the story of a complaint can do.

This book in being *on* complaint is also *on* the university. By saying this book is *on* the university, I mean something more than that the university is my research field or site.[31] I also mean the book is about working *on* the university. I write this book out of a commitment to the project of rebuilding universities because I believe that universities, as places we can go to learn, not the only places but places that matter, universities as holders of many histories of learning, should be as open and accessible to as many as possible. In working *on* the university, I am deeply indebted to the work of Black feminists and feminists of color who have offered important critiques of how power operates within universities, including M. Jacqui Alexander, Sirma Bilge, Philomena Essed, Rosalind Hampton, Sunshine Kamaloni, Heidi Mirza, Chandra Talpade Mohanty, Kay Sian, Malinda Smith, Shirley Anne Tate, and Gloria Wekker. Their combined work has created what I think of as counterinstitutional knowledge of how universities work, for whom they work.[32] Many of these scholars have also provided strong critiques of how universities make use of the rhetoric of diversity as a way of managing differences and antagonism. This book is indebted to these critiques in part because complaints procedures function rather like diversity: when offered as solutions to problems, they are problems given new forms. So many complaints about problems within institutions are resolved in ways that reproduce the problems. So many complaints end up being complaints about how complaints are handled.

So many complaints made within institutions end up being complaints about institutions.

Counterinstitutional work in Black feminist and feminist of color hands is also often *housework*, with all the drudgery and repetition that word entails; painstaking work, administrative work, care work, and yes, *diversity work*.[33] Institutions become what we work *on* because of how they do not accommodate us. My own experiences of doing this work as a woman of color academic have thus been an important resource in researching and writing about complaint. I noted earlier that this book came out of my experience of working with students at my former university (as well as on it; there is no question, *we were on it*). I think of this work as in conversation with the work of those former students, two of whom are now academics, Tiffany Page and Leila Whitley, as well as the many other student activists I have met since beginning this research who are trying to find new ways to address old problems of sexual harassment and sexual violence at universities. As Anne McClintock (2017) describes, "Furious with administrators for protecting their institutional reputations instead of their students' rights, survivors bypassed obstructionist deans, invented new strategies of collaboration, taught themselves Title IX, and with unprecedented clout brought over two hundred universities under federal investigation."[34] So much of the *inventiveness* of student activism comes *from* an intimate knowledge of how institutions work to protect themselves, comes *out* of an experience of being obstructed, whether by procedures or by people.

I have many debts to students. I am deeply indebted to the work of Black students and students of color who have pushed universities to address their complicity with slavery and colonialism by challenging the ongoing use of campus security and police, by asking questions like "Why is my curriculum white?" or "Why is my professor not Black?," by calling for the removal of statues of slave traders or the renaming of buildings named after eugenicists.[35] Some of the students complaining against sexual violence are the same students campaigning against the glorification of slavery and empire. I am inspired by a new generation of Black feminists and feminists of color in the UK and beyond; I think especially of the work of Lola Olufemi, Odelia Younge, Waithera Sebatindira, and Suhaiymah Manzoor-Khan.[36] A feminist ear needs to be intergenerational: we need to become each other's ears. We have so much to learn from each other.

We have many struggles at universities because universities are occupied by many histories. If to complain within the institution is to struggle against it, then complaint shows, to use Angela Y. Davis's (2016, 19) terms, "the intersectionality of struggles."[37] By taking complaints as the shared thread, this research also brings the objects of complaint into view. I noted earlier how complaints can bring a world into focus; you come to see more. Making the act of complaining my focus thus brings what complaints are *about* into focus. Complaint provides a lens, a way of seeing, noticing, attending to a problem in the effort to redress that problem.

We could describe the lens provided by complaint as an *intersectional lens*. Some of the words used to describe the complaint experience, I think especially of the word *messy*, are the same words used to describe intersectionality. We can return to my earlier description of complaint as a crash scene. Kimberlé Crenshaw (1989, 139) describes intersectionality as like a collision of traffic coming from many different directions: "Consider an analogy to traffic in an intersection, coming and going in all four directions. Discrimination, like traffic through an intersection, may flow in one direction, and it may flow in another. If an accident happens at an intersection, it can be caused by cars traveling from any number of directions and, sometimes, from all of them."[38] You cannot always tell who or what determines the crash; for Black women, it could be race *or* sex discrimination or race *and* sex discrimination. If intersectionality is a point about structures, complaints are often an experience of those same structures; we tend to notice what stops us from proceeding, from going somewhere, from being somewhere.

Power is not simply what complaints are about; power shapes what happens when you complain.[39] Complaint offers a way of attending to inequalities and power relationships from the point of view of those who try to challenge them. Although the focus of my study is on how people make use of complaint to challenge power, that is not all I will have to say about power. This book will show the complexities, contradictions, and complications of power through the lens of complaint. We will learn, for instance, how the same complaints procedures used as tools to redress bullying and harassment can be used as tools to bully and to harass. That this happens will not be surprising to feminist readers. We are familiar with how the tools introduced to redress power relations can be used by those who benefit from power relations. The issue is not just that complaints procedures can be used by those with more power, but that complaints are more likely to be received well when they are made by those with more power. Even complications have complications. It can be tricky to work out who has "more power" in this or that instance in part as many who have complaints made against them tend to pass themselves off as victims of a disciplinary apparatus. When this passing is successful, there is a reversal of power.

If power is tricky, complaints are sticky. Those who make complaints and those who are heard as complaining are themselves more likely to be complained about, becoming what I call in chapter 4 *complaint magnets*. So much can stick to you because you complain or when you complain. In the pages that follow, you will read about many sticky situations. I will share stories of those who have made complaints about sexual harassment, racial harassment, bullying, ableism, homophobia, transphobia, sexism, and racism. You will hear how complaints can be affected by the structural position of the complainer (and by *affected*, I am referring not only to where complaints go but whether and how complaints are made), by institutional precarity, poverty, mental and physical health, age, citizenship status, and so on. These phenomena all have distinct academic literatures. I will not be engaging substantially with these literatures within the main body of this book, although I use notes as pointers so you can find relevant sources. I think of myself in this book as thinking *with* those I have communicated *with*. The complainers are my guides; they are my feminist philosophers, my critical theorists, and also my collective.

The words I have collected not only *do* the work; they *are* the work. In the first part of the book, I explore how making complaints teaches us about how institutions work, or *institutional mechanics*. Most of the material I share in this part of the book is drawn from people's experience of going through a formal complaint process, with a focus on what happens early on in that process. My concern throughout this part is with the gap between what is supposed to happen in accordance with policy and procedure and what does happen. I consider how complaints are stopped or blocked by the system set up for handling them. In the second part of the book, I go back in time to explore some of the experiences that lead people to consider making complaints. I consider the significance of immanence: how complaints are in the situations they are about. In the third part of the book, I consider how and why *doors* come up in many of the testimonies. If complaints teach us about doors, doors teach us about power: who is enabled by an institution, who is stopped from getting in or getting through. This part of the book is premised on a simple point: to complain about an abuse of power is to learn about power.

The concluding part of this book turns to the work of complaint collectives. I mentioned earlier that I became part of a complaint collective begun by students. The first conclusion, chapter 7, is written by members of that collective, Leila Whitley, Tiffany Page, and Alice Corble, with support from Heidi Hasbrouck, Chryssa Sdrolia, and others. They describe how and why they formed a collective, which was fluid as well as purposeful, created to push complaints through, to get them out. In the final chapter I reflect on what complaint can teach us about collectivity, how we can assemble ourselves, sometimes without even being in the same time and place. There is hope here; when you hear us together, we are louder. Although complaint can be a shattering—yes, I am picking up many sharp pieces—to make a complaint is often to fight for something. To refuse what has come to be is to fight to be. Doing this work has left me with a sharper sense, a clearer sense, a stronger sense, of the point of that fight.

PART I

INSTITUTIONAL MECHANICS

In this part of the book, I consider what happens when we make or try to make formal complaints. Making a complaint can require becoming an institutional mechanic: you have to work out how to get a complaint through the system. It is because of the difficulty of getting complaints through the system that complaints often end up being about the system.

In talking to different people about their experiences of making complaints, I was constantly reminded of my earlier project on diversity work. In that project, I interviewed practitioners who had been appointed by universities to institutionalize their commitments to diversity and equality. I was not expecting to be reminded of this earlier project in quite the way I was or to quite the extent I was. After all, in the project on diversity I had spoken to administrators who seem structurally to be in a very different position to complainers or complainants.

The data generated by listening to those who make or try to make formal complaints has almost uncanny connections with the data generated by listening to diversity practitioners. I am still learning from these uncanny connections. The complainer does seem to end up in a position rather similar to that of the diversity practitioner, having to administer an unwieldy process (chapter 1) or having to fight the institution to get something through it (chapter 2). The complainer, rather like the diversity practitioner, knows all about stoppages and blockages, where they happen, when they happen, how they happen. In my book *On Being Included*, I described diversity practitioners as institutional plumbers: they develop an expertise in how things get stuck, as well as where they get stuck

(2012, 32). I wrote then that "the mechanical aspect of diversity work is revealed most explicitly when the institution is working: when diversity is blocked, then institutional conversations 'stop' diversity from becoming part of the conversation" (32). In *What's the Use?*, with reference to the same project, I changed the wording slightly. I suggested that "the system is working by stopping those who are trying to transform the system" (2019, 212). Thinking about complaint as institutional mechanics (and the complainer as an institutional mechanic) is a way *to show* what those who make complaints come *to know* about how institutions are working.

In this part of the book, I develop some of the concepts I introduced in my study of diversity, for example, "the nonperformativity" of institutional speech acts, policies, procedures, and commitments. Although in this part of the book I begin with policies and procedures, I am more concerned with describing experiences of the complaints process. Policies and procedures might exist on paper—we can refer to them, point to them—but what happens when you try to follow them or do something with them? As I explore in chapter 1, there is often a gap between what is supposed to happen in accordance with policy and procedure and what does happen. To complain you have to *mind that gap*. In chapter 2, I consider some of the methods used to stop complaints, including warnings, nods, blanking, and what I call strategic inefficiency. None of these methods is an official method; they are usually what organizations represent themselves as committed not to doing.

To find the methodical in the unofficial is in itself revealing something about institutions. We learn *about* institutions from the wear and tear of coming up against them. And we learn *from* the embodied nature of the work of complaint: we can be worn down as well as worn out by what we have to do when we go through a complaints process.

CHAPTER ONE

MIND THE GAP!

POLICIES, PROCEDURES, AND
OTHER NONPERFORMATIVES

What would you do if you needed to make a complaint? Where would you go? Who would you talk to? Most organizations have complaints procedures that lay out a path you are supposed to follow if you make a complaint. To find out how to make a complaint is to find the procedure as well as find out about the procedure; *where* it is and what it *requires* from the one who makes that complaint. You might also find out about related policies in order to make a judgment about whether you have sufficient grounds for a complaint or in order to substantiate a complaint. Policies provide a set of principles and values that are supposed to govern institutions. In my study, those who considered making complaints consulted a wide range of policies, including policies on dignity at work, diversity and equality, harassment and bullying, conflict of interest, and the management of attendance.

If making a complaint often entails familiarizing yourself with policies, making a complaint can involve reencountering institutions through or even as a series of documents. Many of those who make complaints do not simply read these documents; they make use of them either by filling in existing forms, following templates, or making explicit reference to existing policies. One academic says, "In every one of my complaints I used the policies that were given to us by the university." To make use of policies in a complaint is often to point to their failure to be followed. In this chapter, I will consider the implications of this seemingly simple point; how policies can matter to the extent they provide evidence of what is *not* being done. In reflecting on how policies can function as evidence of institutional failure, I develop the concept of "nonperformativity," introduced in my earlier work on diversity (Ahmed 2012). By "nonperformative" I refer to institutional speech acts that do not bring into effect what they name.[1] Working on complaint has allowed me to revisit the concept of nonperformativity in new ways and to explore how the failure to bring something into effect can have rather *strange effects* on institutional life. Those who make formal complaints, I will show, document these strange effects. To make a complaint is often to find a gap, a gap between what is supposed to happen, in accordance with policy and procedure, and what does happen. That gap, we learn, is densely populated. I understand my own task as *minding the gap*; to mind the gap is to listen and to learn from those who experience a process.

1.1 The gap between what is supposed to happen and what does happen.
Photo: Reinhard Dietrich.

A complaint procedure is how you learn what to do, where to go, in order to make a complaint. If policies lay out principles, procedures offer paths. Complaints procedures are often represented as flowcharts, with lines and arrows that give the would-be complainer a clear route through.

Surely, then, to make a complaint is to follow the procedure for making a complaint, a path that has been laid out for you in advance? Things are not always as they appear on paper. Sometimes it can be hard to find the paper. One postgraduate student told me, "It took us forever to try and find the complaints procedure PDF on the database. We knew it existed but it was like a mythical golden egg, we just couldn't find it. And when we did it was so big that even two PhD students spent weeks trying to get through the small print, to find out what the complaint process was." If you can't locate the procedure, you do not know how to proceed. We need to think about the implications of complaint procedures being *user unfriendly*. In *What's the Use? On the Uses of Use* (2019) I explored how use can be a technique; you can stop something by making it hard to use. The less something is used, the harder it is to use. We can think of the example of the unused path: the less it is used, the harder it is to find; you can hardly see the sign for the leaves. A complaint procedure can be like an unused path: hard to find, difficult to follow.

It can be hard to find the complaints procedure. Or you can be told there is no complaints procedure. A postdoctoral researcher wanted to make a complaint about transphobia and bullying by the director of a project team. She contacted Human Resources: "They did not have any complaints procedures. I wrote to the appropriate contact in Human Resources I am resigning because of bullying and transphobia in the project and her response was no, we have never had anything like this before and, as far as I could see, there was no route to do that." You can be told no by being told there is no complaints procedure. Or even if there was a complaints procedure, being told there isn't a complaints procedure would be sufficient to stop someone from proceeding along that path ("there was no route to do that"). Procedures are not simply *there*, available to be followed; they have to be talked about in a meaningful way before they can be taken up or in order to be taken up.

A path can be what unfolds through action: a path as what you have to do in order to get somewhere. A path can also be a path *through* an organization. To make a formal complaint is to enter into an administrative process, which is dependent upon the creation of pathways for

Mind
the Gap!

31

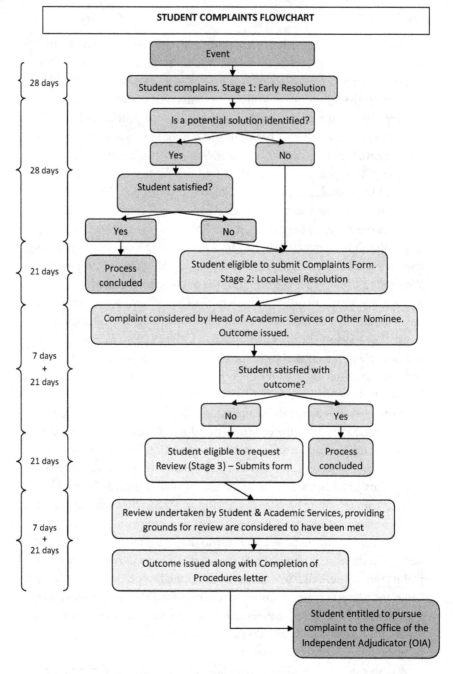

STUDENT COMPLAINTS FLOWCHART

Event

28 days

Student complains. Stage 1: Early Resolution

Is a potential solution identified?

Yes — No

28 days

Student satisfied?

Yes — No

21 days

Process concluded

Student eligible to submit Complaints Form. Stage 2: Local-level Resolution

Complaint considered by Head of Academic Services or Other Nominee. Outcome issued.

7 days + 21 days

Student satisfied with outcome?

No — Yes

21 days

Student eligible to request Review (Stage 3) – Submits form

Process concluded

7 days + 21 days

Review undertaken by Student & Academic Services, providing grounds for review are considered to have been met

Outcome issued along with Completion of Procedures letter

Student entitled to pursue complaint to the Office of the Independent Adjudicator (OIA)

1.2 A clear route through.

1.3 Hard to find,
difficult to follow.

information, sometimes called a postal system, routes and routines for
passing materials between different actors within the organization. By
"administrative process" we are certainly talking about *paperwork*: the
more papers, the more work. The work of complaint is not distributed
equally. A student who made a complaint about disability discrimination
noted, "It's just like a mess of documents and this back and forth and all
this paperwork and me writing these seven pages, seventeen-page letters
itemizing the failures of the university and them just writing the same
letter back in response." Her description teaches us how the creation of
standards by an organization can allow the lessening of effort ("writing
the same letter back") but also how administrative failure can mean more
effort is required by those who make complaints ("itemizing the failures
of the university"). Indeed, she opened her testimony by picking up her
complaint file and showing it to me. She said, "Here is my folder of my
experience of making a formal complaint. Reading through the documentation . . . I was reminded I wrote a history of complaint on it." If to

make a complaint is to write a history of complaint, then a complaint folder is a history holder.

Administrative labor is also communicative labor. In addition to writing your case and collecting written materials to support your case, which might include letters sent to you as well as policies, you have to speak to many different people from your own department as well as administrative departments such as Human Resources, equality and diversity units, occupational health, and staff or student unions. Communication might be a requirement to speak and to write about what happened, to speak *about* the situation the complaint is *about*. To make a complaint you have to keep making that complaint, to give it voice, to give it expression. A complaint can be experienced as the requirement to become expressive. As I noted in my introduction to this book, to express can mean to push something out. The harder an experience, the harder it is to express a complaint. If complaints are a "mess of documents," that mess is *hard*.

Communication is also about hearing: it is about who within the organization is tasked with receiving the complaint. I talked to one administrator about her experience of supporting students through the complaints process. She talked me through the process:

> So, your first stage would require the complainant to try and resolve it informally, which is really difficult in some situations and which is where it might get stuck in a department. . . . And so it takes a really tenacious complaining student to say, no, I am being blocked. . . . If something bad has happened, and you are not feeling that way inclined, you can understand why a student would not have the tenacity to make sure that happens, and to advocate for themselves. They might go to the student union, and the student union is really bogged down. So you can imagine that something on paper that looks very linear is actually very circular a lot of the time. And I think that's the problem. Students get discouraged and get demoralized and feel hard done by, and nothing's getting resolved, and then they are in a murky place and they can't get out.

On paper a complaint can appear linear, a straight line. In reality, a complaint is often more circular (round and round rather than in and out). This circularity is due to blockages: if a procedure exists in order to clear a path, that path can be blocked at any point. Blockages can occur through conversations: if those you speak to are bogged down, you can get bogged down. A conversation can be another wall; a complaint can feel like "talking to a wall," which is another way of thinking about complaint as communicative labor. What is required to proceed with a complaint (in her terms, confidence and tenacity) might be what is eroded by the experiences that led to a complaint ("something bad has happened," "not feeling that way inclined"). What leads you to make a complaint is what makes it hard to complain. In other words, the very experiences you need to complain about are the same experiences that make it difficult to complain.

A complaint is not simply an outcome of a *no*; a complaint requires you to keep saying *no* along the way. Complaints then are rarely experienced as a flow. It might be that at each step, you have to push. One academic describes this: "I had to keep pushing them and pushing them to get their act together. I had to push them because according to their policy there were so many days you had after submitting the complaint for it to be investigated. . . . A month and a half went by since my complaint went in and nothing happened. So, I had to keep pushing." You have to push to get them to "get their act together." You have to push to get them to follow their own procedures, otherwise your complaint can be dropped in accordance with their own procedures.

Even if you follow their procedures, it can feel like you are pushing against a current. This is counterintuitive given that procedures are institutional instructions; they are telling you which way to go. You are being told to go in a direction that slows you down. The gap between what does happen and what is supposed to happen is thus filled by intense activity. You might have to push in order to get them to meet their own deadlines. It is not as if once you push, the work is done. You have to keep pushing, because at each step of the way, you encounter a wall, made up, it seems, of a curious combination of indifference and resistance. If a procedure is represented on paper as a straight path, a complaint can be rather messy and circular; rather like the drawing in figure 1.4, it's a mess, a tangle. You can enter the complaint process but not be able to work out how to get out ("they are in a murky place and they can't get out").

If you have to talk to many different actors within the organization, these actors are not necessarily talking to each other. Another student who made a complaint about transphobic harassment from their supervisor described how they ended up having to administer their own complaint process:

> I am the one who has to arrange all this information and send it to different people because they are just not talking to each other. I had to file the forms in order to get the Human Resources records; I had to do all

1.4 A drawing of a complaint.

the Freedom of Information requests. It was on me to do all of this work, which raises the question of why have Human Resources officers at all because I am literally doing their job. And I am the one who made the complaint and I have all the emotional damage around that to deal with.

The person who makes the complaint—who is often already experiencing the trauma or stress of the situation they are complaining about—ends up having to direct an unwieldy process. The person who puts the complaint forward ends up being *the conduit*; they have to *hold* all the information in order that it can be circulated; they have to keep things moving. We sense a difficulty here given that many of the experiences that lead to complaint can make it hard to hold yourself together, let alone an unwieldy process.

You have to keep making the same points to different people. An early career academic says, "There are like four channels of complaint going on at the same time. But interestingly none of these people seem to be crossing over. You duplicate the complaint at different times: emails, phone calls, occupational health, the union. It is all being logged. It is generating all this material and all this paperwork but actually nothing seems to shift. It's just a file, actually." You end up duplicating the same points to multiple parties because there are no clear lines of communication between those parties. A complaint can be experienced as the requirement to labor over the same points, which are already sore points, points that can become even sorer because of the need to keep making them. And where does a complaint end up? All of those documents, many of which replicate other documents, end up in the same file ("it's just a file, actually"). If a file is what you achieve, and that file sits there, it can feel what you have achieved is sitting there.

When you make a complaint, you end up all over the place, even if all the different paths you follow lead to the same destination, even if all the materials you created or collected end up in the same file. I talked to another student about her experience of making complaints. She had once worked as an administrator supporting students in making complaints, so she had experience with the process from different angles: "It's messy and it's cyclical: you file the complaint, this process happens, which can cause another complaint." Complaints can lead to complaints because of how they are handled. Indeed, a number of people I talked to ended up making complaints about how their complaints were handled. Another student told me, "I went through an official complaints procedure, and that went from a departmental level to the officer of independent adjudicators. I have seen that process firsthand." By going through the complaint process, she "uncovered all these failed processes." And then her complaint became, in her terms, "a complaint about the complaint itself." Another student who made a complaint about sexual harassment from another student was told by a member of Human Resources, "I need to tell you this: the only way you can go with this now, you can't put in a complaint about a student. . . . The only complaint you can put in is if you complain against the university, against the way that this has been dealt with." Being directed to make a complaint about the complaint can be how the original complaint is dropped. It can be how you end up on another route, which does seem circular, round and round, round and about. Complaints end up referring to complaints; you have to keep dealing with what is not being dealt with; yes, once you start the process, it is hard to get out.

Where, then, do complaints end up? I noted earlier how all the different materials generated by a complaint can end up in the same file. And those files can end up in filing cabinets; filing as filing away. One student said of her complaint, "It just gets shoved in the box." Another student said, "I feel like my complaint has gone into the complaint graveyard." A burial can be what happens because you follow the procedure. I spoke to

1.5 Where com-
plaints end up.

one academic who supported a PhD student through a formal complaint process: "The attempt to do things in a proper way is not necessarily effective; it just becomes how things get buried. You are doing things in a discrete way, in a way that maintains everyone's privacy. You can have good procedures in place and it allows things to be buried that shouldn't be buried." Doing things in the proper way, doing what you are supposed to do, can lead, does lead, to a burial. If a burial should not happen but does happen, then burials might not appear to have happened; a burial can disappear along with what has been buried.

The complainer knows a burial has happened. When a complaint is filed away or binned or buried, those who complain can end up feeling filed away or binned or buried. We need to remember that a complaint is a record of what happens *to* a person, as well as of what happens *in* institutions. Complaints are personal as well as institutional. *The personal is institutional.* One academic researcher shared her complaint file with me:

"One of the things I talked about in those documents, I am very open, I was under such stress and trauma that my periods stopped. That's the intimacy of some of the things that go into it, bodily functions like this." A body can stop functioning. A body can announce a complaint. That body is in a document. And that document is in a file. And that file is in a cabinet. To file a complaint can also mean to become alienated from the history that led you to complain, an intimate alienation that you feel in your own bodily being.

The filing cabinet is, of course, not the only place a complaint is stored. Many of those I spoke to also retained their own complaint files.[2] I described earlier how one student began her testimony by showing me her file. An academic I interviewed arranged to meet me after her interview, in person, so she could hand me her file, as she did not have enough trust in the postal system. She handed me documents that she was not even supposed to have, documents she had been instructed to destroy. I have only been able to conduct this research into complaint, I suspect, because many have refused to follow instructions. She was not only handing me documents, however much they mattered. She was handing me a part of her life, a hard part, a painful part. She was handing me emails that had been sent to her, reports that had been written about her that devastated her because of how they portrayed her. She trusted me to read those materials, to be skeptical about that portrayal. I received that file; I saw through that portrayal. I understand myself to be responsible for her file, to take care of it. In my study where I work at home, I have many complaint files, housed in the same place. Those files by coming into my hands ended up together, files that would otherwise have been held apart. Together they contain so much information; they throw so much light on each other. I suggested in my introduction that I hear spillage as speech. My task is to open these files, to spill their contents the best I can.

If bodies can end up in documents, and documents can end up in files, bodies can also be files or perhaps bodies can be filing cabinets, holders of multiple files. What is filed away by institutions can be stored in our bodies, experienced often as weight. *The body of the complainer is a testimony to the work of complaint.* One senior academic explained, "You have a lot of strain and mental anguish which comes out in different ways, and the way that mine came out was in my back. That was when I started having this really bad back problem." The less backing you have, the more weight you have to bear. A back can bear the burden of the weight of a complaint. A back can tell the story of what is required to do this work.

If a complaints procedure offers a path for the would-be complainer, that path can be blocked at any point. It is hard to know whether procedures are a problem because they are followed or not followed. On the one hand, you might have to push because organizations are not following their own procedures. On the other hand, following the procedures seems to lead to complaints being buried. It is thinking from the experience of complainers, what they have to do, where they have to go, that we can reflect on *how* procedures become part of the problem.

The experience of making a complaint throws so much light on what is often made obscure or kept in the shadows. Let's return to the early career academic who described how "all this material and all this paperwork" became "just a file, actually." Where did her complaint begin? Her complaint began because of the failure of her university to make reasonable adjustments to her workload after she returned from long-term sick leave.[3] She complained in order to have the time and room she needed to do her work. She describes the experience as follows:

> It was like a little bird scratching away at something and it wasn't really having any effect. It was just really small, small, small and behind closed doors. I think people maybe feel that because of the nature of the complaint, and you are off work so they have to be polite and not talk about it and so much of their politeness is because they don't want to say something. And maybe [it is] to do with being in an institution and the way they are built: long corridors, doors with locks on them, windows with blinds that come down. It seems to sort of imbue every part of it with a cloistered feeling. There is no air; it feels suffocating.

"It was like": note this *it*. A complaint as something that you are doing can acquire exteriority, becoming a thing in the world; scratching away; a little bird, all your energy going into an activity that matters so much to what you can do, who you can be, but barely seems to leave a trace; the more you try, the smaller it becomes, you become, smaller, smaller still. A complaint is made confidential as soon as it is lodged, so all of this happens behind closed doors; a complaint as a secret, a source of shame, what keeps you apart from others. A complaint becomes like a magnifying glass: so much appears, so many details are picked up by an attention; the geography of a place, the building, the long corridors; the locked doors; the windows with blinds that can come down—these are familiar features of our built environment.

Long corridors, locked doors, windows with blinds that come down: if these are familiar features of our built environment, what is familiar can also be what is suffocating. You don't have enough air, you cannot breathe. If a complaint is made to create more time and more room, a complaint can take time and leave you with even less room. The less time you have, the less room you have, the more conscious you become of who is given time, who is given room. Complaints can thus allow institutions to be registered all the more intensely; you acquire a sense of the institution through an experience of restriction. A complaint provides a *phenomenology of the institution*. You become more attuned to the environment of the institution; you begin to perceive what might have been part of the background.

Becoming more attuned to an institution is how many find a gap between an appearance and experience; in other words, what you experience is not how the institution appears. In describing the work of complaint as "scratching away," this early career lecturer also talked to

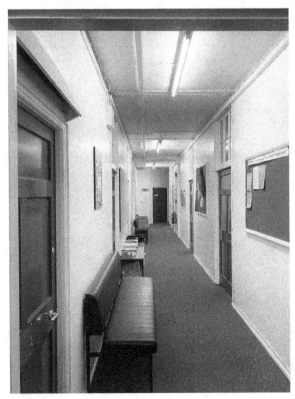

Mind
the Gap!

41

1.6

1.7 Photo: Kim Albright/
Phrenzee.

1.8

me about how she came to learn about the university's own policies and commitments. She detailed her own use of detail: how she went through her university's policies on dignity at work and management of attendance, the university charter as well as her contract "with a fine-tooth comb." Through this process, she was able to demonstrate that the work she had been allocated by her department, "none of that lined up" with the university's own policies. But even though she demonstrated that the university's own policies were not being followed in what she had been asked to do, she did not get anywhere with her complaint.

Even if you *can* use a policy as evidence to support a complaint, it does not guarantee you will succeed. I spoke to another academic who made use of multiple policies in putting together a complaint about plagiarism. She described policy as a trip wire: "That was my experience of the complaint process. As an employer of the university, the minute you try to enact policy that you are told when you are hired to be the vanguards of, to protect the quality of education and work at the university, that in effect it is a trip wire, and that in effect you become the person to be investigated. These policies are not meant." When you try to use a policy to do what it was meant to do, your action sends out an alarm or an alert. To make a complaint is to find out what policies are not meant. You are stopped from using the policy to do something, rather like a trespasser is stopped from entering the building. If a usage becomes an alarm, you are being told that you are not supposed to do that, you are not supposed to be here. You are stopped by becoming "the person to be investigated."

I will return in chapter 4 to how making a complaint can lead you to being put under investigation. It is worth reflecting more on how we learn about institutions from what policies do not do. She describes further: "I was told it was now a formal process. I had to look at all the policies. *I found there was this fog.* It was constant. Every time I found clarity—isn't it supposed to happen in accordance with policy blah blah blah—this has been around ten years, isn't this supposed to happen, and they would be like no." To be told *no* is to be told that however long a policy has been around it is not going to determine what happens. Even when a policy makes something clear ("every time I found clarity") you end up in a fog; a no can be a fog.

If you acquire more of a sense of an institution from an experience of restriction, that sense is not always about things becoming clear. A complaint can queer your relation to the institution, and I mean *queer* in the older sense of the word, queer as strange or wonky; *complaint as a queer phenomenology.* Words that are everywhere in my data are odd, bizarre, weird, strange, and disorienting. To enter an administrative process, interestingly, perhaps surprisingly, can be the start of a rather queer experience: trying to assemble the papers in the right way can lead to odd things happening. One lecturer described what happened during his complaint about discrimination in a promotion case. He noted how documents would suddenly appear in files that had not been there before: "The lawyers had said in my file I had all these negative annual reviews. I thought that was weird as I had no negative reviews." I have collected many stories of documents that mysteriously appear or disappear, which I will be sharing throughout this book. The words we use to describe something tell us about something. He described his experience thus: "I would bend toward the surreal. The situations have been so bizarre. I want to believe there is some research value in that because it is so strange."

I agree: there is research value in documenting what is bizarre and strange. The strangeness of complaint manifests in so many ways; there are so many loose ends that do not line up. What is strange is noticeable because it does not conform to an expectation. I remember from my own experience how disorienting the experience of complaint can be: you have to keep switching dimensions. You are having all these conversations, so many meetings, meetings after meetings, but most people you are working with don't even know what is going on. And you have to keep going back to your other job, your day job, different kinds of meetings; and that world, which is supposed to be the real world, the upright, brightly lit world, feels increasingly unreal, topsy-turvy, upside down.

What makes the experience of complaint surreal is not just the gap between what is supposed to happen and what does happen. It is also because complaints can take you away from what you are used to, what you usually do. A formal complaint can lead you into the shadowy corners of an institution, meeting rooms, corridors; buildings you did not have any reason to enter before become where you go. If complaints can be what you end up doing, where you end up going, the lack of clarity of the process *becomes the world you inhabit*: nothing is clear; nothing seems to make sense; you can't make sense of it. One early career lecturer who complained after being harassed by a professor in her department explains, "It is like being trapped in some kind of weird dream where you know you jump from one section to another because you never know the narrative. I think that's the power that institutional abuse has on you." Making a complaint can feel like becoming a character in somebody else's story; what happens to you is dependent on decisions that are made without your knowledge or consent. This is why making a complaint about harassment can often feel like being harassed all over again, becoming subjected, again, to another's will. You know that what is happening is not what is supposed to be happening, *but you still don't know what is happening*. You can feel like something or someone is pulling the strings, but you don't know what or who.

And you also know that however much you are doing, so much else is going on behind doors that are closed to you. What is going on is *withdrawn*. On the surface, at the front, in the window, the organization might appear to be happily willing to listen to a complaint, hearing the complaint as helpful feedback. Behind closed doors, the atmosphere is quite different. I spoke to two students who made a complaint at an institution that had developed new complaints procedures intended to create a more positive environment for the complainer. I will return in the next section to the significance of changing procedures and policies. They told me, "The tone of the emails is very telling. The tone was horrendous. It was basically like 'Tutt,' stop it [*accompanied by hand gesture*], that sort of attitude, like that tutt if you could make that noise it was in there somewhere." When you make a complaint, you hear that "tutt, tutt," as if you are an irritating fly they are trying to brush away, a complaint as what they will away, a complaint met by a go away.

Behind closed doors, the communication you receive in response to a complaint can be, to use their term, *horrendous*. And even when complaints happen behind closed doors, it is hard to close the door on a complaint. An academic who made a complaint about bullying from her head of department says:

> You don't know what is going to come through the door, when the next thing will break you. It doesn't leave you. . . . It reminded me, some of it you know when you are waiting for the next thing to come in the post. When I've been broke in the past and you worry about bills, when they used to have paper bills years ago, coming through the door, it always used to freak me out. I used to go into a dead panic when I didn't have any money and the bills used to come. It reminded me of that. I always used to expect something to come. I didn't want to open my email. I didn't like it when things come through the door. When I would see the university logo on it, I would go into a right panic about it.

The process is not only exhausting; for many, it is *terrifying* because you do not know what is going to come through the door; you do not know if the next thing will be too much, will be what breaks you. If organizations use doors to contain a complaint (see chapter 5), the complainer cannot close the door on the complaint; materials keep getting through, more and more materials; none of your life, nothing that is yours, can be held apart or kept apart. If complaints can take over your life, it can feel like being taken over by the institution; you experience anything that comes at you as potentially a letter with a university logo.

What comes *at* you is not revealed *to* others. In other words, what is hidden from view is often what is most harmful or violent about the complaint process. In another instance, a senior manager ended up in a dispute with other senior managers. The dispute began as an administrative dispute about how degree classifications were reached at an exam board. It is important to note how administrative dispute can still have *life implications.* If academics come to different judgments on how classifications should be reached, those judgments determine the mark each student gets, and those marks have profound implications for the students themselves. As she described it, "We were talking about students' life chances." An administrative dispute can be a dispute about life. The dispute, I should also add here, did not lead to a straightforward grievance or complaint—although a straightforward complaint might be an oxymoron. But listening to this senior manager's account of the dispute, which led to disciplinary action being taken against her and to her losing her job (for creating "a scandal" and bringing her university into disrepute), has taught me a great deal about how power works within educational institutions.[4]

What is important to note here is how she presented her case or supported her own view of what should happen. She gathered evidence of the university's own policies and procedures: "We looked at the university's procedures. There was one policy document which said [x]. These were clearly written documents. We pointed that out, and still they didn't respond. We were able to say we are working within our capacity to do this and here's your document which says this, and still they didn't accept it." Having evidence of a policy does not get her anywhere—even though it is clearly written and spelled out. In fact, over time she gathered more and more evidence that supported her view *from* the university's own policies and procedures: "Immediately after the decision had been announced, I discovered another policy document on degree classifications. . . . I mean it was really as *clear* as that." She uses the word *clear* again: "It was *clear* to me that they were the ones who were not following their own procedures." It is not just that the policy and procedures were clear, but it is clear that the policies supported her position.

What happened? Even though the procedures were clear, they did not determine the outcome. She contacted the head of the university: "I drew his attention to this. I said it's the university [that] is not following its own guidance, not us." However, she did not get anywhere—the head referenced not the policy but the decision of the board as a "superior body." She persisted not by filing a grievance but by finding evidence to support her understanding of procedure: "I didn't see myself as making a complaint. I saw myself as identifying a problem that affected my school, which I had the power and authority to address and I was addressing it. And I think that the university saw me as challenging them, and I had suddenly become something other than a senior member of management and I was just challenging them." The more evidence she gathers to challenge their interpretation of the procedures, the more she is treated as *being* challenging. In other words, when you have evidence that something is wrong, that can be used as evidence that what you are doing is wrong.

The dispute became a disciplinary matter because she refused to back down: "It was really just saying: back down, you are not going to get anything, so just back down. And I think they were saying that if you want to get something it has to be a different kind of discourse. I am not sure what the discourse would have been, but it would be something other than saying these are your policies and you are bound by them." Having evidence that the organization has failed to follow its own policies and procedures becomes evidence of insubordination because that evidence implies that those who govern the university should be bound by something other than themselves. Of course, we might answer by saying that those who govern or manage educational institutions should be bound by laws, policies, and procedures. What should be the case is not always the case. In making a complaint or in challenging the decision of a "superior body," you are coming up against the emptiness of that *should*. That *should*—should be bound—not only means nothing, but those who suggest it does mean something become insubordinates. Policies become for others to follow. As she explained, "They are not bound by their own policies, and frankly they can rewrite them if they don't like them." She later qualifies, "They don't even think they have to rewrite the policies they don't like." The implication here is that only those who are in subordinate positions are bound or even should be bound by policy. She provided us with a summary of their position: "The position: it is for others. Policies are for others." Those who challenge how power works come to know how power works. *You know that policies are nonperformatives when you try to use policies as evidence of what is not being done.* Knowledge of the emptiness of policy is an intimacy with the workings of power.

Perhaps we are learning what is required to be a good citizen: you are supposed to inhabit the nonperformative, to use the same empty words and phrases, to go along with it. As she suggests, "Whatever you think of the university's procedures, you don't challenge them in that way; *you swallow it.* As far as the university is concerned, because it is the superior body, everything they say is legitimate by reason of it being the superior body. The more you challenge, the more they come back. I also found the more clearly evident the university was wrong, the more I was challenged." The more evidence you have that they are wrong, the more you are treated as being in the wrong, the harder they come down on you. It is important to know what comes down. It is important to share these stories. If our institutional duty is to swallow it, it might take complaint to spit it out. But then again, many who don't swallow it end up out of it, as she did. The ease with which procedures can be bypassed tells us something about the nature of power. Power can be understood as the right to suspend what is binding for others. That right, however, is never articulated as such; it appears as if procedures and policies are binding for everyone.

This ease with which procedures can be suspended teaches us how institutions are reproduced. An early career academic who described to me in acute detail the intense and everyday misogyny and racism in her department also speculated on how her department came to be that way. She said the Human Resources guidelines are often bypassed to enable such-and-such white man to be hired or promoted:

> We have the HR guidelines. I have been on the promotion committee for about five years, I expect, and I saw it in action. Even though we had an HR representative right there and we had these guidelines and people would be saying, "Oh yeah, but he's a great guy, you know, I like to have a beer with him, he really should, he really does deserve Reader, let's go for it." . . . The same thing with the short-listing and interview panels that I was involved in. Someone would say that woman's presentation was outstanding, but really, he's the guy you'd want to have a pint with, so let's make the figures fit. So they'll wiggle the numbers around so even if he just gets one point more, he gets the higher score.

This criterion for appointability—hiring someone you would want to have a pint with—cannot be made official; it would contradict equal opportunities commitments. The procedures are not so much suspended; the right form is still being filled in, but adapted or corrupted: if he doesn't get the highest score, you wiggle the numbers, making the figures fit. The figures are made to fit when a person is deemed to fit. Policies, even those that have been officially agreed on, can be disregarded if they get in the way of what people are invested in doing.

In the next section I turn to diversity policies that aim to intervene in the reproduction of institutions. What we are learning here is how power is often secured through unofficial means. Complaints relating to discrimination have taught me a great deal about *unofficial policies*. I talked to a woman of color academic. She observes that even though many academics of color had received research grants, they did not get the same amount of teaching relief as white faculty. There is supposed to be a principle of equality in determining the allocation of workloads, but somehow (I think we know how) workloads tend to be distributed unequally, in old and familiar patterns: white men professors get more time to do the work that is more highly valued, the work that contributes more to promotion and progression. I will return to speed and promotion in chapter 6.

How, then, are decisions made about the allocation of workloads if they are not the official policies? She introduced a term, *shadow policies*, to explain how she did not get teaching relief while other staff did:

> I found out there is teaching relief for other people. He had shadow policies that were done one-on-one with certain people but not with all people in the department. They made these deals. He would write these policies about workload assignment and that people who are directors of centers could get teaching releases in order to build those centers. And once the centers get built, they put themselves forward as directors for centers and they get more teaching releases.

It is not only that a shadow policy is not the official policy; the shadow is a reference to *how* as well as *where* deals are made. The deals are being made behind closed doors.[5] Deals are also duplicitous: the deal is about one thing (a new center), but it is also achieving something else (teaching relief), with the latter achievement being the point of the deal, achieved without anything ever being said about the nature of that achievement.

Being given relief from doing the less valued work can be secured through a back door. A shadow policy teaches us *how* decisions are made but also *who* makes those decisions. It is not simply that making a complaint means learning how procedures and policies can be bypassed. It is that the bypassing of procedures and policies shapes the environment in which complaints are made.

CHANGING POLICIES

If making a complaint requires learning more about an organization's own policies and procedures, that knowledge is often about what policies do not do, how procedures are not followed or are deliberately bypassed in order to secure a desired outcome. In this section, I hope to explore what we learn from the effort to change policies and procedures. It might seem curious to focus on changing policies and procedures given that complaints teach us how easily they can be bypassed. But those who complain know that even when procedures and policies are bypassed, following procedures is how many complaints end up going nowhere.

If making a complaint requires following the procedures, making a complaint requires using tools that are developed "in house." Complaints procedures could thus be understood as "the master's tools," to evoke Audre Lorde's (1984) terms.[6] When procedures are developed in house, it is not surprising they are often used to keep that house in order. It is also not surprising that those who use formal complaints procedures end up leading an effort to modify the tools. A trans lecturer made use of the UK Equality Act (2010) to challenge his failure to be promoted, making a case that transitioning should be understood as a career interruption.[7] He ended up drafting a new policy on equality for trans staff and students at his university because his experience of making a complaint revealed the absence of such a policy. He said, "Now I am developing guidelines for a trans equality policy. I hope to take this new path." There is much to learn from this trajectory: from complainer to diversity worker. In trying to get a complaint through the system, you end up taking on a role to modify the system.

Complaints by showing the failure of policies, which can include the failure even to have policies, often point to the need for new policies or for amendments of old policies. That this is the case has much to teach us about why complaints end up being so much work: the work of complaint becomes the work to change the institution in which you make the complaint. Many people have expressed the concern to me that if we help organizations develop new policies or procedures to address an institutional problem, we are giving them tools they can use as evidence they have dealt with the problem. Creating evidence of doing something is not the same thing as doing something. I share this concern. Let me return to my earlier project on diversity. I talked to practitioners about their efforts to develop new equality policies and procedures. My task, then and now, is to learn from those who are doing the work, who are *laboring to change policies* in order to bring about institutional change. In one instance, a diversity practitioner is trying to get a new policy agreed so that all members of academic appointment panels receive diversity training:

> When I was first here there was a policy that you had to have three people on every panel who had been diversity trained. But then there was a decision early on when I was here, that it should be everybody, all panel members, at least internal people. They took that decision at the equality and diversity committee which several members of SMT [Senior Management Team] were present at. But then the director of Human Resources found out about it and decided we didn't have the resources to support it, and it went to council with that taken out and council were told that they were happy to have just three members, only a person on council who was an external member of the diversity committee went ballistic—and I am not kidding went ballistic—and said the minutes didn't reflect what had happened in the meeting because the minutes said the decision was different to what actually happened (and I didn't take the minutes, by the way). And so they had to take it through and reverse it. And the council decision was that all people should be trained. And despite that I have then sat in meetings where they have just continued saying that it has to be just three people on the panel. And I said but no, council changed their view and I can give you the minutes, and they just look at me as if I am saying something really stupid. This went on for ages, even though the council minutes definitely said all panel members should be trained. And to be honest, sometimes you just give up.

It takes so much work to get the policy agreed because of the resistance to the policy. In this case, two different kinds of resistance are distinct sequences of an action: an individual action of sabotage (removing the policy from the minutes) is followed by an institutional action of indifference (acting as if the policy does not exist). If the first action had been successful, the second would not have been necessary. The head of Human Resources could have succeeded in stopping the policy if nobody had noticed that he had removed the decision from the minutes. In the end what stopped the policy from coming into use was simply the shared refusal to acknowledge its existence.

The content of the policy that did not come into use does matter. The policy was intended to change the procedure for academic appointments: the policy was supposed to require that all academic members of appointment panels would be diversity trained. For the new policy not to come into use meant that the old policy, which was also the current practice, how things were being done, remained unchanged. In practice, nonperformativity means *the same practice*. If the policy is treated as if does not exist, it does not come into use. But the policy that does not come into use still exists, just as she does, the person who worked hard to get the policy through the system. Indeed, the energy she expended on getting a policy agreed that did not do anything is an important part of the story; it is why I keep telling her story. *It is not just the policy but the work of creating the policy that disappears.*

Even if policies and procedures are bypassed in this or that instance, they still exist somewhere; as I noted earlier, those who make complaints often have to work quite hard to find them. A policy too can be buried. Or a policy can have a virtual life. One academic notes, "A policy can sit there on a website." Policies that just "sit there" are still doing something; sitting can be what they are doing. The gap between what exists and what is in use is another gap those who complain can fall through. I think of the world of the nonperformative as the world of the *as if*: papers keep circulating as if they matter in a certain way, even when they do not, although later they might come to matter in another way. This strange and queer world of the nonperformative is the world those who complain tend to occupy.

That a policy still exists, even when it is not being used, matters. So, for instance, when complaints about harassment or bullying come out in the public domain, many organizations respond by pointing to their own policies as if having a policy against something is evidence it does not exist.[8] This means that a policy that is not in use can still be used as evidence of what does not exist. In my book *On Being Included*, I referred to an example of how a university responded to international students who claimed they had "no proper channels of complaint" to raise concerns about racism (2012, 144). The university spokesperson responded to the students thus: "This could not be further from the truth. The college prides itself on its pastoral care" (144). Commitments can be used as a *rebuttal system* as if they directly contradict the evidence of a complaint, including a complaint about the lack of "proper channels for complaint."

Rebuttals are not always explicit. Sometimes an organization responds to public disclosure of a problem with declarative statements about their commitments, without even referencing that disclosure. This certainly happened when news of my own resignation made it into the press. The college's statement written in response to the media reports began:

> We take sexual harassment very seriously and take action against those found to be acting in ways incompatible with our strong values relating to equality, diversity and inclusion. We do not tolerate or condone inappropriate behaviour towards any of our staff or students, and we work hard to create an environment free of such behaviour. All concerns and complaints are fully investigated with reference to our statutory duties, issues of confidentiality, and guidance from relevant national agencies to ensure that we are compliant with best practice. Moreover, they inform the development of our wider practices and policies to create an inclusive and diverse environment.

If any of this had been even remotely true, I would not have had to resign. It is not surprising, then, that experience of a complaint is surreal and unsettling: when you have evidence that the institution is not following its own policies, the institution can and will make use of its "wider practices and policies" to contradict that evidence.

If policies and procedures can be used as evidence of what does not exist simply by virtue of existing, it should not surprise us that institutions can use complaints as evidence of the success of their own policies. One university writes that complaints will "assist in identifying problems and trends across the University." They then write that complaints will "form the basis of positive publicity, in demonstrating that identified issues have been resolved." When complaints record a problem, they can be quickly folded into a solution, a record of how the university resolved something: resolution as dissolution. The development of new policies and complaints procedures can also be used as "positive publicity." After the launch of one campaign, a vice chancellor announced, "[The university] prides itself on being a leader academically, in terms of research and educationally. It has to be a social leader as well, tackling tough problems such as sexual harassment." Although the statement does not claim leadership on sexual harassment (it says "It has to be a social leader" rather than "It is a social leader"), the reference to its own status as "a leader academically" turns the new policy into an expression of institutional pride.[9]

In hearing how complaints can be wrapped up in the language of solution, I was reminded of the uses of the language of diversity.[10] One practitioner described diversity as a "big shiny apple": "It all looks wonderful, but the inequalities are not being addressed." Diversity can be used rather

1.9 Scratching the surface.

like a complaint procedure, as a way of appearing to address a problem. She also described diversity work as a "banging your head against the brick wall job," suggesting the ease with which diversity travels has something to do with the difficulty of getting through. When you bang your head against the brick wall, it is you who gets sore. And what happens to the wall? All you seem to have done is scratched the surface. And this is what diversity work often feels like: scratching at the surface, scratching the surface.

Complaint too can feel like scratching the surface. We can think back to the image of a complaint as "a little bird, scratching away at something." Scratching can denote scale: it can be used to suggest something small (also fragile) as not having much effect on something big (also hard), like a head against a wall. Scratching can also be a sound, a small, irritating noise created by one thing rubbing against another. Perhaps the diversity practitioner too is heard as a little bird, scratching away. If she is heard at all, she is heard as interrupting the flow of a meeting ("they just look at me as if I am saying something really stupid").

To scratch at the surface is to become aware of how little you are accomplishing. Those who work on new policies and procedures come to know how hard it is to get them to do anything. But even if policies and procedures can be used not to do something, it does not follow that we should not try to develop new policies and procedures. There are many good reasons for changing procedures and policies. This book provides evidence of the need for such changes, and I have learned so much from those who are pushing for them.[11] But that the experience of complaint often means becoming conscious of the bypassing of procedures and policies might teach us the limitations of focusing on changing procedures. You can change how you address a problem without addressing the problem. In fact, if you put all your efforts into changing *how* you address the problem, those efforts can be how problems remain unaddressed.

Does changing procedures and policies change what happens when you make a complaint? My best answer is: not necessarily. One academic put forward a formal complaint about harassment and bullying by her head of department. She did so after her university had invested a great deal of time and money in developing new policies on harassment as well as new complaints procedures. She did so because they had new policies: "I thought, great. The [x] policy has just been implemented. I have a means to complain." New policies and procedures might increase the likelihood that people will make complaints. But if they lead some to complain, they do not necessarily change what happens when they make a complaint. She thought the new policies and procedures, to use her terms, "meant what they state," only to learn they did not.

She described the new procedures and policies as "window dressing." The new procedures and policies allowed the university to appear at the front, in public, as having created a new culture that was more supportive of those who made complaints about harassment. Behind closed doors, the culture was unchanged. We need to remember that complaints are mostly made behind closed doors, the places that are withdrawn from the public gaze. This is why changing the appearance of how complaints are handled can be how you don't change very much at all. She told me that she said to the senior manager responsible for overseeing the inquiry that followed her complaint, "This policy means absolutely nothing."

The issue might be not only that the university had focused much of its efforts on developing a new policy, as if the policy was performative, as if it could bring a new culture into existence, but *how* the policy had been changed. They had appointed a new officer (on a temporary contract) to write that policy. This academic described the appointment of the officer "as part of the window dressing." When she contacted the officer to tell her about the failure of the university to support her through the complaints process, the officer said, "It is not my concern—you have to tell senior management." If you are appointed to write a policy it does not mean you are concerned or are even *allowed* to be concerned about whether the policy is being implemented. A new policy can be treated as a stranger, created by someone who has been brought in, somebody who will go again. Perhaps when they go, the new policy can go with them.

When writing a new policy is deemed sufficient, a policy is insufficient. But there is more to say here. Her complaint was about bullying and harassment from her head of department. The bullying had taken place over eight years. The situation worsened, and she was physically assaulted by him after a meeting. In chapter 5 I will describe that assault in more detail and explain how he was cleared of any wrongdoing. (We always have so much to learn from clearings.)[12] The day after the assault, she attended a Human Resources committee meeting. The meeting was chaired by the deputy head of Human Resources. It was to discuss a new policy on bullying. She gives an account of what happened during that meeting:

> I had a Human Resources committee meeting that was going to be chaired by the deputy head of HR and was all about bullying policies and I went to that. [My union rep] and I then asked to see [the deputy head of HR] after it. In the meeting, I started crying in the meeting, we were supposed to talk about all this material, and I had just been bullied. [The deputy head of] HR tried to get out of a meeting, [but my union rep] said, sorry, this is really serious, you have to make time and meet with us.

Earlier I described nonperformativity as a world you occupy when you make a complaint. It is a strange world; you experience a disconnect between what is supposed to happen and what does happen, between paper and practice. That disconnect can also be *excruciating*. Think of this: you have been bullied and you go to a meeting to discuss a new policy on bullying. Bullying is a profoundly undoing experience, and how bullying affects a person is often the aim of the bully: you are undermined, made to feel smaller, brought down; you are frightened to go to work, to walk down that corridor, to open the door to the meeting room. If you are bullied you have to fight to make it into the room to discuss a new policy on bullying. The experience you have of what is being talked about makes it hard to get to that meeting, let alone be in the meeting to talk about it.

I will explore in chapter 3 how a complaint can be what comes out, given an almost involuntary expression, in the middle of a meeting. It is in that meeting that she asks the senior administrator tasked with developing the new policy if they can meet. That administrator "tries to get out of meeting." The person who wrote a new policy on bullying does not want to meet with a person being bullied. It is not just that what is written on paper and what actually happens are different. It is that the effort to write that paper, to create a policy, becomes disconnected from the problem the policy is intended to address. *This disconnection is cruel.* The concern to create a policy to address a problem becomes a refusal of concern for those affected by that problem. Creating a new policy to deal with a problem becomes another way of avoiding that problem. And by *problem*, we mean *person*; the person who has been bullied becomes the problem to be avoided.

New policies can be old problems given new forms. I am not suggesting here that policies and procedures do not matter; they most certainly do, even if they can be bypassed in specific instances. During our experience of going through a formal complaint process, we pushed hard for a change to the university's policy on conflicts of interest.[13] One student in particular invested a huge amount of her time and energy into trying to get the policy amended. She emailed our complaint collective in frustration:

> I've just checked the college website and discovered that the Conflicts of Interest Policy remains unchanged, a full two years after I first began advocating for it to be removed and rewritten. It still contains this line: "The College does not wish to prevent, or even necessarily be aware of, liaisons between staff and students and it relies upon the integrity of both parties to ensure that abuses of power do not occur." I've lost track now of the number of meetings with management in which I've tried to get this policy taken down and changed. Two years! Has anyone heard about or been shown any new versions of this policy lately?

In the end it took a direct intervention from the equality officer before the old policy was removed, over two years after students first called for the amendment.

There was another problem. The university had appointed someone in Human Resources to amend the policy. There was no conversation between academics and students about the policy and why it needed to be changed. A new policy can be a way of avoiding a conversation about a problem that the policy is intended to address. Nevertheless, as a collective we had many conversations about that policy, including conversations with the person given the task of changing it. In fact, it became obvious from these conversations that the person given the task of amending the policy had been given a limited brief; he did not know why we needed to change the policy; he did not know the context in which that change had become necessary. A new policy can be a way of drawing a line between past and present. The college very quickly began to talk about the cases as "historical cases." A new policy can be a way of making a problem appear to have been dealt with, as if it is in the past.

We kept insisting on the need to open up a conversation about the need for a new policy. I emailed another feminist professor, a senior manager, and a senior administrator in frustration, "[X] who is looking into policy has told one of us ... that he had not been briefed on anything that had happened ... so he is working on policies with no idea of the severity of the situation. That cannot be right, and many of us are very concerned about this, staff as well students." The other feminist professor replied, "Really!!! Has he ever dealt with sexual harassment before? He didn't even have other university policies. Or know their differences." The response of the senior administrator was to justify his selection: "He is an HR legal policy expert who has worked for us for the past 6 months." She then reprimanded us for improper communication: "Can we please keep this off-line now." When the policy did finally get removed, something had been achieved, without question. But it seemed so much work not to get very far given that how the amendment had been achieved, with secrecy, in silence, reproduced the very culture that led to the problems in the first place. And that is a good way of describing what complaint often feels like: *so much work not to get very far.*

It was still important to change that policy. I myself learned about the policy only after I attended that meeting with students. When I got home, I went to the university website to try to find out what the relevant policies were. I didn't know. And then I found it. I was deeply disturbed by how such a sentence could have make its way into an official policy.[14] Later I came to realize just how important it was to remove that sentence because a student had told me she had consulted that policy and understood it to mean that the institution was endorsing the culture she had, as a result of her own experiences, wanted to name and to challenge as "sexual misconduct." It is important to be reminded here that even policies that "sit on the website" can be consulted as expressions of an organization's values. If a policy can be consulted as expressive, a policy can be a technique: it can be a way of shaping conduct by giving permission to that conduct or by refusing to withdraw permission for that conduct.[15]

We needed a new policy to state that such conduct was not institutionally permitted even if a new policy would be insufficient to change the culture. Simply put, it is hard to complain about conduct if institutions state they endorse that conduct, an endorsement that can be in a policy that sits there, becoming part of the background, shared as an agreement.

Even if a new policy would not bring into effect what it named (creating a culture in which such conduct was not permissible), it would still have effects (by giving people a means to challenge that culture).

Policies can be how we support a case for what needs to be done. Let me return to the trans lecturer whose complaint about discrimination in a promotion case led him to develop a new trans equality policy. He was aware that a new policy would not necessarily change the culture of the institution that the absence of a policy revealed. But he also had a sense of the point of developing a policy: "There were no policies of guidelines for trans people. So, in that process, I was creating a conversation. That opened up a lot of awareness of what needs to happen." As we have learned, policies can be developed as a way of avoiding a conversation. But policies can also "create a conversation," a conversation about why new policies are necessary or about what "needs to happen." A policy should not be treated as the end of our work, *what* we are trying to achieve, but as part of our work, *how* we are trying to achieve something.[16]

A POSITIVE DUTY

The environment in which complaints are made is often the same environment complaints are about. In this section I want to consider how equality has become part of that environment. My discussions with diversity practitioners that formed the basis of On Being Included (2012) took place as many practitioners were writing new race equality policies. These policies were required because of the amendment to the law, which changed equality from a negative to a positive duty for all public organizations in the UK. Since the Equality Act of 2010, the general equality duty is now understood in positive terms: "The general equality duty therefore requires organisations to consider how they could positively contribute to the advancement of equality and good relations. It requires equality considerations to be reflected into the design of policies and the delivery of services, including internal policies, and for these issues to be kept under review." "Positive" is supposed to refer to a field of action; public bodies have to demonstrate what they are actively doing to promote equality.

The redefinition of equality as a positive duty has meant that a great deal of effort has been invested in writing new equality policies. Many of the practitioners I spoke to were very skeptical about what was being achieved by writing race equality policies. One practitioner said, "Well I think in terms of the policies, people's views are, 'well we've got them now so that's done, it's finished.' I think actually, *I'm not sure if that's even worse than having nothing,* that idea in people's heads that we've done race, when we very clearly haven't done race." A policy can create the illusion of doing something without doing anything. Note that for this practitioner the problem with writing new policies is not simply because senior management can use them for instrumental ends. She is implying that the problem goes deeper; policies can create a general idea "that we have done race." Another practitioner described a "marshmallow feeling" created as an effect of having a new policy. A policy can create a shared impression, necessarily vague, that a problem has been dealt with.

The redefinition of equality as a positive duty has created more of a gap between how institutions appear and how they are experienced. In other words, equality and diversity are increasingly used to create the appearance of doing something. I noted earlier how complaints, even when treated as negative data or negative speech, can be channeled in a positive direction by being treated as "positive publicity." In other words, organizations can use complaints as evidence of how they resolve a problem even before a problem is identified. When we are talking about "minding the gap," we are learning about the *uses of an appearance.*

The gap between the positive use of equality and diversity and our experience of making complaints felt like a gap we fell through. In the middle of the three years we were trying to challenge the culture of sexual harassment, the college appointed a new equality officer. When we first met, she told me about all the work she wanted to do, positive work, drawing on the expertise of many academics at the college. I just wanted to talk about the problems we were facing in trying to address the culture of sexual harassment. In subsequent meetings, it felt like a disconnect; to me at least, positive action seemed a distraction.

I noted earlier how making a complaint can feel like going against the current even when you are following the organization's own procedures. That current can even include equality as positive action. It was only after students organized a conference on sexual harassment in 2015, which was hosted by the Centre for Feminist Research, and which the equality officer attended, that the currents of equality and complaint began to meet. We began talking to each other about why we needed new complaints procedures and better support systems, and also how the problem of sexual harassment related to institutional culture. The equality officer began to push for change; I have already noted how she was the person who finally got the policy on conflicts of interest removed from the website. When I resigned, I emailed her the following: "You have made such a difference since you have been here! Sorry not to have more energy to sustain the fight. I am really going to try and get colleagues to see why it is an issue that everyone should be working on—not just a few of us—before I go." The point of sharing this story is that it took work, led, as it often is, by students, to enable equality and complaint to become shared currents. That work was about creating a space in which we could discuss the problems rather than simply focus on solutions (solutions; resolutions; dissolutions). The work of complaint can be how we rechannel equality work.

There was another gap that was hard to handle. In 2014, in the middle of the inquiries, I received an invitation to join an Athena SWAN committee.[17] A senior manager wrote to me:

> I do hope you are willing and have the time to work with us on this, as both your academic expertise and your personal insights into potential barriers encountered by women . . . will be invaluable. If and when we proceed with an actual application, we will need to set up a steering group comprising membership from several academic departments. [X] is also very keen that we take this forward and become seen as sector-leading in our practices as well as our theoretical contributions.

I didn't respond to that email, but I was struck both by how barriers are framed as personal insights and by the ambition to become a sector leader on gender equality. I received another email the following year, which was addressed to me and a feminist colleague, which indicated the college was planning to make "an application for the institutional bronze award next year." I felt dismayed when I received the invitation and when I heard of their plan. It made me aware that an organization could go for an award in gender equality while working very hard to stop any conversations about the very serious problems of sexual harassment that had been brought out by multiple inquiries.

In conducting this research subsequently, I have been struck by how many interviewees made specific reference to Athena SWAN.[18] Many experienced as frustrating, even excruciating, the fact that their universities were going for an equality award while they were trying to make complaints. In some cases, the pressure to be involved in Athena SWAN was experienced as bullying. One postgraduate student made a complaint about bullying from her supervisor that included pushing her to do Athena SWAN: "She kept wanting me to do Athena SWAN things. I didn't want to. I was very critical of the diversity agenda. And she kept critiquing me." The supervisor's bullying seemed to be about pushing the student to do activities that would enable the supervisor to achieve institutional recognition and to stop her from doing activities that would not: "She said my work didn't align with the impact work she wanted to do." If an equality award becomes another institutional measure of value, it is not surprising that students and more precarious staff can end up being pressured to undertake that work even if that work does not correspond with their own values. That some can be pushed into doing positive versions of equality work can be evidence of the impact of institutional inequality. Simply put, how equality is done reproduces inequalities.

I spoke to an early career academic who ended up as a cochair of her department's Athena SWAN committee. She did not want to be on the committee because she "did not believe in Athena SWAN." She was "told to do it." She described herself as "the token queer on the committee," which might give us an insight into why she was "told to do it." She describes a meeting:

> We had a meeting yesterday to see where we are with Athena SWAN and my cochair was like, "People are quite unhappy but we are only unhappy with HR. We think things are great in the department." And I was "that's not true, that's not true at all because the heads of school aren't doing anything, when we take it to them the heads of school are stopping it." When my cochair said it's just HR, it's clearly not HR, it is something in our school. And I am sure other people's schools as well.... And our head of school actively tried to prevent us from tackling any of these problems. She actually said to us, "It's okay, all you have to do is list the issues. That's all you have to do to get a bronze award, and then maybe we can deal with some of them in order to get the silver."

In the meeting her cochair denied the problems in the department or school. If there was a recognition that "people are unhappy," that unhappiness was located somewhere else. But she knew this was not true. She knew that people in her department were unhappy with the department. She knew this because she complained about what was going on; she knew this because other colleagues had complained about what was going on. A complaint is evidence that what is going on is going wrong:

> We have [X], who has just been promoted to professor. I have no idea how: he's shouted at me, he's shouted at other women, he takes credit for what women do. Several of us have gone to our current head of school. I went to our current head of school about it as well and she

just said, oh well it is not that big a deal, maybe we'll let HR deal with it if they feel it is necessary. So the person who was suffering the most from this guy because they were working closely together, she was doing all this work and he was taking all this credit. He was bullying her, going into her office and talking to her face. She went to HR to make a formal complaint. They told her they were too busy to accept a formal complaint from her.

She enters that Athena SWAN meeting knowing that there had been attempts to make complaints about harassment and bullying from at least one senior academic in her school. She enters that Athena SWAN meeting knowing that although complaints had been blocked by Human Resources (being "too busy" can be a blockage), they were not about Human Resources. She enters that Athena SWAN meeting knowing the school had recently promoted an academic man to professor even though he had been accused of bullying, plagiarism, and harassment. She enters that Athena SWAN meeting knowing the head of school had tried to prevent anyone "from tackling any of these problems." Think about what that would be like: to be told at an equality meeting that people are "only unhappy with HR" and that "we think things are great in the department," knowing what she knew.

The problem here is not only the denial of the problem here. Going for an equality award can be used to justify *delaying* the effort to deal with the problem of harassment and bullying. (All you have to do is "list the issues" to "get a bronze.") If institutions can be rewarded for listing issues rather than dealing with them, they are being rewarded for not dealing with them. It is also possible for institutions to be rewarded for concealing issues if not listing issues can be used to imply not having them. And so: you can end up in an equality meeting in which there is a refusal to recognize ongoing, institutional inequalities.

When equality is used to contradict the evidence of inequality, equality is inequality given a new face. Some of the people I spoke to talked about how those who gave a face to an organization's commitment to equality were the same people who tried to stop their complaints (most often, it seems, senior white women). Let me refer back to the experiences of the senior lecturer who complained about harassment and bullying by her head of department. A senior woman manager played a significant role in undermining and threatening her during the complaint. She said, "Whenever there's something to do with feminism she is trotted out— she's clearly not a feminist. . . . I thought, it's so ironic she becomes the figurehead." It is an irony that she is a figurehead for feminism given her role in stopping complaints about sexual harassment. In fact, this woman was also the chair of the university's Athena SWAN committee. We need to learn from this: the people who head equality initiatives can be the same people who try to suppress complaints, often by threatening and silencing those who make them.

The face you see when you are stopped from complaining can be the face of an equality initiative. I spoke to a woman of color academic who made a number of complaints about racism as well as sexism throughout her career. She described what happened when she tried to address "the issue of gender" in her department:

> We were having a group discussion of what we need not to be complacent about. I raised the issue of gender. I said, look, even before I came to this department there had been narratives about it not having an inclusive research culture. One senior male professor said, "This is just a personal issue for you." It wasn't put back as a feedback to the rest of the department. That evening I saw the head of department, and I said, I think this is a real issue: women have left and women who are here feel they don't get treated well for promotions and stuff. It's not just a throwaway thing. It's not just an ephemeral thing. And he said, "I would like to throw that issue into the dustbin."

When she first raises the issue of gender, a senior man professor makes it a personal issue. A structural issue is turned into a personal issue as if she is concerned about gender inequality only because she is concerned for herself. And that she raised the issue is not recorded ("it wasn't put back as feedback to the department"). When she raises the issue again with her head of department, saying it's a real issue, not just personal, not ephemeral, he tells her he "would like to throw that issue into the dustbin." I noted earlier that complaints often end up in filing cabinets or dustbins. Issues can also end up in dustbins. But later the same head of department said to her, "We need to do something about gender and equality." She is quite clear about how to interpret this apparent change of position: "It was to do with grant funding." Of course, it is not surprising that organizations are more willing to invest in equality when it is directly linked to resources. And, yes, we can be pragmatic, or strategic, we can argue that all equality initiatives need to be linked to resources so organizations will take them more seriously.[19] But we can also hear in her account a more critical position: that equality when resourced is also *channeled in a certain direction*, a more positive direction, and that this channeling does not mean that issues like gender inequality are no longer treated as rubbish.

The positive model of equality in channeling institutional work in a certain direction can thus make it harder to complain about inequalities. She explained, "I was on the equality and diversity group in the university. And as soon as I started mentioning things to do with race, they changed the portfolio of who could be on the committee and I was dropped." Some words can carry a complaint; all you have to do is use a word like *race* and you will be heard as complaining. In part II of this book I will return to how you are heard as complaining for using certain words. If to use a word like *race* is to be dropped, then to participate in equality and diversity initiatives, you might have to drop those words. In her testimony, she also made reference to another "positive duty": "You are not allowed to be negative about the institution." She was referencing a clause within her university's code of conduct that requires all staff not to say anything that would negatively impact the reputation of the institution. This is how turning equality into a positive agenda can become part of an institutional agenda. A positive duty can refer to a duty to be positive about the organization, including being positive about its commitments to equality and diversity.

This folding in of positive duties can mean the folding out of complaint and those deemed complainers, those who are not willing to speak the happier language of diversity or the emptier terms of nonperformativity. A positive duty can thus be expressed negatively as a duty not to complain or not to complain in such a way that undermines the reputation of the organization. When positive uses of equality are instrumentalized this is achieved not only through marketing or disciplinary regimes that impose being positive (or not being negative) as a duty upon academics. Academics can also be invested in organizations as progressive spaces. One senior woman academic described what happened when she became head of department:

> I ended up on a table full of blokes, heads of department, [the deputy vice chancellor]. They were big kind of cheeses on that table. I was the only woman. The conversation was not what I would have expected from people at a university, especially somewhere like here, which I believed at the time was a good place to be with its attitudes to women. The conversation was like being in a men's club, you know. It was really offensive. They didn't notice me; they didn't even see me. I got out [from] the table and I was almost in tears, which sounds ever

so dramatic. And it disturbed and upset me not just because of who they were but because of the conversation: it was just so offensive.

In being unnoticed, unseen, she was able to see what was going on, to hear how those conversations sound, "like being in a men's club." It was all the more disturbing, all the more upsetting to hear the conversations at that table, at that university, because of what she expected; she didn't expect those sorts of conversations because she believed the university to be "a good place to be with its attitude to women." For her, telling me this story was also about telling me that she no longer had that belief, she no longer believed that university to be a good place for women.

An experience of sexism and misogyny becomes more difficult to process because to recognize what is going on can mean giving up a belief in an organization. It can be a lot to give up, that belief in the organization, that belief the organization you work for shares your beliefs. I spoke to another senior woman academic. She is a visibly disabled, biracial, queer woman. She understood herself to be a diversity hire, that her appointment signaled a commitment to change: "I was brought in to assist with some cultural change, to bring in diversity and a progressive curriculum." But when an organization appoints someone "to assist with some cultural change," it does not mean those within the organization are willing to be assisted:

> I found being the only woman in a senior management group quite a distressing experience. I found there were lots of sexualized conversations. I felt like I was in a latrine. They were really over the top, inappropriate. There were also racialized conversations. They always referred to "the black boy." . . . The dean works in critical jurisprudence, he is a really high flyer and crash hot about feminist stuff, feminist politics and scholarship. He had a double kind of life. It was a bit of shock for me, not the negative attitudes but the way that management was run. I thought someone from a diverse background would actually make a difference, which is why I took up that position. I was the most senior person with a visible disability in the university.

Mind the gap, find the gap: it can be a gap between an appearance of being committed to diversity and equality and the kinds of conversations that are routine; it can be a gap between having a senior manager who is "hot about feminist stuff" and the conduct of that manager. You come to realize that hiring someone from a "diverse background" does not make a difference, that your arrival does not make a difference, even though they can and do use your arrival as a sign of having made a difference. In fact, even if your difference does not make a difference, you are still supposed to be positive, which means overlooking so much negative stuff: all those sexualized conversations, all those racialized conversations. If you complain, especially publicly, you are often deemed to be compromising the attempts made by others within the organization to enable change in more positive ways. Those who embody diversity, who have direct experience of a problem, tend to be more policed the more they try to transform institutions. You can be dropped out of conversations and activities for not doing institutional work in the right way. In order not to be dropped, you too can be channeled in a positive direction.

Feminist work can also end up channeled in that direction. A feminist duty can be expressed as a duty to be positive about the institution. I learned this duty by failing to fulfill it. When I disclosed that there had been inquiries into sexual harassment where I had worked, I was reprimanded not by managers or administrators (who, with one exception, did not communicate with me after I shared that information) but by some of my former feminist colleagues. One colleague described my action as "rash" and said that my action was "against the interest of many long-standing feminist colleagues who have worked to ensure a happy and stimulating environment." If I had publicly identified as a feminist killjoy, I was here identified as killing feminist joy.[20] The college had certainly not provided a "happy and stimulating environment" for those who had been harassed or those who had complained about harassment. She wrote to me again, saying that I should have set up a meeting with other women professors in order to avoid a "fallout which damages us all, now and in the future." We had already called many meetings. That another meeting could be imagined as the solution to a problem teaches us how problems are not dealt with. We learn also from how a complaint, when made public, becomes damaging to "us all," those who are part of the institution and those who identify with the institution. The damage to those who were harassed, to those who complained about harassment, disappears from view.

We need to learn from that fact that it is possible that a disclosure about sexual harassment could be framed as compromising not just the university but feminism. The implication is that feminist happiness *within* the institution depends upon withholding complaints *about* the institution. I began to revisit my earlier experiences of trying to deal with the problem of sexual harassment as an institutional problem. At the first event we held, when students spoke openly about their experiences of sexual harassment and sexual misconduct, another feminist colleague expressed concern to me in private. She said she was concerned that speaking publicly about the problem of sexual harassment in the college would lead to people overlooking the critical feminist work that had historically been done at the college. She was not saying we *should* be silent about the problem of sexual harassment in order to keep sight of the college's feminist history. Rather her concern teaches us how silence ends up being preferred as an orientation.

In order to promote certain kinds of progressive, feminist, or critical work, the evidence of complaint is treated as a secret or like dirty laundry, *what should not be aired in public.* To make a complaint often requires going against what are deemed your duties, including your duty to be positive about an organization and its commitments to equality and diversity. The negativity of complaint thus matters. That negativity is not only a feeling or an attitude. It is a political action: a refusal to use the empty phrases of the nonperformative or to be bound by a positive duty.

CHAPTER TWO

ON BEING STOPPED

What appears on paper as a flow can be experienced as a blockage. In this chapter I want to explore how blockages and stoppages happen and what we can learn from them. We learn how institutions work, what I am calling *institutional mechanics*, by how complaints are stopped. An early career lecturer talked to me about her attempt to make a complaint on behalf of an undergraduate student about the sexual misconduct of a professor. She described her experience of the process thus: "It felt like a game of chess, that we were all on this chess board, and it was checkmate for me; there were no more possible moves. There was no support network there for me. I felt like I was blocked—the position provides me with accommodation, it is where I live, all of those sorts of things, so it would have massive ramifications for everything." Feeling blocked and unsupported is about having nowhere to go with the complaint. It can feel like you have been playing a game with so many moves and that you used them all up. Having nowhere to go with a complaint, no possible moves left, can have "massive ramifications for everything."

How do blockages happen? In chapter 1, I quoted an administrator who supported students through the complaint process. She described blockages as occurring through conversations; a complaint can be "bogged down" if those you talk to are bogged down. She also suggested that the first stage of a complaints process—when persons are encouraged to resolve complaints informally in their own departments—can be "really difficult in some situations." Again, to use her words, this is where complaints "might get stuck." Complaints can end up stuck in the complainer's own department, which is to say, complaints often end up stuck in the first place they are articulated. Complaints are stuck *closer to home*.

I turn to the question of *where* complaints get stuck with specific reference to the use of doors in chapter 5. In this chapter I explore what we can learn from the conversations that happen in the early and informal stage of the complaint process, as a would-be complainer. The would-be complainer is someone who has indicated to somebody within the institution that they are considering making a complaint. Some of these conversations could be called *institutional*; these are the conversations you have to have with certain people because of their institutional role or status: for academics, you might have to speak to your head of department (or another senior academic if the complaint is about the head of department) or the head of Human Resources; for students, you have to speak to a course leader, a supervisor, a director of studies, or a member of Human Resources. Most of these conversations happen behind closed doors; there is no official record of what has been said or even that these conversations have taken place. If an informal complaint does not become a formal complaint, those conversations might as well, from an institutional point of view, not have happened, which might be telling us something about why as well as how they happen.

WARNINGS

In chapter 1 I explored how doing the work of complaint often means "minding the gap," the gap between what does happen and what should happen. A gap can be what you fall through or how you fall through. *Mind the gap* is a familiar instruction to us from trains, trams, and other transport systems. The gap you are supposed to mind is the gap between the train or tram and the platform.

Mind the gap means be careful, watch out, take heed! Warnings are useful techniques for directing or redirecting the behavior of others because they introduce notes of caution predicated not on abstract rules about rights and wrongs but on a person's own health and safety. Warnings are certainly alerting someone about something; they are intended to inform you of a danger ahead. A warning might be telling you *how* to treat a situation (as dangerous). For warnings to be useful they need to be articulated in a timely fashion so that a potential danger can be avoided; in other words, a warning is also an instruction about what you need to do in order to avoid a damaging situation.

2.1 Take care! Photo: Reinhard Dietrich.

Those who make complaints are frequently warned about the consequences of complaining. If people are warned about complaining, they are being told to avoid complaint as a way of avoiding doing something that would endanger themselves in some way. Warnings are all about consequences; a warning might bypass the rights or wrongs of an action by focusing the attention of the person considering complaint purely on the consequences of the action.

Warnings can vary in intonation. They can be articulated softly or be stern and alarming. Let's start with the softer warnings, those spoken in the language of care and concern. A concern about the consequences of complaint is often expressed as "thinking about your career." One student said, "I was also told that if I made a formal complaint, this was the head of department, I had to think about my career." Another student said, "I ended up going back to the chair and saying, look, this is harassment and I am going to file a complaint. And his response was essentially, 'Well we are just thinking about your career, how this will affect you in the future.'" The implication is that to proceed with a formal complaint is *not* to think about your career.[1] Your career is evoked as a companion who needs to be looked after; maybe your career is a plant that needs watering so that it does not wither away. If your career would wither as a consequence of complaining, then a complaint would be careless, even negligent.

Warnings that are expressed out of concern for one's career do not always feel like concern; in these cases, it was quite clear to the students concerned that the concern for their careers was masking some other concern. Whether warnings feel concerned for the welfare of those being warned seems to depend not so much on the words used, or how they are used, but on the kind of relationship that already exists between those who are warning and those who are warned. A junior woman of color academic was warned by a senior woman of color academic about the costs of complaining: "This was a professor who I really trust and who did probably have my best interests at heart and she said to me at that point, don't put in a grievance, you are a young academic, and if you do that now you are going to be known as someone who puts in grievances, you are going to be known as someone who puts in complaints, so just let it go, and work out something informally." This warning evokes the danger of complaint as the danger of how you will become known. The warning is also an instruction about what not to do. She is advised to "let it go" in order not to be known as "someone who puts in grievances" or "someone who puts in complaints."

A complaint is treated as *sticky data*.[2] A warning can be telling you that if you make a complaint, not only will it stick to you, it will be how you get stuck. It is important to stress here that this early career academic understood the professor as having or as probably having her "best interests at heart." Her trust, I think, came out of political allegiance and from a recognition that her colleague, as a senior woman of color, had had a political struggle to get as far as she did. Warnings can be expressed not only out of concern for the well-being of others but out of a sense of being worn. When you have to battle the institutions of patriarchal whiteness to establish yourself you might become wary about complaining because you are wary about being worn. That wariness can be passed on as a warning to others.

When warnings are used to discourage a course of action they also function as more positive directives: you are being encouraged not to complain, to "let it go" by resolving things in some other way or by hoping for some other resolution. Indeed, one academic described not complaining as the default setting: "the default academia thing, the university thing: it will be fine, if we do wait, don't make a fuss." A default is what will happen if you do not change something intentionally by performing an action. Not complaining can thus also be about not performing an action or not altering a setting; not complaining as how things are set. Complaining is often treated as "making a fuss" about something or making something bigger than it needs to be. I will return to the significance of this evocation in part II. Not complaining becomes a virtue, a kind of calm patience, a positive outlook, as if waiting is what would make something fine, as if the best way to approach a wrong is to wait for it to right itself. The flip side of a warning is thus a promise, an institutional version of what I call *the promise of happiness*, a promise that if you don't complain you will go further.

Sometimes you can be given permission to complain and be warned about the consequences of complaint at the very same time. A postgraduate student was considering making a complaint against her supervisor who had sexually harassed her. She goes to the office that handles such complaints: "They were like, 'You can file a complaint.' But then the same narrative: 'Not much is going to happen: he's really well loved by the university; he has a strong publication record; you are going to go through all of this emotional torment.' It was even proposed that he could countersue me for defamation of character. The line was essentially, you can do this, but why would you." What she calls "the same narrative" is skepticism that there is any point in following a complaint procedure, which is articulated by those responsible for the administration of those procedures. There is a sense that even if you file a complaint, what will happen is "not much," no matter what evidence you have in the file. There is a certain kind of fatalism operating here; we might call this a procedural fatalism ("procedures will be procedures!") or institutional fatalism ("institutions will be institutions!").[3] Institutional fatalism tells you that institutions are what they are such that there is no point in trying to change them. That fatalism can be performed through warnings is instructive: after all, warnings are about how you can avoid certain consequences. The implication is that in order to avoid certain consequences, you should avoid complaint: to complain would be to hurtle toward a miserable fate, complaint as fatalism, to leave the right path, the institutional path, to bring misery upon yourself. A prediction that the consequences of complaint will be dire, not only that you would experience emotional torment but that you could render yourself even more precarious further down the line ("he could countersue me for defamation of character"), is also an expectation that those who are institutionally valued will retain their value no matter what, no matter who.

If a complaint is deemed in advance to be dangerous, a complaint can also be framed as pointless, as what will not stop the reproduction of the same thing. A warning that you won't achieve anything by complaining makes a warning about the danger of complaint even more likely to succeed because it suggests there would be no point to putting yourself in danger. And note you can be told "you can do this" while being warned about doing this. Warnings can operate in the realm of the *would* rather than the *could*. Warnings can be translated into questions you end up having to ask yourself: *you* could complain, but, if that's what is going to happen, why would you? A warning becomes about what you would not do if you wanted to protect yourself, your career, and your own happiness.

Sometimes you can be told you should make a complaint and be warned about making a complaint at the very same time. A woman student who was sexually assaulted by an academic man described a warning she received from a woman research assistant:

> She told me that if I wanted to make an official complaint (which I should), she would support me. Yet, she also told me about her own experience of sexual harassment by another professor in another school and warned me about what would happen and what would not. Especially considering this professor's image in the school, she said I should have been ready for the possibility that many people wouldn't even believe me and would accuse me of misunderstanding his open-mindedness and intimacy.

A warning about "what would happen" can be predicated on what has happened. And a warning about "what would happen" can even be offered as feminist knowledge about how sexism operates as a belief system—a knowledge of how much is invested in the professor and his image and how that investment means he will be protected from facing the consequences of his actions (turning even an assault into a fault of perception, a misunderstanding of his "open-mindedness and intimacy"). I think it is important that a warning can be offered in the style of a report. The person who warns you can do so by reporting on what is likely to happen given the prevalence of beliefs she does not herself have and might even oppose. A wealth of feminist knowledge can be translated into a warning. If we accumulate more evidence that she will not be believed, that evidence can be used as a technique of redirection; she can be given even more reasons not to complain.

Even as she is told by her feminist colleague that she *should* complain and that she will receive the support of that colleague if she does complain, she is also being told to "ready" herself for the consequences ("the possibility that many people wouldn't even believe me"). She is being offered what I would call *qualified support*, when someone says they will support something or somebody but then qualifies that support with a concern of some kind. Qualified support might be how some can retain an idea of themselves as being supportive ("she would support me") while withdrawing their support. I noted earlier that warnings are usually telling you to be more concerned with consequences than anything else. The qualification of support is also predicated on a concern for consequences more than anything else.[4] I don't think qualified support is especially supportive; qualified support can be an oblique warning, a warning made without being expressed.

A warning is a technique of redirection: somebody is being directed away from a path they have indicated they might take or they have started taking. One academic described how she and a number of other colleagues decided to make a formal complaint about bullying from a head of department. Whichever way they turned—to Human Resources, to the union, to other colleagues—they were discouraged from taking that route:

> Every time we tried to initiate a formal inquiry someone would stop us and say it is not a good idea to do that. Someone from the union, someone from HR or someone from the university, they would frighten you with the process. I think that's what they do. They would say, most complaints, they go on for a year, the people are so resentful by the end of it they don't want to work in the place and nothing ever happens. And that's the union.

Evidence of the difficulty of a process can also be used to try to stop someone from entering that process. You frighten people into not going through the process by representing the process as frightening. If warnings evoke frightening consequences, they do so by making what is frightening present. You come to feel the consequences of an action before you commit to that action ("people are so resentful by the end of it").

Note again the function of fatalism: a sense that what will happen, will happen; the past is used like an arrow that points to what will happen. You are being told the likely consequences of complaint before you proceed, as if what will happen to you will be the same thing as what happened to others before you: that complaint has led people to want to leave ("they don't want to work in the place and nothing ever happens") and that a complaint will lead to your leaving. Warnings are more likely to work to stop someone if they contain within them a kernel of truth. Predictions can have truth value (people do leave as a consequence of complaint) and function as directives (don't complain if you don't want to leave).

In this example, the union is among many different actors who tried to stop the informal complaints being turned into formal complaints. She continues:

> We keep putting in complaints, but our union constantly discouraged us going down the formal complaint route. We were wondering whether to put in an official grievance, and the union kept discouraging us and discouraging us. It was like they were on the side of the university: it felt like that to us; I don't know what was going on there. You would meet with the union leader and he would say things like, "It's their sandpit; they can decide who is going to play in it."

She experiences the union's effort to stop a formal complaint or grievance as siding with the university (fatalism as a side). You can be left unsure by what is going on but still "feel" that different actors are siding together; siding as stopping. A warning becomes an alignment, how different actors seem to be invested in the same thing, stopping a complaint from going forward.

Institutional fatalism thus offers a way of viewing the organization. Just think of how at the meeting when they are being discouraged from complaining, the head of the union shares a view of the university: "It's their sandpit; they can decide who is going to play in it." Warnings can *reproduce* a view of an organization. In this instance, the act of discouraging a complaint about bullying is an endorsement of bullying, treating the university as a sandpit that is owned; decisions made about "who is going to play in it" as how forms of conduct become right or even rights. Such a way of viewing the organization is how a bully is given permission to bully, as if to say, because of what institutions are like, heads *can do what they like*. Warnings about complaint can not only offer predictions of bad consequences for those who make complaints; they can function as endorsements of the conduct a complaint is being made to challenge. Institutional fatalism could be thought of as a useful tool for those who wish to assert their power within institutions: it is how certain kinds of behavior are deemed natural and inevitable, as being the nature of the game. A complainer becomes by fault and default the one who does not know the rules of the game.

I noted earlier that warnings can vary in intonation. Some warnings are given in a stern and disciplinary tone. One student described what happened when she and a group of postgraduate students tried to make a complaint about harassment from other students: "I was repeatedly told that 'rocking the boat' or 'making waves' would affect my career in the future and that I would ruin the department for everyone else. I was told if I did put in a complaint, I would never be able to work in the university and that it's likely I wouldn't get a job elsewhere." Complaints are framed as self-damage, how you would damage yourself, how you would stop yourself from getting anywhere. The implication is that the damage caused by complaint travels; you are being told you would ruin your career, yes, but you are also being told you would ruin a department or institution. Perhaps a warning is how your own happiness is made dependent on the extent to which you are willing to protect the happiness of an institution.

This student used the expressions "rocking the boat" and "making waves" a number of times in her communications with me.[5] In being warned about complaint, she is being told that "that" is what a complaint would be doing. She explains further:

> All this time everyone had said to us informally, different students and staff members, had said to us, don't do this, you'll ruin your career, you'll be making waves and no one likes you to make waves. . . . At this point, we really realized that, like, oh shit, we started to realize that we could actually get kicked out because of this, we could lose our jobs because of this, and the university was making it quite clear that they are a really big institution and we are four PhD students with not very much power or resources.

A complaint is heard as making waves, as stopping things from being steady. The implication here is that rocking as a motion is more dangerous for those with less stable footing. Warnings can be used to remind people of the precarity of their situation. They can also be used to put people in their place, to tell someone who is bigger and who is smaller (they are bigger; you are smaller) or who will prevail and who will not (they will prevail; you will not). You can be put in your place by being reminded of how easy it would be for you to lose your place. The expressions "making waves" and "rocking the boat" can also be used to imply a deliberate act of causing trouble or controversy; to make waves or rock the boat is to upset the status quo. So if a warning is about the consequences of an action, a warning can also be a judgment that those consequences are intended: that you complain in order to cause damage, controversy, or trouble.

Warnings can function as an increase of pressure. They become what you have to withstand. She described how the pressure not to complain was exerted: "In just one day I was subjected to eight hours of grueling meetings and questioning, almost designed to break me and stop me from taking the complaint any further." You can stop people from doing something by making it harder for them to do something. Breaking someone, stopping them from complaining, can be "almost" part of the design. In other words, the system is designed to make it difficult for people to proceed with a complaint.

When warnings don't work, when they don't stop someone from proceeding with a complaint, warnings are often converted into threats. She told me how, toward the end of the meeting, the head of department made reference to her source of funding:

> And then she said, have you looked at your agreement with the [funding body] because there is an agreement that says that if you appear to be slanderous against the university that's a reason to have your funding withdrawn. And then she said that if you were to repeat anything that happened in this meeting that would be unethical, that would be breaking a code of research ethics, because we haven't had an agreement for you to quote me. So it was explicit: she said, we can take away your funding, we can discredit you as researchers for being unethical for talking about this complaint.

The explicit threat that they would or could have their funding withdrawn if they proceeded with the complaint was tied to damage to reputation. We are back to that positive duty given negative expression as the duty not to say anything slanderous about the university. The threat was also tied to confidentiality: to be threatened in a meeting is to be threatened not to talk about being threatened in a meeting.[6] Indeed, during the meeting the head of department calls her a whistle-blower: "What's happened is a whistle has been blown, and you've blown that whistle. You're the whistle-blower. I thought, that's weird, why is she saying that to me?" It was weird that her head of department called her a whistle-blower because whistle-blowers disclose information about misconduct within an institution to a wider public, while they as students had only made an informal complaint within the institution. To turn a would-be complainer into a whistle-blower is to warn the students about what they might become if they follow that route.

It is important to add that threats do not always need to be made quite so explicitly. You don't have to say: I will or they will take your funding away if you proceed with a complaint. You could just mention the source of funding for a threat to be made. In this case the threat is made explicit with reference to rules, to preexisting agreements or codes, which almost works to conceal where (and whom) the threat is coming from. When warnings become threats, you are being told not only that you will damage your career if you complain but that they will damage your career if you complain.

Such threatening warnings seem rather different from warnings offered as care and concern. Warnings coming from different places still lead in the same direction. Consider also that complaints procedures often come with warnings. I noted earlier that the expression "rocking the boat" can be used to imply a deliberate attempt to cause damage. The figure of the "malicious complainer" also functions as a warning, used to denote those whose complaints are motivated by a desire to cause damage to others. The figure of the malicious complainer has precedence by policy. Many complaint policies not only evoke the possibility of malicious, vexatious, and frivolous complaints; they warn those who would make such complaints that disciplinary action will follow. This is from one university's complaints policy: "Frivolous, malicious and/or vexatious complaints will not be accepted. If we consider that a complaint is frivolous, malicious and/or vexatious, this may constitute a disciplinary offence and would be dealt with under the Student Disciplinary Procedure."[7]

If the figure of the malicious complainer has precedence by policy, some people will be judged as malicious complainers more quickly than others. A woman of color was told her complaint was a "scatter gun," as if she were firing at anybody or anything. Another woman of color told me she was called a "loose cannon," as if the damage caused by making a complaint was a result of a failure of precision. Perhaps the people who are more likely to be judged as malicious complainers are the same people who are more likely to be judged as dangerous. That the figure of the malicious complainer can be used as a warning teaches us how some complaints can be dismissed in advance by being judged as motivated by the desire to cause damage to the whole system and as deriving from a failure to be properly attached to that system.

NODS

Warnings often articulate a no, don't go there, don't do that. In this section, I want to explore how complaints can be stopped by a yes. Consider how complaints policies are sometimes represented as open-door polices. An open door can be a *yes*, come in; we will hear you. But *yes* is not necessarily saying *yes*, go there or *yes*, do that. So we need to ask: What is that *yes* saying? Or what is that *yes* doing?

In thinking about what *yes* is saying, I want to focus on nodding.[8] Many of those I talked to discussed how, when they gave their complaints, those who received the complaints often nodded. Nods seem to surround complaints. We learn from our surroundings. A nod is when you move your head up and down, often several times, to show agreement, approval, or a greeting. One student made an informal complaint about harassment from other students. She described what happened when she talked to her head of department: "He seemed to take it on board; he was listening; he was nodding. Ten days later I still had not heard anything. A space of limbo opened up." It is striking to me how a limbo is described as a space: you make a complaint and that is where you end up; a limbo is what is opened up. To be in limbo is to be left waiting.

I am interested in what the head of department was doing by nodding. Nodding is not the only thing happening. But nodding is how the head of department is communicating that he is listening: nodding as taking (or seeming to take) something on board. The movement of a head up and down seems to be telling the one who is making the complaint that their complaint is not only being received but is being received well. If you leave feeling encouraged, perhaps that is what nodding is doing: nodding is encouraging. If she leaves feeling that he has taken her complaint on board, she does not then hear anything. She has to do what many who make complaints have to do: follow it up; send reminders, prompts. When you don't hear anything, you have more work to do.

Nodding can be nonperformative. In chapter 1 I used *nonperformative* to refer to institutional speech acts *that do not bring into effect what they name*. If a nod can operate in the realm of the nonperformative, then bodies can be in on the act; that is, bodies too can appear to act without doing anything. A nod can be made in order not to bring something into effect. A head does not even have to move for a nod to be performed. Diversity, for instance, could be thought of as a nod, a yes, yes, that does not require much movement at all.

Nodding is not only a specific gesture but is how a yes is performed or enacted. I spoke to an academic about how she came to a decision about whether to complain about the conduct of senior members of her university, including heads of departments and a deputy vice chancellor, around a table. She was the only women at that table. She described how they were "talking about women's bodies, what they look like, what they do to them as men, what they would do to them. Very sexual. Very sexist jokes. Very sexually overt conversations, and I was sitting there as if I was not there." It was a deeply distressing experience, in part as she had assumed the organization to be as progressive as it claimed to be (see chapter 1). She took the matter up by speaking to another deputy vice chancellor and the director of Human Resources: "I had a hearing . . . but I think it was just to placate me." To placate is to calm or to soothe. *Placate* derives from the word *please*, to be agreeable. If a hearing is a placating, then a hearing can be used to calm someone down by appearing to agree to something. Being placated is another way a complaint is stopped. When hearing about a problem is offered as a solution, hearing becomes another kind of dissolution. When these senior managers did not do anything after hearing the complaint—and not doing is an action, not simply inaction—she decided not to take the complaint any further. Perhaps a hearing is offered because a hearing is deemed sufficient to complete the action of complaint, as if to have heard a complaint is to have dealt with it.

We can return to my discussion of how complaints involve communicative labor: you have to keep making the same complaint to different people in the organization. Many people shared stories of making an informal complaint to a line manager, supervisor, or head of department with the expectation that that person would take the complaint forward. An expectation can be what you receive: nodding can be expressed as commitment to take the complaint forward. A postgraduate student told her supervisor about sexual misconduct of another postgraduate student: "She was like, leave it with me; I will have a chat with him. And then nothing happened. I suspect in part it was because there was nowhere for her to go with it institutionally. There was nowhere for her to take it. There wasn't enough." When you leave the complaint with somebody and nothing happens, the complaint stays with them; it sits there. We can recall how policies too can just "sit there." She speculates that her supervisor did not take the complaint forward because "there was nowhere" for her to take it.

Taking the complaint forward can be understood as having to make a complaint even if you are making it on someone else's behalf. This might give us a clue as to why so many complaints end up being sat upon. When one early career lecturer told her line manager about being harassed by a professor in the department, her line manager agreed to speak to the professor on her behalf: "I just want someone to have a chat with him and say, please don't continue with this. And she assured me that she would do that." You can receive an assurance, a nod; yes, she will do that, she will ask him to stop. But her line manager did not say or do anything, and the behavior did not stop. She speculated as to why her line manager did not say or do anything: "Much later I learned because she did not want to complain, nothing happened." People might not pass the complaint on if to pass on a complaint is to make the complaint. She added, "It is hard to have those conversations, because you are the problem and the spoilsport; it is easier not to, I suppose. I never spoke to her about why she hadn't, and it clearly wasn't that she forgot." For the line manager to take the complaint forward by asking the professor to stop behaving in this way would be for her to become a spoilsport, to become implicated in what she was passing on. This early career lecturer acknowledged that being implicated in a complaint can be costly: "There is a cost to saying these things; there's a cost to having that conversation." A complaint might not be passed on given that to pass on a complaint can be to pass on the costs of complaint.

The failure to pass on a complaint might tell us something about how complaints are perceived: complaints are treated as contagious, catchy, as well as costly.[9] A complaint can be deemed dangerous because it can contaminate those who touch it. The sociability of the complaint—how many people are involved in getting a complaint through—is thus key to understanding blockages. Some of those I spoke to used the expression "rocking the boat" to convey not only how they were warned but how they were received. In other words, the person who receives the complaint does not pass it on because they do not want to "rock the boat." The woman professor who was placated by how she felt heard by her deputy vice chancellor described how "he gave it a sympathetic hearing but he didn't want to rock the boat, that was for sure." You can be heard sympathetically. That *but* matters. That qualification of support I referred to earlier can also be a qualification of sympathy. And that qualification is associated with the senior manager not wanting to rock the boat, not wanting to disturb an institutional order or hierarchy. (Her complaint was about the conduct of his peers, of other senior academics.) Perhaps those who receive complaints do not pass them on because they fear they will be caught up in the disturbance.

To pass complaints *on* can also be to pass complaints *up*. An early career lecturer noted, "We don't know where to go and we don't feel confident that anyone is going to deal with it. It's especially when people [are] higher up, the readers and professors. People don't want to rock the boat with them, because they are so important and they bring in this grant money and their names really matter." Not wanting to rock the boat by passing a complaint on can also be part of an effort to maintain positive relationships to those with authority and status. Nods might be used because they are a way of stopping complaints by causing the least disturbance.

Agreeing to something is an efficient way of stopping it from happening because you avoid the costs of disagreement. Another academic brought a complaint to her line manager about how her university handled her sick leave, which turned into a grievance about how she had been treated by her university. She noticed that he kept saying *yes*: "I would say he's a yes-man. So, whenever I'd talk to him, he would say yes, but I knew the yes was definitely not a yes; it was a 'we'll see.'" Perhaps a yes can be said because there is not enough behind that yes to bring something about. "Yes saying" can be understood as a management technique. She described this technique as magical:

> this weird almost magical thing that happens when you speak to people in management when you go in there and you're kind of ready for it, and you are really fired up and you kind of put your complaint, your case, your story to the person, and then you sort of leave as if a spell has been cast, leave feeling like, okay something might happen, and then that kind of wears off a few hours later and you think, oh my gosh. It is like a sleight of hand, almost like a trick, you feel tricked.

The feeling that something might happen can be what is being achieved; to be left with a sense you are getting somewhere is how you end up not getting anywhere. A nod can be an attempt to extinguish a fire, to calm as to cool things down. (We learn from this about how a complainer is heard as *fired up*, which might be how complaints are not heard.) A yes can stop a complaint from progressing by diffusing the energy of the one who complains. You can allow a complaint to be expressed in order to contain the complaint.

The management of complaint is thus the management of its expression. A woman of color academic talked to me about PhD students who made an informal complaint about the behavior of professors at research events. The students had stopped coming to research seminars. When they were sent a reminder that attendance was compulsory, they wrote a letter saying "they actively choose not to go these seminars because they were designed for a handful of senior white men in the department." Academics discussed that letter among themselves: "The first thing the director said is that we must defend ourselves. Perhaps these people didn't attend the sessions because they found them too intellectually challenging." This response to the complaint enacted what the complaint was about. She commented on the response of other academics to his comment: "There were a lot of nods." The nods indicated a shared agreement that the complaint masked the failure of the students. These nods seem more performative, bringing something into existence; an agreement becomes shared, a wall built from shared sentiment.

During this discussion they decided to offer the students an "open meeting." She described the point of that meeting as "just about calming them down." She added, "The very people setting up the meeting are the people they are talking about." As I will explore in more detail in chapter 5, *who* receives a complaint is often sufficient to explain *how* it will be received. The official rationale for the meeting is that it gives the students a chance to express themselves. But remember those prior nods, that wall; how the complaint had already been dismissed; how they responded to the complaint about their behavior in the mode of self-defense ("we must defend ourselves"). The point of the open meeting is not to hear the complaint but to enable its dismissal. To dismiss means to send away. You can send the complaint away by letting it out. I think of this mechanism as *institutional venting*. Once the students have vented their frustrations, once they have got complaint out of *their* system, the complaint is out of *the* system. Venting is used as a technique for preventing something more explosive from happening. The mechanism is rather like a pressure relief valve, which lets off enough pressure so that it does not build up and cause an explosion. You let a complaint be expressed to avoid an explosion. A complaint can be thought of as steam: puff, puff. In being let out, a complaint disappears, becoming air. A hearing can be a disappearing; we are back to those magic tricks; puff, puff.[10]

You can manage complaints by managing *where* and *when* they are expressed. Another tactic is to turn the complainer into an informant. A senior woman academic who made a complaint about bullying from her head of department described the response: "[They] told me to report any instances of corruption to them. So of course, I reported these things and they did nothing." Being told to report instances of something gave her something to do. And they did nothing. When she told me this, I felt a shiver down my spine because I recognized something from my own experience. During the inquiries, I had been told by a senior administrator to report any further instances of misconduct to him. And I did report further instances because there were further instances. And I realized how useful it was to them that I did this not because they intended to make use of the information but because they did not. By ensuring that I passed any information I gathered to them, they could ensure that information would be deposited in a safe space, that is, in a file where nobody else would find it.

The management of complaint can also be about controlling to whom complaints are expressed. I noted in my discussion of warnings that if the complainer persists, a warning is turned into a threat or the threat that is already in the warning is made more explicit. If nods don't lead to nothing, in other words, if a complainer persists in making the complaint, nods can be withdrawn. One academic indicated that she intended to make a formal complaint about bullying and harassment by another academic. Initially she was met with sympathetic responses. She described the "initial sympathy and concern from various offices and individuals" as "largely rhetorical." She was implying that sympathy could be given because it was empty; words can be said because of what they do not do. We learn what the initial sympathy was doing by how that sympathy was withdrawn. When she persisted with making a formal complaint, she was received less sympathetically. She said, "The more insistent I was on filing a formal complaint, the more resistant the institution was to addressing my concern; confidential, informal mediation was strongly preferred, because it involves neither fact-finding nor fault-finding." Formal complaints are *data-full*; the complainer is required to gather evidence to support the complaint. In this case, the data included information about bullying and harassment by another member of faculty who was highly valued. To move forward to a formal complaint is to *present that data*. She noted, "On multiple occasions, someone who had initially seemed to be supportive withdrew support or concern—after I had shared sensitive information." Sympathy is withdrawn, no more nodding, as an institutional resistance to receiving "sensitive information." I am interested in how data can be sensitive, how data can touch an institutional nerve. I will return to sensitive data in due course.

In writing and speaking about complaint, I too have been surrounded by nods. One time I gave a lecture that included a discussion of nodding as a nonperformative. The lecture was funded centrally, so there were a number of senior managers in attendance. They were seated toward the front of the lecture theater. Afterward some students came up to me. (Thank you to all the students who come up to me!) They had been seated behind the senior managers. The students observed that the senior managers had been nodding throughout my lecture, including nodding during my discussion of nodding as nonperformative. If you are nodding about what nodding does not do, your nodding is still not doing something. The students were at the tail end of a long and difficult complaint. And they told me that the management had enacted the same tactics that I was describing in the lecture. What then was their nodding doing? Perhaps a nod can be about a public performance; it can be about being seen as giving approval. A public nod can be made because it can be easily withdrawn when you are behind closed doors, which is where complaints are mostly made. If nods can be withdrawn in time, they can also be withdrawn in space. Nodding can be about recognizing a problem insofar as the problem is safely construed as being somewhere else or as coming from someone else. A nod can be how a problem is enacted by the appearance of being heard.

We can return to my discussion of what follows when equality becomes a positive duty: how the same people who express commitments to equality in public can be silencing those who complain behind closed doors. Many of those I have spoken to have versions of this difficulty: minding the gap between what is supposed to happen and what does happen is often about learning what public nods are used to conceal. When a nod is performed well, it does not even appear as a performance, and you know that others, those who are not where you are, doing what you are doing, might be convinced. You know that a nod might be convincing because of a story it can be used to tell; those who are working in the institution, who want to be convinced, can find in the nod a reason for hope, a reason not to give up on an idea of the institution as being warm and inclusive.

BLANKING

Many of the responses to complaints at the early stage of a complaint process are articulated as a no or yes, no don't do that, yes do that, both of which can be used as techniques to stop a complaint from going forward. We need to explain how apparently opposing commands, yes and no, can have the same effects. Most people who complain will receive a yes and no at different points in the time of their complaint. That timing is not necessarily sequential (yes, then no; or no, then yes). In one instance students turned their complaints about racism, which included complaints about the failure of the university to deal with their complaints about racism, into an occupation; they took over a building, the administrative hub of the university. The senior management agreed to a meeting to discuss the students' complaints; they appeared to be willing to give the students a hearing. It turned out that they were pursuing legal action to try to force the students out of the building at the very same time. When yes and no are articulated at the same time, they point in the same direction. A yes can be used as another way of getting the students out.

You can receive a yes or a no or a yes and a no. You can also receive neither a yes nor a no; in other words, you can receive no response at all. I am calling the response of no response *blanking*. To be blanked is to be ignored; you might be treated as if you are not there by someone you would expect to acknowledge you. Sometimes we use the word *blanked* to describe how we forget something in the moment we try to recall it.

Blanking can be an action performed in relation to written and spoken complaints. You can be blanked in person. A senior academic made a complaint about bullying from her head of department. Her head of department had told her he was recording their conversation during the conversation. In a subsequent meeting with administrators, she asked about this recording: "They just stared at me, they didn't answer, they did not speak, which I just found quite extraordinary." A blank stare can be how you are received; you say something, and they say nothing back. This is not *ordinarily* what happens in conversations during meetings ("I found it quite extraordinary"). She is turned into a spectacle by not being heard ("they just stared at me"). By not saying something in response to what she says, it is as if she has not said anything. When you say something, it needs to be acknowledged as having been said. This is what blanking can be doing: when someone says something, you can stop what they say from being said by acting as if they did not say it.

By not acknowledging the person who makes a complaint, you do not acknowledge a complaint. When I noticed how blanking was being used as a method of stopping complaints, I realized I had written about blanking before, even though I had not used that word. One of the examples that I referred to in the introduction to this book, which I first wrote about in *Living a Feminist Life* (2017), was from the film *A Question of Silence*. In the scene, a woman is seated at a table of men. A reminder: she says something and no one acknowledges what she says; a man says the same thing, and he is congratulated. Some are blanked as a matter of routine: they might as well be silent as they will not be heard as saying something if they do. We call that routine *sexism*. One of my examples from chapter 1, which I first wrote about in *On Being Included* (2012), was also about blanking. A diversity officer was blanked when she reminded academics that a new equality policy about academic appointments had been agreed on. When she reminded them, she says, "they looked at [her] as if [she] was saying something really stupid." The diversity officer is an administrator; the woman at the table, a secretary. To become an administrator or a secretary is to be blanked: to assume that role is to be assumed not to be there to say something.

Blanking can be built into a system. When you try to change the system, you encounter what is built in; that is, you are blanked. When the diversity officer is blanked, it is not only she who disappears; the policy disappears too. It was only necessary to blank the policy because it came to exist, that is, because of her work (as well as the work of others) to bring it into existence. The policy is blanked because the previous efforts to stop the policy failed.

Blanking is often used when other methods for stopping something do not succeed. A postgraduate student described a number of failed attempts to get her complaints about harassment and bullying taken seriously. In her last attempt, she felt more hopeful because her complaint was received in a sense that reflected how it was made, that is, with a sense of urgency. When hearing the complaint, a member of Human Resources responded affirmatively, "Yes, you really have a case we can explore and investigate: how would you feel coming back to talk to our director later today?" That yes did what yeses tend to do: she felt encouraged. On the same day she talked to the director of Human Resources: "I felt really supported by him. . . . He also said this isn't the first complaint like this he'd heard within the institution and that he'd heard similar complaints within our division." She assumed that if her complaint was not the first complaint, it would be taken more seriously, it would have more weight.[11] He also gave her a commitment that they "would follow up with me to have further conversations because they wanted to further investigate this. I thought, this is great, this is already moving faster than my process here. This is great, this is awesome." But then she did not receive any more communications: "Not even a response to an email, not even 'I have got your email, I am looking into it.' Nothing. Nothing." Nothing can be achieved by nodding. A nod is followed by a blank. In fact, she received no more responses to any subsequent attempts at communication.

Blanking can come quite late in a series of actions. Blanking can be a sign that someone has persisted with a complaint, persisted beyond warnings, beyond nonperformative nods. Blanking can also be an accumulated history. An Indigenous academic had been trying to put forward a grievance about the sabotage of her tenure case by a senior white academic. Despite numerous attempts to initiate an inquiry, she did not get anywhere: "I had to send an email to her with the subject line in all capital letters with an exclamation point, my final email to her after seven months. THIS IS A GRIEVANCE! THIS IS A GRIEVANCE! And her obligation under the university rules and the process is that she has to put it forward. She did not. She did not put it forward." A complaint does not go forward because it is not put forward by those who receive the complaint. That capitalized subject heading has much to teach us about hearing. Sometimes you have to shout because you are not heard. If you have to shout because you are not heard, you are heard as shouting. If you are heard as shouting, you are not heard. The effects of complaints not being heard make it even less likely that complaints will be heard; you become worn out, worn down, by the struggle to get a complaint through.

Blanking can be a matter of how you are received. If a complaint is not received as a complaint, then a complaint is not recorded as a complaint. Blanking is about what blanking effects, the erasure of the signs of complaint. (I think of blanking as like an eraser used to remove marks from the page.) The verbs *erase* and *delete* appear often in my data in relation to quite a range of different activities.[12] One academic talked about how the officers who were handling her complaint kept going on vacation at key moments: "Every time they go on holiday, it's a reset. It almost as if the memory is erased." Another senior academic noted how often the people handling her complain would go on leave: "And then it turned out that [she] was going to be on leave until mid-August. It was strung out for one and a half months with me not knowing what the outcome was." When the people who are handling your complaint leave, your complaint goes with them. If your complaint does not return until they do, there is a chance your complaint will not return when they do.

Blanking can be how you erase the data. Or blanking can be how you fail to record the data. I spoke to two students who participated in a collective complaint about sexual harassment in their former department. A meeting was set up in response to their initial complaint. They described what happened:

STUDENT 1   They didn't record it or take any notes. I think there were one or two lines written.
STUDENT 2   It was very odd.
STUDENT 1   You did feel it was a kind of cozy chat.
STUDENT 2   Very odd, very odd.
STUDENT 1   They were sort of wrapping the conversation up, because it had gone on, and I said, this is us making a formal complaint, and there was a shift in the atmosphere. And I said, we do want to follow it up as a complaint.

Informality can be used as a way of setting a tone, trying to discourage an informal complaint from becoming formal, turning a complaint into a casual conversation that can be more easily wrapped up. The failure to take notes in the usual manner, so that they can be written up as minutes, is useful to the organization; if you do not follow the usual procedures for conducting meetings, you stop a record from being created and filed. We are learning the utility of a certain style of institutional response to complaint, how a casual and informal approach can be an attempt not to register that a complaint is being made. If the meeting is conducted without an agenda, perhaps the atmosphere is the agenda. It is then as if the complainer is requiring an adherence to rules and conventions, or as if the formality necessary to make a complaint is itself a form of antagonism (not having a "cozy chat," not being friendly). A formal complaint would become what someone makes because they are being unfriendly. Note how when the students made clear that they *were* making a formal complaint there was a "shift in the atmosphere."

Atmosphere can be used as a way of creating an impression that a complaint is not being made or that a complaint does not need to be made. In other words, atmosphere can be a technique. The technical matters. Another method of stopping a complaint is to declare a complaint "not a complaint" on technical grounds. To be more specific, you can say that a complaint is not a complaint because it does fulfill the technical requirements for being a complaint. A member of staff made a complaint about bullying that involved her head of department as well as other colleagues: "The complaint was about the head of department, the dean, the faculty dean, and the research office because for me institutionally they were the problem." This experience of institutional bullying had been devastating, and she suffered from depression as a result. It took her a long time to get to the point where she could write a complaint. She described what happened once she was able to put her complaint in: "I basically did it when I was able to, because I was just really unwell for a significant period of time. And I put in the complaint and the response that I got was from the deputy vice chancellor. He said that he couldn't process my complaint because I had taken too long to lodge it." Some experiences are so devastating that it takes time to process them. And the length of time taken can be used to disqualify a complaint. Many complaints are not recorded as complaints because they do not fit or meet the requirements.

Blanking can be used as a method in interpersonal communication; to blank someone is to blank their complaint, not to reply or respond to someone when they say something, because they say something. Blanking can be procedural; it can be how an organization does not record a complaint. Blanking is about what is not left behind by a complaint. Another way of making the same point: blanking is how you are left with a blank disk; despite all the activity, all the sound, there is no trace.

I want in this section to explore how the inefficiency of complaints systems can be strategic. As I listened to stories of trying to make formal complaints, *strategic inefficiency* was the term that came to mind to explain what I was hearing. I kept hearing of unexplained and excruciating delays, confidential folders being sent to the wrong person or being posted with incomplete addresses, whole complaint files mysteriously disappearing, or meetings that were not properly recorded or that were assembled haphazardly in contradiction to policy and procedure. (We have already heard about such meetings.) I was listening to the sound of machinery: the *clunk, clunk* that was telling me that inefficiency is not just the failure of things to work properly but is also how things are working.

I had wondered about the *work* of inefficiency before, how inefficiency could be understood as an achievement. One time during my first year as a lecturer I was in the departmental office. An administrator was trying to find someone to mark a course. I was curious. I asked why Professor X was not marking the course given he was the course leader. The administrator gave me a certain kind of look, a look that said, "That's a long story, but I can't tell it to you." Later I talked to another academic. She told me that everyone knows that Professor X can't be relied on to mark his own courses—if you ask him to, he won't do it. She told me about the time a whole set of exams was found behind his chair, perhaps carelessly discarded, perhaps carefully hidden. I came to learn over subsequent years that Professor X was rarely given administrative work: even when he was named director of such-and-such program, he did not actually do the work (though being director still counted as part of his workload). When administrators participated in distributing Professor X's work to other staff (always more junior, usually women), it was not because they thought Professor X was special or wise or important. It was because they cared about the students and they did not want the students to suffer the consequences of his inefficiency. Professor X, however, was still benefiting from his inefficiency; he was being saved from doing certain kinds of work, administrative work or what we could call institutional housework. Having his time freed from that work meant he had more time for the work that was more valued: time for research.

Many years later, when I was visitor at an elite university, I was sitting at the back of a lecture theater. It was a grand room: there were portraits on the wall of old white men in gowns: same old, same old. I was watching someone fiddle with a projector. It just would not work. And something struck me: how organizations that are often so profoundly inefficient at some things can be rather remarkably efficient at others. I was thinking about how difficult it was at this university to get quite basic tasks done: to get the technology to work, a lecture theater heated, a syllabus circulated in advance. And I was noticing how those portraits on the wall and those who were gathered at the meeting tables, the dining tables, all kinds of tables, seemed to reflect each other rather smoothly. The narrowness of an assembly can be its own achievement, a sign that some systems are working. The engines of social reproduction still seem to run smoothly even when other things fail. We can turn an observation into a question: Is there a connection between the inefficiency in how some things are run and the efficiency with which institutions reproduce themselves?

Let's return to one of the common experiences shared in the previous chapter: that if you make a formal complaint, you are often left waiting. You might be waiting for a response to a letter, waiting for a report into an inquiry, waiting for an outcome or for somebody else to make a decision. A common word for describing this time of waiting is *dragging*; a complaint keeps dragging on, taking up more and more time. I think of that time as a heavy bag: the longer it takes, the heaver it becomes; what you have to carry around, what you can barely carry; time as becoming heavier. This weight matters. Just remember that complaints are hard to make, and you are often warned against making them; those who proceed tend to do so out of a sense of urgency. A complaint is usually a last resort. And a future can be what is at stake; a decision about a complaint can be the opening or closing of a door (see chapter 6). Everything can stop when a complaint is ongoing; you can put your life on hold, or you can feel your life has been put on hold.

It is not just that complaints take a long time. Complaints often take much longer than they are supposed to take if they were conducted in accordance with policies and procedures. The gap between what is supposed to happen and what does happen is also a lag; when a complaint is put forward, you often end up lagging behind where you are supposed to be. In that lag, the person who initiates a formal complaint is often very busy; as I described in the previous chapter, you have to keep pushing. You are waiting, but you are also reminding, prompting, sending inquiries; asking questions, questions after questions: What is happening? What is going on now? A wall gives concrete expression to an experience of being stopped. A wall can be thought of not only as hard but as slow. *You can encounter resistance in the slowness of an uptake.*

By using the term *strategic* I am suggesting that the slowness of an uptake can be useful and purposeful. One student described how her university took seven months to respond to her complaint and then another seven months to respond to her response to their response to her complaint. (If it had followed its own procedures, it would have taken no more than three months.) This student had her own explanation for what was going on: "It is my theory they have been putting in the long finger and pulling this out, dragging this out over unacceptable periods of time, *to try and tire me out so that I will just give up.*" The point of tiring the complainer seems to be to get her to retire her complaint. Exhaustion becomes a management technique: you tire people out so they are too tired to address what makes them too tired.

The time it takes to make a complaint might be time some people do not have.[13] I spoke to a student about another case in which the organization had lost a whole file that held information into a large-scale inquiry into harassment. That file was lost alongside a number of other files. The organization's way of accounting for the missing files was that "there was a problem in Human Resources." If inefficiency can be a tendency, a way of working that has become habitual such that it does not require special effort for things to be lost, acquiring that tendency is useful or convenient. If an inconvenient history can be erased by the failure to keep records properly, the failure to keep records properly is convenient. It is also the case that inefficiency can be used to imply that a file that had in fact been removed was just lost; losing all the files could even mask the deliberate removal of one. That it would be impossible to know whether this is the case—whether or not the loss of all the files was used to mask the removal of one file—might be teaching us something about the utility of inefficiency. Inefficiency can be used as evidence that you have not removed evidence. And thus inefficiency can be how evidence of the removal of evidence is removed. A bumbling professor who is always losing the exams becomes a bumbling university that is always losing the files.

I noted in the previous section that complaints can be dismissed on technical grounds. This is often achieved through the use of deadlines and time lines: a university can claim that complaints were not submitted in time (even if it fails to meet its own time lines). It is important to add that technical requirements are not always made in advance even if they are supposed to be. One senior academic describes "long periods of time when there [was] no response" from the university to which she had submitted a formal complaint. But she added, "Then they would give you a week to get back to them. And you know these are arbitrary deadlines."

An arbitrary deadline is one that is pulled out of the air. And of course, if the deadline is not only tight but unexpected, you might not be able to make it or you might have to rush to make it. A student told me how her university gave her "a tiny timescale" to respond to a report that it took a very long time to produce: "That's not part of the procedure. They were just making it up as they go along." To make it up as you go along, to bumble along, can be a technique for catching people out. It can be easy to fail to meet the requirements if you are not told the requirements or if the requirements are made up along the way.

By discussing strategic inefficiency, I want to do more than describe what is being achieved by the failure to administer complaints in an effective way. I also want to use this term to describe who is going to be more affected by that failure. Another student describes multiple delays in her complaint: "Months went by. Nothing. They really botched my complaints procedure just by virtue of missing their own deadlines." A botched job can be your life.

In the previous chapter, I suggested the drawing in figure 2.2 can be a description of the complaints process. It can also be the picture of your life; your life can be what unravels, thread by thread. This student was an international student. She was waiting for her complaint to be processed while her visa was running out: "Ten days before my visa was about to run out, I applied for a new visa. And they were like, how can we give her a visa? She is on probation. You have to have good standing to get a visa and they were like, this complaint thing is open." The longer the complaint is kept open, the more she has to lose. She describes further, "I had no money, I couldn't work. Every week they were like, we will give you an outcome next week, then the next. I couldn't renew the lease where I was renting. I really couldn't continue with my work as I wasn't sure I could stay. Everything depended on the outcome of the complaint. I was like homeless, staying with a friend on a couch. And it ended up being a six-month process." For students and staff who are more precarious because of their residential or financial status, a delay can mean everything topples over; a whole life can unravel, thread by thread; you can be left homeless, even more dependent upon the goodwill of others. The impact of delays can be devastating, and there can be more and more additional effects. In this case, the student's complaint file went missing. The university explained the lost file as being the result of job turnover because she was given a new complaint officer during the complaint. A new officer should not mean a lost file: efficiency is about the creation of filing systems so that materials can be retained and located. Neverthe-

2.2 A picture of a life.

less, it is worth noting that this university (like many other organizations) had a high turnover of staff working in Human Resources on student complaints. And this in itself is telling: inefficiency can also be an effect of how a university does not support those who are employed to do certain kinds of work; inefficiency can be an effect of not looking after staff properly, which can lead to the failure to acquire a long-term institutional memory. Inefficiency can be an effect of constantly making changes to procedures for doing things so that no one acquires a stable footing. Inefficiency (strategic or otherwise) can be an effect of underfunding and the institutionalization of staff precarity, which is also about the unequal distribution of precarity; some are protected from having to keep moving or from having to keep up with the constancy of changes to procedures.

It is important for me to stress this point as there are many committed administrators trying to do their best for students and staff who have complaints and grievances. The failure to support those who are supporting those who are making complaints is an institutional failure, a failure that gets passed around and passed on. In this case, the student did take her case to the Office for Independent Adjudication.[14] They recommended that the university "improve its record keeping." There is nothing wrong with this recommendation. But we learn from it how the failure to support those who are most precarious is framed as *an administrative failure*. For some, an administrative failure is a life disaster. If complaints can be stopped by what appears to be administrative failure, complaints teach us who organizations are *for*. By this I mean: those for whom an organization is built are also protected from doing certain kinds of administrative work or from the consequences of doing such work.

Students and staff with disabilities often have to rely on complex administrative processes in order to secure the "reasonable adjustments" they need to be able to do their work, which means that administrative problems can stop you from being able to do your work. Inequalities can be reproduced by the extent to which staff and students have to enter administrative processes to acquire what they need to proceed. A student with a chronic illness talked to me about the additional work she had to do in order to secure reasonable adjustments. In doing that work, she learned all about the institution; she learned about what I have been calling strategic inefficiency: "I uncovered all these failed processes. You register with disabled services, disabled services get your docs, and then they send a memo to your department, and then something else happens with it. And what was supposed to happen was that it was supposed to go from Disability Services to the disability liaison administrator, who was just the head secretary, who would then cascade it around relevant staff but who never did that." When you do not have an efficient system for passing information around, memos get lost; again, what is supposed to happen does not happen. The more units and staff are involved, the easier it is for something to be lost. And a lost memo can mean you too can end up lost in a system. She noted how "everyone is rubbish in tracking disability." The consequences of rubbish systems for keeping track of things are very different depending on who or what is being tracked. Strategic inefficiency can be how some disappearances are not counted by being deemed "lost in the system."

If you have to complain because of failed processes, you have to enter yet more failed processes. She had to complain about how her complaint was handled: "The complaint hinged on them not giving me the time. I said, you should have given me more time, more than a week, to do all this paperwork. You can't then get pissed off with me when I don't do the paperwork, and moreover you can't do that for a PhD student who is registered disabled." And she commented wryly, "Yes, I was interrupted, but if I stop being a student, I don't stop being disabled." If organizations take too long to respond to complaints, they can also require those who complain to respond in a manner or time that is not possible given their needs and circumstances. The ableism that leads you to complain, not being given the additional time and support you need, can be reencountered when you complain, not being given the additional time and support you need. You are not given the support necessary to proceed, and you are not given the support necessary to complain about not being given the support necessary to proceed.

And so we also learn that those who have the least need to complain tend to be those who can most afford to complain, and those who have the most need to complain tend to be those who can least afford to complain. There is a connection between the discriminatory effects of inefficiency and the efficiency with which organizations reproduce themselves as being for certain kinds of people: those whose papers are in the right place, those who are in the right place; those who are upright, able, well-resourced, and well-connected.

CONCLUSION: SENSITIVE INFORMATION

When the effort to stop a complaint from being made fails, that is, when a complaint is made, there is an effort to stop the complaint from getting out. When you make a complaint, you are often warned not to disclose the "sensitive information" the complaint contains. Warnings about complaint can convert very quickly into warnings about disclosure.

I received such a warning about the danger of disclosure *after* I had disclosed information in the form of a short post on my blog explaining my reasons for resigning. In other words, I was warned about not disclosing more information. I did not share much information. But even saying that there had been a number of inquiries into sexual harassment was sharing more information than had been shared in public before and, from the point of view of the organization, sharing too much. I did not consciously identify myself as a whistle-blower nor identify my action as blowing the whistle, but that was the effect of my action, and that was how my action was subsequently described by others.[15] Perhaps I wasn't warned before I blew the whistle because it was expected that I, as a professor, however resigned, would express my institutional loyalty by keeping quiet. But there is no point in resigning in silence if you are resigning to protest silence. I will return to how professional norms of conduct are about silence, "keeping a lid on it," in chapter 5.

I received a number of warnings during the period after I announced my resignation but before I officially left my position. These warnings varied in intonation from intimidating and stern to worrying and concerned. Some warnings came from outside the university. I was warned, for instance, by a number of journalists. One journalist wrote to me, "Resigning a professorial post is a pretty big deal—do you worry that you will be blackballed for taking this kind of stance?" Questions *put to* someone can be heard as assertions because of what they *put out* there. You can hear "Do you worry?" as "Are you worried?" or even "You should be worried!" To be blackballed is how a candidacy is opposed in secret ballots in organizations such as gentleman's clubs. Would resigning in this way, taking this stance, mean I would cease to be employable by a university or any other gentleman's club? I didn't ask myself that question, but I know how I would have answered it. If speaking out about sexual harassment made me unemployable (as an academic), I was willing to become unemployable (as an academic).

The warning that stopped me from sharing any more sensitive information was made by someone with an institutional position. I was warned by a senior administrator that if I shared any more information about the inquiries, it could or would be used by one of the people who had been the subject of inquiries as evidence that the university had breached their side of the confidentiality agreement. In other words, I was told that *my* act of leaking information would be evidence of *their* breach. That warning worked as I did not want any of those who had been the subject of inquiries to benefit from my actions even though I knew that it would not have been true: the information I had to share did not come from what the management or administration had told me but from the students themselves who had shared their experiences with me, as well as from my own experience of what happened during the inquiries. We learn from warnings that work: they need only to conjure a risk. Most of the information I had I did not share; I have not shared.

The effort to stop a complaint is the effort to control the flow of information. A senior academic who made a complaint about bullying and harassment from her head of department that did not get anywhere, despite the evidence, because of the evidence, considered taking her story to the media. She was warned against taking this route by a colleague she had worked with closely, whom she trusted and who was himself outraged by the institution's response to her complaint. She said, "I was urged to go to the press, but [he] said, it is bringing your institution into disrepute; they can get you on that." I noted in the previous chapter how a positive duty can be expressed negatively: you are not supposed to do or say anything that would bring your employer into disrepute. A positive duty can thus function as a warning system; to disclose the sensitive information contained in a complaint is to fail that duty: "they can get you on that." She could not afford to fail that duty. She had been bullied for many years. But she was a single mother; she needed this job; she did not think she could get another job because the effect of the bullying had meant not doing the kind of work that would have made her more employable. She did not go to the press; her complaint stayed put.

Many of those I spoke with had signed nondisclosure agreements, which are sometimes called gag orders, ways of resolving a complaint by enforcing an injunction to be silent. NDAs can be considered continuous with the techniques for stopping complaints discussed in this part of the book; they are the tail end of a much longer process. NDAs can function explicitly as forms of bribery: a bribe is a gift that is intended to influence action corruptly. One lecturer told me how she decided to sign an NDA despite her own political desire to write about what happened after she made a complaint about racial discrimination. She was offered a sabbatical in return for signing the NDA. She needed that sabbatical to recover from the complaint: it had been a deeply harrowing experience, and she was left depleted and exhausted. A complaint can often end up leaving you even more deeply under the influence of the organization because what you need to survive organizations can be what they can provide.

Bribery is a part of this story. I referred earlier to how a head of department warned four students about the costs of complaining during a harrowing meeting. At one point, she changed tactics, as one of the students explained: "Then the next thing came, and she said I have still got some money, so how would you like to organize a massive international conference, and it would be 'feminism by stealth.' She said, we can give you money. Who would you want for your dream list of academics to come and do this conference? She said, that way you can educate everyone about women." This student told me they began talking excitedly about how they could use the money, who they could invite to the conference, before it dawned upon them what was going on. The head of department did not need to say what she was offering explicitly; they realized what she was offering from how they were affected. In becoming excited about the offer, they had been distracted from the complaint. Note also how the possibility was offered as an alternative, perhaps more positive route ("that way you can educate everyone about women"). They came to realize they were being offered a bribe; they would be given a feminist conference, resources to use for their own purposes, in return for not proceeding with that complaint.

Bribery teaches us how silence is incentivized. In another case, a senior researcher who made a complaint about bullying was considering whether to take her complaint to the ombudsman. She received a letter from the head of the organization in which she had made the complaint. The letter was an invitation to collaborate on future research grant applications. The letter did not make status of the invitation as a bribe explicit. At first, she was enthusiastic. The letter was a promise: it seemed to offer a path forward so that she could continue doing the work she wanted to do. But then she talked to others: "When I talked to other researchers, that's when I found out, this offer of working and collaborating with them, with them knowing how passionate I was about my work, was conditional on me not going to the ombudsman." She came to realize what was being implied: in return for not doing something, she would get something. The condition of an offer can be not taking a complaint any further.

All of these examples of bribery tell us something about institutional culture; bribes are not a special case. In return for silence, you are promised what are widely considered to be the most highly valued resources for academics (money for research conferences, sabbaticals, research grants). When you are rewarded for silence, you are rewarded for compliance. The word *reward* derives from *warder*, to guard. Think reward, think warden: to be rewarded as to guard or to be under guard. You are rewarded for watching what you say or do or watching what others say or do. Rewards are tied not only to surveillance but also to reproduction. A system is reproduced by rewarding those who are willing to reproduce the system. When you are unwilling to reproduce that system or when you refuse not to watch what you say, when you disclose sensitive information, it is made harder to get anywhere. This is why to learn from those who make complaints is to learn about *institutional mechanics*, not only how institutions work but how they are reproduced.

PART II

THE IMMANENCE OF COMPLAINT

In the first part of the book, I focused on people's experience of making formal complaints. It was important to start with people's experiences of making, or trying to make, formal complaints as that was my starting point for the research. But of course, complaints are not the starting point even if they are the start of something.

Complaints can be thought of as being *about* something, as intentional or directed toward objects.[1] What complaints are about precedes them, even if what precedes them is ongoing. If complaints are about what precedes them, they have a backward temporality, we might even say a queer temporality. Complaints require going backward or "feeling backward," to evoke Heather Love's (2007) terms. Going back can mean going all over the place. Erin Grogan (2020, xiv) describes how "a queer critique might understand time as looping and folding, zigging and zagging, circling back, and moving sideways."[2] Queer time and the time of complaint seem to loop in similar directions. To make a complaint, you have to go back over something *because it is not over*.

If complaints take us back, we too need to *go back* to make sense of them. In this part of the book, I back up my analysis somewhat. I go back, "zigging and zagging," to borrow Grogan's turn of phrase; in going back, I too end up all over the place. In going back, I am following complaint in another way. There are many ways of telling the story of complaint. As I noted in my introduction to this book, it can be difficult to know where to begin the story of complaint when it is difficult to know when a complaint begins. We can recall here that a complaint can be an expression of grief, pain, or dissatisfaction, something that is a cause of protest or outcry, a bodily ailment as well as a formal allegation. We have already learned how this latter sense of complaint as formal allegation brings up more affective and embodied senses. A complaint might be how you say *no* to something, whether in speech or in writing or even through nonverbal communication: complaints as objecting, calling out, contesting, naming; questioning; withdrawing, not smiling, not laughing; groaning, and so on.

In this part of the book, I reflect on the significance of the immanence of complaint. Immanence implies what we are in, immanence as presence or even the present, but it can also imply what remains, immanence as what carries on from the past, what has not been transcended or what we are not over. In these two chapters, I will go back over some of the experiences that lead people to make complaints, with "complaint" being understood in an expanded sense as different ways of expressing dissatisfaction with a situation. I also consider how the work of trying to transform institutions is framed as the work of complaint whether or not it is understood by the person doing the work in those terms. In chapter 3, I focus on how complaints *come out* in the situations they are about. In chapter 4, I consider how complaints are *sent out* into those same situations.

The *where* of complaint is thus close to the *what* of complaint. A complaint has much to teach us about *where*, about where we are dwelling. *To dwell* can mean to live in a particular place or in a particular way. *To dwell* can also mean to linger on something or to delay. Given that complaints are understood as negative, to complain is to dwell on something negative. Perhaps we can think of complaint as trying to change how people reside somewhere, which requires an act of dwelling on the problems with or in that residence. From this, we learn: trying to change a dwelling is given the quality of being negative or even destructive, to complain as a negative dwelling.

CHAPTER THREE

IN THE THICK OF IT

You might make a complaint because you are in an intense and difficult situation. What a complaint is *about* is a situation the person who complains is often still *in*. You might make a complaint because you do not want to remain in that situation; a complaint can be an effort to get out of a situation you are in. Trying to get out of a situation can sometimes make that situation even more intense and difficult. This is why I have titled this chapter with the idiom *in the thick of it*. To be in the thick of it means to be in a situation where it is most *intense*; it means to be in the most *crowded* of places. The idiom *in the thick of it* can also reference how much you have to do; it can mean to be occupied or *busy*. What do we learn from complaint, or about complaint, by considering complaint as *intensity*, as *crowded*, and as *busy*?

In this chapter my aim is to reflect with those I have spoken to about some of the experiences that led them to consider making a complaint. For those who take their complaints forward, who go to or through the systems I described in the first part of the book, the story of complaint begins long before they reached that point. Perhaps a complaint is put forward somewhere in the middle of a long journey: that middle can be a muddle. The experiences that lead to complaint and the experiences of complaint can be hard to untangle; they are often part of the same experience. In this chapter I work as slowly and as carefully as I can with the tangles in the testimonies.

I suggested in chapter 2 that the time it takes to get a complaint through the system needs to be understood as part of the system. If the complaints process is long and drawn out, it is more likely that a complainer will tire out. The effect of the process can be the point of that process.

If it takes time to make a complaint, it takes time to reach a complaint. I have already noted how formal complaints can require you to keep saying *no* over and over again. You have to work hard to keep that *no* going. A *no* can also be what you have to reach. When a complaint is about something, you first have to admit *to* something, to recognize something as being wrong, as what you need to complain *about*. Before you have any conversations with others, you might first have conversations with yourself about whether something is wrong. A complaint might begin with a sense of something not being quite right, with an uneasy feeling, with discomfort, unease, or concern. You might sense something is not right without being sure of yourself. A complaint story might begin with being unsure about whether what you are experiencing is something to be complained about.

A master's student begins her new program with high hopes and expectations. And then "it started." "It started I would say in the second or third lesson I had with Professor X. There were certain signs that rang alarm bells for me, and my first reaction is, stop being paranoid, stop being a feminazi where everything is gendered, you know, you are probably reading too much into this, you need to take a step back. What I started doing was questioning myself first rather that questioning his behavior."

When an alarm bell rings you are hearing a warning; the sound of a bell announces a danger in the external world even if an alarm bell is what you hear inside your own head. It does not always follow that you take heed of what you hear. Her first reaction is to question herself rather than his behavior. She tells herself off, even; she gives herself a talking to; she tells herself to stop being paranoid, to stop being a feminazi, *to stop being a feminist*, perhaps. It is striking how in questioning herself, she also exercised familiar stereotypes of feminists as feminazis, with the implication that gender is a judgment that is imposed upon a situation from the outside. External judgments can be given voice as internal doubt.

We learn from what is possible: it is possible to identify as a feminist and worry that gender is an imposition.[1] Sometimes we do encounter that judgment from others. Contrast her account with that of a feminist PhD student who made a complaint about the conduct of another PhD student. When she went to a meeting with administrators, she could see that judgment on their faces: "I think they thought almost that I was looking for it, like a feminist thing, you are always overreacting, blowing things out of proportion because that's what you see everywhere." All it takes to be seen as seeing gender everywhere is to see it somewhere.

Returning to the experience of the MA student, it took time for her to realize that her first impressions were right. Her sense that something was amiss, which was followed at first by telling herself not to be paranoid, was confirmed by what she kept encountering. She describes how the syllabus was occupied: "He left any thinker who wasn't a white man essentially until the end of the course."[2] A syllabus can tell you who is being valued, what is valued; who comes first, who has priority. You can come up against a structure in a syllabus. Many of us are familiar with such structures. Perhaps structures can take time to reveal themselves: "And then by week five I was like, no, no, no, no, things are wrong not just in terms of gender; things are desperately wrong with the way he is teaching, full stop." Her first reaction was to say no to the bell, no to *no*. But when she realizes she was right to hear that something was wrong, those *no*s come out, more of them. I think of those *no*s, all four of them, as the sound of an increasing confidence in her own judgment: "It was a progressive realization that it wasn't just me being paranoid." Perhaps once you get a single *no* out, other *no*s follow. What has been suppressed can be more quickly expressed.

A progressive realization can be about where you locate the problem. In realizing she was not being paranoid, she relocates the problem to the program, from her mind to the world. It can take time to reach a complaint because it can take time to trust your own mind. But even if the realization is progressive, it is not straightforward. As I will discuss in more detail in chapter 4, when she communicates that *no* to the professor, questioning the syllabus, asking questions about gender and race, he became verbally abusive. What follows the questions you raise can lead you back to where you were before, to self-questioning. She describes: "I felt afraid. He hadn't touched me. He hadn't physically abused me." Fear can be magnified by not being able to evidence what you encounter. She explains, "So, then I started getting afraid, I started questioning and doubting myself." We can feel the absence of evidence as fear.

Some forms of violence, however hard they hit you, do not appear to others. If other people can't see it, that it happened, you might ask yourself, Did it happen? Another student wrote to me about her experience as an undergraduate. Her course tutor had sent her texts that did not seem quite right: "At the time, I did not see (or decided to ignore) any odd behaviors and remarks that made me uncomfortable (paying close attention to my habits and mannerisms and commenting on them as well as my appearance, being genuinely insulted when I would occasionally refuse his offer to get me a coffee, insinuating that I might walk in on him naked, suggesting that he could put some sunscreen on my back when there was no need for it)." It is interesting: the implication that she "decided to ignore," which is bracketed, or "did not see" what was wrong, what was making her uncomfortable. If you decide to ignore something, you must first have seen it. Maybe it is possible to experience yourself as having seen something and not having seen it at the same time; maybe the bracket is telling us something about the ambivalence of catching something: to-ing and fro-ing, seeing and not seeing. After all, sometimes seeing something can make something more real; you might have to confirm to yourself that you have seen something; the second time you see something can then be experienced as the first time. Sometimes we might try to convince ourselves that we haven't seen what we have seen: not seeing something twice as not seeing something at all.

A complaint can be what it takes to make something that is happening "real," which means that sometimes not making a complaint, not getting to or even near *that* point, is how something remains not real. Maybe you need to miss something in order to cope with something. But it is a very difficult and precarious situation because of what you are missing: "It was only on my last day of being an undergraduate student that I realized all the cues I had been missing. [He] sent me this text message to my phone: 'Sleep with me.'" He came out with what she had been trying not to see. Even then, it can take more than coming out with it; she has to receive what is being said. She replied to his message, "What, no," and he said later it was a mistake. She tried to rationalize it: maybe it was a mistake. Believing him would be better in some way than taking what he said literally, which would require going back over all that had been said in the past, changing her own understanding of what had gone on before. To accept his explanation would allow her to go on as if what happened did not happen. And she wanted to go on; she wanted to go to graduate school. And so she kept it a secret; she put it to the back of her mind. She did not tell anyone, her partner, her parents, her department:

I graduated top of my class and am still in touch with many of the other teachers from the program. I was terrified that they would somehow find out and that I would be judged by the rest of the faculty for causing drama. I felt as though my academic success would be put into question and as I had planned to apply for graduate school, I needed to maintain good relationships with the program in order to get good references. It did not even occur to me at the time to report it to the university (not that I would have known where or who to go to as I was technically no longer a student having finished my degree) or anyone else. I kept it a secret from my partner, for years as I felt like it would put my integrity as a student and as a partner in question. I never told my parents who remember him fondly as he was a mentor to me; they are proud that I was able to make these kinds of connections with faculty members. I fear that they would doubt my success.

So many complaints are not made because the person who would have to make them knows that to make them would be to be derailed; it would mean not being able to go where you want to go. The warnings we heard about in chapter 2 made by officials thus echo, for those who get that far, warnings that have already been made, including warnings you might have given to yourself, that to complain would be to "put into question" your academic success, that to complain would jeopardize what you need to progress (see also chapter 6). The warnings that are already "out there" can be already "in here": we take them in, we take them on. The warning not to complain is part of a wider cluster of warnings addressed especially to girls and women: you are warned about the consequences of not being agreeable, not putting others first, not trying to maintain relationships with others. A warning can thus be a worrying; you worry that to complain would be to suffer a judgment as "causing drama," that to complain would lead to a questioning of your integrity, that to complain would compromise your connections, professional as well as personal. To keep those connections might depend on preserving an idea of what you have received from others; so much has to be concealed to preserve an idea of happiness. You might keep something secret because you do not want to challenge other people's investments—those of teachers, partners, parents—which are also investments they have in you and your happiness. Even a memory can be an investment: she knew her parents "remember him fondly" because they thought he was a good mentor. A complaint might not be made in the present because it would mean dislodging not only the future but the past. The emotional work of not complaining when you have something to complain about can also be about trying not to recognize what is present. When you make something secret, you have to keep that secret. To keep a secret might also mean to keep something secret from yourself, a secret as how you put something aside: to put aside as to hide. We learn: what is put aside is often what is closest to the bone. In chapter 1, I explored how bodies can store what institutions file away. Bodies can also store what minds file away, which is how we come to feel the truth of something in our bones.

We carry our complaints with us, whether or not we made them. We can be burdened by the complaints we do not make. The student went on:

> I proceed[ed] to start a graduate program in another city, fell into a severe depression, and had to put my studies on hold. I had a hard time reading my male professors (were they just trying to help me out? being friendly? was that *too* friendly? literally just doing their jobs and teaching me? am I reading too much into that glance? is he standing too close to me?). My understanding of reality and boundaries were thrown into question and I still feel uncomfortable trying to read people and their intentions. I don't trust my intuition anymore as it failed me when I was younger. I wonder if any of the other teachers were able to notice anything off. . . . Was it just me who did not see it or could others sense something off? And if they did, why did no one speak up?

Complaints can come out as expressions of doubt. You begin to lose confidence in yourself; the boundaries become unclear; you cannot trust your judgment. Even if it has become this way because someone you trusted betrayed the boundaries, you can end up feeling that you betrayed yourself. The difficulty you have in getting to a complaint becomes a difficulty you have in relation to the world; everything becomes questionable; you feel questionable; your intuition is no longer a guide, no longer giving your clear instructions, about what to do, where to go. You cannot trust anything, anyone, yourself, other people. When everything is thrown into question, a question can be a load, what you end up having to carry around.

The experience of reaching complaint, which can be an experience of not getting there—not complaining is part of an experience of complaint—changes your relationship to yourself as well as the world around you. If you have a sense of something being wrong, you might then check in with others. What did you think of this? Is that what you think? These are conversations with peers: you speak to those you trust rather than those with an institutional position, although sometimes a trusted peer can have an institutional position. A senior woman, a professor, a head of department experiences misogyny and sexism at a table. One of the professors says things that are particularly offensive. She checks in with friends and colleagues. This happened; this is what he said. The responses lead her to doubt herself: "The person who was the main protagonist in the banter, I was told he couldn't be. You must have imagined that because he is married to a real feminist." You must have imagined that; it can't be true; it couldn't be. She knows what happened. She probably knows that men who are married to "real feminists" can be sexist, can be misogynists. But then, external voices can be internalized as doubt.

To proceed (and she did, although her complaint stalled later) she has to put those voices aside, not to believe them. What if the experiences you need to complain about have shaken your confidence? She said, "It does shake you; you think, oh am I making a fuss, should I make a fuss? I have already made a massive fuss at my previous institution, which went on for months." So many of the people I spoke to made use of this expression, *making a fuss*, as if to complain is to be fussy, to be too particular, demanding even, as if a complaint makes something bigger than it needs to be or as if you are making yourself bigger than you are.[3] You might try to keep the complaint secret in order not to make a fuss. One early career lecturer said, "I felt frightened to tell other people. I don't know why. I did feel really frightened. I did not want to kick up a fuss. I didn't want to make a big scene. I don't like that anyway. I don't like to feel that a lot of people would have known what was going on." You might avoid talking about what you are going through to avoid making a spectacle of yourself. And it is not that you would be wrong: those who complain are often perceived as making a fuss, making something out of nothing. Another early career lecturer was told, "You look like somebody who is causing a fuss."

There can be so much work to do before you can trust your own judgment. Those times you have not been heard: you don't leave them behind. One postgraduate student told me, "I would wonder how much is going to be a repetition of not being taken seriously, not being heard." She was an international student, with an Asian background. Her experience of studying was of being heard over, looked over. When you have not been heard, you wonder about the point of speaking out, of expressing yourself. Hearings can be walls; you have to push very hard to make a complaint if that's how you have been heard before.

An early career lecturer is being harassed by her head of department through anti-Semitic and homophobic humor:

I think she thought she was being funny. I have a very obviously Jewish last name, and my family is Jewish, and I am not religious but anyway it is my background, I am Jewish. She made a lot of comments, Jewish jokes and stuff about Jews being stingy and that kind of thing. . . . And I am openly gay and she thought that was something she could tease me about, and she was always saying about other people, do you think he's gay, do you think she's gay, so there was a lot of things.

"I think she thought" means she has an idea of why this person is speaking like this; so much abuse can be intended as "being funny," which gives us an idea of the utility of intentions. A sense of "being funny" can enable some to keep saying things that are demeaning and derogatory to others. These forms of verbal harassment "had been going on for years." And those comments were made in front of other people.

She wonders whether that is just how people talk. I have learned from talking to people how ways of speaking and behaving that seem at one level *obviously* problematic can still be justified as how things are or how things are done. An international student, for instance, arrived at a new department only to find professors being intimate and sexual with students in front of staff and other students. No one seemed to be paying any attention, to show signs of noticing that something was amiss. She said to me, "I thought at first maybe this is how they do things in the UK." Sometimes it is the *unremarkability* of the behavior, how other people are not remarking upon something, not objecting or showing signs of objecting, that can make you wonder whether what is happening is not objectionable after all. Leila Whitley and Tiffany Page (2015, 42) have noted how the absence of objections to sexual harassment can work "to normalise sexual harassment in the university environment." The absence of other complaints can make it even harder to recognize there is something to complain about. This also means that complaints can be stopped by stopping other complaints.

Trying to explain away a problem can give you more of a sense of what the problem is because, to put it bluntly, the explanations fail. We can return to the experiences of the early career lecturer. She realizes that how her head of department talks is not how she herself talks or even how her head of department talks to others: "And I realized, I don't talk to any of my colleagues like that. And I am not sure she talks to other colleagues like that. Why is she doing that to me?" But even if she questions, "Why is she doing that to me?" that question leads to her questioning herself: "And I am like, maybe I am being oversensitive. You can see I am starting to take the blame on myself, oversensitive, I can't take a joke, blah, blah, blah, you know the kind of thing you kind of tell yourself when you are just trying to get over it." You can end up giving instructions to yourself, telling yourself not to make something bigger than it needs to be, warning yourself not to be sensitive. Getting over it can be an injunction you impose on yourself. When she decides to make a complaint, she has a conversation with a member of Human Resources. And what is said to her she has already said to herself: "So I went to talk to our HR person and she was really quite nasty to me and told me that [the head of department] brought in a lot of grant money and was very important to the university and there was no way they were going to talk to her about any of this, and I was just oversensitive. And that's what you had been saying to yourself anyway." The instruction not to complain can be internalized, because that is what you had been taught, that to complain is to be oversensitive, to be easily affected, easily hurt, bruised, damaged. What others say to you repeats what you have said to yourself. What you say to yourself repeats what others have said to you.

The work of complaint can involve an internal process of coming to terms with what you are experiencing. Even if you have to complain about something that is being done to you, whether by somebody else or by a structure that is enabling somebody else, you still have to come to terms with yourself. A complaint can feel like an existential crisis, a life crisis. The conversations you have with others are relayed endlessly as conversations with yourself. I noticed in listening to people's testimonies how often people sharing their complaints with me put on "other voices," so when they told me what the head of Human Resources said or what their supervisor said, they would change their voice; it was like I was listening to a chorus. And that is probably because making a complaint can feel like *becoming a chorus*; all those conversations take up time and space in your head; more and more voices, they become loud, louder still.

I am talking to a postgraduate student based in small progressive university. She talks about the time it took for her to get to the point of realizing she might need to make a complaint. She is a queer woman of color. She is the first person in her family to go to university. She has had to work really hard to get to where she is. She has had to fight to get here. She is being advised by someone she admires; he is well-versed in critical theory, in feminist theory. He is a good mentor. He gives her critical and engaged feedback on her writing. Having fought to get here, she is where she wants to be. She knows where she is going; she knows what she has to do to get there.

Still, something is not right. In describing how she came to realize something was not right, she has to go back. She has to go back to explain how *over time* she came to that realization:

> Over time my relationship with my advisor was very precarious. He positioned himself as a feminist, critical scholar, someone who was kind of holding that space for women, and then over time, and I am sure you are quite familiar with this narrative, over time, I think it was almost a kind of grooming process for him, over time with our academic meetings he wanted to have them more and more in non-academic spaces. So, it moved from, "Oh you know, I don't want to go to campus today, parking's terrible, why don't we meet at this coffee shop that's near campus," and then a while after that it would be, "Why don't you just come over to the house, and we'll meet there." It was on a small doctoral program, and a lot of our faculty–student relationships happened both on campus and off campus . . . so at the time, and especially because it happened so gradually, I didn't really read that what he was moving through was actually a grooming process, trying to see how far he could push that boundary. It moved from on campus to slightly off campus, to his house, to dinners out. And then at some point, I am thinking, this feels really uncomfortable to me, it was feeling more and more uncomfortable.

Grooming is a word that tends to be used retrospectively: grooming describes a process that has an end in sight, and until you reach the end it is hard to notice the process. The process works by not making the end clear until it is too late. It took time for her to realize that the boundaries being pushed back were the boundaries she needed to protect herself. She was not expecting that pushing back to be anything other than what he said it was (the parking was bad, it was easier to meet off campus); after all, he represented himself as a feminist, as her supporter, as giving her space. *Mind the gap* can also refer to the gap between how someone appears to be and how they are being: that gap can be useful; it can be instrumentalized. Some can abuse the power they have been given by how they do not appear. It can take you time to realize what is going on because what is going on is not *that* different from what usually goes on; it is not unusual for academic work to take place in nonacademic spaces; it is not unusual to have casual conversations mixed in and mixed up with work conversations. But looking back, going back, she could see what was happening retrospectively. Clarity could be achieved from the vantage point of the present, given what came next, given what followed.

If the time of complaint is slow, so too is the time of harassment. Harassment does not always reveal itself fully, at once, at first. So much follows this simple observation. Harassment is not always (or even not often) a singular event, striking as a departure from what usually happens. Harassment can be enacted as a series of actions performed over time, the difference between each action being slight, a small, almost undetectable difference. The pushing back of boundaries—from office to the coffee shop to the house—is gradual. The boundaries that are being pushed back are spatial, but they are also behavioral; there are small changes of behavior, intimacy as intimation, little signs of something, ways of speaking, ways of doing ("it was feeling more and more uncomfortable").

Harassment does not reveal itself fully, all at once, to the person being harassed. Harassment often works by not ever being revealed to others. So many people I have spoken with who have made or considered making complaints about harassment had experiences of being met by an insistence that the person who harassed them was a nice or good person. These are some of the comments people have received: "He's always been so good to me"; "He's been so supportive of me"; "I can't believe it, he's so nice"; "He's so sweet"; "His children are so nice." When people are saying they don't believe this person did that because this person is not like that, this person is good, they are really saying this person is good *to* me or *for* me. In chapter 1, I noted that complaints can challenge other people's investments in institutions. Complaints can also challenge other people's investments in persons. When you complain, you encounter a wall of investment. Positive profiles of persons can be used both to deny harassment and to defend investments in persons. Denial can be a best defense.

You might also be asked, "Why did you not complain *earlier* or *sooner*?" Those who complain about harassment might even ask themselves the same question. Another postgraduate student said, "That is part of the culture of silence. You didn't see it that way then. Why did you not bring it up sooner?" The longer it takes to see it, the less likely you are to bring it up when you do see it. Earlier and sooner: When are they really? Small changes, small spaces; it can make it hard to detect something in the present. Being late, noting something later, can be as early as noticing something can be. Harassment is performed in such a way that it is made hard to detect. And then the feeling you are left with—that this is not right, something is not right—becomes isolating as well as inconvenient.

It is hard to overstress the inconvenience of complaint. You might be asked, "Why don't you just change supervisors?" Or "Why don't you just leave?" It can be hard to leave. It can be hard to change supervisors; the person you work with is often the only person you can work with. Let's return to the experience of the postgraduate student who was harassed by her advisor:

> And again it's in a small academic department, and I imagine it is true for a lot of academic departments, you really don't have a lot of choice in terms of who you work with. You do particular kinds of work and there's a person you work with. So I kept working with him, and it started to get more aggressive, both verbally and sexually aggressive, so we would go through these cycles, where I was writing, if I would I have a face-to-face meeting with him, and he would be just praise and great and mentoring and all that stuff, and then literally a few minutes after I would leave the office he would text me something, "I can't get you off my mind," those kinds of texts, and I just wouldn't reply to him.

It is not that all the behavior is harassing, aggressive; sometimes it is going well, the supervisions are going well. In these moments, she feels a sense of relief, even hope, that it is going to be okay, that she is going to get what she needs. But then it switches back, and she is back to where she was before: the inappropriate messages, the pushing, pushing back. It is a precarious situation. It can take time even for the obvious to reveal itself, that he is doing what he had been doing all along:

> And it's odd to think back—in this moment, this seems absolutely insane to me—but at the time it was part of the culture of the department we had. You know, another professor I had met with earlier in the program said, you know, that he had to keep a big wooden table between him and his female students so he would remember not to touch them. And then another of our longtime male faculty is notorious for marrying student after student after student. And that was within all this rhetoric of, like, critical race studies and, you know, pedagogy of the oppressed. As I am recounting it to you, I just wanted to say that it is so jarring to look back on it because it looks so very clear, from this hindsight perspective, but in it I was trying, I was the first person in my family to go to college, graduate from college and work on higher education, so I think, I think I had accepted some level of abuse, for the majority of my life, in academic settings. It's almost as if there is this known quantity, that some amount of violence, really, comes to you, as part of the process of going through it.

It is only afterward, in hindsight, that it becomes clear; it can be jarring to give an account of what was unclear after it has become clear. But the story unfolds in the time it does. When what you experience "at the time" is part of the culture, you don't identify it at the time you experience it. The harassment, the misconduct, which was institutionalized, expressed in the idea that senior men would need a big wooden table in order to remember not to touch women students, is happening at the same time that all the critical work is happening, the work that led her there, to that place, that supervisor. The same time, the same place. The place where this is happening, that history of harassment sedimented in a table, is the same place where the critical work is happening and where the rhetoric of critical work is being used to describe what is happening; critical race studies, pedagogy of the oppressed.

We are back to complaint as minding a gap, finding a gap. It becomes clear that critical work is about rhetoric, that there is a gap between rhetoric and reality. Clarity can be *jarring* because it was not always so; it is clear that it was not always clear. Maybe others might have known earlier, or before, that it was just rhetoric. She is the first person in her family to go to university; she believed that universities were progressive; perhaps she is not protected by what we could call *middle-class cynicism*, the cynicism of those who are entitled. An entitlement to things can be expressed in the suspension of belief about the value of things. Or maybe it was not clear because the violence she encountered there was a violence she was used to from elsewhere, the violence of everyday life, the violence of having to make do, the violence of having to get by. Violence can be a "known quantity," you come to expect a certain amount of it. What you are used to often does not appear; it is not striking.

You have come to expect it. You have come to accept it. She knows something is not right, but you can try not to know what you know because of what it means for that to be the case, what you would have to give up. She tries to handle the situation: "I tried very hard to keep all of the meetings on campus, and to keep the door open." She keeps the door open, an actual door, at the same time she closes another kind of door; we might call this door *the door of consciousness*, trying to shut out what he is doing. Note how doors can hold a contradiction; keeping the office door open is an admission of a truth that she handles by not letting it in. But sometimes you can be hit by the truth of the situation:

And so at some point he crossed even more boundaries and he started sending nude photos of himself, ass shots, penis shots, and I basically, I mean I basically froze, and I felt quite alone, I felt there was not much I can do. . . . I felt like, I don't know, it is hard to explain, I felt like I would take myself down by admitting to the kind of violence he was enacting. There was some way in which I encoded, took on his abuse and silenced it myself because all my earlier attempts to have it understood were completely negated and it felt like, that I must have made it happen somehow, that something I did was creating the context for this to happen.

Those who are the recipients of violence from others often come to feel, are made to feel, responsible for what happens to them. You can be a feminist and know that you are *not* responsible, but still feel responsible. She begins to feel that, responsible, somehow, that she made this happen, somehow, that she brought this on herself, somehow. The time it takes to reach a complaint can be a feeling of becoming implicated in what you would complain about. It is an isolating feeling ("I felt quite alone"). When your previous attempts to "have it understood," to try to stop it, to say no to it, are negated, you can end up feeling more rather than less implicated; it keeps on going; he keeps on going. The complaint can be experienced as something you would be doing to yourself, how you would end up hurting yourself, your own career, your own prospects. Even admitting something is happening can feel like *taking yourself down*: if to admit something makes it real, then to admit something can feel like becoming your own killjoy, getting in the way of your own progression.

A complaint can then feel like an alarming exteriority, what you have to do to get out of a situation, yes, but also what comes *at* you, what would mean giving up on something you had fought very hard *for*. In describing how hard it can be to reach a complaint, we are describing the effects of what you have to complain about. Harassment is often hard to recognize as harassment. Or perhaps harassment is hard to recognize until it reaches a point (the sending of naked photos or sexually explicit messages) that you cannot not see that this is what is happening, although then, even then, it is still possible to excuse the behavior, or to allow others to excuse the behavior (it was a mistake; that's what he's like). We are back to the same point I made in chapter 1, a point I will keep making from different angles: what a complaint is *about* is what makes it hard *to* complain.

COMING OUT

I have learned so much from listening to the struggles people have to reach the point when they can complain about something, whether or not they enter into a formal complaint process. The time taken to reach complaint can be experienced as becoming *implicated* in some way in the situation. In other words, the time taken can be registered retrospectively as a feeling of guilt, a feeling as a questioning: How could I let this happen? How could I have gone along with it? A complaint can feel sticky: the longer it takes to make it, the more it sticks to you. A complaint is a sticky situation. If it takes time, also work, to reach complaint, to recognize something is wrong with a situation, it takes time, also work, to change that situation. The work of recognition can also be the *recognition of work*, of how much work it will take to get out of a situation.

To reach complaint, however, is not like reaching a point on a straight line; once you have reached it, you have made it. Reaching complaint is not the end of a struggle, even a struggle you might have with yourself. I noted earlier how we can put aside, or put away, what is hard to handle. To reach complaint is to face up to what is hard, to allow what is hard to come to the front. Complaint can thus involve a heightening of consciousness. Even if you have to battle to achieve consciousness of what is hard, even if you have achieved that consciousness, consciousness can still be hard. Simply put, it can be hard to be conscious of what is hard. It can be a problem to be conscious of a problem. In *Living a Feminist life*, I suggested that feminist consciousness can feel like being *on* is the default position: you are always on, always on it, noticing what is going on (Ahmed 2017, 30). It can be exhausting being on it, which means sometimes we might switch off. If we are busy, we cannot always afford to be *on it*, and by *on it*, I am thinking of the heightened consciousness that comes with, or through, complaint. It is important to remember that the work of complaint (including the work of reaching complaint) is work you are doing when you are still at work, when you are still trying to do your work; you are trying to hold yourself together.

Holding ourselves together can also be an achievement. In the first part of the book, I noted that complaints, wherever they go, often end up in filing cabinets, those handy containers. We too can become containers. I talked informally to a woman professor about complaints she did and did not make. She attends a meeting for senior managers. She is the only woman around the table. She is used to this; this is business as usual. The usual is the structural in temporal form. If you were to complain about structures, you would be complaining all the time. To complain about being the only woman at a meeting would be to complain all the time. When you are used to something—and you have to get used to it if it keeps happening—that problem can recede, become background. Sometimes, then, *not* noticing something is a reflection of how much we know about something. But then one of the men at the table makes a sexualizing comment about chasing a woman around a dark room. She describes how the comment became a bonding moment between men: how the atmosphere in the room changes, with laughter, interest, as if they had been brought to attention. Even when you are used to it, it can hit you, that wall; the sexism, heterosexism, bubbling away at the surface of so many encounters. She does not say anything. She does not do anything. After expressing her feelings to me, of rage, alienation, disappointment, also of sadness, she says, "You file it under 'don't go there.'" We file away what makes it hard to do our work in order that we can do our work. And that is what many of us do: to keep doing our work, we file away what is hardest to handle, creating our own complaint files.

Our complaint files are full of what we have already noticed. The file "don't go there" tells us where we have been. A complaint file can be filled with the complaints we have but do not make, which is another way of thinking about how we carry our complaints, how complaints become heavy. But there can be a point we reach when it is too much; it is too hard, too heavy. A complaint might come out when we cannot keep hold of it, ourselves, the situation. Let's return to the testimony of the queer woman of color who is being harassed by her supervisor. I noted earlier that she handles the situation by keeping the door to his office open, trying to control where and how they meet. But handles can stop working:

> I was sitting with another colleague at another lunch another day and [my supervisor] started texting me these naked photos of himself, and I think I just hit a critical mass of, like, I just can't handle it anymore. I said [to my colleague], just look at this, and she was just like, you know like, completely speechless. . . . And then, like, it suddenly started to seep into me, into her, in this shared conversation about, like, how horrible and violent that I am having to receive these things, right, and so that basically put a process in motion.

A handle can be what we use to stop violence directed at us from seeping or leaking into us. When the handle stops working, the violence seeps in; it seeps into her and into her colleague, into their conversation, into the space in which they were having that conversation. A critical mass has to be reached before anything can be set in motion.

When violence gets *in,* a complaint comes *out.* A complaint can be what it takes to bring the violence out. Bringing the violence out can be experienced as coming out all over again, as making yourself suffer, again. She said, "I think I started to believe that if I came out with this in a public way, that my own career would suffer."[4] You have to keep coming out; you have to come out as somebody this happened to, to come out as somebody who is complaining that this happened. In chapter 1, I discussed how complaint is a form of communicative labor: you often have to keep making the same points, telling the same story, to many different people. If we think of these points as coming out, as disclosures, an act of making information known, sharing what has been secret, we learn how the requirement to communicate can be *retraumatizing*. To have to keep coming out with it is to have to keep going over what happened, to make it present, over and over again.

Stories of how complaints come out are rather bumpy stories. Coming out is rather bumpy. Queer and trans folk know that coming out is not a one-time event; you have to keep coming out because of how the world presumes a certain kind of body. You might have to correct pronouns being used for your partner or for yourself, coming out as that tiring work of correction. Correction is often heard as complaint: as being negative, assertive, demanding. Coming out can involve an intentional disclosure, but that's not always how coming out happens. Sometimes you have to admit something to yourself before you can admit something to others; sometimes you are outed by others and you have to deal with the consequences; sometimes you don't know when you will come out with it.

We learn from how, when, and where complaints come out: *we learn what it takes to reveal something*, what it takes not to keep a secret. For a complaint to come out "in the thick of it" can mean a complaint can come out when you are busy; you might be in the middle of a meeting. If some of the work around complaint might seem or feel like internal work (the conversations you have with yourself), complaints often come out *at* work, *in* social situations. These points about internality and sociality are related: if you are trying to hold something in and that effort fails, a complaint is expressed; what was kept apart is shared. In another instance, a junior woman academic is being sexually harassed by a senior professor mainly through verbal communication. The professor arrived at the university at the same time she did: "He was much older, late fifties early sixties. It was a big thing in the university: what a coup, we have got this extraordinary professor; he was on the side of the angels." This new professor began communicating with her in a way that felt increasingly uncomfortable. She did not want to make the situation worse; she described his behavior as mildly irritating; annoying, yes, distracting. His behavior, however mild she perceived it to be, was still getting in the way of her being able to do her work. And she wants to do her work:

He made me feel uncomfortable, and at the time I didn't know it was okay to say, please can you give me some personal space, that's not appropriate. Because I wasn't saying no, I really didn't know how to negotiate this. He clearly read that as "all things are go here." The comments became more overtly sexual, to the point where he made this strange comment about wanting to suck my toes, even I, naïve as I was at that point, went, oh shit, this is not, this is really, really not okay in the work environment.

She did not know how to tell him to stop, even if what he was doing seemed small, perhaps because she felt smaller than him. He was a professor, "on the side of the angels," no less; she a junior lecturer. Hierarchies can make handling harassment hard, which is how hierarchies enable harassment. But she wants the behavior to stop: "All I wanted at that point was for someone to talk to him and say, you need to stop this. Like that's what needs to happen. So, I went to my line manager, who was a woman, and said this is going on, this is making me feel really uncomfortable and I don't know how to handle it." The harassment she is dealing with, however minor she understands it to be, is already seeping in. She wants it to stop; she wants him to stop. And she makes an informal complaint to her line manager because she cannot handle the situation. She asks her line manager to talk to him, to say, "You need to stop this." It is her line manager who sits on the complaint, who does not want to make the complaint. I noted in chapter 2, with reference to this case, how a complaint can be stopped because other people do not want to pass the complaint on. When an attempt to stop harassment is stopped, the harassment does not stop:

> And then I was in a meeting with my line manager and her line manager and we were in this little office space, like a glass fishbowl-type meeting room, and then the main office where all the staff desks were, and he emailed me and I made a sound, *eehhhhh*, there's no way to articulate it, someone's just dragging your insides like a meat grinder, oh god, this is not going to stop, and I made that sound out loud, and my line manager's line manager said, what's happened? And I turned my computer around and showed him and he said, for fuck's sake, how stupid do you have to be to put that in an email? You could see a look of panic on her face. Like, crap, this has not magically gone away.

I think back to how *yes* can work rather like magic, making a complaint go away, disappear into air, rather like steam: puff, puff. If the complaint can be made to evaporate, the harassment "has not magically gone away." A complaint came out in the middle of the meeting, not as an account given by someone to someone, but as a sound, *eehhhhh*, a gut-wrenching expression of a *no*, or even a *no, not again*, or even a *no, enough is enough*. That sound, that *eehhhhh*, pierces the meeting; that meeting taking place in the little glass room, a fishbowl, where they can all be seen. Something can become visible and audible, sometimes even despite yourself; a complaint is what comes out because you can't take it anymore, you just can't take it anymore, your insides like a meat grinder: a complaint as how you are turned inside out.

The sociality of how complaints are expressed is another way of considering the effects of how complaints are contained. A complaint can be expressed rather like a snap; you hear the sound of something breaking.[5] If that sound sounds sudden, it is because of what you did not hear before, the pressure of what came before. Her sound became an alert, leading to a question: What's happened, what's up? The sound she made led to that question, and she answered that question by turning her computer around. Her line manager's line manager saw what she had been sent. And note how the problem once heard was implied to be not so much the harassment but that there was evidence of it ("for fuck's sake, how stupid do you have to be to put that in an email?"). A sound becomes a complaint because it brings to the surface a violence that would otherwise not have to be faced.

We can think of those windows with blinds that come down (see chapter 1). I suggested that they are not only a familiar feature of a built environment, that they might be telling us something about how institutions function. Institutional blinds might be how some things remain out of sight; it becomes a norm that the blinds are down. An institutional blind is what stops you from seeing or facing something that is happening within the institution. The violence was already there, in the room, in what she had been sent. Violence is often dealt with by not being faced. It is then as if the complaint brings the violence into existence, forcing it to be faced. Perhaps this is why complaints are often heard as forceful. For those who received the complaint, who heard the sounds she made, it was the complaint that alerted them to violence. A complaint is how violence is revealed; a complaint raises the blind.

Once raised, the complaint then acquires a life of its own. She did not initiate a formal complaint, but a complaints process began. I will return to what happened in the final section of this chapter. We learn from the way in which complaints can come out, tumble out, fall out, right in the

3.1 Institutional blinds.

middle of a meeting, in the thick it. Some complaints can involve an intentional action: you make a complaint about something; you bring that complaint to the right person; you follow the procedure you are supposed to follow, even if others do not follow the procedures, even if they do not pass the complaints on. It is because her attempt to deal with the situation did not get anywhere that her complaint came out in another way. A complaint can be expressed involuntarily; for her, it came out as sound, *eehh-hhh*, because she couldn't take it anymore, what she had to keep receiving.

A complaint can be how you are received when you are not willing to receive something. A postgraduate student attends a two-day conference held off campus at the beginning of a new academic year:

> The atmosphere of the two days was really oppressive. It was the cultural shift I recognize as I came through the doors. There was a lot of touching going on; shoulder rubs and knee pats. It was the dialogue. They were making jokes, jokes that were horrific. They were doing it in a very small space in front of staff, and nobody was saying anything. And it felt like my reaction to it was out of kilter with everyone else. It

felt really disconnected, the way I felt about the way they were behaving and the way everybody else was laughing. They were talking about "milking bitches." I still can't quite get to the bottom of where the jokes were coming from. Nobody was saying anything about it: people were just laughing along. You start to stand out in that way; you are just not playing along.

You can open the door and be hit by it: a change in atmosphere, intrusions into personal space, words out and about. The sexist expression "milking bitches" seemed to have a history. Each time the expression is used, that *history is thrown out like a line,* a line you have to follow if you are to get anywhere. When laughter fills the room, like water in a cup, laughter as a holding something, it can feel like there is no room left. To experience such jokes as offensive is to become alienated not only from the jokes but from the laughter that surrounds them, propping them up, giving them somewhere to go.

Just by not laughing, not going along with something, she started to "stand out." I think this is very important: a complaint can be registered before anything is even said or without anything being said. A complaint can be expressed by how a body is not attuned to an environment or by how someone is "out of kilter with everyone else." When other people are going along with it, you are being told there is nothing wrong with it. Perhaps some people laugh in order not to stand out. When people laugh and you do not laugh, you end up stranded, exposed. Being stranded is part of the experience of complaint, a sense that you have been cut off from a group that you had understood yourself to be part of; you come apart; things fall apart. Being cut off can also be a judgment made about the complainer, who can appear as a figure just because she is not laughing, not going along with things, not getting along.

All it takes is not laughing, not smiling, to appear to be complaining.[6] And to appear to be complaining is not only to stand out; it is to become the object of attention. It is because she experienced what was already in the room as violent that the violence was then rechanneled in her direction. One of the students "specifically went for me, verbally, at a table where everyone was eating lunch. It was a large table with numerous amounts of people around it, including staff. . . . I was having quite a personal conversation with someone [on a topic related to her PhD], and he literally leaned across the table or physically came forward, he was slightly ajar to me, he was really close, and he said, 'Oh my god I can see you ovulating.'" Because she does not find the jokes funny, because she expresses that she is not condoning the behavior, because she is not happy with what is going on, he comes after her. Her personal space is invaded, words flung out, flung at; she is reduced to body, pulled back, woman as ovaries; she is not allowed to do her own thing, to converse with others, to be occupied as a student. To belong might require getting along or going along with something. If those who do not participate in violence become the targets, a method of avoiding becoming a target of violence is to participate in it. This is how harassment often works to recruit others. You might take part in the harassment, become party to it, to avoid being harassed. This student describes what followed her experience:

> I think the staff member knew I was deeply upset by it. I pretty much left the table. And he [the staff member] followed me out and started a conversation, and this is when probably in hindsight it started to get difficult, in that the staff member started to lean on me; immediately he said to me, oh you know what he's like, he's got a really strange sense of humor, he didn't mean anything by it, and the implication was I was being a bit oversensitive and that I couldn't take a joke, and that I need to sort of forget about it and move on.

Note that there is an effort to stop the student from complaining *about* the situation *within* the situation. Warnings do not just come after you have indicated you might make a complaint: they can be articulated in the situation you are in. Warnings too are imminent. She is told not to say anything, not to be oversensitive, not to do anything, not to cause trouble. The content of what he said is dismissed as form, as just an idiosyncratic style of expression (a "strange sense of humor"). Offensive speech is often treated or justified as banter, as if words can be stripped of their histories. Those who are harassed are then required to strip words of their histories. There can be violence in the requirement to overlook or be unaffected by violence. The staff member by leaning on her not to complain is positioning himself *with* the harasser, treating the verbal onslaught as a joke, as something she should take and keep taking. The harasser physically comes forward; the staff member leans on her; the response to harassment is harassment. Harassment can be the effort to stop someone identifying harassment as harassment, which means that the person who identifies harassment as harassment is harassed all the more.[7]

The actions of the staff member in trying to stop her from complaining could be described as *institutional harassment*. It is not simply that she was leaned on not to complain but that she was leaned on by somebody with an institutional position. Institutional harassment describes not only how those within institutions participate in harassment by trying to stop complaints about harassment from being made, but also how the resources of the institution are mobilized to increase the pressure on those who are trying to make complaints about harassment.

In chapter 2, I discussed how attempts are made using a diverse range of methods to try to stop an informal complaint from becoming a formal complaint, which means stopping a person from proceeding with a complaint, which also means, to put it bluntly, stopping a person by whatever means necessary. One student gives an account of a meeting with her head of department after she had made an informal complaint about the conduct of her supervisor: "He framed it as an informal chat. And it wasn't at all. It was an interrogation. It felt like a scene from a Mafia film." Complaints, including those about scenes of violence, can be scenes of violence. Another student, who took her complaint all the way through the system, said, "They are hoping each time they will get me to stop. So there is a risk they will bankrupt me. They are trying to bankrupt me, a single mother on a low income. They know I don't have any money, and they are using that to try and stop me." By force, we are talking about the deliberate effort to deprive someone of what they need to make do, to live. You make it harder to complain "each time" by making it more costly to complain. In other words, one method for stopping a complaint is to make complaints unaffordable.

This is why making a complaint teaches us about power. Power works by making it hard to challenge how power works. That escalation of force is not only a consequence of complaint but a method for stopping a complaint. Escalation is the *increase* in the amount of force being applied to try to stop the complaint. Sometimes the increase of force operates as a deliberate attempt to stop someone ("they are using that to try and stop me"). Force can also be increased not by coming from a single point but by spreading outward. In other words, the force used to try to stop a complaint increases because it widens; more people are applying it. *Institutional harassment* can also be used to describe this process: the longer a person persists with a complaint, the more actors tend to participate in exerting the pressure not to complain.

How complaints are handled leads to the widening of pressure points. When someone makes an informal complaint, the response is often to alert other people about the complaint, including those who are complained about. What follows a complaint then depends upon the reactions of those who have been alerted about it. Even if these reactions are an effect of how a complaint is handled, they tend to be treated as outside the formal complaints process and thus as beyond the responsibility of the organization.

Those who are the objects of a complaint are sometimes alerted that a complaint has been made by being told by the person who received the complaint (who might or might not disclose names; how people handle this seems to have little to do with procedure). For example, a PhD student discussed with her supervisor how she was bullied by a professor in her department:

> I discussed this over with my supervisor (male), who urged me to file a complaint. My supervisor was supportive, but at the same time I also felt that because of their own personal dynamic this incident was kind of used by him to have proof of that professor's bullying behavior. . . . I think this professor must have been made aware about the complaint because he tweeted another disparaging remark sometime later—that if you were pursuing a PhD and couldn't handle criticism you shouldn't be a PhD student in the first place.

Complaints can be caught up in the internal politics of the department. You can be encouraged to complain or discouraged from complaining because of agendas that are not your own; conflicts or tensions between members of staff can influence how complaints are received.

When we think of complaint "in the thick of it" we are also thinking about how complaints can be *caught up* in the dynamics of a situation; when a complaint is *caught up*, you are *caught out*. She could tell that the professor "must have been made aware" of her complaint from comments she read on Twitter. How can you know those disparaging comments are about you? Sometimes you just know; a commentary can lean in the same direction as the bullying. Complaints often lead then to unofficial forms of communication—rejection, criticism, including criticism that you can't handle criticism—either addressed directly to the person who made the complaint or indirectly through social media or through unofficial communication networks such as gossip and rumor. It is important that when she read "some disparaging remarks" on Twitter, she knew who he was referring to. What follows a complaint can also be what the complaint was about: being disparaged, criticized, being told you can't take it, being told you can't make it.

So much negative data about the complainer is not revealed to the complainer; data too, even unofficial data, can be under lock and key, kept where the data is made, behind closed doors, sometimes coming out as vague allusion on social media or in social chit-chat, sometimes not. An early career lecturer who made a complaint about sexual misconduct by another lecturer in her college (he had begun a relationship with one of his undergraduate students) describes how the lecturer concerned began talking about her behind her back: "The backdoor stuff didn't stop. I would hear from other people that he'd been in the pub saying this, that, whatever about me, and it started to have a real impact on me." A backdoor conversation might be rather like the shadow policy discussed in chapter 1: how conversations generate alliances, affecting decisions that become official, without themselves being official.[8] A student who made a complaint about harassment at her college calls the campaign to demonize her "backdoor slander."

Complaints are made even harder because of what follows being known as someone making a complaint, what surrounds complaint: informal conversations, gossip, rumors that circulate to pathologize the complainer or anyone deemed the origin of a complaint. An academic who was forced out of her post said, "If people say things enough it becomes real."[9] What is repeated acquires force. What people say about you becomes part of what you have to deal with. Even if you don't know what is being said about you, even if you don't know who is saying what, you can *feel what is being said* in how people react to you, speak to you, address you, in sideways glances, how you are dropped, the invitations you stop receiving, how you are dropped from texts, how they stop referring to your work, how they turn away when you turn up. A Black woman who made a complaint about racism described people turning away from her in the corridor: "It was interesting to see, like, all of my colleagues, not like they were ever, like, oh hi, but so many of them did this [*puts her hands up*] and walked around me, like, you know, danger approaching." It is like you become a wall that others have to walk around. What you do not hear you can still feel; you feel a wall; a feeling can be a wall.

When people are alerted that a complaint has been made, the person who is deemed to be the origin of the complaint is treated by others as endangering others. A complaint can thus lead very quickly to an escalation of the situation a complaint is trying to address. We can return to the example of the early career lecturer who made an *eehhhhh* sound in a meeting that led to her line manager's line manager witnessing the harassment. A sound can be an alert. A complaints process followed that alert—a formal process that she did not herself initiate. She uses the word *imploded* to describe what happened: "And that is when it just imploded into—I can't even." You do not have to initiate a formal complaint to be imploded by a complaint process. She became isolated: "One by one, with few exceptions, colleagues started to turn against me." She is called to a meeting by Human Resources. During this meeting, she realizes she will have to leave:

> And this meeting dragged on and on and it was sort of going through all the points, and my boss wasn't in it, wasn't party to it, and it became clear at this point that something is going on beyond what I am involved in. That was the first time I realized the level of mess that is accompanying this. The professor disappeared; he was suddenly not there anymore. Whether he had been suspended or whether he quit, I never knew. But the story he had told to my colleagues was that he had been forced out by me. He's come to this country, to take this job, and he'd been pushed out and made to feel like his professionalism was challenged. You've heard all of this a thousand times.

A story can be familiar. We have heard it before because it has happened before. What can become clear is that you do not know what is going on; you are not party to it. A realization can be a realization of the mess. What happens to a complaint is often about who is able to tell the story of what happened that led to a complaint. She continues, "By this point there was just this colossal destruction in the team and I was desperate to get out of there because there was no way of having any professional respect from these people because every conversation was tainted by 'you're the woman who got a man to leave because he said he wanted to suck your toes,' which at no point was what happened, but of course there was no opportunity to talk about it." Even though she did not initiate the complaint, she was deemed to have forced him out, and there was no way for her to challenge the narrative. In practice confidentiality, which is often justified as necessary to protect those who complain, means that those with more connections have more control over how the complaint is framed. The story of what happens to a complaint is often the same story complaints are about: who controls the situation, who controls the narrative.[10]

Being deemed to have forced him out is how she ended up forced out. The university conducts an inquiry into what happened. An inquiry, more meetings, more times she is required to tell the story:

And it really was: tell us exactly what happened, tell us what happened to you. Someone was minuting all of this, and I was faithfully told, you will receive a copy of this report, you will be told what's happened institutionally and what we are going to do to make sure this does not happen to anyone else. And it was never forthcoming. And after that big meeting, I was taken for a cup of tea because I was so upset, I was so humiliated and desperate, really, desperate, by someone in Human Resources, and we went and sat in this empty big university cafeteria, and I was crying, and I remember being frightened about how much it was going to cost me to move house. I was only renting, but to break my rental contract, if the landlord wouldn't let me out, and the sheer cost of having to move again. And as I was crying the first conversation about money happened. It was very gently done. It was, well, funny you should say that, and maybe there is something we could do to help you with those costs. And it was a weird feeling because I had watched enough legal drama to know, hang on, what, this is weird, but we'll write to you about that, we'll find some way to sort of help you. I said I never want to come back into this university again, and she said, you don't have to, you can walk out today, you've got your stuff, you don't have to come back into any other meetings.

When you tell the story of a complaint, you watch yourself, you go back. She watches herself being walked into a conversation, being walked out of the meeting, being walked out with her stuff, being walked out of her job, gently: we can help you with that; we can get you out of that. In whatever way a complaint comes out, the person who experiences what the complaint is about is often the one who ends up out. And we need to think about that: what it means to end up out, to lose a job you love, a home; a life can be what unravels because you did not manage to keep something secret.

The experience of being forced out because of a complaint she did not initiate stays with her. The next time a senior professor said something objectionable, she does not put up with it, nor does she ask someone else to ask him to stop:

In the environment I am in currently, and I can't believe it, skeevy older academic tries this flirty thing again. . . . This time I have no time for this shit. Because I have no time for it—I teach students all day about intersectional feminism—I wasn't rude to him, I didn't embarrass him, but he has now put in a complaint against me for harassing him as a straight white Christian man. Why? Because I wouldn't be nice enough, I was described as dictatorial. I went from being the problem because I didn't say anything to being the problem because I say things. I am still not saying, good god that's inappropriate, will you stop it? I am saying, no, I am afraid that won't be possible. But even that, still cloaked in nice-girl politeness, is a problem.

Her experience of being ostracized as a result of a previous complaint leads her to become less willing to participate in feminine acquiescence to the demands of a senior academic man. Even becoming less willing to participate in something, a gendered division of labor, for instance, can make you more vulnerable to being complained about. She was still, in her view, performing "nice-girl politeness." But because she did not say *yes*, she was heard as saying *no*, "being the problem because I say things." That *no* can be sufficient to be identified as a harasser or even as being dictatorial. Perhaps those who are privileged, who have been taught they are entitled to a *yes* (a "straight white Christian man"), hear that *no* or that *not yes* as damage, as sufficient cause for complaint.

If saying *yes* can be a way of avoiding being harassed, saying *yes* can also be a way of avoiding being accused of harassment. Not saying *yes* can lead in the seemingly opposite direction of having to make a complaint or having a complaint made against you. I will return in the next chapter to how those who complain become the objects of complaint. I noted earlier that violence can be redirected toward those who show they are not willing to participate in violence. We now learn that a formal complaint can be part of the redirection of violence. This is why to offer a full and feminist account of the politics of complaint we have to go back, to what happens before a formal complaint, as well as to go around, to show how complaints come out of a wider struggle or are part of a wider struggle over what is permissible to do or to say.

I want to return to the example of the postgraduate student who was harassed by another postgraduate student at an off-campus conference. We learned from her experience how complaint and harassment become all tangled up: she complained because she was harassed; she was harassed because she complained. Even though she was leaned upon not to complain right from the beginning, she went on to make a formal complaint. She spoke first to her head of department. The head of department then talked to the two students who instigated the harassment, telling them a complaint had been made, though he didn't name the person who made it. Those students did not make a countercomplaint to her complaint, although they could have taken that route. Instead, they went on a rampage, using social media to campaign against anyone they thought might be the source of the complaint, which included many students who did not know anything about it. She describes what happened:

> A chain of events started that was much worse than what originally happened. It really escalated. They began to post messages, really awful messages, essentially trying to find out who was calling them out behind their back. It started off a conversation that the entire program got involved in, so that everyone could see all the messages. At the same time there were a lot of private conversations going on. People started to talk about who had actually made the complaint. The phrase they started to use was "bad apples." There are a few bad apples complaining. And then they started to use "man-haters." And then they said we were a group of women who were just oversensitive. And then it turned into "grasses get slashes." So it became quite violent. And they were talking about the women who complained as vermin who needed to be shot.

The increasingly violent messages were addressed to "the women who complained." The implication of the violent instruction "grasses get slashes" is that to complain to someone in authority is to be disloyal not only to the persons who were complained about but to the whole group. Those who complain are positioned as cutting themselves off from the group. I noted in my introduction to this chapter that *in the thick of it* can refer to where a situation is most crowded. A complaint can gather crowds, crowds of those who are assumed to have participated in that complaint, a crowd of those who gather against those who are assumed to have participated in the complaint. Any women who identified themselves as feminists were treated as the potential source of the complaint, the would-be complainer becoming the could-be complainer. Another woman I spoke to noted, "They had immediately assumed that the women who had put in the complaint were the women in their year that were doing feminist research, so they went onto Facebook and went onto their e-list to start to attack them even though they had not put in a complaint." Being near a complaint (for example, by a perceived proximity in politics) is enough to be targeted. This gives us a clue as to why many people try to avoid proximity to complaints and complainers: they fear being targeted.[11]

The could-be complainer is also the feminist complainer, feminism itself being charged with complaint through the exercising of old and familiar negative stereotypes (feminists as "man-haters"). Feminist complainers are called vermin, polluting agents who need to be eliminated. The circulation of the figure of the could-be complainer or feminist complainer meant more and more students were caught up by it. The use of the expression *bad apples* is suggestive. It implies a complaint is like an internal rot; to stop a complaint is to stop the rot from spreading. To stop a complaint is to stop it from being passed on, one to another, as if a complaint can spread like an infection.

Perhaps feminism is treated as an infection, what causes a complaint to spread. What is spreading is the story of what causes the complaint to spread. Those with institutional positions, heads of departments as well as senior lecturers, participated in the spreading of that story. The head of department describes the complaint as a feminist militancy:

> She said even before you put in this complaint, and now you've put in this complaint, you've really separated yourself from this department. She said, even by having a knitting club (and men and women were in the knitting club) that was already a sign of separating yourselves from the department. She said, what do you want, do you want your own women's space, trying to make [out] it was some kind of militant feminism. Obviously, it was a feminist project, but what we were asking for was equality and safety and people to feel welcome in that space.

Past activities are swept up as symptoms of having "separated themselves," as if their complaint was a result of not being better integrated into the department.[12] Even a mixed-gender knitting club can become a sign of a subversion-to-come. One way a complaint can be dismissed is by magnifying the demand; a demand for "equality and safety" is treated as wanting to bring an end to what or who already exists, or as separatism, as wanting not to share a space or a culture. In other words, the escalation of the violence directed to those who complained can be an escalation of what a complaint is demanding.

If some senior academics participated in the spreading of the story, they participated in the escalation of violence. Participation can be denied by the denial of violence. One of the students explained, "Even when threats of violence were made, it was implied it was just talk and it didn't mean anything." Verbal violence, which can include threats of physical violence, is often deemed not to mean anything at the very point it is identified as violence. Remember the member of staff who had followed her out of the room, who had discouraged her complaint by saying, "He didn't mean anything by it."[13] Not intervening to stop the escalation of violence needs to be understood as how violence escalates. Doing nothing is doing something. Another student who participated in the complaint after the first stage commented on the stance of the subsequent head of department:[14] "And she said, I can't be seen to side with either student, so we can't formally take a line on this. And we were like, how can they not formally take a line on sexual harassment?" Not taking sides is taking sides: it is trying to stop the complaint about harassment rather than trying to stop the harassment.

Escalation can be an escalation of force used to stop a complaint. The escalation of violence can also occur through the justification of violence; in other words, when actions are justified, the violence is enabled, repeated, and intensified. The violence escalated because the student did not go along with it, because she was perceived as complaining. The violence escalated because the students who were abusive were alerted that a complaint had been made. The violence escalated because of the refusal of those in positions of authority to intervene to stop the violence escalating, because the violence was treated as one "side of an argument." The violence escalated by being disputed or by being treated as disputable. Each step is part of the same structure. The more steps taken, the more of the structure is revealed.

There are more steps, more of a structure to be revealed. In the meeting with the head of department, the students were told, "I don't need to talk to you about discourse analysis and poststructuralism, and we can all do a discourse analysis on x, and we'd all come up with very different meanings." We could call this a theoretical justification of violence: using current theories to imply that interpreting "milking bitches" as an offensive or sexist speech act is just one interpretation among a universe of possible interpretations. When I consider such *theoretical justifications*, I think again of institutional blinds.

I suggested earlier that an institutional blind is how violence is not seen. A complaint can be how the blinds are raised, forcing violence to be seen. We now learn: it is not that blinds stop violence from being seen. The blinds come down *because violence is seen*. Justifications can be blinds, ways of not seeing the violence revealed by a complaint.[14] To make a complaint is thus often to notice blinds; *you see what is pulled down over what you see.*

It is not surprising that justifications are so revealing (of a concealing); someone is called upon to justify something when they are required to do so, that is, when questions are asked or complaints are made. To complain is to receive many justifications. The head of department's comment is the kind of justification that I have heard over and over again, both in my

3.2 You see what is pulled
down over what you see.

study of complaint and in my own experience of trying to challenge sexism and racism in the wider public domain. A common justification for
using offensive terms is that terms have different meanings. I have heard
lecturers or students justify their own use of racist terminology, including
terms we know by letter (I will not share the letters; a history can be the
violence of a repeated letter) as an attempt to give those terms new meanings or to show that they can acquire new meanings. The justification of
violence *is* how that violence is repeated. *The justification of violence is
that violence.*

The transition from "he didn't mean anything by it" to "it didn't mean
anything" to "we'd all come up with very different meanings" is teaching
us something about how and why meaning matters. The implication is
that to complain about what such-and-such person said is to *impose* your
interpretation upon others. I think what is going on here is another version of stranger danger. In earlier work I suggested that stranger danger
is used to imply that violence originates with outsiders (Ahmed 2000,
2017).[15] It can also be used to imply that those who identify violence "on
the inside" do so because they are outsiders. The use of words like *racism*

and *sexism* become understood not only as impositions from the outside but as attempts to restrict the freedom of those who reside somewhere, the freedom to interpret what words mean and to do as they say.[16] To complain at the university is to be treated as ungrateful for the benefits you have received from the university: the freedom to make your own interpretation, the freedom to be critical, academic freedom.

If escalation can be another method of stopping a complaint, escalation includes not only the increase of force but the denial of force. The use of the method of escalation can be thought of as another version of coming out: it is how the organization reveals itself, shows itself, what it is really like, who it will support and enable. We learn not only from *who* is supported but from *how* they are supported, how ideals (such as academic freedom or criticality) can be reused to justify ways of speaking or acting that are not only the object of a complaint but what most universities say they are committed to opposing. Coming out is also a matter of consequences. All of the four women who made the complaint left the program; the two men who harassed them remained. The woman who was harassed at the table because she did not participate in the sexist humor did not just leave the table or the program; she left the academy. She left in part because of what she learned *about* the institution from how it responded *to* her complaint. She described this process: "I lost my rose-tinted glasses, the way I saw those spaces being a place of excellence. I thought they were welcoming of difference. I had worked really hard to get to that space. When you come from the kind of background, I have— no one had been to university to do a degree." Seeing the institution more clearly for her meant leaving the institution. It meant giving up a path, a trajectory that she, as a working-class woman, had had to fight for.

Perhaps here we can see how the very expectation that universities will be "welcoming of difference," that is, will be what they say they are or what they appear to be, means that going through a complaint is experienced as the loss of an idea of the university. Perhaps she was not protected by what I called earlier *middle-class cynicism*, a disbelief in the value of things as an expression of an entitlement to them. Complaint can be a continuation of the fight of working-class students and academics to get into the university.[17] She also described the costs of making a complaint for her compared to the costs for students who were harassing her: "Those guys, they were quite financially secure. They came from much more privileged backgrounds than I did. I am a white working-class girl from a council estate, so when I ran out of money, I ran out of money." Complaints become all the more difficult if you do not come from a privileged background—you can run out of money as well as time and energy. We are back here to the reproductive logic of strategic inefficiency (chapter 2): the more costly and time-consuming complaints are, the harder it is to make complaints for those with less means. Those who most need to complain are those who cannot afford to complain. Those who most need to complain and cannot afford to complain often leave.

Those who complain might leave because of what or who remains. And when those who complain leave, what or who they complain about remains. The escalation of violence against those who complain about violence is how violence remains.

CHAPTER FOUR

OCCUPIED

You might have to make a complaint because of how a space is occupied. When you challenge how spaces are occupied, you learn how spaces are occupied. That occupation becomes a *lesson*, what we learn from complaint, tells us that it is not always obvious *how* occupation is achieved or even *that* it is achieved. Sometimes it might seem obvious: there can be a sign on a door that tells us a facility is currently being used.

Spaces can be occupied without the use of such signs. Spaces can be occupied by being intended for specific purposes. When spaces are intended for specific purposes, they have bodies in mind. Perhaps we can more easily tell whom spaces are intended for when those for whom they were not intended turn up. In *What's the Use? On the Uses of Use* (2019), I use an image of a post box that has become a nest as an example of what I call *queer use*, how things can be used in ways that were not intended or by those for whom they were not intended. The birds turned a small opening intended for letters into a door, a queer door perhaps, a way of getting in and out of the box. Of course, the post box can become a nest only if it stops being used as a post box; hence the sign "Please do not use the box" addressed to would-be posters of letters. I am aware that this is a rather happy, hopeful image. Queer use is rarely about just turning up and being able to turn a box into a nest or a room into a shelter. To queer use, to open up spaces to those for whom they were not intended often requires a world-dismantling effort.

4.1 A sign on the door tells us when the facility is in use.

4.2 Queer use: things can be used by those for whom they were not intended.

Complaint describes some of that effort. A complaint can mean having a fight on your hands. You might have to fight for room, room to be, room to do, room to do your work without being questioned or being put under surveillance. You might have to fight for a syllabus that does not enact your disappearance or to have portraits on walls or names on buildings that do not celebrate your dispossession. That fight can be how we acquire wisdom: we know so much from trying to transform the worlds that do not accommodate us. And *trying* seems the right word; it can be trying. But that fight can also be just damn hard. When you have to keep fighting for an existence, fighting can become your existence.

We can inherit a fight for existence, which is also to say, we can inherit the effects of complaint. We might not now be able to enter some doors, some buildings, some institutions, some universities if others before us had not complained. And we have often had to create our own feminist programs because of how institutions were occupied once we got here. But we can turn up in feminist spaces and find that they too are already occupied. I think of Audre Lorde in 1978 turning up at an event to commemorate the thirtieth anniversary of the publication of Simone de Beauvoir's *Second Sex*. She agreed to speak; she does speak, on a panel, "The Personal Is Political." But she finds that the panel is the only panel where Black feminists and lesbians are represented. Lorde takes a stand; she makes a stand. She uses the time and the space she has been given to make a critique, perhaps a complaint, about the time and space Black feminism and lesbianism have been given. That critique, perhaps a complaint, was to become one of Lorde's best-known essays, "The Master's Tools Will Never Dismantle the Master's House." In that essay, Lorde (1984, 110–11) asks a question: "What does it mean when the tools of a racist patriarchy are used to examine the fruits of that same patriarchy?" She tells us what it means by showing us what it does. When a feminist house is built using the tools of "racist patriarchy," the same house is being built, a house in which only some are allowed in, or only some are given room. Lorde stresses that those who are resourced by the master's house will find those who try to dismantle that house "threatening" (112). An attempt to open up a space to others can be threatening to those who occupy that space.

A complaint can be how we learn how the house is built. *Complaint as diversity work*: the work we have to do because we are not accommodated; the work we have to do in order to be accommodated. It might seem that the work of dismantling described by Lorde and the work of accommodation are quite different kinds of political and institutional work: if the former is about bringing the house down, the latter seems to be about enabling more people to enter the house. Things are not always as they seem. Complaint teaches us that for some to be accommodated requires dismantling an existing structure or modifying an existing set of arrangements.

MISFITTING AND COMPLAINT

You learn how a structure is built when you do not fit that structure. A complaint can be what you do *not* have to make if you fit, if you are enabled by a structure. For those who do not fit, a complaint might be what you have to make before you can get in. Rosemarie Garland-Thomson (2014, n.p.) describes not fitting or misfitting as follows: "A misfit occurs when the environment does not sustain the shape and function of the body that enters it. The dynamism between body and world that produces fits or misfits comes at the spatial and temporal points of encounter between dynamic but relatively stable bodies and environments. The built and arranged space through which we navigate our lives tends to offer fits to majority bodies and create misfits with minority forms of embodiment, such as people with disabilities." You have a fit when an environment is built to accommodate you. When you are accommodated, you don't even have to notice that environment. You are a misfit when there is an incongruous relation of your body to thing or body to world. In an earlier article, Garland-Thomson (2011, 592–93) describes misfitting as "an incongruent relationship between two things: a square peg in a round hole."[1] When you try to fit a norm that is not shaped to fit your body, you create an incongruity; you become an incongruity. Fitting becomes work for those who do not fit; you have to push, push, push, and sometimes no amount of pushing will get you in.

The work of "pushing to get you in" is a good description of the work of complaint. An academic describes how she keeps pointing out that rooms are inaccessible because they keep booking rooms that are inaccessible: "I worry about drawing attention to myself. But this is what happens when you hire a person in a wheelchair. There have been major access issues at the university." She spoke of "the drain, the exhaustion, the sense of why should I have to be the one who speaks out." You have to speak out because others do not, and because you speak out others can justify their own silence; they hear you, so it becomes about you; "major access issues" become your issues.

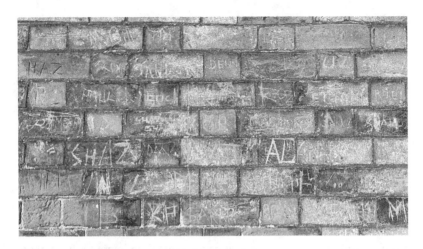

4.3 Learning about structures.

She has to keep saying it because they keep doing it. But it is she who is heard as repeating herself, as if she is stuck on the same point. A complaint is heard as a *broken record*. Maybe we need to enact how we are heard; we might need to break their record. I think back to those scratches on the surface, how diversity work often feels like scratching the surface, complaint too; we can recall the description of a complaint as "a little bird scratching away at something." Sometimes a scratch, a superficial mark on the surface of something, can be sufficient to stop it from working. Scratches can tell us how things are working.

If to complain is to scratch at the surface, to complain is to learn about structures. A complaint might begin with *a feeling of structure*; you notice a structure when it stops you from getting somewhere or from being somewhere: it can hit you; we are back to that wall. Some have to complain about the structures that enable and ease the progression of others. A feeling of structure is an experience of coming up against something that will not move. Kay Inckle (2018, 1373) describes how this immobility—for example, not being able to move a session into an accessible room—is justified:

> During my career I have been told that I cannot be scheduled into wheelchair accessible teaching rooms for a variety of reasons including: that to do so would involve "disrupting" someone else and changing their timetable (even though they are not a wheelchair user and therefore do not specifically need that room); that accessibility is not a "first priority" of timetabling; that I will have to "make do" with a "not

ideal" room (e.g. one which has no emergency egress); that the university could deem it "reasonable" to expect me to go downstairs on my bottom in some situations rather than reorganising my timetable to ensure I have reliably accessible rooms (the last was said by an "Equality Officer" in defence of timetabling).

As a wheelchair user who is registered disabled with her employer, Inckle should be provided with an accessible room. She should not have to ask for an accessible room because she has not been given one; her needs should have been already accommodated in the scheduling of times and spaces. Complaint can be the work some have to do to get what they need, work they should not have to do.

We need to listen to what is being said here, to the messages that Inckle has been receiving over her career as a disabled academic ("I have been told that"). Messages too can accumulate. We need to pause at the idea that it could be thought reasonable to expect that she, a disabled academic, should "go downstairs on [her] bottom," an idea that is expressed by an equality officer, someone who not only knows about the organization's equality policies, and might even have helped to write them, but is responsible for implementing them. It can be deemed reasonable for some people to be humiliated in order not to dislodge others. Inckle's work helps us to understand ableism not only as a structure that is there (like a building), although ableism is a structure that is there (like a building), but also as what is perpetually justified and reproduced *by* those who are enabled by that structure.

In chapter 3, I described how hard it can be to recognize harassment; harassment can disappear by being near what ordinarily happens. Structures can function as sources of harassment. The word *harassment* comes from the French word *harasser*, "to tire out" or "vex." In early usages it "suggests the infliction of the weariness that comes from the continuance or repetition of trying experiences, so that there is not time for rest."[2] Structures are about what is repeated. When there is a "repetition of trying experiences," then structures are exhausting as well as humiliating and degrading. The structures that are exhausting and degrading for some can be the same structures that enable or "free" others. Complaints have much to teach us about structures; the work some have to do just to get through is harassment; the "repetition of trying experiences," the "infliction of weariness."

You can be exhausted by not being accommodated; you can be exhausted by the work you have to do in order to be accommodated. I spoke to one student about doing this work:

The reasonable adjustment duty is really clear that the reasonable adjustment is supposed to bring some kind of parity between disabled people and nondisabled people, but they experienced my need for adjustment as making their lives a complete pain in the ass, and they wanted at the very least groveling gratefulness on a daily basis in order to continue providing it, preferably considerably more than that. I think if I had turned up with some kind of cheerleaders for them, I think then maybe they would have thought it was acceptable.

I suggested earlier in this book that it is hard to overstress the inconvenience of complaint. Asking for accommodations is framed not only as causing inconvenience to others but as *being what you cause*: an inconvenience. You have to smile as if in compensation for the inconvenience. Not showing signs of gratitude, not being a cheerleader for the organization, not fulfilling what I called in chapter 1 "the positive duty" is sufficient to be heard as complaining, as being negative, "a complete pain in the ass." A complaint is how you are received because of how you are perceived. A complaint can be about not having the right stance or not displaying the right attitude. Note her wording here: "they experienced my need for adjustment as making their lives a complete pain in the ass." A need can be negation. To have needs that are not met by an existing arrangement is to become needy. An existing arrangement can be what protects some people from the judgment of being needy; worlds can be assembled to meet some people's needs. The implication is that by asking for a modification so that you have what you need, you are imposing yourself upon others; you are even putting yourself before others.

You can become a sore point because of what you need. If you say what you need, a sore point becomes the same point. This student did end up making a formal complaint to get the adjustments she needed, although the work of complaint began before that, long before that; it began with her need for adjustments that were registered as complaint. *A complainer arrives before a complaint is made.* I will return in due course to the significance of how complainers precede complaints. She described how, when she formalized her complaint, the eye of the institution landed upon her:

They had dragged the whole thing out and treated me hideously and they would be like, oh we see you have had a friend over last night, maybe you could write more essays if you tried harder. They were just brutal. They got loads of letters from my doctors and so on [saying she] has to have extensive medical procedures, and loads of things take a long time and she doesn't have the same amount of energy as everyone else and she's got these genetic incurable conditions and the only way to manage them is to have a lower level of activity in daily life. And they wanted pie charts of how long it takes me to go to the toilet—wildly, intrusively bizarre requests.

Having the eye of the institution landing on you is to be subjected to more and more requirements; you have to tell them more about yourself, give them intimate details about your life, about going to the toilet; you have to turn yourself into data; even pee can end up a pie. Indeed, she talked to me about what she would *not* complain about given her own knowledge of the intrusiveness of the complaints process: "I wouldn't make a complaint about toilets because I feel that being cross-examined about whether I am humiliated by pissing myself in toilets is too much." A complaint can require you to share what is humiliating about an experience. It can be humiliating to share what is humiliating. Sometimes you might avoid making a complaint as a way of avoiding further humiliation. As I pointed out in chapter 2, the work some have to do to complain about the inaccessibility of institutions can make institutions even more inaccessible. And in drawing the complaint out, the person who is trying to get what they need is being treated cruelly, subjected to the humiliation of being asked about humiliations. Whether or not your complaint is about harassment, to complain is often to be subjected to harassment, that "infliction of weariness."

When you complain, your own body is turned into testimony, as revealing something about yourself as well as about the situation in which you find yourself. I spoke to an early career academic who went on long-term sick leave. She began to encounter difficulties in how her department handled her return to work—they made no adjustments to her workload. And in this process of having, in her terms, "to administer [her] own sick leave," she began to realize, "I was not just a person who was off sick. I was a person with a grievance at the way I was treated by the university." After she left her post, she was diagnosed with autism. With that diagnosis in mind, she reflects back on the responses to what she had asked for:

A lot of the things I was asking for, adjustments that could have been made in my job, even without the diagnosis, if they had been listened to, they call it reasonable adjustments, the language of it always makes me laugh, if some of that could have happened instead of people saying, yes we will do this and yes we will do that and then nothing really happening, if some of that had happened and some of this had been listened to and manifested by actually reducing hours properly, and actually monitoring, and actually doing some of the very basic things I was asking for, I think I probably would have still had a job. And maybe the last five years of my life would not have been profoundly stressful, for different reasons, for financial reasons. So yes, it makes me feel quite angry, sad, a lot of that is still around it.

She shows that "even without the diagnosis," how she was treated was wrong, causing her profound stress, leading her to lose her job. She should not have needed a diagnosis to receive "the very basic things" she was asking for. Although she does not assume that if she had the diagnosis earlier it would have made a difference to the outcome of her complaint, the diagnosis does make a difference: it sharpens her sense of the injustice of how she had been treated; it helps her to diagnose what was wrong with the institution, to make an *institutional diagnosis*. She demonstrates that the failure to listen, to respond to what she needed to do her work was a structural rather than personnel problem. In other words, the failure to listen to what different people need to do their work is how a narrow idea of what people need to do their work is *imposed* by the institution.

The work she has to do to secure what she needs to return to work, to do her work, ends up being the work of complaint. She speaks to a physician from occupational health: "I think his sense was that if I was well enough to stamp my foot and complain then I was well enough to work. So there was this equation between being well enough to articulate and being active in terms of making sure I was getting the right support. . . . If you are really good at making complaints, you must be well enough to go to work." Stamp my foot and complain: because she could hear how she was being heard we too have the opportunity to hear something: how a complaint is audible as a tantrum; how the complainer is cast as spoiled; how a grievance is heard as a grudge. Note how being active as well as being articulate can be used against you *as if you speak too well to be unwell*. The discrediting of complaint or testimony is often enacted by making the complainer the object: you chip away at her testimony by casting doubt on her ability to narrate her own experience. A complaint can be discredited when the person who makes a complaint is too coherent and capable. Or a complaint can be discredited if the person who makes a complaint is not coherent enough or capable enough. You can be too much or not enough. A postgraduate student who made a complaint about disability discrimination was told in a letter that she had, and this is a direct quote from the letter, "misinterpreted her own interpretation."

You can be treated as if you can't even understand your own testimony or as if you do not know the content of your own mind.

There are different ways a complaint testimonial can be discredited. The word *complaint* can denote "an illness or medical condition especially a relatively minor one."[3] In being heard as complaining, the quality of being minor is transferred to the object of the complaint, such that the mere fact of making a complaint is used as evidence that the person who is complaining is suffering from a minor condition. Being able to complain about an oppressive situation can be used as evidence that you are not really oppressed by a situation. The expression "suffering in silence" can be descriptive (those who suffer *do not* speak) but also normative or prescriptive (those who suffer *should not* speak). To give expression to suffering can then be used as evidence of not suffering or not suffering properly. A complainer in being expressive becomes a moaner, moaning about minor matters. And maybe too the quality of being minor is transferred to the subject of a complaint; the one who makes a complaint can become a minor condition, an irritant in the fabric of institutional life. *Minor* also seems to evoke the minority: complaint as the discourse of minorities. And indeed, this hearing is telling; those deemed minorities are often heard as moaning about minor matters; the complainer as minor evokes the complainer as privileged (again, as if to say, to be suffering would be not to be able to complain at all). Minorities are often understood (by those who are privileged) as privileged or as being given special privileges.

We can return to the conversation between the early career lecturer and the physician from occupational health. She describes how she refused to sign a report he wrote: "He was shocked I think that I complained to him in the room face-to-face. He was dictating the letter to the computer, which was automatically typing it, and I think he was astonished that I said I am not going to sign it." I think of her refusal to sign that letter, to agree with how he expressed her complaint back to her: the words he read out loud, his words, the computer automatically typing those words, his words; the different ways you can be made to disappear from your own story. A complaint is more likely to be received as justified if you allow others to articulate that complaint for you, if you passively receive what those with authority give to you. Perhaps to make a complaint without becoming a complainer (I will return in due course to the question of who becomes a complainer) requires being receptive. A complaint can require saying *no* to those with authority who in receiving your complaint will use their authority to retell the story. In saying *no*, a complaint provides evidence of insubordination.

We end up repeating ourselves. You have to keep saying it because they keep doing it. A *no* can be harder to keep saying if you don't feel you have a right to keep saying it. Even though she was making a complaint, she did not herself feel confident about her right to do so: "There is something else which is something to do with being a young female academic from a working-class background: part of me felt that I wasn't entitled to make the complaint—that this is how hard it is for everybody, and this is how hard it should be and if it isn't hard then it is not work." To question one's entitlement to complain can be to question whether one has the right to expect anything other than more of the same (if it is hard, that is how it should be). Those with a strong sense of entitlement do not tend to question their entitlement to complain.[4] Perhaps this is why those with a strong sense of entitlement tend to dismiss complaints *as* expressions of entitlement.

In the previous chapter, I considered how a complaint can be the continuation of the fight working-class students and academics have to enter bourgeois institutions. A fight to get there can also give you a sense you don't have a right to complain when you get there. If part of her felt she was not entitled to complain, she has to fight all the more, she has to fight against that part of herself, that inheritance of a classed as well as gendered history; she has to fight to complain in her own way, using her own terms, just as she has to fight for what she needs to do her work. So yes, a complaint can be a continuation of the fight by other means.

BECOMING/UNBECOMING COMPLAINERS

The complainer can appear before a complaint is made. This is how a complainer can acquire further meaning or value very quickly: the complainer as moaner, the complainer as minor, which speeds her dismissal. In chapter 2, I introduced the figure of a would-be complainer as the one who has indicated to herself or to others that she is considering filing a complaint. We are now learning: you can become that figure without giving any such indication. *A figure too can be a file*; the complainer is a rather stuffed file. If you then make a complaint, you are picking up an already stuffed file. As Leila Whitley and Tiffany Page (2015, 43) have observed, "When a woman files an objection to sexual harassment, she becomes in the language of the institution a woman who complains, and by extension a complainer." There are many ways to file an objection. If you ask for a modification of an existing arrangement, or if you ask for a change to your workload so that you can do your work, so that you can return to work, you are heard as filing an objection, as complaining, being negative, even mean.

The sharper the figure of the complainer, the more she comes into view, the blurrier the background. *What* the complainer is complaining about thus often recedes from view. To complain is to try to make what a complaint is *about* stand out. We can draw here on Paulo Freire's ([1970] 2000, 83) radical pedagogy: "That which had existed objectively but had not been perceived in its deeper implications (if indeed it was perceived at all) begins to 'stand out,' assuming the character of a problem." To make a complaint is to try to make something stand out, to assume the character of a problem. So often the person who makes the complaint is the one who ends up standing out, "assuming the character of a problem." A student who made multiple complaints about bullying and sexual harassment (you have to keep complaining if you don't get anywhere) described how in complaining you draw attention to yourself: "You draw attention. You draw attention to the inequities, the power situations that are present, the things that you know people should see, but the minute you draw attention to them the attention is drawn to you." If as soon as you draw attention to structures you draw attention to yourself, the structures do not come in view; *you* do. We can recall the words of the disabled academic who "worried about drawing attention to [her]self." And we might recall the words of the postgraduate student who described how she started to "stand out in that way" when she did not laugh at a sexist joke (chapter 3). You can stand out by not participating in something, by not being in agreement.

The figure of the complainer also functions as a diagnosis: if a grievance is heard as a grudge, then a complaint is often understood as masking a personal failing of some kind. An early career lecturer describes this dynamic:

I have been told I have a chip on my shoulder, that I've got a chip on my shoulder because I am Jewish, that I have a chip on my shoulder because I am foreign, living in this country and you're upset about Brexit, or because you're gay and you are just looking for the problems. And you start thinking, am I looking for these problems? I just turn it inwards: is it me, is it my fault? I lie awake at night thinking, is it actually a problem with me here?

It is as if you keep making the same points, which quickly become sore points, because you are invested in being sore. If you keep making the same points because you keep encountering the same problem, it is not surprising that you can end up feeling that the problem is you.

Once you have become a complainer it is hard to unbecome a complainer. And having become a complainer is often to find more and more sticks to you. A lesbian academic became head of department; she is the first woman to be head of department, let alone the first lesbian. She is new to the department:

> I was the first female head of department and everything became stuck to me. The fact that there had been fire doors put in all the rooms to replace the solid wood ones, ones with windows in, that was my fault, that was me wanting to spy on people. The fact that faculty was going over to electronic calendars, and I said, what do you think, shall we use these, how shall we use them? That was me wanting to spy on people.

I will have more to say about doors in part III of this book: there is so much more to say about the stories they tell. The solid doors were in fact replaced after a number of cases of sexual misconduct and sexual harassment. She mentions LGBT groups at her university who knew "why those solid doors were turned into windows." Whatever the story these doors could tell, and doors have stories to tell, the doors end up sticking to her.

Complaints have a lot to teach us about how "negative affects" are sticky as well as picky; you can be picked on by what you are stuck with. She is introduced as a lesbian head of department by a student: "There was some discussion of that with colleagues, like I had some banner to fly, pushing students to get involved with this." The figure of the pushy minority has an institutional life for a reason: you are registered as imposing yourself on a situation.[5] For some to be is to be judged as imposing. You can become a complainer just by being called a lesbian head of department.[6] She added:

> If you have a situation and you make a complaint, then you are the woman who complains, the lesbian who complains, and it gets in the way of being in the role: being a good colleague, a good mentor, a great teacher, a supervisor. And you can feel the change in your voice and the dynamic in meetings. And you don't like to hear yourself talking like that, but you end up being in that situation, again. And you think, it's me, and you think, no it's not, it's systematic, and you think, it's me.

That conversation you have with yourself—it's me, it's the system, it's me, it's the system—takes time. And it can feel like everything is just spinning around. Spinning, spilling: maybe you reach a point, a breaking point, when it spills out. To fly off the handle can mean to snap or to lose your temper. If the handle breaks, you become the one who can't handle things.

She continues, "And then of course you get witch-hunted, you get scapegoated, you become the troublesome uppity woman; you become the woman who does not fit; you become everything the bully accuses you of, because nobody is listening to you. And you hear yourself starting to take that, not petulant tone, [*bangs table*] come on. You can hear them saying, oh there you go." A diversity practitioner had said something very similar to me: that she only had to open her mouth in meetings to witness eyes rolling as if to say, "Oh, here she goes." Both times we laughed: it can be a relief to have an experience put into words. It was experiences like that that became the basis of my equation *rolling eyes = feminist pedagogy*. Even when we laugh, we know that to be followed by rolling eyes is to be followed by eyes. We can feel the weight of scrutiny as the expectation that *that* is what you would say.

To become a complainer can also mean becoming the object of other people's complaints.[7] Members of her department submitted an informal complaint to Human Resources identifying her as a bully. It should not surprise us that a "pushy minority" can morph into a bully. Bullying often works to create a narrative about a person as behind whatever is deemed problematic. She was a new head of department; she was trying to make changes to the culture of that department. Any modification introduced by a person can be used as evidence they are pushing their own agenda.[8] It can be difficult from the outside to identify who is bullying because bullies often represent themselves as bullied.[9] The effect of the bullying, which included framing her as the bully, was to make her feel isolated. Although she knew she had grounds to make a formal complaint, in particular about the role of a dean in enabling the situation, she did not: "It was really hard. I was just on my own. It is like the world becoming completely weird all around you. And your basic integrity questioned: the reasons you do a job like this, you just want to do a good job, what you want to put right. Everything is utterly strange." In the end, she hired a "crack employment lawyer" and won a case of constructive dismissal.[10] Even though informal complaint was one of the tools used against her, she still understood herself in career as well as life terms as a complainer, as someone who felt compelled to complain about injustice, even though she did not make use of complaints procedures in that instance. She said,

"I have got to make a point, to draw this to people's attention." We are back to complaint as an effort to draw attention to a problem.

Given that drawing attention to a problem makes you into a problem, complainers are often complained about. In fact, the more you have to complain about, the more you are complained about. The figure of the complainer becomes a *complaint magnet*. To become a complainer is to attract complaints, to receive as well as make them, or to receive them because you make them. If you use words like *racism* or *sexism* that point to structural injustices in your teaching or research, you are not only heard as complaining; you are likely to have complaints made about you. Those involved in teaching gender or race studies or teaching gender or race in other courses are likely to have had numerous informal complaints made against them because of what or how they teach. Complaints you might have received include: there is too much feminism; this is too biased; this is too political. These kinds of complaints are not typically made using formal complaints procedures but informally, using faster and easier methods—for example, by sending emails or letters to members of a department or through student evaluations.[11]

Note the nonreducibility of the figure of the complainer to the making of informal or formal complaints; if you can become a complainer before you make a complaint, or even without making a complaint, you can make a complaint without becoming a complainer.[12] In chapter 2, I referred to complaints as *sticky data*. Perhaps it is the complainer who is sticky; the negative data of complaints does not stick to everyone who complains or is perceived as complaining.

It is because of the costs of becoming a complainer that some might seek not to become complainers, which can be rather hard given how the figure of the complainer can turn up before we do. A woman of color explains, "I think with a person of color there's always a question of what's this woman going to turn out like. . . . They're nervous about appointing people of color into senior positions. . . . Because if I went in my sari and wanted prayer time off and started rocking the boat and being a bit different and asserting my kind of culture, I'm sure they'd take it differently." Some forms of difference are heard as assertive, as if you are different only because you are insistent on being different ("I'm sure they'd take it differently"). Even wearing a sari or wanting a prayer room can be heard as "rocking the boat." We can place this use of the expression *rocking the boat* alongside its use in warnings about complaint (chapter 2). Difference from something can be heard as a complaint about something: *difference as complaint*. And complaints about something can be heard as differences from something:

complaint as difference. You can rock the boat just because of how you are perceived to be; any difference is registered as trying to destabilize things, to stop things from being as they are. And you can rock the boat by questioning how things are; any complaint is registered as a product of not trying to assimilate to the culture of an institution.

Given that rocking the boat can make your own passage unsteady, you might try to avoid rocking the boat by minimizing signs of difference. I have called the labor of minimizing signs of difference *institutional passing.* Maybe you don't wear a sari; maybe you don't ask for prayer time off. You might smile. A smile, I suggested in the previous chapter, can be where you deposit the complaints you do not make. A smile can be a file. You might have to work hard to contain yourself. Not complaining becomes another kind of institutional labor when you know you have something to complain about. You might avoid using the word *racism* even though it makes sense of your experience or perhaps even because it makes sense of your experience. A woman of color academic talked to me about how and why she avoided complaining at least in the early part of her career. She said she had "observed when other women of color have complained and asked questions they have been viewed in a negative light." Knowing how complaints can be sticky, as well as picky, she gave herself instructions not to complain: "I told myself to shut up. I told myself not to talk, not raise questions and just be invisible." When you have something to say but realize it would be costly to say it, you have to keep telling yourself not to say it. Institutional passing can be the effort to maximize the distance between yourself and the figure of the complainer. You might try to pass not because you identify with them or wish to be one of them but just because it is safer not to stand out.

If becoming a complainer means increasing the chances of being complained about, unbecoming a complainer is also an effort to reduce the chances of being complained about. To unbecome a complainer is a project for those deemed complainers. I talked to a professor of color who did not herself make a complaint but who, in her previous post, supported one of her PhD students who made a complaint about sexual harassment. She did not make a complaint, though she had a lot to complain about as one of only two academics of color in an otherwise all-white department. She described "not complaining" as part of the culture of that department: "There's an agreement between people not to rock the boat. People would talk about the institution as a kind of legacy project and would imply that you just didn't understand how the institution was formed.

The implication was that you have to be respectful of how this place was organized and what its traditions were essentially. And if you were not abiding by that it was because you had not been there for ten years." To make a complaint would be to provide evidence of being a newbie: someone who has not been somewhere long enough, who has not internalized the norms of the institution, a complainer as the one who has yet to fall in love with the institution.[13] There is an interesting implication to pick up here about complaints and time. Maybe after you have been in an institution for a certain length of time you are given permission to complain. Or maybe it is assumed that if you have been in an institution long enough you will no longer complain because the project of the institution will have become your own.

She did not complain about the university or department when she was a member of that university or department. This was not, however, because the project of the institution had become her own. Not complaining can be trying *not* to show that you have *not* internalized the norms of the institution. Not complaining can be a sign of how much you have to complain about. She decides to leave because not complaining about problems did not make them go away. The other academic of color from the department also resigned at the same time. She submits a resignation letter, which took the form of an informal complaint about how racism and sexism were part of the culture of the institution. What happened? "After we resigned, they said we were the wrong kind of people. This is the two brown people in the department of around fifty people." Being the wrong kind of people was used to explain and dismiss that complaint. The right kind of people were the white kind of people, the kind of people who would not complain about racism: white, right, right again. If some complaints are dismissed by being deemed to come from people who are too new to abide by, or respect, an institutional legacy, some people will be dismissed as complainers no matter how long they have been in an institution. In other words, you can become a complainer by virtue of not reproducing an institutional legacy.

A HOSTILE ENVIRONMENT

So much of the work of complaint is work we would not have to do if institutions were as committed to creating open, accessible, and inclusive environments as they claim to be. This is why complaint has so much to teach us about nonperformativity; the failure of policies to bring about what they name. As I explored in chapter 1, complaints often happen in the gap created when what is supposed to happen does not happen. Inckle (2018, 1372) opens her important article, "Unreasonable Accommodations," by referring to this gap: "Many universities promote themselves as positive environments for equality and diversity, and yet this is not the experience of disabled academics." There is a gap between how universities promote themselves as positive environments for equality and diversity and how universities are experienced by disabled academics. We are learning more about the gap between an appearance, a positive environment, and what some experience, a hostile environment.

A complaint is often necessary in order to address not only the failure of an environment to be open and inclusive but the hostility of that environment. Why evoke the term *hostile environment*? Many harassment policies use the term to define a work culture that is undermining and degrading to a person or persons. What is important, then, is that harassment, even when perpetrated by an individual, has general effects. In the UK, the term *hostile environment* was used by the government as the name of a policy on illegal immigration. Theresa May, when home secretary in 2012, described the policy as "to create here in Britain a really hostile environment for illegal migration."[14] The use of a term that was already definitional of harassment was in fact instructive, teaching us how harassment became national policy. The category of "illegal immigrant" is a racializing category; you can be Brown or Black and born here and still be told to go back, to go home. In other words, racial harassment can be an official national policy, the right to interrogate those who appear not from here.

A hostile environment is not always an official policy. A hostile environment can be masked by official policies. I pointed out in chapter 1 how policies that are not in use can still be used as evidence of what does not exist. When diversity is used to create the appearance of being welcoming, diversity can mask the hostility of an environment. An Indigenous student began her PhD on an Indigenous studies program:

> In the early days it was, I look back upon it now and I think, I was naïve, I naïvely believed that this was a program, because it was Indigenous studies, and there are all these ethics and goals and objectives of Indigenous studies programs, especially a PhD program, that they are engaged in decolonization. So I thought they would welcome a critical

analysis, I thought they had seen my research project, that they would know who they were getting when I walked into the room, as a mature woman who knows who I am, who has a political analysis, a critical analysis and who can use my words.

She turns up, an Indigenous student in an Indigenous program, and she finds she is not welcome, that her critical analysis is not welcome, that her words are not welcome. She is the only Indigenous person in the room. And the classroom is occupied:

> The way the dynamics were unfolding in the class, with the one student, I just couldn't handle it because she would say these egregious ignorant things about Indigenous people, constructing us as objects to be studied, and I'd be like [*grimaces*], why are you even in this program? The professor would never say anything. And I certainly didn't feel safe to say anything, but there would be times when I would, when something was said and I could respond to that, then I would strategically challenge that, but I never opened it up.

As I pointed out in chapter 3, there is a point you reach when handles stop working; the violence you have to deal with gets in. When violence gets in, a complaint comes out. She described what happened:

> You start seeing these patterns, and I wanted to start questioning them, you know, white supremacy in the classroom, white privilege in the classroom that's not being called out or tackled, constructions of Indigenous people in the classroom that are very colonial. Challenging rich white people in the classroom did not bode well for me, especially with the white privilege of the professor, who refuses to believe that Canada is still colonizing Indigenous peoples and who is part of the system who has been doing Indigenous research as a social scientist forever. There's a power there that didn't bode well for me. I complained about the professor; that didn't go very well in the sense that nothing happened about it, but I wanted, sensed slowly that I was being constructed in these really awful ways: [she's] a problem, [she's] aggressive, [she's] scary. . . . It is only in the last few years when I have had distance, geographical distance and emotional distance, that I can see that I have been constructed as this monster, and I think, what have I done, I've challenged the structures, the racial structures and the patriarchy, so I have questioned these things, and never in a hostile way, you don't have to be hostile, you just have to ask the question and people respond so violently. So it's been very, very painful.

She knew before she began to call out the patterns that it would not "bode well," but it is still "very, very painful." The one who complains about white supremacy, who challenges structures such as patriarchy, or who even questions "these things," is heard as hostile however she speaks. You are heard as hostile if you do not pass over the structures that stop you from being able to be in the room. The word *hostility* denotes the strangers, coming directly from Latin *hostilis*, "of an enemy, belonging to or characteristic of the enemy; inimical," from *hostis*, in earlier use "a stranger, foreigner."

The designation of a complaint as hostile can create a hostile environment for a complaint. But officially you might be welcomed; even your complaints might appear to be welcome. A hostile environment can be covered over by the signs of diversity. And we can be required to provide that cover, to smile. If a smile can be a file, or how we pass by not appearing as complainers, we don't always smile. Heidi Mirza (2017, 44) describes how her university kept using her smiling brown face: "Visual images of 'colourful' happy faces are used to show the university has embraced difference. My 'happy' face appeared on the front of the university website—even though every week I asked for it to be taken down, it still kept popping up" (see also Swan 2010). It is not just that you have to work not to appear. You have to work in order to stop your own experiences of harassment from being covered over.

I talked to a Black woman about her experiences of racial harassment that led her to leave the school in which she had been based. She noted that they kept her picture up on their website. She had to ask them to take the picture down: "After I left it took them over a year to take my picture off, my profile from their web page. Because of course the head of school said she refused to do it because of marketing. I said, I am not a marketing strategy or part of a marketing strategy. That's the first time I used *racist*, that's a really racist comment, so take my picture down now." Being used as a marketing strategy is itself a form of racism, your face becoming their brand. She has to use that word, *racism*, to give the problem its name, to get them to stop. It is racism that leads her to use the word *racism*. It is so important to learn from this: how often the words we use to name things come after, how they are interventions, *racism* as a word you use to stop the reproduction of the same thing.

It is not simply that a positive environment is *not* what those who embody diversity come to experience, although that *not* covers so much of what is difficult. If you embody diversity, it makes it harder to challenge the hostility of the environment. A postdoctoral researcher, a woman of color, wanted to make a complaint about racial discrimination. But she was hired as part of a diversity program. And she knew that the program was precarious: "I don't want to do something that is going to threaten a program that is supposed to diversify the faculty." Diversity as a promise to transform the institutions often ends up being located in students and scholars of color who are assumed to be here because we bring diversity with us, however we are hired. And that can make it even harder to address the problems we have when we get here, which are not unrelated to the problems we have getting here. She uses the term *coercive diversity* for how the university wanted to make use of her body and her research as evidence of its diversity while undermining her work as a colleague, as an early career academic, as a human being.[15] As she described very powerfully, diversity can be about "pretending to give a fuck about people of color just for optics." Pretense can be about a visual appearance. You end up feeling implicated in that pretense: "What is the work of the complaint, even keeping that in my mind, it is labor, it is the work of diversity; it is not paid, it is punished. These institutions are designed to function in this deeply dysfunctional way. It is like chipping away at the foundations of white supremacy. I am trying to chip away at it with my fingernails." You are supposed to do this work, but you are punished for doing the work; you are punished for doing what you are supposed to do. And the walls you chip away at, the walls of white supremacy, do not even appear to others. The work of chipping away is the work of trying to make the walls appear. But diversity can be how you appear, which is also how white supremacy disappears, again: diversity as what you are asked to do as well as be.

Diversity can be where you end up. We often end up on the diversity committee because of who we are not: not man, not white, not cis, not able-bodied. The more nots we are, the more committees we end up on. If you end up on the diversity committee, you can end up under more surveillance. We can recall the example from chapter 1 about how a woman of color was dropped from the equality and diversity committee for "mentioning things to do with race." Just using *that* word can be sufficient to be heard as a complainer. She also described her experience of working on a special issue of a journal on decolonizing her discipline. She received feedback from a white editor: "The response of the editor was 'needs to be toned down, not enough scholarly input to back up the claims they are making.' Basically, get back in your box, and if you want to decolonize, we'll do it on our terms." Being dropped from the diversity committee for "mentioning things to do with race" is continuous with being told to tone it down on the decolonizing special issue. The white editor in making a judgment about her scholarship, "it needs to be toned down," "not enough scholarly input," is also giving her an instruction: tone it down, be more scholarly. We could call the issuing of instructions the performance of *decolonial whiteness*.[16] Whiteness can be just as occupying of issues or spaces when they are designated decolonial.

Whiteness can be reproduced in the spaces where it is supposedly being questioned. You even have to do the work of questioning the terms of their terms ("if you want to decolonize, we'll do it on our terms"). If you don't use their terms, or if you question their terms, what happens then? You might be dropped; you might be stopped. But the questions you raise are turned into questions about you. She describes: "Whenever you raise something, the response is that you are not one of them." I suggested earlier that some become complainers by virtue of not reproducing an institutional legacy. Another way of putting this: the complainer becomes a stranger. When you are a stranger, however long you have been somewhere, you are deemed to have come later or to have come after. It is not that "raising something" makes you not one of them. You are *already* not one of them. When you raise something, perhaps you use the word *race*—although let's face it, for people of color, turning up is enough to bring race up—you reconfirm a judgment that has already been made.[17]

A reconfirmation can be an amplification. A complaint seems to amplify what makes you not fit, picking up what you are not, becoming more evidence—not that they need more evidence—that no matter what you do or how far you go, you will not be "one of them." You complain because you do not belong here. And your complaint becomes evidence you do not belong here. When the judgment that you do not belong here has already been made, you have to work hard not to provide evidence to support that judgment. She explains further: "To retain your post you have to be whiter than white. You are not afforded any goodwill. You have no scope for error. You don't have any scope for being a bit foggy. The level of scrutiny is so high. Someone else could fuck their student and get away with it." I will turn to the "someone else" in part III of this book. But that expression *whiter than white* is telling us something: how whiteness becomes clean, good, pure, yes, but also for people of color, how you have already failed to be those things, or how easily you come to fail, because when you are under scrutiny, anything can be used as evidence of failure, any mistake you make, or anything quirky, irregular, queer even, can be confirmation that you are not meant to be here.

Having no room for error can mean having no room. A Black student said, "There wasn't any room for error. Even if you hadn't really made an error, you were under a magnifying glass, any woman who is not white. It was so extreme." Indeed, I noted in chapter 1 how making a formal complaint can be a magnifying glass; so much appears, so many details capture your attention. That magnifying glass can end up on you. You end up being policed, your body, your tone, heard as wrong, as in the wrong. She continued, "It was like you are on a different volume and they can't hear you, and the panel was criticizing my tone and I was called aggressive and said that I was being threatening. They tone-policed me in their formal response." You can be tone-policed on a diversity committee. You can be tone-policed in a decolonizing special issue. You can be tone-policed on a complaint panel. What you encounter when you make a complaint is *more* of what you encountered *before*.

For many, to complain is to become more visible and thus more vulnerable. To be under scrutiny can feel like those around you, who surround you, are waiting for you to trip up. And maybe it feels like that because it is that. Shirley Anne Tate (2017, 59) offers a powerful description of navigating the white academy as a Black woman, being seen by "the White eye only, an eye that constantly has the Black woman academic body—individual, collective and epistemological—under surveillance for any sign of trouble, any possibility of a claim of racism to break the uneasy White conviviality of academia." To stand out, to be seen, is to live under "the sign of trouble." Given that complaining can make you stand out even more, complaining can heighten your sense of being targeted at the very moment you try to stop yourself from being targeted.

Making a complaint can lead you to be under more interrogation. Indeed, when complaints identify a wrong, interrogation is often made into a right. A woman of color academic files a complaint about academic misconduct against a postgraduate student who plagiarized her work. The student was a man of color and he was supervised by a senior white man in her department. She receives a report from the interrogation committee and asks a friend who is a legal expert to read it: "She came back and she said you know how it goes in rape trials don't you. And I said yes. And she said this letter is asking you questions on the grounds of why you should not have been penetrated. You basically have to defend why you should not have had this happen to you, despite all the evidence." It is a painful connection to make, between what happens in a rape trial and what happens in an academic misconduct case. Pain can be that connection.

Having evidence of being wronged does not stop you from being judged as in the wrong. When a woman of color's work is stolen, she is made responsible for that theft as if she caused it to happen, as if she invited it. Consider that ideas are often assumed to originate with some people, ideas as becoming seminal; perhaps ideas are passed down a line from a white man professor to his student. In claiming misconduct against that professor's student, she crosses that line. Perhaps it is inexplicable to the professor, and to those who fall into line, that a woman of color has ideas that would be deemed worth stealing. Perhaps if she has ideas, those ideas are judged as not really her own ideas, or not even ideas; her work becomes just there for the taking; unmediated data, uncultivated nature. And then when she claims her ideas have been taken, she is questioned as if there is something wrong with her claim. And it is not far from there to here: if there is something wrong with her claim, then there is something wrong with her.

When some people complain they are wronged, they are treated as being wrong. You become a suspect; you become suspicious. A trans student of color makes a complaint about sexual harassment and transphobic harassment from their supervisor, who keeps asking them deeply intrusive questions about their gender and genitals.[18] Questions can be hammering; for some to be is to be in question. These questions were laced in the language of concern for the welfare of the student predicated on judgments that they would be endangered if they conducted research in their home country. Racist judgments are often about the location of danger "over there," in a Brown or Black elsewhere. Transphobic judgments are often about the location of danger "in here," in the body of the trans person: as if to be trans is to incite the violence against you.[19] Over there, in here: for trans people of color, the point of intersectionality can be everywhere.

Questions can be judgments; they can pile up until you have no room left. When they complain, what happens? The student said, "People were just trying to evaluate whether he [their supervisor] was right to believe there would be some sort of physical danger to me because of my gender identity . . . as if to say *he was right to be concerned.*" The complaints process can lead to a reiteration of yet more intrusive questions. The same questions that led you to complain are asked because you complain. These questions make the concern right or even into a right, a right to be concerned. So much harassment today is enacted as a right to be concerned. We have a right to be concerned about immigration (as "citizens"); we have a right to be concerned about sex-based rights (as "adult human females"). A right to be concerned is how violence is enacted, a violence premised on suspicion that some are not who they say they are, that some have no right to be where they are, or to be as they say they are, that some have no right to be.

A complaint is put out into the same world a complaint is about. You encounter what you complain about when you complain. I am speaking to a PhD student informally. She told me she had objected to how a lecturer was communicating with her: he was overly intimate. He sent her an email from a private Hotmail account and suggested they "meet up during this or the next weekend in the evening." She communicated to him that she found his style of communication to be inappropriate. His response: "As for meeting in the evening and its combination with [personal email], this is how we do it here at the department (ask our MA students). Perhaps your department has some other norm which I do not understand. Also, your religion might be a problem." Note the assertion of "how we do it here" as an answer to questioning how he was doing things. Note the implication that an objection is an expression of a difference in norms. And note how her religion—she is from a Muslim background—is used to explain her objection. When your complaint is explained away, you are explained away. We are back to the complainer as stranger, the complainer as foreigner, the complainer as not from here, not really from here, not.

It might be that some complaints can be received by being made foreign. A woman of color academic talked to me about her head of department's response to a student who had experienced racism:

He said he was sympathetic because of Brexit and started talking about Muslim students being attacked on the bus. I said the department is reproducing a culture that isn't inclusive no matter how sympathetic you are. If you had an experience on the bus you are not going to come back to the department and tell them about it, are you, if it's the same department where when you have a cup of tea, the white people go to a different part of the room?

It seems a complaint about racism can be received sympathetically if racism is elsewhere, outside, on the streets, on the bus. She makes a clear connection between how racism operates here—white people going to a different part of the room—and the ease with which it can be identified elsewhere. As Crystal Fleming (2018, 46) has observed astutely, "racism is always someone else's crime." Although the head of department was able to say he was sympathetic to students who experienced racism on the bus, she knows those same students would not bring complaints about racism to a department organized by racism.[20]

Some complaints about racism are not made because of racism. Another Muslim student of color wrote to me about how she does not feel she belongs at her university: "I know that as a Muslim woman of color who wears her religion on her sleeves in a pervasive white space, I have never felt that I belong; my feeling of displacement has never escaped me." She does not get the same number of classes to teach that other students get; she does not get the fellowships that other students get. She is an international student; she is also a mother, so not getting the same classes, not getting fellowships, meant not having enough to get by or make do. She lodges a complaint about racial discrimination: "After I made a complaint against them, I felt all sorts of overt discrimination, as if the complaint made everyone free from the mask they used to put on when they were dealing with me before." The mask she is referring to could be described as diversity, a mask of politeness. When the mask of diversity slips, racism comes out. When you make a complaint, a judgment that has been made is given freer expression. Complaints teach us about diversity at the point that the mask slips.

So much comes out when the mask of diversity slips. A woman of color academic describes how her research expertise was used to secure funding for a project on diversity. Once the project was funded, she is shut out: "If you are a mascot, you are silent. Everything you are amounts to nothing. You are stuffing, if that, a skeleton with stuffing. . . . I was kept out of the frame of the management structure; I had no control over how the money was spent, who was being employed, who was being invited to the advisory board. I was effectively silenced." You are stuffing, a skeleton with stuffing. You are supposed to be silent; you are supposed to symbolize diversity, or perhaps you provide the raw materials that can be converted into theory only by those who can pass into whiteness. What happens when the stuffing speaks? What happens when those who embody diversity theorize for ourselves? She told me what happens. She documented seventy-two instances of racial and sexual harassment directed toward her because she refused to be silent. Harassment can be the effort to silence those who refuse to comply, to try to stop somebody from speaking: to shut her up as to shut her out.

In this section I will explore how dismissals of the complainer that we have already encountered—the complainer as moaning about minor matters, the complainer as malicious, the complainer as stranger—are directed toward those who make informal or formal complaints. I want to catch the figure of the complainer where she is most at work in the middle of doing a certain kind of institutional work. I call this work *nonreproductive labor*: the labor of trying to intervene in the reproduction of a problem. One academic suggests complaint is how "you can stop something from happening or try to stop something from happening." In chapter 2, I explored how complaints are stopped; here I explore how complaints are an effort to stop something from happening.

Given what we have already learned about how complaints are dismissed, it is worth asking: Why complain? In reflecting on their complaint experiences, many people offered answers to the question "Why complain?" even though I did not ask that question. A complaint testimony can provide an answer to that unasked question. A woman professor who made a complaint about bullying from her head of department, which led her to have to leave her job, said:

> Apart from anything else at a personal level I can live with myself.[21] I wouldn't have been able to live with myself just coping with that situation and letting it happen. I could have gone the other way and just protected myself, and just said, can I take my sabbatical early and get out of there? That would have been another strategy, but that wouldn't have been me to do that, so I couldn't have done that. I didn't feel I had options really. I had to complain. It wasn't like a choice. For me, if I saw something that was so wrong, I couldn't not do anything.

A complaint can be how you live with yourself because a complaint is an attempt to address what is wrong, not to cope with something, not to let it happen, not to let it keep happening. You refuse to adjust to what is unjust. A complaint can be a way of *not doing nothing*. I think the double negative is often the terrain of complaint ("I couldn't not do anything"), a complaint as saying no to doing nothing. Doing nothing about "something that was so wrong" is to let that wrong happen.

A complaint comes out of a will or desire not to let something happen, to let it happen as to let it keep happening: violence, an injustice, a wrong. When complaints are made about a situation someone is in, they are often made because the person who complains does not want somebody else to find themselves in that same situation. A Black woman who made a complaint about racism said, "It was something I had to do because of my politics. A wrong had been done. I had to make sure it had been put right even at my own personal expense, it turned out. I'd still do that again. I'd do it for another person, not for me. If the same thing happened, I would do it again. I wouldn't change my mind on it or say no, I didn't notice anything. I wouldn't do that." She would complain again not for herself but for another person despite what happened to her, perhaps even because of what happened to her. When you know how hard it is, you know what you have to do. You do not want those who come after you to have to go through what you went through. Note also: a complaint can be a refusal not to notice something. Noticing too can be political labor; to intervene in what is wrong requires noticing it is wrong. Noticing something can be what we do for others.

A complaint can come out of a sense that unless you complain, the same thing will keep happening. In other words, a complaint can be what you have to make *to stop the same thing from happening.* "The same thing" could be thought of as an institutional legacy. If you can become a complainer by virtue of not reproducing an institutional legacy, as I suggested earlier, not reproducing an institutional legacy could be described as *the work of complaint.* I want to return to the testimony of the MA student who took time to get her *no* out in response to how her syllabus was occupied (chapter 3). Why did she eventually make a formal complaint? She complains because she "wanted to prevent other students from having to go through such practice." Of course, before she got to that point, she had to first identify the practices she wanted to prevent. The work of her complaint began as work she had to do on herself, to get that *no* out, to admit something as being wrong, to admit something. But she then decides to say *no* to her professor: "I brought this up and he said, well last year there were no women on the syllabus, so be happy with what you get. Why should I be grateful that there were two women in a syllabus of ten weeks! In the statement he revealed just how little respect he had for female thinkers. They are there to shut the students up, not because he genuinely wanted to teach them or because they have something to offer."

A response to an informal complaint is how she finds out about previous complaints. The implication is that you should be happy for what you receive. We are back to the expectation of gratitude. Diversity becomes a gift not only in the sense of what some give but what some give up (giving up their syllabus organized around white men). When diversity becomes a gift, diversity is registered as an imposition on freedom. The implication is that she is lucky the syllabus included some women thinkers because if students had not complained there would be none. Those women thinkers are added on; they are "tokens." When he introduces one of those two women thinkers at the end of the course, he prefaces his comments by saying, "She is not a very sophisticated thinker." In the case of the other woman thinker, "he kept talking about mankind, mankind, mankind, mankind." "At one point one of the feminist students put her hand up and said, when you talk about mankind, are you talking about humankind or are you talking about men? And he said, no, no I am talking about humankind, and then he went on to say mankind. You're like, come on, you were told, somebody put their hand up and told you, come on, you can do better than this. And he couldn't."

Even when a point is made, an issue is raised like a blind, the discourse remains unchanged; *mankind* is still used for *humankind*. An old syllabus, an old word, an old policy: these habits *hold* despite the modifications. The modifications made in response to previous complaints can end up reproducing the structure the complaints were about. He keeps saying "mankind, mankind, mankind," saying what he said he was not saying; maybe that's the point at which the record is stuck, *man, man, man*, that broken record. It is the complainer who is heard as making the same point, which becomes a sore point, because of what is not heard; the repetition of *man* is not heard as the repetition of the same point. And the modifications made, adding women at the end, lucky you having women at the end, can be a form of silencing. Modifications, made grudgingly, can be a way of shutting people up ("they are there to shut people up"), made to be used as evidence to counter the evidence of complaint.

When we are talking about the *immanence of complaint*, we are also talking about how the more we challenge structures, the more we come up against them. This is how: to try to intervene in the reproduction of a structure is to learn how it is reproduced. Even indicating that you want to write an essay about gender and race is heard as complaint. A complaint then is not just how you are received but how you are heard because you have not received something, not digested something, not taken it in. Sarah Franklin (2015, 29) suggests that "the force of sexism as a means of reproduction is achieved through means of either prohibition or cultivation to *select a path*—for example by blocking a conversation or an argument when it flows in the 'wrong' direction, or enabling the 'right' kinds of thinking or critique by creating spaces for them to move into."[22] You are heard as complaining if you are not willing to go in the right direction. You end up with no space "to move into."

To go in the right direction is often a matter of reception; you are supposed to receive whatever the professor gives. The MA student has an essay tutorial with the professor. Remember she had already asked questions about the lack of gender and racial diversity on the syllabus. You can arrive into the room as a complainer, which is another way of learning how a room can be occupied by complaint. What happens? He shouts at her, "If you write on those fucking topics you are going to fucking fail my course. You haven't fucking understood anything I have been talking about if you think those are the correct questions for this course."[23] The swearing, the rage; she is brought down; he is trying to bring her down. Her questions, her feminist questions—she is interested in gender, in race—are the wrong questions. The violence he directs toward her is also a judgment he makes about her: "But then he says, wait, you know what, you're so fucking old, your grades don't really matter, you're not going to have a career in academia, so write whatever essay you wanted to write. You are going to fail, but it doesn't matter, right, you're not here to get a good grade, you are not here for a career, you're obviously here because you want to learn, so write whatever it is that you wanted, it doesn't fucking matter." The complainer, who is questioning the syllabus, becomes the feminist who gets the questions wrong, becomes the old woman who might as well be wrong, who is too old for it to matter whether she got it wrong, because she can't proceed, she won't proceed. I will return to how his actions stop her proceeding in chapter 6.

You can be undone by a judgment: "And then I left in tears. It is not true that I am too old to have a career. It is not true that my grades don't matter. How dare he decide that based on any of my physical attributes. How dare he say that to any student, it doesn't matter if they are seven or seventy?" I noted earlier that complaining often means drawing attention to yourself at the very time you draw attention to structures. We can see here how that attention can fall the way it so often falls, on your "physical attributes." We can consider the significance of that judgment: that she is "so fucking old." The complainer becomes not only a nag but a hag.[24]

The complainer as a hag or an old woman has come up in other accounts. A woman professor who participated in a collective complaint against a senior academic man for sexual harassment, sexual assault, and sexual misconduct was told by his union representative that her "maturity in age had a bearing on [her] statement against him, as [she] was envious of younger women." The idea that the complaint comes from envy is, to use her terms, "unbelievable really," or it should be unbelievable. Feminism is often framed as suffering from envy, as if women become feminists because we are not desirable to men. The implication is that the complainer wants what they complain about and that they complain only because they don't have it.[25] The figure of the hag is thus doing something, allowing a complaint to be framed as deriving from disappointment; the complainer is treated as a rejected or jilted lover. She is not pleasing, so she refuses to please; she is not agreeable, so she refuses to agree. When you raise issues, when you raise that blind, you find out about techniques of reproduction; you find out how proceeding is dependent on agreeing, on valuing what those who teach value, how having somewhere to be, somewhere to go, requires being agreeable.

In chapter 3, I described the escalation of violence against those who complain as a method for stopping complaints. Methods for stopping complaints are also methods of occupation, how spaces remain occupied in the same old ways. I am speaking to a woman of color academic. She had set up a writing group in her department because she wanted to create a more collaborative research culture. But the meetings became dominated by senior men: "What I found in each of the meetings were senior men who were bullying everyone in the room." The bullying takes the form of constant belittling of the work of more junior academics as well as postgraduate students: "The first session someone was being just really abusive about someone's PhD, saying it was rubbish." Racist comments are made: "I'm from London and London is just ripe for ethnic cleansing." She describes how people laughed, how the laughter filled the room. She comments on these comments: "These were the sorts of things being aired." These were the sorts of things, sentences as sentencing, violence thrown out as how some are thrown out. Even the air can be occupied.

What do you do? What to do? She decided to make a complaint because she "wanted it recorded" and because "the culture was being reproduced for new PhD students." A complaint becomes a recording device; you have to record what you do not want to reproduce. This is what I mean by complaint as *nonreproductive labor*: all the work you have to do in order not to reproduce an inheritance. She gathers statements from around twenty people in her department. A complaint can be a collective.[26] A meeting is set up in response to her complaint. At that meeting she is described by the head of human resources as "having a chip on her shoulder," as if she complained because she has a personal grudge.[27] Yes, those chips have come up again. The more nots you are, the more committees you are on. The more nots you are, the more chips they find. If we keep chipping away at the old block, no wonder they keep finding those chips on our shoulders. She added, "They treated the submission as an act of arrogance on my part." It is as if she puts a complaint forward as a way of putting herself forward; the complaint is treated as self-promotional. So, it is not only that in making a complaint, you come to stand out. A complaint is treated as how you are promoting yourself. Women of color are often judged as self-promotional. Some do not have to promote themselves in order to be promoted (see chapter 6). A structure can enable promotion. And if you challenge those structures, you are the one who becomes self-promotional. Her complaint goes nowhere; the issues are, in her words, "swept under the carpet."

Sweep, sweep: I think of all those issues under the carpet. So many issues, so many complaints. In chapter 1, I described how many complaints become complaints about how complaints are handled. Jennifer Doyle (2015, 33) observes that "the filing of a complaint often leads to the filing of more complaints—counter-complaints and complaints about the complaints process." The immanence of complaints—complaints are made in situations that complaints are about—could be well described as a crash site: to complain is to collide into other complaints. Another way of saying this: some complaints get uptake; others do not. Marilyn Frye (1983, 88) describes anger as akin to a speech act: "It cannot 'come off' if it doesn't get uptake." Some complaints get uptake, which is to say, they come off, they survive a collision.

Whose complaints get uptake? Whose complaints survive a collision? I communicated informally with a woman academic who made a complaint against a colleague for academic misconduct and bullying. She describes his conduct after a relationship they had went wrong: "[He] systematically undermined me at work, including removing me and my academic ownership from a research council project we had won together." She decides to make a formal complaint after finding out that a number of students were putting in complaints against him for sexual misconduct and bullying. Sometimes it takes other people complaining to realize the point of complaint. She realizes that he needed to be stopped from doing the same thing because what he did to her, he had done to others. But the university, in accordance with its own policies and procedures, treats each of these complaints separately. The atomization of complaints procedures can be how abuses of power remain unrecognized. She is the only academic who submitted a complaint. He submits a countercomplaint against her, "saying [she] had bullied him." And it is his countercomplaint that gets uptake:

I think what's interesting in my case is the way that the Equality Act was leveraged against me (e.g. he claimed I was the bully). The fluffy terminology of university policies (if they feel upset, it is bullying) was used to his favor here: e.g. being made responsible or called out on your behavior obviously is upsetting (like a gender equivalent of white fragility) and it makes it so easy to DARVO [deny attack and reverse victim offender] and flip victim and offender. He went off work sick with depression and anxiety, which was used as "proof" of how my bullying affected him (rather than the fact that he was depressed and anxious about having multiple women file complaints about him— the emotional impact of which for him doesn't make the complaints wrong). It was like his distress was worth so much more than mine, because mine were cheap female emotions. The whole thing felt so misogynistic.

This is a very powerful description of a very old problem. The technologies we have available to challenge abuses of power—from complaints procedures to antidiscrimination policies to equality polices to the very languages of harm and oppression—can be used to deflect attention from abuses of power. Those who abuse power given to them by virtue of their position can use the technologies intended to challenge abuses of power to abuse power. A bully with a complaint procedure is a bully with another weapon. Power is also the ability to influence how we are received. When some people matter more, their feelings matter more ("his distress was worth so much more than mine"). We are back to the *significance of immanence*. You don't need to complain about not being taken more seriously if you are taken more seriously. But if those who are taken more seriously complain, then their complaints are taken more seriously.

That some complaints get more uptake reproduces the very problem that other complaints are intended to redress. Let's return to the problem of hostile environments. Complaints about hostile environments might be necessary in order not to reproduce hostile environments. But complaints about hostile environments are often made in hostile environments. In one instance, a trans student made an informal complaint that their department "had made it a hostile environment for [them] as a trans student." The complaint came about after the student had questioned the department's sponsoring of a trans-hostile group on campus. The student was asked to attend a meeting in which the complaint was treated as "a difference in opinion on this topic." They said, "[It was] as if I was having some kind of tantrum for not getting my way rather than it being a fundamental issue about existence." Their complaint went no-where—it did not get uptake or initiate a formal process.

A student who was part of the trans-hostile group made a counter-complaint about the trans student for harassment and bullying. Her complaint was directed against an individual who made a complaint about an environment. And her complaint got uptake; a disciplinary process was initiated and was dropped only at the very final stage. What was striking was how flimsy the case was against the trans student, as well as how much it depended on surveillance of that student outside college life; for example, evidence included Facebook pages they had liked. After the first hearing, the trans student received a letter that said, "One of the outcomes could be that you might get expelled." The student could hear the threat in the identification of a possible outcome (because there was a threat in the identification of a possible outcome) and sought support from the wider trans and trans-inclusive communities.

When you disclose more of a problem, you become more of a problem. An additional item was then added to the disciplinary case against the trans student: "They were saying that I lied about being threatened with expulsion. . . . They said that by writing the letter I have connected the university to transphobia and for bringing them into disrepute for suggesting they might be transphobic." Note again how responses to complaints often enact what complaints are about: you can be threatened with expulsion for saying you were threatened with expulsion.

When a complaint about a hostile environment collides with another complaint, that collision reproduces the hostile environment. To identify an environment as hostile is to be identified as hostile, as causing dam-age. You can become a "malicious complainer," even though the complaint that is taken forward is not your complaint but the complaint made about you. And so we learn: it becomes more damaging to call a person, department, or institution transphobic than to be transphobic. We also learn: not all complaints are nonreproductive labor. In fact, complaints are more likely to get uptake when they are made against those who are trying to intervene in the reproduction of a problem. Reproduction is also about immanence: what is reproduced tends to be what we are in. Whether or not a complaint gets uptake can depend on the extent to which the environment of the institution in which the complaint is made is made part of the problem.[28] When you make the environment part of the problem, your complaint becomes more of a problem.

We learn how the house is built from those who have to fight to be accommodated, to fight so they can enter a room or have room. The complainer as figure is sticky, also picky, loaded with affect and value: the complainer as moaner, as minor, making something from nothing, much out of little; as a stranger or foreigner, not one of us, as endangering us. The more value is acquired by this figure, the more complaint is treated as self-revelation, the less attention is given to what complaints reveal: the structures, the walls, history made concrete.

To learn *from* those who try to intervene in the reproduction of something is to learn *about* reproduction. To stop a system from being reproduced, you have to stop it from working. You have to throw a wrench in the works or to become, to borrow Sarah Franklin's (2015) terms, "wenches in the works." When you throw your body into the system to try to stop it from working, you feel the impact of how things are working. We learn how those who try to stop a culture from being reproduced are stopped. But in learning this, we also learn that reproduction is not inevitable, nor is it smooth, despite the failure to stop something from working. It is the erasure of failure that can give an impression of inevitability, of smoothness.

Diversity itself is often the smoothing of an appearance. Remember the post box that had become a nest? There could have been another sign: "Birds welcome." That sign would be a nonperformative if the post box was still in use because the birds would be dislodged by the letters, a nest destroyed before it could be created. Diversity is *that* sign: "Birds welcome." "Minorities welcome!" Just because you are welcomed, it does not mean they expect you to turn up. You might turn up only to be told, "Get back in your own box." When diversity is *that* sign, diversity is doing more than covering over the hostility of an environment. Diversity *is* the hostility of an environment. All it takes for some to be dislodged or dispossessed is for what usually happens to happen. Comments, jokes, assertions, questions—who are you, what are you doing here, where are you from—they are a hostile environment. They function as the letters in the box, piling up until there is no room left, no room to breathe, to nest, to be. From the letters we learn not only that the occupation of space is material, that dispossession is material, but that occupation and dispossession are achieved by the same materials. In this part of the book, I have shown how dispossession is made immaterial by those who occupy space.

4.4 Diversity as a
nonperformative.

So much violence is made immaterial, small, insignificant, "on par with a handshake," "he didn't mean anything by it," the door is open, come in, come in. When diversity is *that* sign, diversity describes the materiality of dispossession.

For some to be in the room requires stopping what usually happens in that room, otherwise they would be, as it were, displaced by the letters in the box. Complaint as nonreproductive labor: to open spaces up you have to stop what usually happens from happening; you have to stop the same letters from being posted. Nonreproductive labor is often a labor against an appearance. Officially, complaints too are welcomed; we are back to *that* sign: "Birds welcome." "Minorities welcome." "Complaints welcome!" Remember, a welcoming would be nonperformative if the post box was still in use.

Complaints too can be displaced because what usually happens still happens, because the letters keep being posted. I want to return to the example of the Indigenous student who made a complaint about white supremacy in her classroom. What happened to her complaint? She made an informal complaint by writing a letter to the professor:

> I can't remember what the point was, but at one point I was just done with this white supremacy in the classroom, with this ignorance, and this lack of responding to it. I was expected to sit there and be in it, and accept it. So I went home and wrote an email to the professor. I told him what the issues were. I said I wouldn't be able to come back into the classroom until these matters were addressed. And he never responded to me. He never responded to me, but I got a phone call the next day from one of the women in the course. . . . She said, so Professor X came to class today and he read out the email you wrote about us. So he never emailed me back to say, thanks, I am going to deal with this, this is what I am going to do. No, he printed out the email and read it aloud to them. So she called me and she called me out on it. . . . Of course I am stunned, and then she starts crying, she starts crying on the phone, and I just remember sitting there and looking at the ceiling, thinking, are you kidding me right now? You are calling me to tell me that the professor did this, and you are telling me about how I should communicate about these problems in the future? And know you are crying because you feel like you are racist, that you are worried that you are racist.

A complaint can be a point you reach when you can't take it, when you are "just done with this," the violence that makes it hard to be in the room. But rather than respond to her, the Indigenous student who called it out, the white professor prints out her letter and reads it out to the class, the same class she was complaining about. He does so without her permission. I think of that complaint, that letter, being read out by him. I think of what he is *expressing* in doing that. She is complaining about what is taken from her; white supremacy as the theft of space. And then her complaint is taken from her, turned into another way he expresses himself. White supremacy can be enacted in the response to a complaint about white supremacy; you can be dispossessed from a complaint about dispossession.[29] And the consequences are the cause: you are back to where it started, having to deal again with what you had to complain about, the centering of whiteness, white tears, the racism of denying racism, hurt feelings, white supremacy performed as hurt feelings.[30] She is told off, called out for calling them out, for complaining in the wrong way.

A classroom can be a post box. In writing that letter, she is trying to stop the same things from being posted: white supremacy as occupying of space. But the letter ends up being what is posted. A complaint about the letters in the box becomes another letter in the box. This is why to hear complaint is to learn about occupation. What usually happens keeps happening because those who try to stop it from happening, who complain about the hostility of an environment, are stopped. To post that letter, to make that complaint, can mean to end up being displaced.

PART III

IF THESE DOORS COULD TALK?

The title of part III of this book is an allusion to a film, *If These Walls Could Talk* (1996, directed by Nancy Laura Savoco and Cher).[1] In this film, different generations come and go through the same house. The walls are not only containers of a human drama; they witness the unfolding of that drama, as we do. I have replaced walls with doors, though really, the walls led me to doors. It was walls that caught my attention in talking to diversity practitioners: brick walls, institutional walls, walls that work to convey how we come up against the institution when we try to transform an institution. If walls came up in my project on diversity, doors have kept coming up in this project on complaint. You might have noticed how often doors appear thus far. Many people describe how complaints happen behind closed doors. If we put our ear to a closed door, we might be trying to overhear those who are speaking inside the room. What if we were to listen to the door rather than through the door?

I have been listening to doors.[2] I began talking to people about complaint while I was writing a book, *What's the Use?* (2019), on the uses of use. Working on complaint and the uses of use at the same time shaped both projects. Doors are a tangible connection. Doors teach us how things are supposed to function, for whom they are supposed to function. My discussion of doors in *What's the Use?* was inspired by scholarship in disability studies on usable and accessible doors. Aimi Hamraie (2017, 19) writes in *Building Access,* "Examine any doorway, window, toilet, chair or desk . . . and you will find the outline of the body meant to use it." Hamraie usefully names this outline "the normate template" (19). Those who don't assume the shape of the norm know the norms; norms become walls, tangible; they can hit you when they stop you from entering. You can be addressed by a door. If the door is not intended for you, if it is too heavy or narrow for you to use, you notice the door. That doors are everywhere in my data is telling us something: we tend to notice doors when we cannot open them, when they stop us from getting in. When you cannot use something, you notice something.

We can consider how systems of racial, class, and gender segregation enlisted doors to do certain kinds of work, how doors can be used to direct human traffic, go this way, go that way. Different people might be required to use different doors to enter the same building; when an entry is marked out as being for servants and tradesmen, the main entry, the main door, the front door, the unmarked door, is the master's door. The master's door can be a white door; the back door, the Black door. Kimberlé Crenshaw's (1989) classic essay on intersectionality tells a front door/back door story. She describes an encounter:

> One of our group members, a graduate from Harvard College, often told us stories about a prestigious and exclusive men's club that boasted memberships of several past United States presidents and other influential white males. He was one of its very few Black members. To celebrate completing our first-year exams, our friend invited us to join him at the club for drinks. Anxious to see this fabled place, we approached the large door and grasped the brass door ring to announce our arrival. But our grand entrance was cut short when our friend sheepishly slipped from behind the door and whispered that he had forgotten a very important detail. My companion and I bristled; our training as Black people having taught us to expect yet another barrier to our inclusion; even an informal one-Black-person quota at the establishment was not unimaginable. The tension broke, however, when we learned that we would not be excluded because of our race, but that I would have to go around to the back door because I was a female. I entertained the idea of making a scene to dramatize the fact that my humiliation as a female was no less painful and my exclusion no more excusable than had we all been sent to the back door because we were Black. But, sensing no general assent to this proposition, and also being of the mind that due to our race a scene would in some way jeopardize all of us, I failed to stand my ground. After all, the Club was about to entertain its first Black guests—even though one would have to enter through the back door. (161)

They bristle, expecting not to be allowed to enter through the door because they are Black, because they have been there before, only to find she has to use the back door "because [she] was a female." Given that to identify a problem could cause problems "due to our race," she does not say anything or do anything ("I failed to stand my ground").

Crenshaw's door story tells us how physical barriers can function differently over the course of a life trajectory. You can be taught by history to expect a barrier. You can encounter history as a barrier. Doors are not just physical things that swing on hinges, although they are that, they are mechanisms that enable an opening or a closing. These mechanisms, I will show in this part of the book, are not always obvious. A door can even be closed by appearing to be open. The diversity door is such a door, as I explore in chapter 6. Doors can be, to borrow again from Audre Lorde, "the master's tools," teaching us how the same house is being built.

In part II of the book, I explored how complaints challenge how the house is built, for whom the house is built; in this part, I explore in more depth how houses are built around certain bodies, to support them and to enable them to do what they are doing, considering the relation between sympathy and machinery, doors and backs, locks and hands. In chapter 5, I consider how actual doors are evoked in accounts of sexual and physical assault. I then show how academic networks, collegiality, forms of loyalty, function as doors, the same doors, which will allow me to deepen the analysis of institutional mechanics offered in the first part of the book. I then turn to the question of who "holds the door" as a way of asking who can progress within the system and who cannot. Doors, in other words, teach us about how power can become concentrated or handy, power as that which can be held over others, despite or even by appearing to be dispersed.

CHAPTER FIVE

BEHIND CLOSED DOORS

COMPLAINTS AND INSTITUTIONAL VIOLENCE

In listening to complaint, I have been hearing about where complaints happen. An early career lecturer describes how "the majority of the complaint happened behind closed doors or via communication like email or conversations that were private from other members of staff or other colleagues." The expression "behind closed doors" can refer to the actual doors that might need to be closed before someone can share information in confidence. It can also be used to signal how information is kept secret from a public. This expression tells us not only *where* complaints happen but *how* they happen. She refers to "closed door–type complaint procedures" and explains, "In my department there were more than a handful of staff who were there complaining about the same issues, but all of us were doing it not in silence but in an atomized way, so that none of us knew actually that we were all having similar problems and were making similar complaints." Doors can be how offices are turned into atoms; complaints can be made smaller if those who complain are kept apart.

Her account also demonstrates that if "closed door–type complaints procedures" are intended to keep those who complain apart, they do not necessarily succeed in doing so. Even when procedures are used to atomize, to individuate and to separate, complaints can lead you to find out about other complaints: similar complaints, similar problems. As soon as we start reflecting upon atomization as a process, as soon as we learn that we have been kept apart or how we have been kept apart, we cease to function as atoms. It is thus not surprising that she refers constantly in her testimony to doors: doors appear because she herself noticed what doors were doing.[1] Doors provide clues that something is going on that is supposed to be kept secret. And so: you can find out that others are complaining by noticing doors, by noticing the effort to stop you from finding out others are complaining. She describes, "I was just frightened and I just allowed myself to go through it very privately, and I hit all those doors along the way, and just came out very guarded by it." When you keep hitting all those doors, the same doors that are supposed to keep communication private ("going through it very privately"), those doors become not only part of the complaint but part of the person who made the complaint. A door story, which is also her story ("hitting all those doors"), is a story of becoming guarded.

A complaint can be how you learn about institutional violence, the violence of how institutions reproduce themselves, the violence of how institutions respond to violence; yes, we can be hit by it. All of the chapters in this book are concerned, in one way or another, with institutional violence. In chapter 3, I used the term *institutional harassment* to describe how institutional resources are mobilized to stop those who are trying to make complaints such that those who are trying to make complaints feel the institution as weight, as what comes down on them. In this chapter, I explore how violence is performed not only in meetings by those who exercise seniority in the form of instruction, often weaponized as reprimands, threats, and warnings, but also in languages, spaces, and styles of conduct that might seem, on the surface, rather convivial. The complainer comes to know institutional violence as not only over *there*, exercised by disciplinary regimes imposed by senior management, but *here*, closer to home, implicated in warm (even cherished) ideals such as solidarity, loyalty, and collegiality.[2]

The connection between *there* and *here* can be made through doors. In this chapter, I begin by juxtaposing three different accounts of sexual or physical assaults taking place in offices or corridors in which doors are a crucial part of the detail: solid doors, locked doors, doors with difficult-to-use latches or handles. The detail provides a lens: how we can see what is going on that would ordinarily be obscured. After zooming in on these doors, I then zoom out, showing how these doors point in the direction of other doors, other means by which violence is contained.

THE SAME DOOR

Doors can be how you are stopped from getting in. Doors can be how you are stopped from getting out. I am speaking to an academic about the first complaint she made when she was a student. One of her lecturers on her course had been making her feel uncomfortable.

Door Story 1
A tutor at my college had been harassing me verbally, well, it was more a case of going up to that line beyond which it would be pretty clear what he was trying to do. It was just a case of trying to push

5.1 The same door. Photo: Kim Albright/Phrenzee.

*that line and inveigle his way into my confidence, in getting me to
meet him off campus. I was not comfortable with it; I didn't seek
it. . . . And while he wasn't involved in any way in delivering any
of my teaching or supervision, he still found ways of talking to me,
and presented it very much as "I am just being friendly here." We
are always taught, aren't we, to be polite and considerate and the
least troublesome as possible. And he was very much inviting my
confidence, sharing confidences with me, not that I wanted them,
and then presented it very much as "Why would you not want to
spend time talking to me," so that it would construct me as being
very rude and brusque and antisocial. And then one afternoon, I
went into his office to talk to him about something. It was an office
a bit like this but without any glass, with a door that opened inward
and opened on a latch. And he pushed me up against the back of a
door and tried to kiss me, and I pushed him away, it was an instinc-
tive pushed him away, and tried to get out of the room, and it was
a horrible moment because I realized I couldn't actually, it was very
difficult to operate the latch. And so I left and I ran down the stairs
and gathered my thoughts as I got to the next floor. I walked into
the common room and just talked to whoever was there about anything. He must have thought I was quite strange at the time, because
it wasn't very coherent. And I heard him follow me down and just
turn around and go back up again.*

The door appears in the middle of her account. It is important we don't
start with the door. She begins by sharing what she sensed, her sense
of being uncomfortable. As I explored in chapter 3, our bodies can tell
us when something is not quite right, when something is wrong. When
consciousness becomes a door, we resist hearing what our bodies are telling us. Resistance can be its own kind of hearing, slow and bumpy; you
might catch a glimpse of a structure when you are not quite ready for it
to be revealed. She senses a line is being pushed. A line can be pushed by
"just being friendly"; a push can be disguised as "just being friendly." He
keeps trying to find out more about her: "He's interested in psychology,
so he was trying to find out about family background. . . . He'd met my
parents at graduation, and all of this kind of stuff, so he was talking, asking me about them." The effort by a lecturer to become intimate with a
student is experienced as intrusive because it is intrusive. He suspects she
is a lesbian: "That was something else that drew him to me. . . . Perhaps
he thought I needed to experience the right contact with the right sort of

person and that would sort me out." Perhaps being a lesbian is heard as closing a door; you do not want to be intimate with the man lecturer, to have sex with him; that closed door is treated as an invitation, as if that door is closed only because it has not been opened by him.[3]

Even when you are made uncomfortable by a situation, you can still find it hard to get out of it. We learn from how hard it can be to do what you need to do to protect yourself. *Who* you are taught to be, *how* you are taught to be, polite, considerate, not troublesome, as a girl, as a student, is how you become more vulnerable, less willing or able to stop someone from pushing the line you need to protect yourself. When you know that to say *no* is to be judged as antisocial, it is hard to say *no*.

If you are trying not to be antisocial, if you are trying not to cause trouble, you might end up entering spaces that make you more vulnerable. She enters his office. She told me about the office by comparing that office to the office we were in. The offices were like each other but for the glass. I think of the absence of glass: you can't see in; you can't see out. The absence of glass leads us to a door, how it opened; getting in, getting out. A door creates a space that is withdrawn from others; a door provides a surface against which somebody can be pushed. He pushes her onto the door; he pushes himself onto her. To get out she has to push back. And the door she is pushed against won't open; the latch won't open. Getting stuck: a "horrible moment" can last a very long time. She did get out of his office, but it was hard. And she gets out not only by walking away but by talking away: she makes her way into a common room, talking to whoever is there, saying whatever came into her mind, getting away by entering into discourse.

Can that be what doors do: stop us from entering into discourse? Behind closed doors: harassment happens there, out of view, in secret. A door can turn an office into a private room, not a common room. Doors have something else to teach us: they teach us the significance of complaints about harassment being lodged in the same place the harassment happened. A door is shut on her. The same door is shut on a complaint; the same door. She decides to make a complaint. First, she talks to a friend, and then to a representative from the students' union. Under guidance, she writes and submits a letter. That letter could be called an informal complaint. If she went on to a formal complaint, that letter would have become the first stage of a formal complaint; stopping a complaint can be a matter of formality. That letter was *about* what happened; it *came out* of conversations about what happened. Letters, as we have been learning, have their own complaint biographies, stories of where they go, where they do not go. Where did her letter go? It went to the dean. And what does the dean do? "The dean notified the head of department, and there was obviously some discussion going on there. The dean basically told me I should sit down and have a cup of tea with this guy to sort it out." So often a response to a complaint about harassment is *to minimize harassment*, as if what occurred was just a minor squabble between two parties, what can be sorted out by a cup of tea.

A complaint was passed between senior managers. I will return in the next section to the significance of it being obvious to her that there was "some discussion going on" between the head of department and the dean. We have already learned how what is said when you make an informal complaint can be decisive. There is a pattern to what might appear a matter of informality, what just happens to be said on the day—shrugs, nods, replies, suggestions, resolutions. She does not proceed to a formal complaint. That letter might have ended up in a file, her file or his; or it might have been discarded. We don't know. But whatever happened to that letter, her complaint was stopped and he was not. Now I say her complaint was stopped rather than she was stopped because she did go on to have a career; she is now a professor. But this experience of being assaulted when she was a student stayed with her: "I thought I got a first because of academic merit, but then after this happened I remember thinking, but hang on, maybe not, maybe this was some sort of ruse to try and keep me in the institution so he could keep the contact going. . . . It starts undermining your own sense of your academic merit, the quality of your work and all that kind of stuff." Being harassed by a lecturer damages your sense of self-worth, intellectual worth, leading you to question yourself, doubt yourself. Her complaint was stopped, she was not, but she carries that history with her.

Her complaint was stopped; he was not. What happened to him? She tells us: "He was a known harasser; there were lots of stories told about him. I had a friend who was very vulnerable. He took advantage of that. She ended up taking her own life." She ended up taking her own life. So much more pain, so much more damage at the edges of one woman's story of damage. He went on; he was allowed to go on, when her complaint—and for all we know there were others too; we do not know how many said no—did not stop him. He has since retired, much respected by his peers, no blemish on his record. No blemish on his record, no blemish on the institutional record, the damage carried by those who did complain, or would complain if they could complain, is carried around like baggage, slow, heavy, down. To hear complaint is to hear from those weighed down by a history that has left little trace in the official records.

Another story, another door. This time a student was sexually assaulted by a lecturer after he locked the door.

Door Story 2

I just crossed the corridor and knocked on the door, and he welcomed me with great joy and offered candies, which he always carried around with him to give out. . . . A casual and informal talk turned out to be an extremely close physical contact, including him taking pictures of my hair and my face, constantly hugging and lifting my entire body, touching his erected organ to my back, and trying to kiss me (when I rejected kissing him, he held my face tightly and said, "Come on, what is the difference between kissing on cheeks or lips?"), etc. Maybe this was some minutes, but for me it was hours, as I felt that I was completely frozen. Time froze, I froze. I was totally unable to move. I remember the only thing I could do was to push him away, saying "please" repeatedly. At some point I wanted to reach the door, but I was like a stone, while my brain was trying to process what my body was experiencing. Everything was wrong, disgusting, disappointing. Anyway, after probably so many times I repeated that I wanted to leave, finally he released me and I approached the door, but I realized it was locked. I panicked more (because I realized it was sort of "planned," because they were not allowed to lock their offices with people inside, of course) while he was trying to persuade me to sit down, talk, relax and have another candy. After he realized that I was quite shocked and petrified, he had to open the door and I just ran out and left the school immediately, sobbing.

When you are assaulted it can be hard to process what is happening. She is welcomed into the office, with joy, so much positivity, how sweet. A welcoming can be the beginning of violence, a friendly chat becoming physical contact, taking pictures, taking something from her. A body can become stone, heavy, hard; time can be frozen; a body can be frozen. She tries to push him away, saying *please*, that word, that polite word, that word that has its own history, trying to please, being pleasing, becoming part of an effort to say no; *please don't*. A *please don't* is not enough to stop him. She tells him again and again that she wants to leave. And when she is able to move, to react, to reach the door, to try to get out, she finds the door locked. She panics; the locked door tells her what he had planned; she knows you are not supposed to lock the door with someone inside.

You can be stopped by your body, stopped by a door, stopped by a lock on a door. She did get out, but it was hard. What then? What to do then? At first, she did not consider making a complaint. But eventually, years later, after coming out to a friend who in turn told her about the abuse she suffered, she decides to make a complaint. She first speaks informally to her head of department and then sends a letter to the dean. After some time, a committee is assembled. She details that committee, who was on it, what happened on it:

> To cut the long story short, I went to this meeting and basically it was just another horrendous experience. There were three heads of department (all women, by the way) and the dean, and they started interrogating me. First of all, I immediately understood that this as-saulter teacher was a good friend of all of theirs, because of the way they talked with me and mentioned him. One of the professors said, laughing, for instance, "Ah, X, he is always like this, isn't he? Always very seductive and funny.... He has always been like this since we were studying together.... He also touches me when talking, what so? ... Well, he always calls me as such and such, so, it's him!," while the other was saying, "Ah, I know him for so many years, it must be some misunderstanding, for sure," while the other was just smiling and nodding, before even having heard what I had to say.

A meeting can be an interrogation. And an interrogation can be made on behalf of a good friend. It is not simply that they *are* his friends; they are *telling* her he is their friend; that history of intimacy is brought into the room. Being told of their friendship is being told how her complaint will be received. It is not only that a shared history is casually evoked ("studying together," "I have known him for years"), but that evocation is offered as justification: we know him; he also touches me; he is like this; he has always been like this. The evocation of a shared history is how a complaint about assault is dismissed, smiling, nodding. As I noted in chapter 2, a nod can be a nonperformative, as if to say, "If you knew him, you would forgive him." Relationships can be sedimented history, how some are known to each other "for so many years," how that knowledge can be used to do things, to stop things. A complaint can be stopped because of what is shared, who is shared: loyalties, personal, professional. If what does not get out is built in, what is built in is not just about the building, bricks and mortar, the wood of the door, the glass in a window;

it is about relationships, intimacies, and connections. This is why we keep finding hands and backs as well as locks and doors in the stories.

Another story, another door. A senior lecturer has been bullied by her head of department over many years; he has shouted at her, accused her of being insubordinate when she questions his suggestions; taken things from her that she values, such as courses and positions; dismissed and devalued the work she is doing, the new programs she has introduced. She has already been to the union. They give her instructions, tell her what to say if he starts shouting at her again. He is her head of department. She cannot avoid him. She attends a meeting:

Door Story 3
So then he started to yell, and I stood up and said what the union had told me to say, and I burst into tears and I was really sobbing very loudly. . . . You go out of the office and then to the left is a little passageway to the door. So I went up to the front door. It has two locks that you have to turn in two different directions, and I had all my bags on me, and then up behind me came these pair of hands and pulled my hands off the lock, and I thought, God, what is going on? . . . He then grabbed me by the left arm and pulled me down the corridor, saying, "Don't go, don't go." I was saying, "Do not touch me. Get your hands off me." And then I couldn't get to the door, I couldn't get to his office because he was blocking the way, and then he wrapped his arm around me, and so I was constrained with my arms by my sides. I thought, I don't know what to do. . . . He was standing there, and then he suddenly, he let go, and he had this look on his face, like exasperation, like I had been a naughty child. And I didn't know what to do. I thought, if I try to go to the front door again, he may grab me again.

The lock turns in two different directions; it is hard to know which way it turns, which way to turn. She has probably noticed that lock before, that it was hard to use, but now, now that she needs to get out quickly, that difficult lock matters even more. She fumbles: her bags are heavy; it is taking too long. And hands come up, pulling her hands off the lock, the lock becomes a hand, a hand a lock, what stops her from getting out. She is pulled off the lock, pulled down the corridor; she has nowhere to turn. She does get out, but it is hard.

And then, what then, what to do then? In this instance, she does submit a formal complaint. What happens then? He is suspended during a formal inquiry. And what does the inquiry find? He is cleared of wrong-doing. Instead, he is described as having "a direct style of management," as if being physically violent is like blunt speech, being rough as a way of expressing himself. What about the assault itself? The assault is described in the report as "on par with a handshake." On par with a handshake; *on par* equals *equal*. A physical assault is turned into a friendly greeting. Violence can be removed from an action by how an action is described. Description can be a door. There is so much violence in this removal of violence. The deputy head of resources reads that sentence out to her in a meeting: "[He] read two paragraphs orally that you can read in the extract I sent you. He read that what he had done 'was on par with a handshake,' that was the conclusion, and that he was going to be returned to his position as head of department." I think of him reading out those words, that description of the assault on her, to her. I think of how you can be hit by words.

The violence took place behind closed doors. She tries to bring the violence out, to complain as to bring something out from behind the door. That violence is shut back in. The violence of the action is how the violence is shut in. I noted in chapter 3 that a complaint can bring the violence that is in the room to the surface; a complaint can force violence to be faced, which is how (also why) complaints are heard as forceful. But the institution can use force to stop that violence being faced. The force revealed by a complaint is directed against the complainer; his expression, which tells her how she is seen, a naughty child, willful, is how the institution comes to sees her. If they turned an assault into a friendly greeting, on par with a handshake, violence is treated as her projection, as a problem with her description, as a problem she introduces. He is returned to his position. They cannot force her to leave, but they encourage her to leave. And she knows that if she stays, she would keep encountering him. Eventually, she moves to another department. When violence is shut in, those against whom that violence is directed are shut out.

PARTICIPATION AND PROTECTION

The doors in these stories, the actual doors, have something to tell us about how harassment happens; a door can be used to create a space freed from the scrutiny of others, or to protect some from the consequences of scrutiny when the doors don't stop that scrutiny, which is to say, when an informal or formal complaint is made. What enables abusive behavior is thus what conceals that behavior. A postdoctoral researcher described a meeting for her project team in which the project leaders routinely bully and harass the researchers on the team. She decides to leave: "In the final meeting of the project that I attended before I resigned, they were really shouting at us, accusing us of all this off-the-wall stuff. It was in her office, the door was closed, and in hindsight I wish at that moment I had said, can we halt this meeting and get an impartial person in here or, like, open the door, like there's clearly something wrong. I wish I had interrupted what was happening." An open door can be the promise of an impartial person, a way of interrupting the conduct, what is off-the-wall can be the wall, by giving witness to it. So much injustice is reproduced by the elimination of the witness.

The elimination of the witness is how you ensure violence is not seen. Ensuring violence is not seen is a way of protecting some people: if you can't stop their abusive behavior, you stop the behavior from being seen. It might be that some people are protected because of how violence is not seen. One student told me that a feminist academic said she couldn't support her in making a complaint about harassment by an academic because "she did not know enough." If you don't know enough to support a complaint, that lack of knowledge is doing something. Not knowing enough can be how you end up protecting someone, which also means you can protect someone by not knowing what you are protecting them from. It is not only that you can participate in violence without knowing about it; not knowing about violence can be how you participate in it. It is because complaints are made behind closed doors that many who are working within the institutions in which those complaints are made often do not know the scale of the problem.

When complaints are stopped in order to protect someone, protection is the aim as well as the consequence of an action. I spoke to an administrator about what happened when his university received multiple complaints from students about sexual harassment and bullying by three academics from the same department. One of the academics, the most senior academic and the former head of department, kept his job; the two other academics did not. The administrator told me he thought the fact that two of the academics had left their posts "had sent a strong message" to the wider academic community that sexual harassment and bullying would not be tolerated. I asked him what message was being sent by the fact that the most senior professor had not had any disciplinary action taken against him. He did not answer my question directly but told me that the official line was that "there was not enough evidence" to take the complaints forward, but that "unofficially," "he did not get away with it.

He had a very difficult meeting with the vice chancellor." Of course, no one knows "he did not get away with it" because no one knew about that "very difficult meeting." The protection of the most senior academics can take the form of keeping the consequences of complaint secret; if he is reprimanded, that action is performed behind closed doors. If "he didn't get away with it," he did get away with his post, his pay, his pension as well as, perhaps most crucially, his reputation. I say *most crucially* because the university in protecting the reputation of the professor was also protecting its own reputation; they were protecting their investment, which was in him.

Let me return to door story 3. I noted earlier how the violence of the assault was removed by being represented as "on par with a handshake." What is also striking in this case was how the institution made use of the language of protection. The senior lecturer said, "We had a number of meetings where they just kept being unable to say how they will protect me. They kept saying that they had a duty of care to protect him as head of department." The word *protect* comes from *cover*, "to cover, to recover." His hands on the lock became the hands of the organization; in giving him cover, the violence is covered over. A complaint can be discarded, a complainer disciplined, in order to protect someone. She was aware that the sexist culture of the department was the culture of protection: "The men got protected and the women got persecuted if they didn't turn off the light kind of thing." An important detail in this case is that the head of department was a Black man. Protecting the head of department can be about protecting the more senior person; it can be about protecting men. But it is important not to pass over race. She herself did not pass over race: "The university was so afraid because he was Black. They did everything they did to protect him because they were fearful of that, because they don't understand racism, how it works in institutions." The university seemed to be protecting him because they anticipated he would lodge a complaint about racism if they did not. The implication is that the university protected him to protect itself.[4] Racism is often treated as damaging the reputation of an institution (Ahmed 2012). You might stop one complaint that has been made in order to stop another complaint from being made that would be deemed riskier to the reputation of an institution.[5]

We can return to door story 1. As I described earlier, after the assault she submitted an informal complaint; as with many complaints, this was as far as she got or it got. She was dissuaded by the dean from taking her complaint any further. But at the time I interviewed her, at a point much later in her career, she had begun the process of making a collective complaint about what had happened when she had been a student over thirty years earlier. We might call that collective complaint a "historic complaint." She came to this decision because of conversations she had with two other former students from the same department. They had been in conversation about their experiences of sexual harassment as undergraduates. Sexual harassment had been in the news, as a result of the #MeToo movement and other feminist activist campaigns within universities.[6] In chapter 8, I will return to the significance of how, when stories of sexual harassment come out, more stories come out. I ended up speaking to all three of these women about their past experiences as well as about what happened when they tried to communicate with the university in which they had been based.[7] They spoke to me of their friend who had ended her life, who had a relationship with one of the lecturers that had ended very badly. I did not meet her, but she is part of their story.

Between them, it turned out, they had experiences of harassment, assault, misconduct, and grooming from five different men in the same department. At the time, they had not known the full extent of each other's experiences; they did not know what each had been through. Yes, doors can turn offices into atoms. The effort to stop complaints from being made is an effort to stop people from knowing about each other's experiences. The student who was assaulted behind a closed door, who is now a professor, said that lecturers treated having sexual relationships with students as a "perk of the job": "There was a culture at that time of male members of staff just treating it as the opportunity to sleep with students, to harass students, to bring sexuality into the teaching situation. It was like a 'perk of the job,' something the students used to just deal with by joking about it, but it was just awful really, that kind of culture." Dealing with something that has become normalized, a norm, a perk, a benefit, often requires laughing it off, laughing off what is "awful really." If laughter can be a form of *institutional passing*, laughter can pass over many different kinds of awful.

This expression, *a perk of the job*, was in fact used seven times in testimonies given to me. The expression is often used to refer to the expectation that being a lecturer meant having access to sexual relations with students, or perhaps we could just say access to students (to their bodies, minds, as well as labor). One lecturer who supported students in a complaint about sexual misconduct by a senior man in her department told me, "During this process, other female colleagues began to approach me from other departments; they told me time after time similar stories of seeing students destroyed after sexual relations with senior men. It was like I was suddenly made aware of something akin to a pedophile ring in operation at the institution. Many of these men had social as well as professional links with each other. They were 'in the know,' nudge-nudge, wink-wink, perk of the job." This idea that having sex with younger students is a "perk of the job" becomes a sexual as well as professional intimacy between men who conduct themselves in this way, being in the know, "nudge-nudge, wink-wink," as a kind of *homosocial* bond, to borrow from Eve Kosofsky Sedgwick's (1985) *Between Men*.

The expression *a perk of the job* is used not only to characterize a shared attitude or common practice but in defense of those attitudes and practices. Another woman academic supported a group of students who made complaints about sexual harassment and sexual misconduct by an academic. He gave her this defense: "He came up to me and said, 'It's a perk of the job.' I couldn't believe it. He actually said it to me. It was not hearsay; 'this is a perk of the job.' I can't remember my response but I was flabbergasted." We need to learn from how *perk of the job* can be mobilized as a defense against a complaint about sexual harassment and sexual misconduct. The implication is that having sex with your students is like having a company car; it is what you are entitled to because of what you do. A complaint can then be interpreted as a *contradiction of an entitlement*: the right to use or to have something.

We can begin to appreciate how harassment is built into the system, part of the job, a perk of the job. When complaints about harassment are not made, the harassment does not stop. In the case of the three students, when they found out they had each had similar experiences in the past, they decided they wanted to speak to the university in the present, in part because they had heard from a current student, "This guy is still behaving in the way that you describe." The university did not ask any of the current students about their experiences; they said current students would have to come forward of their own accord. But as one of the former students I spoke to noted, "People are not going to come forward and corroborate unless you can create an environment that people feel comfortable doing that. You are not going to know what's going on now." Perhaps the university did not want to know "what's going on now."

As I listened to their combined testimonies and thought more of the student who I could not speak to—I am glad I know her name even though I cannot share it with you—who had taken her own life, I felt the devastation, that this was devastating, how this was devastating. They shared with me instances after instances. When you have instances after instances, we are talking structure, not event, or structure as well as event, because when you are assaulted, it is an event. One of the students suffers a devastating bereavement. She becomes more and more intimate with one of her lecturers. He began to make comments about how she looked, what she wore, her lipstick. As soon as she completed her studies, they began a sexual relationship. It took her a long time to realize that she had been groomed, that he had exploited her vulnerability; as I noted in chapter 3, the end of grooming is kept out of sight during the process. She kept a diary, which eventually became a record that was passed on to the institution. I will explain in due course how the inquiry made use of that record.

Another of the students was assaulted by her course tutor at the end-of-year party: "He said, I will give you a lift home. . . . I left the car and he pushed me up against the wall and his hands were up my top." This same lecturer had assaulted another of the students I spoke to, also at an end-of-year party: "It's like him thinking, I will get away with it." Getting away with it, she added, "that seems to be the culture: What can I get away with?" She did not consider making a complaint at the time: "No, it was part of the course; it was something you had to put up with. It was almost: that's what they do." Sexual assaults become part of the course; that's what they do. The task of the students is to put up with it, to get used to it, to try to minimize the harm or to avoid situations where they could be harmed. She describes another incident that happened in the head of department's office: "I walked into his office, and this was the head of department, really revered, his finger just went down my back, hovered where my bra was, and then went further down, and then he carried on." Down her back: he puts his fingers on her, showing her what he can do, what he would do if he so willed, if he so wished. I think of his fingers there, hovering at her bra strap, his fingers communicating something about who he is, what he can do, what he feels he is entitled to do. I think of the message she is receiving about what she can expect from him, the head of department. I think of the harassment that happens behind closed doors; down her back, the back of the institution; the back of the door.

The back of the door; we are back to the door. We can return to the assault on a student by a lecturer who had been a member of the same department behind a closed door that opened inward with a latch that was difficult to use. Her informal complaint, as I noted earlier, was passed between the dean and the head of department. In her words, again: "The dean notified the head of department, and there was obviously some discussion going on there." We don't know what was said in those discussions; they too happen behind closed doors, the same place the harassment happened. But we can think of the head of department who ran his fingers down another student's back. She said, "They are going to have each other's backs." When they have each other's backs, *their backs become doors*. To say their backs become doors is to say that the relationships they have with each other close the door on the complaint. Those who receive complaints about harassment can be those who *participate* in harassment. They are, in other words, receiving complaints about themselves; to close the door on the complaint is *to keep the door open for themselves*, to enable their own conduct.

The question of *why* complaints are stopped leads us rather quickly to the question of *who* receives a complaint. It is not only that complaints are received by the colleagues of the person whose conduct is under question. *Complaints are often received by those whose conduct is under question.* Participation is how some end up providing cover for others. Participation is a kind of covering over, another form of protection; to participate in something with someone is to protect someone from something. This is why to address how sexual harassment is normalized, becoming part of institutional culture, is to give an account of the same mechanisms that stop complaints from getting through. This is why speaking to those who complain is to learn how cultures are reproduced.

When we talk about culture, we are not talking about something that is inert, already there, given, but actively being maintained through and in relationships. Sometimes by *culture* we might seem to be referencing some intangible thing; it exists, but it cannot be touched, given an exact description or value. What is intangible to some is tangible to others. I think of the expression *in the air*, which is often used to describe shared sentiments but which can also be used to indicate what will come to happen. Perhaps by *culture* we are thinking of what is in the air, or what is aired; what is shared is what will come to happen. I think back to the woman of color lecturer who made a complaint about the use of sexist and racist comments at research events (chapter 4). She said, "These are the kinds of things being aired." When the air is occupied, the air is stale. The room has become stuffy; history is stale air. I think of another lecturer I spoke to who taught an undergraduate course with an older white man. She described how he made use of his own body in the seminar room—often putting his leg up, "like he is airing his crotch to the whole room." What is aired is how a body occupies space. And she talked about the course materials: "Written down in the handbook was an answer to last week's question which was framed in terms of 'if you have applied case x versus y instead of case a versus b you have gone straight for the orgasm and missed the foreplay.'" Sexualized talk becomes a way not only of occupying space but of framing course materials. These materials too are products of a certain kind of history, not just an educational history but a social history, an effect of relationships that have sedimented over time, history as becoming material: ways of acting, speaking, teaching that we might call *conduct*.

By *conduct* we are not referring simply to behavior. The root of the word is from Latin *conductus*, "to lead or bring together." This is an early definition of conduct: "To *conduct* is to lead along, hence to attend with personal supervision; it implies the determination of the main features of administration and the securing of thoroughness in those who carry out the commands; it is used of both large things and small, but generally refers to a definite task, coming to an end or issue: as, to *conduct* a religious service, a funeral, a campaign."[8] To conduct is to lead or direct action in a way that determines the main features or functions of administration. That heads of department keep being evoked in the data matters. Another head of department said to a professor in his department, a professor who was subsequently accused by many students of sexual misconduct and sexual harassment, "I don't care what you do, as long as you don't fuck my wife." This head of department was giving permission to a member of his staff to harass students, to do whatever he wished or willed, by enacting harassment in the form of an instruction. By saying "don't fuck my wife," he was treating another woman, who was also, as it happened, a professor at the university, a colleague no less, as his possession, a sexual thing. Harassment operates as entitlement: as the right to use or to have something. When you describe an entitlement as harassment you are understood as depriving somebody of what is theirs; the complainer as killjoy could characterize this deprivation. This is why many who say *no* end up being harassed all the more. As I discussed in chapter 3, harassment can be the effort to stop you identifying harassment as harassment.

To deepen and thicken our understanding of conduct is to consider conduct as the *transmission* of values, information, energy, and resources. Some become *conductors*; that is, information, energy, resources travel through them. When you challenge a person's conduct—which can include their course materials as well as how they talk, what they do with their bodies—information, energy, and resources are directed at you, to try to stop you from getting anywhere. You also might lose access to the information, energy, and resources you need to do your own work. What is brought against a complaint is the weight some have acquired by virtue of what they have already received from the organization.

COMPLAINTS AND COLLEGIALITY

We need to think more about *who* as well as *what* is protected. To have each other's backs is to give support, loyalty, to back each other up. Backing is often about defending a colleague against a complaint. This was certainly evident in door story 2: when the student attended a meeting with professors and a dean, they didn't just speak *as* colleagues of the man she put in a complaint about; they spoke *of* being colleagues. They brought that collegiality into the room. When complaints are received by the colleagues of those whose conduct is under question, collegiality becomes cement in the wall, a binding agent. But what about when the person who makes a complaint is also a colleague? It is no accident that one of the most used words for those who complain is *uncollegial*. In door story 3, the woman who made a complaint after being assaulted by her head of department was repeatedly described as uncollegial. When a complaint about an assault is understood as uncollegial, the assault itself is not. As soon as the person who is assaulted complains, as soon as she uses the word *assault* to describe his action, she is no longer treated as a colleague; she is no longer deemed worthy of protection.

We need to think about what is treated as collegial (and what is not), who is treated as collegial (and who is not). Collegiality can be about developing positive relations, a sense of goodwill and trust, among colleagues; it can offer a way of resisting the impulse of egoism and individualism. Collegiality might even imply the opening of a door, offered as a promise to treat incoming members of a department *well*. But collegiality, however open as an aspiration, or even by being open as an aspiration, can still end up being restricted to some, those with whom one shares something, whether that something is history (remember "I have known him for years") or a set of qualities loosely defined as *culture* or *character* (what we are like, what we like).

This restriction is not simply about who is protected as a colleague; it is about who can become a colleague in the first place. I have noticed that when there is a wide departmental problem of harassment and bullying, there is often an informal or casual culture around hiring. In chapter 1, I showed how it becomes usual to suspend the usual procedures in hiring and promotion cases. An early career lecturer told me how people would talk about such and such candidate as "he's the guy you'd want to have a pint with." Sometimes you hire people whom you like, or who are like those who are already there. Informality matters at many levels. The suspension of formal procedures can be what enables some to get in. Informality also matters in terms of spaces and how they are occupied (being at the pub, having a pint). You suspend a formal procedure to enable someone to be hired who could be the kind of person you would want to spend time with in those spaces where you like to spend time.

Or you might hire people because they are already your friends, or friends of friends, or partners of friends. The university becomes *a web of past intimacies*. These intimacies can be mobilized when complaints are made. The senior lecturer who was physically assaulted by her head of department described her department thus: "So much cronyism. All friends had been employed who were not equipped to be in a university space, who couldn't get funding and who ended up in the department. . . . We had four or five friends who ended up in the department, so the culture was very tricky. They were also very defensive about getting support or starting conversations." Hiring your friends: hiring becomes wiring; who is hired is also about what conversations happen or are allowed to happen. A culture is tricky because friends are sticky; they tend to stick together.

When some colleagues are friends, they are who end up being defended. Perhaps defensiveness relates to a sense of being of the same kind, a family, a close unit, related. One lecturer said her university was organized around married couples. She creates a map: "I study all the charts; I created maps, power maps. I started to see that [the university] has an invisible map of a power structure that is shared by more than twenty married couples." I think we learn from how married couples can be a power map, a way of distributing power across an institution. When you make a complaint, you often learn about how power is wielded. One PhD student talked to me about a complaint she made about harassment and bullying from a married couple, one of whom was her supervisor. Her supervisor had previously been the postgraduate student of the professor she then married. There is another history there, another web, another weave: students becoming partners of their professors; married now, his colleague now, his student before. She describes their behavior as a unit as "coercive intimacy." In meetings, in common rooms, they would often share intimacies through sexual humor as well as jokes about bodily functions: "They share all these intimacies, and they bring them all into the room, giggling, even the poo jokes, imposing something intimate into a public." I have noted how violence often happens behind closed doors; doors can be used to create a private space within a public institution. Violence can also be the imposition of intimacy within an institution ("imposing something intimate into a public"). It is a way of saying, "This meeting is ours." A common room becomes a private room.

It is not only that a married couple can impose their intimacy upon others; that intimacy can be instrumentalized, used to stop complaints from being made. One student said, "I have been here since I was seventeen years old. I grew up with them. I can't do anything." Students become like children; to study in a department, to study *under* someone, is to acquire a sense of loyalty. Perhaps loyalty can be understood as the affective expression of debt: you are loyal because of what you owe; you are loyal because that's who you know.[9] To progress as a student becomes akin to growing up: progression, how you go, how far you go, is made dependent not only on internalizing a set of norms, duties, and priorities but on expressing them through action or inaction. By describing inaction as expression, I am referring to how *not complaining* becomes a positive duty not just to an institution but to another person: you don't complain because of what you owe; you don't complain because that's who you know.

Not complaining can be how you receive what you need from those who can provide it. I want to return to the example of the postgraduate students who made a complaint about sexual harassment by other postgraduate students (chapter 3). The postgraduate men were protected; they stayed; they continued to receive support and benefits. The women who complained left. We can ask whose backs were becoming doors given the students being protected were not colleagues or not yet colleagues. The student who was harassed and the student who was the harasser shared a supervisor. In the first instance, the supervisor supports both students. But when the initial complaint became a formal complaint, the supervisor "began to advocate for [him] in the formal complaint process." By giving support to the student who was being investigated for harassment, the supervisor withdrew support from the student who had been harassed. She experiences that withdrawal as devastating.

Collegiality can be a promise: you treat some more than others as would-be or could-be colleagues. Perhaps support was given to the students who were most promising. The story of harassment does not, then, begin with one student harassing another student. One of the students I interviewed talked to another woman from the same program who, she found out, had earlier made a complaint about harassment by the same student.[10] That woman she spoke to describes how a "lecturer had come around and was asking people about their topics. She had said she was interested in feminist studies and the lecturer had responded, 'Feminism is a dirty word.' It was done publicly in that group, and [she] was like, 'It set up the tone and gave them permission.'" It gave them permission. Note that permission can be tonal, a more performative version of a nod: yes, we can say that; yes, we can do that. The student who was later to call women "milking bitches" and who was to harass the student who was not willing to go along with it, with him, had been enabled, even encouraged, to do so. You can be rewarded for following a line or for reproducing an inheritance. And so we learn: a promise can also be a matter of reflection. The students who are protected, who are promising, are those who reflect back the image of the professors, laughing, joking, feminism is a dirty word, women are milking bitches. Harassment can be a reflection: how some say yes, see, we are like you; yes, we are on our way to becoming you.

Those who complain about harassment are treated as naughty willful children who need to be disciplined or straightened out. One of the women told me what was said during one of the grueling meetings: "The line I really remember was 'we are not going to leave until we get this sorted' because we were treated like four unruly girls who needed disciplining." Another of the women who complained said, "I always felt they were treating us like siblings who were having an argument." Harassment and bullying in universities are often explained in ways similar to how violence in the family is explained, either by being projected onto strangers who can be removed (as if to remove them would be to remove violence) or by being made familiar and thus forgivable.

The institutional fatalism I have been describing throughout this book, which converts a description (*this* is what institutions are like) into an instruction (accept *this*), is also often familial. In other words, you are supposed to accept harassment and bullying because that is what families are like. One lecturer described an incident:

> It was really weird. It was in the school office, and he started talking about one of my classes, and he said, "The external examiner said something," and I said, "I don't actually agree with the external examiner" . . . and he said, "Well fuck you, you don't fucking know anything, the external examiner is a major professor, fuck off, who the fuck do you think you are talking about him like that in front of other people." . . . I later found out that the external examiner was one of his closest friends. So I went to the head of school and I said this happened, and she said, "You know, [he] is like the naughty uncle of the school. That's just how he is, you just have to let it go."

The naughty uncle appears here as a figure, as familiar, but also as an instruction to her: to let it go, not to complain, to accept the shouting and abusing behavior; this is how he is, how we are, what will be. Perhaps then complaints are stopped by being turned into a family secret.

The family can also be used to stop complaints by being positioned as that which would be damaged by them. A woman academic I communicated with informally had her work plagiarized by a colleague. She finds out later that he had also plagiarized the work of another woman academic. The chair of the department gave them both "the same line," which was "to keep quiet about it because [he had] a family." She files a complaint. The first stage of the complaints process is an inquiry to decide whether "the case warrants investigation." In the inquiry, the mediator "kept reminding me, a lesbian, that [he] has a wife and child." She could hear what she was being told, that by complaining she would damage not just him but his family. Perhaps that reminder is being addressed to her as somebody assumed not to have a family in need of protection. In the end, her complaint is not investigated. I suspect much academic misconduct is not investigated, and is thus enabled or reproduced, in the name of the protection of the family.

Complaints can be stopped to sustain a bond, whether familial or collegial. Bonds can be binds. I want to return to the experience of the woman of color academic who made a complaint about racism and sexism in her department. She was told by the head of Human Resources that she had "a chip on her shoulder" (chapter 4). She had heard this before. In another instance, after she presents a paper on the emotional labor of diversity work (presenting papers on emotional labor is emotional labor), a white woman professor in the audience responds in a hostile manner, accusing her of having "a chip on her shoulder." If making complaints can take you into meetings with Human Resources, what you encounter there can be what you have already encountered in academic settings.

She has allies in the audience, two white women who did critical work on race. She says that although they had heard what had been said they "could not recognize it." They defend their white colleague: "She got wrong-footed," "She didn't understand," "We like her." *Wrong-footed* is used to imply that the white woman colleague made a muddle of her words. Racism is often heard as an error message, as inexpressive: *not* what a person is like, *not* what an institution is like. She tells me what she would have liked to say to them: "You've just witnessed somebody abuse somebody because they have expressed their experience of racism, and your problem is you can't hear what you've just heard." The racism they cannot hear is then treated as if it is not there: "They probably deleted it from their memory." This deletion is what enables them to stay loyal to a white colleague; when they have her back, they turn their backs on a woman of color who is also their colleague. In chapter 2, I explored how institutions can delete complaints through blanking: complaints are deleted from institutional memory. Deletion can be personal as well as institutional. Racism is deleted by white people when its acknowledgment would compromise their sense of collegiality with other white people.

You don't notice what would get in the way; whiteness as a way of viewing the world can put racism behind closed doors. In another instance a Black woman had been racially harassed over a long period of time by her white head of department. You will hear more details about that harassment in chapter 6. She has a meeting with a white colleague who has just become her new head of department. This colleague refers to the "history" between this Black woman and the former head of department, another white woman: "I want you to reconcile with her because, after all, she is my friend and colleague and all she ever did is write you some long emails." Note how the former head of department is evoked possessively ("my friend and colleague"). It is important that the appeal was being made by a white woman on behalf of a friend and colleague, her white friend. The white friend enters the scenario as a figure, loaded with value and significance; she is appealing. The problem is not simply that the white woman is saying what she wants ("I want you to"). The expression of desire is also a management tactic: she is giving an instruction, telling a Black woman, who is also a colleague but is *not addressed* as a colleague, what to do, what to say.

The restriction of collegiality to those of a certain kind, our kind, the same kind, is how collegiality can function as a means to protect some and not others or even some from others. She continues, "What I learned from the complaint process was that white organizations always seem to protect white people because in protecting the one white person they are protecting the whole institution from any claim that there is any racism happening at all. There is always this massive PR exercise."[11] When we talk about protecting the institution, we are also talking about protecting some colleagues more than others, or even some colleagues *against* others. We are talking about how protecting one person can be the same thing as protecting the whole institution. There is a history to who becomes that person. *There is a history to who does not become that person.*

Throughout this book I have explored the mechanisms whereby complaints are stopped. I am now suggesting that collegiality is one of those mechanisms. Sympathy is part of the machinery. Their backs become doors; their hands become locks; bodies and machines are so entangled that it can be hard to tell a lock from a hand, a back from a door: to tell them apart or to take them apart.

When attempts are made from those higher up in a hierarchy (such as heads of department) to stop complaints, we need to understand those actions not only as top-down bullying from management. Heads of department can also be those whose conduct is under question or can be colleagues or close personal friends of those whose conduct is under question. This is why it is too easy but also wrong to identify management or Human Resources as the source of the problem of how complaints are dealt with or not dealt with (though they are often part of the problem). I want to make a stronger argument: the identification of complaint with management can be used as a method for stopping complaints. Academic networks are protected by identifying complaints with the management of those networks.

I talked to a group of students informally. They described to me how they were dissuaded from lodging a complaint about sexual harassment. They were told that any complaint would be repurposed by senior management as a tool to be used against "radical academics." This was a very successful method: for the students to express what they felt, a political allegiance to the academics, being on the same side, against the same things, required them not to complain about the conduct of those academics even though they objected to that conduct. Note here that those who complain often have the same concern that their complaint will be used by hostile management to justify decisions that those who complain would not make.[12] It is an understandable concern: any evidence of wrongdoing by a person or in a department has the potential to be used for ends that are not knowable in advance. But that concern is instrumentalized because if it is used to stop complaints it is also used to enable the conduct that the complaints, if made, might have stopped. And then, those who do make formal complaints about harassment or bullying by academics are often treated as managers, disciplining "radical academics," trying to stop them from expressing themselves freely. The complainer as manager is a way of diagnosing complaint itself as a will to power. In other words, a complaint is treated as an exaggeration of injury, how the structural is used to disguise the personal, in order to discipline others, to restrict their freedom, and to contain how they express their desires.[13]

The complainer as manager borrows and builds from the figures discussed in chapter 4: the complainer as moaner (moaning about minor matters), the complainer as malicious (intent on causing damage), and the complainer as stranger (not one of us). The figure of the complainer as manager helps to explain what might seem at first like a curious finding: the use of the word *neoliberal* to dismiss the complainer and, in particular, the student complainer. One student who made a complaint about harassment by a professor in her MA program said, "My complaint was called neoliberal." Her complaint was called neoliberal by other students in the program. The other students also said that the complainers "needed to be in 'solidarity' with those whose education was now being disrupted, not the other way around." Neoliberalism can be mobilized to judge those who complain as motivated by self-interest. Not complaining about harassment from a professor then becomes judged as being in the collective interest, a way of holding on to the professor by keeping silent about his abusive behavior. She was also told it was questionable to complain, as to complain is to "turn to the institution" and to "seek support" from it. To make a formal complaint can be judged as "using the master's tools." We can also remember that some academics position themselves as counterinstitutional, as working against the neoliberal institution, refusing to comply with its bureaucratic impositions. (Equality too can be treated as just another bureaucratic imposition.) This positioning is convenient because it allows abuses of power to be framed as counterinstitutional, even radical. Entering into an institutional process by submitting a formal complaint can be framed in advance as institutional complicity, as becoming the manager's accomplice.[14]

The designation of complaint as neoliberal can also be used to imply that to make a complaint is to behave like, or to become, a consumer. Another student who made a complaint about bullying and harassment from a professor in her MA program said, "The idea that would come up is that I was somehow being a very neoliberal person, the idea of the student as a stakeholder." When a student making a complaint about harassment is treated as a student acting as a stakeholder, treating education as an investment, the university as a business, complaints about harassment are made akin to not liking a product. Complaints about harassment can be minimized and managed when filtered as consumer preference. She added, "Maybe I am just a perfect neoliberal subject. Or maybe I am a person who doesn't want to be abused." What is striking is what she is revealing: how not wanting to be abused, complaining about abusive behavior, can be judged as being "a perfect neoliberal subject." We need to learn from how neoliberalism can be used to picture the person who does not want to be abused and who acts accordingly.

I have suggested that when a complaint forces violence to be faced, force can be used against the complainer to stop violence being faced. Force can also be assumed to *originate* with the complainer. The diagnostics of neoliberalism is central to this achievement of originality. The figure of the complainer is treated as a symptom of a more generalized structure of violence, whether institutional, managerial, or neoliberal. When complaints against academics are made, they can *pass themselves off* very quickly as the ones being forced, being forced out or being forced into compliance by a disciplinary regime. I am using the word *pass* deliberately here. Passing often works because it is an approximation of something real. Not only do such disciplinary regimes exist, but many of us share an understanding of them as compromising educational values.[15]

The designation of the complainer as neoliberal is useful because so many working within educational institutions share a critique of neoliberalism as damaging institutions. If a complaint is designated as neoliberal, the complainer can be identified as damaging universities not because they damage their reputation, which would be a neoliberal model of damage, but because they threaten progressive educational values or even the idea of the university as a public good.[16] In other words, complaints about harassment are *passed off* as compromising values: critical, radical, even feminist values. One student who put in a complaint about harassment was told, "You are going to ruin any chance for this innovative work continuing." The effort to stop a complaint can be justified as giving support to innovative work. I think it is very important to understand how this works given most of you reading this book would, like me, want to do what you can to support innovative work. We might think of institutional violence as happening over *there*, enacted by those who would or could direct that violence toward us, as critical thinkers, say, subversive intellectuals even, but that violence is right *here*, closer to home, in the warm and fuzzy zone of collegiality, in commitments to innovation, radicality, or criticality, in the desire to protect a project or a program.

If a complaint about harassment is made about staff working in a feminist program, the effort to stop that complaint can then be justified as necessary for the continuation of the feminist program. But feminism can also be treated as part of a managerial and disciplinary regime that is imposed upon others to restrict their freedom; in other words, feminism can be treated as neoliberal.[17] Equality can be dismissed very easily as audit culture, as tick boxes, as administration, as bureaucracy, as that which can distract us from creative and critical work and can even stop us from doing that work.[18] I think the word *neoliberal* also becomes attached to other words, including *feminist, prude, uptight, moralizing, killjoy,* and *policing.* These words might seem quite far apart. But we have already learned how neoliberalism is used to picture the complainer as individualistic. Being a prude, uptight, and moralizing can thus be part of that same picture: the person who is unwilling to give herself to others or to participate in a shared culture is judged as putting herself first.[19]

These terms are used because they are already in circulation; they are floating around, in the air, ready and spare, available to be picked up because of what they have been used to do, what they can be used to do. The overlaying of negative terms can turn neoliberalism itself into a feminist plot designed to suppress and contain the movement of free radicals, as if the very designation of conduct as "harassment" is simply another way of controlling and constraining expression. The complainer becomes, if you like, a feminist manager who is imposing moral norms upon others, disguising her own will by deploying the language of injustice. In most instances, the diagnosis of the complainer as neoliberal happens retrospectively, after a complaint is made, or is made as part of a generalized critique of feminist activist work around sexual violence. That diagnosis of neoliberalism can also appear in advance of a complaint being made. Those diagnostics, in other words, can be used as techniques of persuasion. An undergraduate student was persuaded to enter a sexual relationship with a senior man professor: "The first time he touched me he closed his office door. I thought it was strange that he closed the door. We weren't doing anything wrong. I pondered, Why hide this? He informed me that the university's 'sex panic' was the reason: predatory neoliberal policies encroaching on our freedoms. I nodded. The door remained closed after that." Here the closed door is deemed necessary because of "neoliberalism policies" as well as "sex panic," a term that associates neoliberalism with a narrow, moralizing, feminist agenda. Policies are treated as the police. It is implied that the door is closed because of how certain forms of conduct (such as having sex with your students, that perk of the job) have made rights into wrongs.

Even though feminism can be associated with neoliberalism as well as managerialism, it is worth noting that some feminists can be persuaded by this reframing of complaint as a disciplinary technique used against radical academics. I have read many letters of support written by femi-nists on behalf of colleagues who have been accused of sexual harassment or sexual misconduct. We need to understand how this can happen. In one instance, multiple complaints were made by students against an academic man, which included allegations of rape, sexual assault, domes-tic violence, and sexual harassment. He was able to convince many col-leagues that he was the one being harassed. I communicated informally with four women involved in making that complaint. A woman professor said, "His narrative was apparently that he was being accused of making sexist comments and the 'feminazis,' us, were out to get him." We are back to how much control of the narrative of the complaint matters and how much control is what the complaint is about. The case against him was also described as a witch hunt. This use of terms like *feminazis* and *witch hunts* will be familiar to feminists: we only need to consider how quickly #MeToo was framed in this way, as a persecution of innocent men by a feminist mob. We also know how often sexual violence is dismissed as sexist speech, as if the complaints were reducible to how he speaks or expresses himself.[20]

What is really notable in this case is how much support he received from feminist colleagues (some of whom had public roles in developing new policies on sexual harassment). Those who supported him by writ-ing letters on his behalf did so without even hearing from the students who had made the complaints: "Many colleagues, about sixty-eight to seventy, came forward on his behalf to suggest that really, he was a 'good guy,' just a regular 'Northern Cheeky Chappie,' maybe a bit of a rough dia-mond. . . . They had no idea of what he was being accused of, other than what he offered up to them as his own narrative." We have already heard how sexual as well as physical violence can be framed as blunt speech. These descriptions, "rough diamond," a "Northern Cheeky Chappie," were used by academics in letters of support submitted on his behalf. We can hear what they are doing. They are intended as rebuttals. They are used to imply that the complaints derive from a failure of feminists to ap-preciate how he was expressing himself. They are used to imply that the failure to appreciate how he was expressing himself is a form of snobbery or class prejudice. The figure of the complainer as privileged, as moaning about minor matters, discussed in chapter 4, is working hard here. That figure is also about missing persons: some of the women who complained were middle class, some were working class. An early career academic from a working-class background described to me how enraging it was to be positioned as middle class, as if "working-class women never complained," as if working-class women did not have their own militant feminist history and were not themselves instrumental in the battle to recognize sexual harassment as a hostile environment in the workplace in the first place.[21] The complainer becomes not only a figure but a fetish, cut off from this history of those who had to complain about sexual harassment in the workplace in order to do their work.

We have more to learn from the utility of the figure of the complainer as moaning about minor matters. In another case, a man of color left his position after complaints were made by students about harassment and bullying. His departure was publicly represented by supporters as being a result of a complaint made by a single white student who didn't like how he expressed himself. I spoke informally to the students who were involved in the complaint process. I learned from them that complaints were made not by one student but by a group of students, including students of color, and related to Islamophobia and racial harassment as well as sexual harassment and bullying. The use of the figure of the privileged white complainer, we could call her Karen, can stop students of color from being heard; it can stop complaints about racial harassment from being heard. Another student wrote to me about another case involving a complaint made by a professor, a man of color. He was the object of multiple complaints by students for sexual harassment, including sexual assault. In this case, the students shared information about the conduct of the professor with other students because of the failure of the complaints system to uphold their complaints.[22] Their action was described by faculty as "attacking a colleague" and as "lynching," an extremely problematic use of that word for multiple reasons, including for how it evokes a history of racist violence against Black men specifically and how it implies that the complainers, who were all students, were a lynch mob.[23]

Complaints about assault can be treated as an assault. As such, the person who is complained about is turned into the one *really* being persecuted, whether or not complaints are made using official channels. When complaints are put forward, however they are put forward, many charges fly around. We are familiar with these charges: they are old and familiar forms of antifeminism. We need to account for how feminists can exercise the same rhetorics when they are called upon to protect colleagues. This can happen, it seems, not just because people suspend their political beliefs and commitments when their own colleagues and friends are the ones whose conduct is being questioned (although that suspension does matter). I want to turn here to the Grimm story of the willful child to make sense of how this can happen. I have drawn on this story before (Ahmed 2014, 2017).

Once upon a time there was a child who was willful, and would not do as her mother wished. For this reason, God had no pleasure in her, and let her become ill, and no doctor could do her any good, and in a short time she lay on her death-bed. When she had been lowered into her grave, and the earth was spread over her, all at once her arm came out again, and stretched upwards, and when they had put it in and spread fresh earth over it, it was all to no purpose, for the arm always came out again. Then the mother herself was obliged to go to the grave, and strike the arm with a rod, and when she had done that, it was drawn in, and then at last the child had rest beneath the ground. (Grimm and Grimm 1884, 125)

The willful child: she has a story to tell. In this Grimm story, which is certainly a grim story, the willful child is the one who is disobedient, who will not do as her mother wishes. If authority assumes the right to turn a wish into a command, then willfulness is a diagnosis of the failure to comply with those whose authority is given. The costs of such a diagnosis are high: through a chain of command (the mother, God, the doctors) the child's fate is sealed. It is ill will that responds to willfulness; the child is allowed to become ill in such a way that no one can "do her any good."

In this story, the arm that keeps coming up inherits willfulness from the child. The arm keeps coming up until it too is beaten down. In *Living a Feminist Life* (2017), I reconsidered this story as an institutional parable. I have noted already how those who complain are treated as willful children who need to be straightened out. A complaint could be thought of as an arm that is still rising. This grim story is of course *not* the story of feminist complaint. It offers a warning: be willing or you will be beaten. It offers an invitation: *identify with the rod and you will be spared.* So much violence is abbreviated here; so much silence about violence is explained here, as if by not bringing up violence, not noticing it, not mentioning it, you might be spared.

Even if the Grimm story is not the story of feminist complaint, those who are doing the work of complaint can hear something about their own experiences in it. One student wrote to me about her experience of sharing in public the names of harassers; she was forced to remove the posts and to issue a statement that she regretted the allegations. She does not regret them. She writes, "I feel like the willful child, the one in the Grimm fairy-tale you write about in *Living a Feminist Life*, the rod beating her down, beating her arm down, the arm's still fighting to live, while the body is dead. And then she rests. That willful child is me. I had to get into a settlement. I had to remove the posts." They do what they can to stop you, to stop you from raising your arm, from making a complaint. One of the women I interviewed, who made a complaint about bullying, told me that reading the Grimm story helped her to understand what happened to her: "Reading of it was upsetting but at the same time it makes sense. They are hurting me because I am raising my arm." If you raise your arm in order to lodge a complaint about violence, that violence is directed back at you.

I am bringing this story up here because it allows me to show vividly how passing operates. Those who have complaints about harassment brought against them *pass themselves off as the arm in the story*, as the ones being beaten by a disciplinary regime. The complainers are then treated not as raising their arms, refusing to be beaten, protesting violence, but as the rods, the managers, the police, the prison guards. I think this passing is successful because many academics identify themselves as the arm in the story, as potentially harmed by a disciplinary apparatus because of who they are or the beliefs they hold. If you have had an experience of the institution coming down on you, you might be sympathetic to those who frame complaints made against them as the institution coming down on them. When collegiality with harassers is performed, it is a sign of how the passing succeeds, how the complaint is framed, who is controlling the narrative; the arm and rod switch places. Those who complain about harassment often end up feeling all the more stranded—they are all the more stranded—because the sympathy they would expect to receive from those with whom they share an allegiance is withdrawn from them and given to those whose violence required them to complain in the first place.

DAMAGE LIMITATION

I have described how doors can be used to shut violence in. We can return to how the expression *behind closed doors* is used figuratively to imply how information is kept secret from a wider public. Keeping our attention on doors allows us to connect different kinds of activity that occur around complaint that might otherwise seem disparate and unconnected. In this section I explore how solutions to a complaint (such as the use of reconciliation or mediation) can operate as doors to shut the violence in, as well as how many of the activities that happen after complaints (such as reports produced by independent inquiries) can function to close doors, to keep complaints secret from a wider public.

Let's return to door story 1. That an assault of a student could be "sorted out" by the student having "a cup of tea" with the professor who assaulted her has much to teach us. The resolution of a problem can be how the problem *is passed over* as if what occurred was just a minor thing. You treat a problem as slight by making the resolution light. And I think of the "cup of tea" not only as a way of making something slight but as a signifier, an English signifier of reconciliation, of how you sort something out. Reconciliation can function as a management technique, used as a way of "sorting it out." Recall the example of when a white academic said to a Black academic, "I want you to reconcile with her because, after all, she is my friend and colleague and all she ever did was write you some long emails." She had in fact been racially harassed by the former head of department, another white woman, for many years (see chapter 6). This white woman, by expressing her desire for reconciliation ("I want you to reconcile with her"), is also offering an interpretation of events ("all she ever did was write you some long emails"). A key tactic for minimizing harassment is to present harassment as a style of communication: long emails might be annoying, but the implication is that they are not harmful or serious.

The work of reconciliation often falls upon those who have been harassed: it is the Black woman who is given the task of reconciling "with her," the white woman who harassed her while she was her head of department. The problem here is not simply that those who are harassed are expected to do the work of reconciling themselves to the situation they are in (to reconcile with her as reconciling yourself to a situation), although that problem is quite a problem given that the situation *is* the harassment (reconciliation with her as reconciling yourself to being harassed by her). Reconciliation does not just happen once you have reached a certain point in a longer sequence. Reconciliation is often there from the very beginning as an expectation or appeal. The appeal to reconcile or to be conciliatory is another way of appealing to someone not to complain. The expectation that she will smooth things over or keep smoothing things over is how she is required to maintain a relationship that is damaging. An expression of desire for reconciliation might appear to be a friendly gesture. There is nothing friendly about this gesture. If she does not return the desire for reconciliation, if she is not willing to smooth things over, moving on, getting along, getting on, she becomes the one who has not only broken a connection but refused to repair it.

An expression of a desire for reconciliation sometimes takes the form of apology. In one instance, a professor makes an apology to a master's student who had lodged a complaint against him for bullying and harassment. You heard about her experiences in part II of this book: he shouts and swears at her, but she is afraid, because his actions left no evidence. His apology is unsolicited. It is inserted into her complaint file: "And the other thing they did is send me that letter by x. I didn't ask for any contact from that man. He is a bully. He already lives in my nightmares." If the letter was an apology, it was also a form of contact and communication; the letter allowed the professor to take up space in the way he had already taken up space ("he already lives in my nightmares").

Why was it significant that the letter was an apology? What apologies are doing depends on how they are worded.[24] Those who apologize do not have to say *what* they are apologizing for, or if they do say, they can do so in such a way that the problem is made slight or about how someone is affected rather than what that person caused: you might apologize for hurting someone's feelings, which makes the hurt feelings the problem as well as the obstacle to reconciliation. She gives an account of the apology she receives from the professor: "I think they thought I would accept it as a real apology. Reading it, it is not an apology. He did exactly the same thing he used to do in seminars. . . . I am just going to capitulate in such a tone that tells you that I don't believe a word you are saying, therefore not giving you the respect of recognizing that you might have a valid point." An apology for bullying can be extension of bullying; you can be telling someone how little you think they are worth by appearing to concede in such a way that intonates that their complaint is not "a valid point." If the violence he enacted did not appear to others, the apology can be another way the violence is made to disappear. Note as well that the action she is identifying as problematic is not only the apology but the insertion of the apology into her complaint file ("I think they thought I would accept it"). Finding that letter in the file is to be put under pressure to accept it, to move on with it, to get on with it.

When reconciliation becomes a mode of governance, abuses of power are treated as minor squabbles or as the product of poor communication that can be resolved by better communication.[25] When harassment is minimized by being treated as a style of communication, reconciliation can be experienced as the enforcement of communication. One student is considering making a complaint about sexual misconduct by her former tutor. She is told her options would either be a formal complaint, which she does not "think would lead anywhere without tangible proof of physical assault," or "writing him a letter directly." She does not want to write such a letter: "I have no wish to reopen channels of communication with

X as I have successfully cut myself off and I do not want to start a conversation with him or give him a chance to explain himself." To be asked to communicate, whether in writing or in person, with the person who has harassed you is to be asked to reopen channels of communication that you closed to protect yourself.

I noted in chapter 3 that harassment and bullying are often treated as a conflict between parties, as different viewpoints that ought to be heard, as if you are hearing different sides of the same story. We can now deepen the analysis of what viewing harassment or bullying as a viewpoint means practically for the persons being harassed or bullied. In one case of bullying by a head of department, members of the department were invited to mediation: "The deputy vice chancellor then said, I am going to give you this gift, I have arranged for you to go to this hotel, and I have arranged for this person, a negotiator, to sit with you and sort this out. I had been bullied and called in so many times by this guy. I just thought, I am not going to a mediation meeting with this person." Being asked to enter mediation is represented as a gift. The gift is proximity to the person who is being abusive; she is being asked to be in the same room with him, to sit with him, as if all that is needed to resolve the problem is time and proximity. We need to remember that both verbal and physical harassment can be represented as self-expression. To be asked to be in the room with someone who has bullied you is to be asked to witness a bully being given more opportunities to express himself.

The refusal to take sides by treating bullying as a side of an argument that needs to be heard is to side with the bully. Another woman professor said, "If somebody is being bullied by another member of staff, they don't take sides, they don't go into the situation, they don't look at what's happening, and they don't say, well, if this behavior is unacceptable, this is putting pressure on this person. All they will do is look at the situation and say, your account contradicts your account. I've nothing to do with it." Pointing to contradictory accounts is a way of not doing anything; it is a way of not intervening in the situation. She adds, "There have been a number of times when I have been going into a managerial role myself and have been basically told, whatever you do, don't get involved in conflict between staff. That is just carte blanche: it's a bully's charter just to do what the heck they like." Not taking sides, not intervening, is how bullying is enabled; it is to give bullies "a charter just to do what the heck they like."

Treating an abuse of power as a difference in opinion that can be resolved through informal communication not only operates as a form of damage control; it is in fact damaging. Formal inquiries can also be used to limit damage in a way that is damaging. We can return to door story 1 and the subsequent complaint made by a group of students many years after they experienced harassment as undergraduates. The university set up an independent inquiry into their complaint. All three women provided testimony. In the subsequent report, only one of the testimonies is referenced. One of the women said of her testimony, "It's been erased completely: it's not there." Another said, "There's not even a sentence." The report stated that there was no need for further investigation into current practice in the department because current students had not come forward with complaints. Indeed, the report implied it would have been up to these students to have provided such evidence, even though they were reporting on their experiences in the 1990s. As the former students who gave us door story 1 described it, "What they have effectively done with that report is identify one rogue member of staff who's been encouraged to take retirement, and then of course 'they've dealt with the situation,' and the reason they left all of our testimony out of the picture is that they didn't want to accept exactly why we wanted to talk to them about it in the first place, which was that this all was *the face of culture*." In effect, the report was a means by which the university was able not to deal with the situation by appearing to have dealt with it.

It is worth adding here that the report did not simply fail to include the testimony of some of the former students. It was written in such a way that implied sympathy with the organization. The report reads rather like a reference for the university. Perhaps it reads like that because it is that. For example, the report references the commissioning of the inquiry as evidence of what the organization was doing to deal with the problem. An inquiry can be used rather like a policy: as evidence of what is being done or as self-evidence. One of the former students, now a professor, describes how the university then used such actions as evidence that the situation had been addressed: "[The university] now has a very nice patch on its intranet telling staff what happened, and it all looks cleaner than clean because of all the action they have taken in the past six months. And frankly they haven't addressed the situation at all." I am interested in her evocation of *the intranet*: communication about the house is kept in house. Communication can be used to clean up a mess, which implies that complaints about harassment are treated rather like dirt, "matter out of place," to reuse Mary Douglas's ([1966] 1994, 35) reuse of an old definition of dirt. It is not just that activities undertaken do not address the problem; *they are a way of not addressing the problem.*

If the report was written in such a way that implied sympathy with the organization, it was also sympathetic with one of the harassers, the only named person who was still a current member of staff (although he was later quietly retired). The inquiry found that there was no evidence to support the argument that this lecturer had groomed the student, even though they had her diary, which provided a record of conversations. What I want to pick up here is how the sympathy was given to him by how the report repeated some of the lecturer's own explanations of his conduct. Take the following paragraph:

> She mentions in her diaries his referring on more than one occasion to her lipstick. I also accept X denies he was flirting but rather that he was being friendly. The diary entries show she was attracted to him whilst finding his behaviour unsettling at times. My finding is that he was familiar and perhaps over-familiar towards her. I reject the suggestion that he was attempting to build an emotional connection to gain X's trust for the purposes of sexual exploitation. X's compliments might be outside the type of behaviour expected to take place in the normal course of a tutorial, but rather than necessarily pointing to a sexual or abusive intent, objectively his behaviour could be demonstrative of a means of boosting her confidence.

This is a clear instance of sympathetic identification. The report is confident in accepting his explanation that he was "being friendly" and even suggests that his behavior *objectively* could be considered "a means of boosting her confidence." The author concludes that the professor was "familiar" with her, and even qualifies the possibility that he was being "over-familiar" with a "perhaps." I have noted already how much harassment (including assault) is justified as "being friendly." Those who experience such behavior as violence, as harassment, or indeed as sexual exploitation or grooming are thus framed as *having misunderstood a friendly gesture.* Note also how the apparent attempt to be neutral in a report—to treat each party as having different viewpoints—is what transforms the view of the person accused of harassment into something objective; when he is given a view, his view disappears as view and becomes instead how something is recorded ("objectively his behaviour").

The sympathetic identification with the harasser is doing something more than being sympathetic: to declare "it was friendly" is to clear him of any wrongdoing. I have suggested that doors are used by institutions to shut violence in. Inquires too can function as doors; that is, they can be used to shut violence in by taking the viewpoint of the harasser while disguising that they are doing so. In our third door story, the report on a physical assault described the assault as "on par with a handshake." And that was how the head of department described his own action: he said to the person leading the inquiry that he knew the contact was "unwelcome" but that he was "intending to console." The institutional use of friendly terms to describe violent behavior is thus a repetition of the same terms that enabled that violent behavior. I have in my files many such examples of confidential and public reports that offer sympathetic identification with harassment. That identification is often also how organizations are cleared of wrongdoing, which is to say, it is how they clear themselves of wrongdoing.

When independent inquiries are used to clear organizations of wrongdoing, those inquiries are not independent. Another academic described this problem as a general problem with how universities use the category "external" when they are hiring the same people as consultants. She described how universities develop "all these cozy relationships." Ranks can be closed because of how someone external is appointed as well as why someone is appointed. In another case, for instance, a white man with no expertise in equality or sexual harassment was appointed to head an inquiry into a senior professor who had multiple complaints against him for sexual harassment. When an administrator was asked why they appointed someone without the relevant expertise, she replied, "Because we cannot be seen to be conducting a witch hunt." Antifeminist rhetoric can be used to justify hiring decisions: if the effort is to manage perception, trying not to be seen *in that way* is what allows him to *get away* with it.

Formal inquiries set up to deal with a complaint can be used to limit the damage caused by a complaint. We can return to the example of the four postgraduate students who made a complaint about sexual harassment from other students. Following their complaint, the department commissioned a review. What did the review find? It presented the department as a warm and inclusive environment. The person who wrote this review did not talk to any of the students who made the complaints. As one of the students described it, "They randomly selected people from each year that didn't include anyone who had been involved in the complaint about sexual harassment or any of the people who had been vocal about issues of racism in the department." You can preserve a view of the department as inclusive by not including the views of those who would challenge that view. In other words, the more you exclude, the more you can appear inclusive.

The report referred to sexual harassment as the "it" problem. As she described further, "A strong theme throughout the inquiry was the problem that 'it,' the critical event, had caused. It is not the remit of the report to comment on it, the critical event. The report then refers to the 'it problem.' The 'it problem' was not the problem of the awful moments of humiliation and sexual harassment. The 'it problem' was us, the complaint." A report can manage not to name the problem but still identify the problem as those who name the problem. A report can be a repair job. And the damage being repaired is not the damage caused by the harassment but the damage caused by the complaint. Leila Whitley (forthcoming) has usefully described how organizations respond to complaints about sexual harassment as "the displacement of harm." The harm experienced by the person harassed is displaced as harm to the institution. Damage limitation as a tactic for handling complaints can operate to minimize *and* displace harm.

Damage limitation is not only performed by how complaints are handled in informal or formal inquiries. Damage limitation can also be achieved silently or through silence. Sometimes silence requires silencing. In one instance, a lecturer was told that even communicating with students who put forward a complaint about sexual misconduct from a senior member of her department would be in breach of her contract. She called the university's initial response an instruction: "Delete all email correspondence related to the cases, do not under any circumstances respond to allegations in any way, shape, or form. Basically, shut up. Keep quiet. . . . I knew many of these students, I had taught them, I wanted to support them, but I was told that to communicate with them would be in breach of my contract." Perhaps she had to be told that communicating with the students would be in breach of her contract only because she was communicating with them or at least indicating an intent or desire to do so. Even to give support to a complaint can be understood as in defiance of your duties. It is not simply that codes become disciplinary when we fail to follow them. Rather, when we fail to follow them, we come to know them.

Damage limitation can thus be achieved by virtue of how people are already working or how they are supposed to be working. Professional norms of conduct can be about "keeping a lid on it," that is, working without saying or doing anything that might damage the reputation of an institution. You might be asked to keep up that silence in response to a complaint. Silence can then be about protection—protecting the reputation of the institution, protecting the reputation of colleagues, or self-protection, protecting your own reputation or your own resources or your relationship to the institution or to colleagues. I think of Lorde (1984, 41): "Your silence will not protect you." Your silence will not protect you, but it could protect them, those who are violent, or those who benefit in some way from silence about violence.

It is not only administrators or managers who make silence an instruction. In another instance, a student submitted what was described by a member of her department as a "Me Too letter." The letter contained information about abusive behavior from a highly respected member of the department. It also referenced a prior history of complaints against that member of the department. Colleagues were instructed by written communication as well as word of mouth not to talk about the letter. One lecturer wrote, "The department is essentially falling in formation behind [the professor], who claims that any discussion of the letter would be unhealthy for the department. So, no one speaks about it—or at least no one speaks to me about it." The professor who made the instruction not to discuss the letter as it would be "unhealthy for the department" was, in fact, a senior feminist academic. Many have relayed to me that feminist colleagues, often senior feminists, often senior white feminists, were among those who told them not to speak in public about cases of sexual harassment, in other words, who told them to "keep a lid on it."

It is also possible to "keep a lid on it" while appearing to speak, to open a conversation, or to offer a critique. A postgraduate student described how being critical was self-definitional for her department as long as critique pointed elsewhere: "We are a very critical department, but if those things are happening here, we can't talk about it; if they are happening elsewhere, burn the system down." Critique has a particular utility as a mode of damage limitation because it allows people to sustain an idea of themselves as being critical while being silent about "those things happening here." She added, "The closer to home it is, the less likely they are to take action." You can keep it up, keep the house up, while being critical; you can burn it down as long as it is somebody else's house. In one instance an event was organized by a feminist department that was about "dismantling" the cultures of sexual harassment. The draft program for the event included a list of proposed speakers. One was highlighted as a potential speaker because although she had "referenced" problems at the university, she had done so "not obviously." They did not want the problems at the university hosting the event to be made too obvious. You can reproduce structures at the very same time you appear to critique them.

5.2 Feminism in the academy (letters in the box).

When a critique is used as evidence that structures are not being reproduced, structures are being reproduced.

A house, a home, a building, a shelter: we can return to the image of the post box that has become a nest. When I think of feminism in institutions, I rather imagine feminists as the birds nesting. But when feminists keep complaints in house, treating the data contained by a complaint as a secret, as what must be kept secret, they have become not the birds nesting but the letters in the box.[26] Those who complain are positioned as trespassers, as disturbing a feminist environment. And complaints are treated not as straw, part of a feminist nest, but as messy matter.

Damage limitation can be about limiting the damage caused by a complaint to the reputation of institutions or colleagues. But damage limitation is not simply about uses of happy diversity, the production of shiny brochures, or the requirement to tell positive stories about universities and their commitments (chapter 1). Damage limitation can be performed in the same places where we do more critical work; it can even be performed through that work. Giving support to those who make complaints can also be done in such a way as to limit the damage caused by complaint. One student who made a complaint about sexual harassment commented, "The support was all being done discretely. I felt like that was the exact opposite of how it should be dealt with. It was like this secret little thing we have got to fix." Support too can keep complaints secret, can keep secrets. When support is given behind closed doors, support is given in the same place the harassment happened.[27]

Behind closed doors: this expression points to how those who complain end up contained. The term *damage control* is useful in accounting for the violence of containment. This term is typically used in emergency situations. A ship might be at risk of sinking perhaps as a result of the rupture of a pipe or hull below the water line. Damage control is used to stop the ship from going down by locking off the damaged area from the ship's other compartments. The containment of damage is necessary to stop the ship from sinking. The complainers are perhaps located *here*: in that damaged room, keeping the whole thing afloat by what they are expected to take in and take on. When doors are used to hold and to contain the complaint, they function to keep the whole thing afloat. If it takes a political movement to open these doors, it takes a political movement to survive the consequences.

CHAPTER SIX

HOLDING THE DOOR

POWER, PROMOTION, PROGRESSION

A master's student is talking to me about her experience of making a complaint about the conduct of a professor in her department. She had undertaken the MA with some hope that she might go on to do a PhD and become an academic. Toward the end of her testimony, she said of that prospect, "That door is closed."[1] By the time I spoke to this student I had collected fourteen testimonies. I had already noticed how often doors were coming up: actual doors, solid doors, doors with difficult-to-use handles. Once we notice something coming up, we tend to listen for it. It was because I was listening for doors that I heard the door in her expression. This expression is, of course, quite an ordinary expression. When paths are no longer available to us, doors become figures of speech: we say, "That door is closed." It is the idea of a door as the opening or closing of a path or possibility that I explore in this chapter. To open a door can refer to the opening of an actual door by one person so another person can enter. To open a door can also be used to indicate somebody has created an opportunity for somebody else. The word *opportunity* itself evokes doors deriving from *port*, implying a harbor but also a gateway or a way in. If doors need to be opened for some paths to be possible, doors are how we indicate barriers to progression.

An opportunity can be figured as a window. A window of opportunity is the time you have when you can do something, when something is possible. When that window closes, a possibility is no longer available. Windows, like doors, are passages; they can be opened and closed, although windows are not usually intended for the passage of persons. The word *window* comes from a combination of *wind* and *eye* and has been compared to the old Frisian word *andern*, literally meaning "breath-door," a window as a hole that allows the passage of air as well as light and sound. Windows enable the circulation of fresh air; a breath-door is how a room breathes, as well as how we can breathe more easily when we are inside a room. In chapter 5, I talked about how rooms can become stuffy because of how they are occupied by histories: history as becoming stuffy; history as stale air. To understand how rooms are occupied by history is to explain how rooms will be experienced differently by different people depending on their relation to that history. In the same room, some can breathe; others not. Windows and doors help us to think about how worlds are built to enable some to breathe more easily than others. They help us to think about who is given paths in the sense not only of routes through a difficult terrain, but also of possibilities that can be reached.

When we ask who "holds the door" to the institution, what, then, are we asking? In her conversation with Ruth Frankenberg, Lata Mani describes two different incidents of arriving at her university after hours. She is writing from the politics of her location: an Indian feminist working in the United States. In the first instance, a white man professor opens the door and refuses her entry: "He cannot let anyone in off the street, God knows what I might do" (Frankenberg and Mani 1993, 296). In the second instance, a Filipina woman cleaning the corridor opens the door: "She looks up at me, smiles, and without a word opens the door for me" (296). When race, gender, and class intersect, the effect is bumpy. In one moment, you are not allowed in because of how you are seen (off the street; you could be anyone). In another moment, you are allowed in because of how you are seen (a professor; you are someone). Same door; two different people holding the door. Depending on who encounters who, you are in or not in. But it is the professor who holds, as it were, the door to the institution, who decides who can reside there, who can be legitimately employed there, not the cleaner. When we consider who is "holding the door" to an institution, we might be thinking of how actual doors are used to stop some people from entering. We might also be thinking about power and legitimation: *who decides who resides.* In this chapter, I explore how power works through the literal and figurative senses of "holding the door," drawing on testimonies offered by people at different stages of their academic careers: postgraduate students, early career scholars, midcareer scholars, professors, and retired academics.

ENTRY DOORS

To become an academic requires going through many doors, as those of us who are, or have been, academics know very well. You get through one door and, hey, there is another. In this section I explore entry doors, the doors you have to go through before you become an academic or in order to become an academic.[2] Doors can feel like hurdles: what you have to get *over* to get *in*. You are marked, judged, evaluated; you have to pass examinations in order to have a passage into a profession. Marking systems are control systems: you are learning, acquiring knowledge and skills within a specified field, yes, but you are also assimilating rules for conduct, some of which are written down and some of which are not. (We often come to know unwritten rules by not getting them right.) You learn how to write, how to cite, who to cite, where to publish. You are given bearings, ways of navigating a field often represented as territory. You are being taught how to present yourself, how to speak, how to ask questions, who you should speak to. You are being given advice on what to do (and what not to do) in order to go further or faster in your career. To be given career advice is to be told not only where you can go but what you would need to do to increase your chances of getting there.

Think of how you are told to do something "because it would be good for your cv." We are encouraged to think of academic careers as having exteriority, as what you have to care for in order to have somewhere to go. A career is treated as a potentiality, a precarious, fragile thing. I think of an academic career and I think of a jug that could be easily shattered if it was left too close to the edge. The precarity of academic careers is far from a fiction: it can be very hard to establish yourself, to acquire a stable footing, and you know that however many people enter the academy, many more won't make it. Even if precarity is not a fiction, precarity can still be instrumentalized, used for specific ends, made into a reason to do something or not to do something.

I explored in chapter 2 how many are warned about the consequences of complaint. Warnings about complaint are not exceptional utterances but part of a cluster of speech acts we call "career advice," a set of instructions about what to do to maximize your chances of getting in. If you are encouraged to treat a career as a fragile thing, you might become hyperaware of what you need, who you need, to establish yourself. This hyperawareness can be internalized as *no* to complaint. A PhD student told me, "You can't complain against your supervisor, you can't be that PhD student if you lodged an official complaint against your supervisors. These are the people you are going to rely on. . . . As one academic said to me, your supervisor is not just for your PhD; it's for your life." If a supervisor is for your life, a complaint against a supervisor could be the end of that life, at least your academic life, your institutional life. A complaint can thus be framed in advance as *career suicide*, or what I have called *institutional death* (Ahmed 2019, 195): a complaint as how you would reach the end of the line.

This student did in fact make a complaint about her supervisor, but only after she decided to leave that program and that university: "The complaint was the last resort. And the complaint was the thing I could do because I knew I was going to withdraw. I wouldn't have been able to do it unless I knew I was going to leave. And even then, it screwed up my references; my CV has a big gap in it." Complaints leave traces by becoming gaps, empty spaces on a CV. An empty space can in fact be full of activity, but that activity cannot be listed without compromising your career. You cannot put "made a formal complaint" on your CV, although I wish you could because making a formal complaint requires so much institutional skill, knowledge, and dexterity.

Treating warnings about complaint as part of a cluster of speech acts called *career advice* helps to clarify what these instructions are doing. An MA student was considering whether to make a complaint about the conduct of the most senior member of the department. It was she who said, "That door is closed" in reference to doing a PhD. In part II of this book, I described some of the experiences she had that led her to consider making a complaint. She speaks to the convener of the program. The convener says to her, "Be careful. He is an important man." Be careful: a warning not to proceed is a statement about who is important. Importance is not just a judgment; *it is a direction.*

Warnings not to complain function as door stories: you are being warned that to make a complaint about "an important man" would be to close the door on your own career. Note how doors matter as futural objects; in order not to close a door, to keep a future open, you are told to avoid certain choices in the present. The warning "Be careful. He is an important man" could be heard as a promise: the student could benefit from "an important man" by withholding her complaint. The warning could also be heard as a threat: to complain about "an important man" would mean the door would be closed on her by him. In the same conversation, the lecturer says to the student, "If you don't like the way the master's is being taught, you could always leave." The student knew what she was being told: "I was being given an ultimatum: shut up and put up or leave." *Lump it or leave it* becomes the maxim; it can be made explicit because it was already implied. To indicate you are considering not shutting up, not putting up, is to be shown the back of the door.

The back of the door: we are back to the door. In the end, she did not make a formal complaint during the year in which she was undertaking her MA. She understood what she was being told: to make a complaint about "an important man" would not bode well for her own performance. Instead, during her MA she tries to put up with it: "What I ended up doing was shutting up and putting up. And for the rest of my master's, I just put my head down, put my tail between my legs, and avoided him as much as possible." To avoid complaint when you are in the thick of it, when you are in the situation the complaint is about (or would be about if you were to make it), means avoiding so much else; you might have to avoid being in certain kinds of spaces, especially informal spaces; you don't go to seminars or events in case he will be there; you end up, in effect, not being able to participate in the program. As she describes, "I felt like I couldn't access this course because he was teaching it." Harassment is an access issue.

It is important to add that she did not just receive a message about what not to do to do well by being warned. She herself had noticed that doing certain kinds of work meant doing less well: "Students who had written essays on race or gender didn't seem to get marks that were as high as students who had written on other topics." Marking systems are how power can be held: yes, no, do this, don't do that. For an MA student not to receive "marks that were as high" can mean not being able to progress to a PhD. If students who write on "race or gender" routinely do less well, there is a lessening of the likelihood that that kind of work will be able to take root or flourish within a discipline or field. If that work does not take root, it is harder to follow that route, especially if you are at the beginning of an academic career. Students are given a route to the extent they are willing to write on "other topics" that reflect back what has been taught: not race; not gender. Remember: harassment can be a *reflection* (chapter 5).

Instructions about what we have to do to do well tell us about value systems. What would you do if you did not share the values of those evaluating you? Would you go ahead and write an essay on gender or race if it meant you were likely to get marks that were less high? This dilemma of whether or not to be strategic will be familiar to many who do not share the values of their evaluators. I would locate the dilemma of complaint *here*. If you would be slowed down by working on categories such as gender and race—categories can be complaint holders or complaint folders—then to speed up might require not using those categories. Many students have described to me how they were directed away from doing certain kinds of projects, often by being told such projects would not get them very far.

You can be given such messages in the middle of a complaint. A postgraduate student was in a meeting with her head of department and other students about a collective complaint they had made about sexual harassment in their program. You have heard about this meeting already (chapter 2). She described how the head of department "started to conflate feminist research with complaining about sexual harassment" and how they "kept trying to separate it by saying, we are not really here to discuss whether feminist methodologies are valid or not; we are here to discuss acts of violence and sexual harassment." Being warned not to complain about harassment becomes very quickly a warning not to do certain kinds of research including feminist research: "She started saying that feminist, gay, Black theory was all old-fashioned. . . . If you do that you are never going to have a career." *Old-fashioned* does a lot of work as a judgment: that kind of theory, that kind of research becomes old, slow, tired, as if to say, if you do that, you will end up *behind*. If a career requires keeping up, then a career requires giving up that kind of theory. In chapter 2, I explored how the flip side of a warning is a promise that if you don't complain, you will go further. In chapter 4, I showed how those who try to stop a system from being reproduced are stopped. We can now bring these arguments together: *what you are told you need to do to progress further in a system reproduces that system.*

Those who do not reproduce the system risk not passing, let alone not progressing. I suggested in chapter 4 that some become complainers when they do not pass. To indicate that you want to write an essay on gender and race is sufficient to be heard as a complainer. It is worth pausing here to be more precise about what it means to be heard as a complainer, drawing upon what we have learned by following this figure thus far. If writing an essay about gender or race is heard as complaint, then writing an essay about gender and race is heard as moaning about minor matters (gender and race studies as grievance studies); as being malicious or destructive (decolonizing the curriculum as vandalism); as evidence that you are a stranger (that you do not belong here or that you are not from here); or as trying to manage other people's expression or to restrict their freedom (gender and race as the *imposition* of categories not only on fields but on others). Readers involved in the projects of gender studies and race studies will be familiar with these hearings.

We can return to the example of the MA student warned about "an important man." I have already noted that she decided not to proceed to a formal complaint while she was still enrolled in the MA program because she wanted to maximize her chances of doing well: "I was afraid that if I put in an official complaint at this stage, it was going to be extremely detrimental to the grading of my work. He wouldn't be able to be impartial about my work. I decided that after my master's, after the grades had come in, then I would make an official complaint, when the danger that it would negatively affect me would be removed." Her plan to avoid making a complaint during the year of her MA did not work, however, because she was already viewed as a complainer. Although she had asked for him not to mark her dissertation, he did. And the mark she received for her dissertation was much lower than the marks she received for any of her essays. Her subsequent formal complaint was made in part because he marked her dissertation; she had asked for this not to happen because she thought she would be penalized for writing about the wrong topics, for being the wrong kind of student. And that is what happened. She ended up making a complaint because of the consequences of being understood as having already made one.

Many who make complaints experience direct forms of retaliation. It can be hard to evidence such experience. Retaliation can be concrete (such as lower marks), but even then, to make that claim is often to be met with disbelief (he wouldn't do that; it couldn't be that). It can be difficult to establish a causal connection: that you received lower marks *because* you complained. But more often than not, retaliation can be about what you do not receive; retaliation can be about *missed opportunities*, doors that are not opened, what does not come your way. Opportunities can be what you miss in making a complaint. It can be hard to provide evidence of what is missing.[3] As this student put it, she "sacrificed the references." And that is when she said about the prospect of doing a PhD, "That door is closed." References can be doors: how some are stopped from progressing. That door is closed: she understood herself as having been stopped from getting into the academy (she did not have the marks; she did not have the references) as penalty for complaint.

It would be hard to point to a single action that closed that door. Did the closing of the door begin with her indicating she wanted to write her

6.1 References can be doors, how some are stopped from progressing. Photo: Kim Albright/ Phrenzee.

essays on gender and race, what he called "the wrong topics"? Did it begin by her questioning who was missing from the syllabus? Did it begin by sharing with the course leader that she had a problem with his teaching? These questions would locate the cause of the closed door in her action. And that *is* how so many closed doors are explained, as a result of what such-and-such person was not willing to do or not willing not to do. We need to explain the closed door differently. If these doors could talk, that is what they would be telling us: how power can be held even if it is not a possession as such, by whom power is held, power as yes or no, a door open, a door closed. Power is the power to determine who can proceed and who cannot, for whom a door is opened, for whom it is not.[4] Even when power is not what someone simply *has*, power can be acquired; doors teach us about the nature of this acquisition. It is not simply that the professor is holding the door, which he then closes on the student as penalty for complaint (although that is indeed an important part of the story). When the door is closed on her, the door is kept open for him. And the door is kept open for him by colleagues who are willing to close the door on her complaint, the kinds of doors I referred to in chapter 5, institutional doors that shut in what he is doing so he can keep doing it.

When we hear the statement "He is an important man," we might assume the speech act points to whom it is addressed. After all, as I noted in chapter 2, the point of warnings is to give the person who receives them time to change an intended course of action. But if the door is kept open for him to the extent that others are willing to shut the door on her, the point of the speech act might be in its delivery. Let's think more about the lecturer who delivered the warning. She was certainly *holding the door* for the student, not only in the sense that as program convener she could influence whether or not that student could proceed but also by giving instructions about what the student needed to do (or not to do) to get through. A door is always a scene of instruction. The lecturer is a relatively new and junior member of her department, far junior to the professor. She is a woman of color; he is a white man. For the door to be open to the lecturer, for her to proceed, she might need his support. The door she is holding for the student could be understood as the same door that she, as a junior lecturer, will need to get through. The warning she gives could thus be a warning she has received about what she would need to do in order to get through.

Thinking of the one who delivers the warning as receiving what she delivers helps to complicate the scene of "holding the door." It might be that for some to open the door to complaint would be to shut the door on their own careers. This possibility is often registered by other people as concern. A number of students talked about their concern that junior lecturers could be compromising their careers if they were to support student complaints about harassment by senior academics. A postgraduate student talked to me about the support she received from a junior woman academic: "I feel uncomfortable because women are asked to do the emotional labor of complaint so often."[5] She added, "I don't want to put her in an uncomfortable position that might affect her career on my behalf." Some complaints might be stalled out of concern that the people who are most likely to support them are the same people who would be most compromised by them.

We can return to the example of the MA student who received the warning "Be careful. He is an important man" from her program convener. She also talked to me about the support and solidarity she received from her supervisor (a junior member of staff on a temporary contract) when she told her about the abuse from the professor, a conversation they had on the stairs because they happened upon each other. But the supervisor then requested that they have a subsequent conversation on the phone so the student "wouldn't have a record of it in writing." "She sounded scared on the phone, and with the backtracking she did, my initial thought was, who has got to you, how has the discourse of solidarity which we had on the stairs when I revealed to you the abusive behavior changed?" The student had her own explanation of the change: "She was already in a precarious situation herself"; "she has a mortgage, two kids." Also note that precarity can make it harder not only to make a complaint but to support a complaint, especially if the complaint is about the conduct of permanent or senior members of staff. It is not only that complaints are caught up in the internal politics of departments, as I described in chapter 3. The path of a complaint might be the same path established by internal hierarchies; the line through is a line up (also down); doors are held open or closed depending on who needs who to get through. If you are lower down within an institutional hierarchy, you will need the support of those who are higher up to move up, which means there is so much that you cannot say or do without compromising your own trajectory. Of course, many of us know this, but knowing this is not sufficient to changing this.

When we are talking about power as *holding the door*, we are talking not only about how some are enabled and others impeded but also about how those who are enabled become indebted. Debts can be passed on, passed down. And doors can be deals: for the lecturer to keep the door open to her own progression, she might need to keep the door open for "an important man"; she might need to demonstrate her loyalty to him by *willing his importance*. In responding to the student's informal complaint, the lecturer also described the professor as "really well meaning. He's a really nice man," as if the student in making a complaint had misunderstood his intentions or as if it would not be nice to complain about somebody nice. We are back to how positive profiles can be used to defend someone, as a defense of a relationship or an investment (chapter 3). When doors are deals, debts become duties. Shutting the door on a complaint can be about demonstrating you are willing to protect him. The speech act "he is an important man" can be saying "I am willing to make him important" and thus be saying "I am willing to protect him." We are back to how backs become doors. You are supposed to *have the back* of someone who is *holding the door*: to have their backs, to back them up.

The acquisition of debt can be achieved through the creation of an implication. I talked to a lecturer informally about a case of sexual misconduct and sexual harassment by a "star professor" from his university; he too was "an important man." I was struck by one short statement the lecturer made: "He was everywhere." By this he meant: the professor seemed to have his hand in everything, to fill every pocket of the institution; every prize, every scholarship awarded, every distinction or achievement by a student or more junior colleague had his name on it. I think of another conversation with a student who had been harassed by her supervisor. She said that whenever she achieved something, he implied "it had something to do with him." He too implied he had a hand in all of her achievements. You can acquire power by virtue of an implication: you only need to imply you opened the door for someone for them to acquire a sense of debt and duty.

I think of narrow corridors. They can be what you have to go through to get somewhere, to reach an open door. A professor can become a narrow corridor: who you have to go through to get somewhere, who you have to go through to reach an open door. A going is often narrated as a gift. Those who abuse the power given to them by virtue of position often represent themselves as being able to open the door for others. When an open door becomes a gift, an open door can also be a threat. To be told

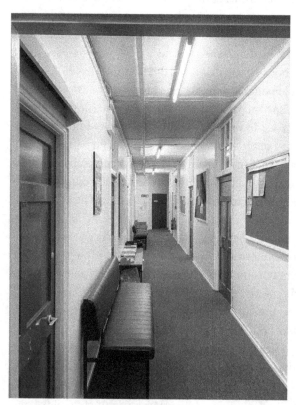

6.2 Who you have
to go through.

someone can open the door is to be told they can close the door if you do not do what they want you to do.[6] Power can thus work in positive and negative registers at the very same time: a yes when offered can be withdrawn; an opening is also the potential of a closing. You might be told that a positive reference from "an important man" will be worth a lot, that it will get you far; it might get you into an esteemed university. In a story of what a positive reference can do for you is lodged a more sinister story of what you might not be able to do without that reference.

We know that references *can be* used to stop people from progressing because they *have been* used to stop people from progressing. It might be that someone, as the MA student did, sacrifices the references. Or it might be that the reference written for you closes the door on you. A PhD student says, "There have been horror stories I have heard of people asking for letters for recommendation and people saying yes and then sending awful letters." It can be hard not to hear a warning in a horror story. It can be hard not to be concerned that what has happened to others could happen to you: "That's the other fear I have, is that someone will say yes and then won't write a good letter." A *yes* can be how a *no* is enacted while being withdrawn.

When references close doors on academic progression, that closure usually comes after other closures. In chapter 4, I gave an account of the experiences of a Muslim student of color who did not get the same number of classes to teach, nor the fellowships, that other students did. She is an international student; she is also a mother with child care responsibilities. Not getting the same classes, not getting the fellowships, meant not having enough to make do. When she makes a complaint about racial discrimination, the situation worsens, the mask of diversity slips. She decides to change programs. But she needs the support of the professors from the program to get into another program. She described what happened:

> When I decided to leave the program and transfer to another, many of my professors did not want to write me a reference letter. Only two of them agreed to write me letters. Shockingly, I discovered later when I got rejected by all the ten programs that I have applied to that the letters were not flattering at all. When I asked them to share the letters with me, one refused to share it and the other sent it to me. She wrote that I am "good at transcribing data," nothing at all about my research, awards, the paper I was working with her on, nor about the classes I took with her. It was a short and very weak letter.

A door can be shut by the refusal to provide a reference. A door can be shut by how you write a reference. A short and weak reference is another kind of no, a no performed as a weak yes. Power can work through what might seem like a light touch: all you need to do to close a door is to write a less positive reference. The content of that less positive reference matters. The reference says she is good at something; it says she is good at "transcribing data." We are back to how those who embody diversity become data, diversity workers as data collectors. In this becoming, so much is gone: gone the intellectual labor, gone the learning, gone the collaboration. Doors: how we explain what is gone, what has been erased or made to disappear. When a door is closed, there is an erasure of an erasure.

We need to remember that she had to make that complaint because of doors that had already been closed, because of opportunities she did not receive as a Muslim woman of color. Institutional passing might mean being willing to pass over doors. (We stop ourselves from talking about being stopped.) Sometimes you can't even afford to pass because not getting the same opportunities means not having enough to get by, let alone to get through. But then, when you complain about how doors are closed, more doors are closed. Note again: the actions that close doors are performed behind closed doors. So much of the data, including data about who is reduced to data, remains confidential unless somebody works very hard to get the information out. This means that: *the actions that close doors are not always perceptible to others.* A closed door might itself be imperceptible; it might seem that there is nothing stopping anyone from getting in or getting through. Or it might be that the effects of the actions are perceptible, but the actions are not: when someone has stopped, it can then seem as if they stopped themselves.

NOT BEING PROMOTED

You have to go through many doors to become an academic. These doors are the *same doors* used to stop complaints. Once you become an academic, there are certain points you reach in a forward progression. We call these points *promotion*. Each promotion is a door; it can feel very heavy; you have to work hard to open it. Sometimes no matter how hard you try, you cannot open it. You come to know that the door was not intended for you from the difficulty you have opening it. In this section I draw upon the testimonies of those who have made complaints about not getting a promotion.

The set of instructions called "career advice" do not cease to matter once you become an academic, even after you have secured a permanent position; these instructions continue to matter as a backdrop of warnings as well as promises. You have to work out what to do to give yourself the best chance of moving up the academic ladder. Perhaps we learn what these instructions are telling us when we fail them. A trans lecturer considered making a complaint after not getting a promotion and went to his union. He was told that "because [he] was trans [he] would never be promoted." This telling is another version of fatalism: an acceptance of the reality of discrimination being offered as a prediction that you will never progress. An effect is treated as the cause: "because I was trans." Think of the weight of that *because*, as if being discriminated against because of who you are is because of who you are. Being who you are can thus acquire the status of complaint (*being as complaint*): being trans as closing the door on yourself, putting yourself in harm's way. In his testimony, he described transitioning as moving between different zones of discrimination. Before he transitioned, he experienced the ordinary and routine sexism I have been describing throughout this book: "being pushed out and side-lined in terms of my career." He describes what it was like to witness colleagues who "make use of sexual jokes" only to be quickly promoted. In transitioning, he enters a different zone: "I started transitioning and he fired me." He suggests discrimination against trans people is "given a green light." A green light is a yes, how discrimination is enabled: yes, do that; yes, go there. A green light is opening the door to closing the door on him: yes, we can stop him.

Some have to put in a great deal of effort to stop being stopped, to stop them from stopping you. The effort to stop discrimination is part of how discrimination is discriminatory. He adds, "I appealed against the [denial of] promotion, and that led me to more work." As we learned in chapter 1, he ended up a diversity worker, writing a trans equality policy for his university because his complaint revealed their failure to have one. Complaints, as I have been showing, are slow and laborious. If you have to complain because you are not promoted, you are complaining about being slowed down or stopped, which means you are slowed down even more by having to challenge what slows you down. As ever, we learn from loops. So much inequality is enacted through or even as speed. Who progresses more quickly often depends on who conforms to an expectation of who will progress more quickly. When a door is opened for you, you do not even have to notice the door. This in itself might explain why complaint testimonies are so full of doors: you have to make a complaint because (or when) you are stopped from doing the work you want to do.[7]

Complaints teach us who has to do "more work" to get through and thus who is spared from having to do "more work" to get through. I have learned about what it means to be spared from doing "more work" from talking to those who are not spared. In *Living a Feminist Life* (2017, 125) I defined privilege as an energy-saving device. To be spared of the need to complain is to save energy. You don't have to complain about not getting promoted if you are promoted. When you have to complain you have to expend time and energy doing what others are saved from doing. One student described her complaint as "a real energy zapper." If you have to complain about not getting promoted, you are expending more time as well as energy challenging how you did not get further without getting any further. In fact, the time you have to spend appealing not getting a promotion can mean having less time to do the work that might speed up a promotion (less time for research, for example).

It is not only that not getting a promotion slows you down by the requirement to do more work, but that each time you are slowed down it affects what happens (or does not happen) subsequently. He gets a new post: "They used the fact that I hadn't been promoted to bring me in below." Slowing can be accumulative: the more you are slowed, the more you are slowed. Being slowed down can lead to getting stuck: if you don't get one thing, it can lead to not getting something else later on. As he says, "Things kept getting repeated."

A complaint biography can be about what gets repeated; it can be about what gets stuck or about getting stuck. A retired academic gave me her complaint biography in three chapters, each chapter corresponding to a different institution in which she worked. In her career, sexism and ableism intersected to slow her down. I want to give a sense of how complaint becomes part of a career trajectory by traveling with her, following the route she took in her testimony. The first part of her biography relates to her experience as a postdoctoral researcher. Her supervisor or mentor is beginning to make her feel uncomfortable:

I started to get the distinct impression he was becoming obsessed with me. He would come up to my office with some spurious thing he wanted to talk to me about, and he would sit there in my office for an hour and would start talking to me about all of his problems. I felt like I was being treated like his emotional handmaiden really. I was feeling a bit uncomfortable about the relationship, that maybe he saw it as not an entirely professional relationship.

I described in chapter 3 how many stories of harassment begin here, with a sense of something, an impression, sometimes distinct, an uncomfortable feeling. She senses that how he treated her, "like his emotional handmaiden," was not as it should be, that it was not "an entirely professional relationship." Her office became a place in which he deposited himself. So many stories of harassment of students by academics begin like this, with the needs of a professor, with him taking up time, your time, to discuss "all of his problems."

Discomfort can be wise. She knows she needs to get out of the situation. She did not consider making a complaint: "One of the issues for me early on in my career when I was in extremely insecure employment, basically I was a contract researcher for a number of years before getting a more secure job, was, I didn't complain. Things happened and I didn't complain and I felt pretty much at the mercy." Many do not complain as they do not feel they can afford to complain (although, as we have learned, many complain although they cannot afford to complain because they cannot afford not to complain). Harassment often happens in the way that it does because people can't afford to complain; they are "at the mercy." This is why those who abuse their power often pick out or pick on those who are more vulnerable or those whom they perceive to be more vulnerable.[8]

She knew enough to know it would be unsafe to stay in that position. Not being able to complain can lead people to leave (just as complaining can lead people to leave). If she was to have a chance of getting a new academic post, she would need a reference from him. In order not to close the door on her career, she did not explain to him (or anyone else) her reasons for leaving. Many do not complain because they cannot afford to "sacrifice the references," to borrow the words from the MA student discussed in the previous section. It is not just that a good reference will open the door. It is that in order not to stop yourself from having a chance of getting a good reference, you have to shut the door on complaint. She stops herself from disclosing her reasons for leaving so that she has somewhere to go. Because she needed to get out, because of the harassment, she did not feel able to negotiate a better salary in the new position: "They had me over a barrel in a way: they knew I really needed to change jobs, and I wondered whether they would offer a man the job on a lower scale than he was working at, but I didn't have much choice in the circumstances, so I took the job, but I was then advised to apply immediately for promotion, back on the scale I had been at previously." When you need to leave you are less able to negotiate a salary that is appropriate to your skills and experience. If harassment is why you need to leave, harassment can increase the chances you will not receive an offer appropriate to your skills and experience. Again: slowing down can be cumulative.

She accepts the new job at the lower level in part as they told her she could apply for a promotion straight away. A new job, one door, a new job, another door: "I did that. I had a very good application and was confident I would get the promotion." In order to get that promotion, she will need references. She asks her former supervisor: "I had asked him if he'd be a referee for me and he had said, he'd written back, whenever you need a referee, I would be happy to support you." But when she speaks to him later, he says, "You won't get it." She asks him why he said that. He replies, "I wrote a letter saying they shouldn't give it to you." It was for her a shocking experience: "I was really, to put it bluntly, gobsmacked. I didn't know what to say, I was so shocked. And obviously I was really, really upset. I fell down in the street three times on the way to the station. I was just shaking and I was in complete shock. I am sure people must have thought I was drunk or something." This part of the story might not seem to be a story about complaint or the consequences of complaint. She did not make a complaint; she left rather than making a complaint; she kept the door open by not disclosing to him the problems she had with how he was behaving. But leaving can be heard as complaint, saying no to somebody, withdrawing from them, not doing what they want you to do, not being what they want you to be, "an emotional handmaiden really." All she had to do to be penalized and punished was to leave, to make herself unavailable to him.

The attempt to stop her promotion—to offer to support her by writing a letter and then to use that letter to tell them not to give her a promotion—teaches us how harassment works. If you do not agree to it, if you are not willing to receive an advance, a door is shut on you, or there is an attempt to shut the door on you. A yes, "I would be happy to support you," can be how a no is enacted, how he can acquire the power to stop her. That *no* can be a retaliation for leaving. In this case, the effort to shut the door on her career failed. And it failed because the head of her department saw the letter before the meeting: "I thought it would be a shoo in, he said, but when I saw the letter, I thought, I have got to be at the meeting." She continues, "And he went and advocated on my behalf. He said, I have poached her from this institution and this is sour grapes." It took somebody else to name the action as "sour grapes" for the action not to work: "He managed to persuade the rest of the committee to ignore it." But think of this: how many letters are sent out that succeed in stopping people from progressing because of what people do not do; they do not turn up to meetings to advocate on behalf of others. She states: "I'd seen lots of things that I didn't like in higher education, particularly toward women, but that direct experience of somebody trying to obstruct my career in the most unfair way really took me aback." When you encounter an obstruction, a hand coming down, a lock on a door, trying to stop you, trying to shut you out, you learn what is possible, what injustices are possible, how a possibility can shape the institutions in part because of who is no longer here.

In her second institution, the second chapter of her biography, she relays to me another experience of not being promoted. She is invited again to submit her materials, this time for promotion to a full professorship. But during the process, the university works out a new algorithm, leading to the decision that only one person would be put forward for promotion even though a large number of people had been encouraged to apply. All that work on making her case led to nothing: "My application for promotion had been put in the bin." When your application is put in the bin, you can end up feeling binned. Of course, she wasn't the only one affected; everyone except for the one person who was put forward was denied promotion. She contacted other people "who were in a similar situation. . . . [But the head of department] refused to see us as a group but saw us individually." As I noted in chapter 1, procedures can be used to atomize, to individuate, and to separate. That atomization repeats what a complaint would have been about if they had been allowed to file one together: "So who did get put forward? And of course, it was a man far less qualified than any of the women who had applied." The justification for putting one individual forward is probably familiar to many feminist academics: "The head of department's argument was that he had very important contacts, very important contacts in the community. . . . In order to keep this guy, they had to give him the promotion because they didn't want to lose him."

They didn't want to lose him: a door is opened to him because of who he brings with him. The "very important man" has turned up again; we learn how his importance is predicated on his connections. The door opened for him is the same door that is closed on the others. A door can be closed because of who you do not bring with you. And when that door is closed on them, it does something. A closed door can be how you are told you are not valued or valued less, how they do not value you enough to want not to lose you: "That had a terrible effect on me. I became really depressed because I was so angry, and so disappointed and so anxious." We are back to the additional effects: being slowed, being stopped, becoming depressed.

But she does keep going; she tries again. This time, she does succeed. But then she receives another letter: "I got a letter from Human Resources that although the professoriate committee had awarded me the professorship, Human Resources weren't going to allow it to go through. They said because I had a mental health disability, I wasn't in a fit state to carry out the responsibilities of a professor." Such a letter is against the law, an explicit example of disability discrimination, but that does not stop the letter from being sent; it does not stop her having to deal with the consequences. She has to fight it or accept it: "I thought, fuck you lot, I am going to fight you over this because you are breaking the law." You have to fight for what is yours by right. So much injustice is enacted in the fight some have to receive what is theirs by right.

She does initiate a complaint process at this point; she has the "institutional conversations" I discussed in the first part of this book: "So I first went to my head of department and I said, look you are breaking the law. This is blatant, illegal discrimination. And he was like, there is nothing I can do; Human Resources have decided." Saying there is nothing he could do is of course doing something. Later a motion was passed "that the head of department should pass a letter on to Human Resources insisting the professorship be awarded, and he never did that." In the earlier chapter of her complaint biography, the letter sent by her former employer was an attempt to stop her from being promoted. Here not sending a letter was how she was stopped; the effects were as potentially devastating. A letter can be sent in an attempt to close a door. Not sending a letter can also close a door: different actions, similar effects.

Some people need to make much more of an effort to get through the same door as others; power is how we name this differentiation. An effort can be compromising: if it is more effort to get through, it can take too much out of you. When she did not get the support she needed, she became ill: "I was still off sick at the time, and planning to come back, and it made me ill again." The person who wrote an access-to-work report "said it was one of the worst cases she'd seen." She finds out that the person who wrote the report is phoned by the Human Resources Department asking them "to withdraw the access-to-work report on the basis it could be used against them in court as evidence." I commented at this point, "It could be used as evidence because it is evidence." An independent occupational health doctor wrote a letter to HR saying "it was complete rubbish" that she couldn't undertake the duties of a professor. It was a long, time-consuming, and draining process: "HR was hostile all the way. They were just digging in and sitting tight." In the end, after she indicated she would take them to an employment tribunal with the backing of her union, Human Resources backed down.

Even when you get through, the work you have to do to get through can destroy something: your relationships with colleagues, your relationship to a department, to a university; "You begin to lose trust in people when they are not prepared to back you up in that kind of way." She knows they value her work—she was, after all, awarded the professorship: "I know I was a really valued member of the department. I made a massive contribution to the research assessment exercise. I was very much one of the leading lights in Britain and internationally. I made a big contribution to their esteem factors." Being valued for what you bring, and being supported in what you do, can be quite different things. She came to understand the absence of support not just as an individual failing but as the culture of the institution. Not rocking the boat, not complaining, becomes how you avoid endangering yourself and your own career: "The interpretation I put on it was that they were all just too scared to oppose management in any way whatsoever, that they were not going to do anything that vaguely felt like them putting their own necks on the line."

She decides to look for another job: chapter 3. This time, she has more behind her, including more feminist knowledge. She knows women professors are paid less; she knows she needs to fight to make sure she is appointed at the scale appropriate to her expertise: "I knew the situation of female professors. I know they get paid a lot less than male professors, and that is often because they don't ask for enough money, so I asked for a big lot of money I knew I wouldn't get, and I got a very favorable salary." But being promoted, being paid well as a professor, does not mean you are treated well or even treated as a professor: "But from the very moment I started working there, I found I was up against a constant low-level exclusion and harassment by my male colleagues." She discovers that all major decisions were made by a small group of men, who met among themselves, writing those shadow policies, discussed in chapter 1, during shadow meetings: "So I started trying to have my lunch with them. I thought, I am going to break into the circle and try and fight my way in. But that didn't work. They would just get up and go [*both laugh*], which isn't surprising really. They didn't want a girl to come to the boys club, so they just held it somewhere else." You can't break in. Tables can be doors: you join their table and they use your entry to exit. Perhaps they exit through the back door; a "back door" used in this way refers to how decisions are made by being kept secret.

There are so many doors in these stories. One of the senior man professors finds out about her salary: "He's going knocking on everyone's doors asking how much you earn because he found out what my salary was and it was more than his, substantially more than his, and he'd gone berserk about it and was actually knocking on people's doors saying, do you know that the two highest paid people in this school are both women? He was outraged by this and expected other people to be outraged by it." I think of that door story, how it follows from other door stories; if we have to force our way in, to break in to get in, they force that door open, the same door. The outrage that women colleagues could earn more, more than men, more than he does, more than most do, leads to doors being knocked on, doors being wrenched open; her salary becoming news—Did you know? Did you hear?—an expectation that the outrage would be shared, that this is not how it should be.

When a hierarchy is not reproduced, it causes disturbance. Not being promoted is not then simply a story about who is enabled and who is not. It is a story about the institution. It is a story about how hard some have to fight each step of the way. In chapter 1, I referred to an Indigenous academic who had to shout in an email, "THIS IS A GRIEVANCE! THIS IS A GRIEVANCE!" Her testimony offers an extraordinary account of how the violence of the university as a settler colonial institution, the struggle to be promoted, can be a struggle against white supremacy. She talked of the kind of work she was given—service work, committees, diversity work—and the kind of work she was not given: "I was being downloaded with all this academic service work. What is going on? This seems really oppressive to me, there is no way I am getting the research done, I am so overloaded with responsibilities and committees and heavy service work on top of my teaching." I noted earlier that much inequality is enacted as speed: some are slowed down because of what they are asked to do, and what they are asked to do is partly about who they are assumed to be. As an Indigenous woman, a racialized Brown woman, she has had to battle for everything, but especially for time, for the time she would need to do the kind of work that would enable her to be promoted.

To battle for time is often to battle perception: how they perceive you, what stories are told about you. She said, "My head is creating a narrative in my department that is based on stereotypes of the Native, that I was irresponsible, that I was using them and not contributing. It was a false narrative and I had documentation." To challenge these false narratives takes time: having evidence, collecting evidence. Her word to describe the institution was *brutal*. And to battle what is brutal is to risk becoming more brutalized.[9] As I noted in chapter 4, a formal complaint can be understood as part of an institutional battle. We might have to battle to change the institution so it is more accommodating. We might have to battle to get through the institution, those doors we call promotion. *These can be the same battles*: for some to get through a system requires changing the system.

The grievance or formal complaint she made related to what happened when she applied for promotion. Let me share more details about what happened. She had submitted her curriculum vitae for her academic review: "I received a phone call after the file went to the standing committee that there was a huge emergency with my cv. The chair had a meeting with me. The cv was not the cv I submitted. The cv had huge blank spaces; it was like someone had used a return tab; *it was completely sabotaged*. This was not what I turned in." The word *sabotage* means "to destroy something deliberately," often with the intention of obstructing someone. Sabotage has come up a number of times in my data; the person who makes a complaint knows what has been removed; they have evidence of that removal, blank spaces in a document as traces of something. It could have been possible that she was not alerted to the problem, that it was not treated as an emergency that needed to be dealt with. And then she would have assumed she had been assessed on what she submitted. This is why hands do not always appear in these accounts; so many acts of obstruction happen behind closed doors.

And she was indeed told she was lucky to have the chance to resubmit the cv. She had a meeting with the chair of the standing committee:

> Don't say another word, don't talk, you should be lucky they are allowing you to submit another copy. He sat there for thirty minutes and degraded me, and yelled at me. Anything you say I will report it and I will say you are being resistant. He sabotaged three Indigenous faculty members. One lost his tenure. Another did not get tenure; they forced him on the teaching line. He said, do this and it will be okay. So I did it. I didn't ask any questions after that. I was demoralized and frightened and terrified that this would continually be the narrative, that I was ill-fitted for a tenure position, that I was incompetent. It went forward. The letter that came back from the dean and president was that the evidence was there of my record, but there was a problem with my cv and if I didn't resolve it by the next review that

would be it. That was when I began having severe mental and emotional collapses. I was very angry about what happened, but I was still not able to talk about what happened. A colleague looked at my cv and she said, you have got to be kidding me, you submitted this, it's a joke, the template he gave me; this is laughable, this will never make it for the senior committee, never, we are going to rewrite it. She became my mentor.

I have noted how harassment happens behind closed doors. We can hear that here: she had a meeting in which she was yelled at, degraded, by a person with institutional authority. And he then gave her a template which she followed, a template that meant the cv she submitted would not meet the requirements. Even though her record was there, the cv could lead to the judgment that she was "ill-fitted for a tenure position." You can direct people along a path that leads to a locked door. When you have to battle the institution, you notice the patterns (the repetition of what we come up against). She had seen the same person, a senior white man, doing the same thing to other Indigenous faculty; she knew what he was trying to do, why he was trying to do it.

Sometimes hierarchy can be habit, creating a pattern; the same people end up being promoted without any additional work or effort on their part. At other times, hands come up to stop something from happening that would deviate from that pattern, to stop a promotion that would be registered as unseemly, a cause of outrage, a disturbance in the right order of things: right, white, the white order as an order of things, a colonial order. A fight to be promoted can be a fight against history; a white settler colonial history occupies the university as well as the land.

THE DIVERSITY DOOR

Experiences of not being promoted are hard to untangle from experiences of harassment. Harassment does not simply take place behind doors. Harassment takes place *around* doors because doors can be opened or closed at each point of a progression. Some are harassed when they go for promotion because in going for promotion they are deemed to be getting above themselves.

We can return to Lata Mani's description of not being allowed into the university building by a white male professor; he says "she could be anyone." We have learned there is so much more at stake in "holding the door" than who lets who in. The white man does not just hold the door to the building; he holds to the door to the profession. The door used to stop someone from entering the building can be the same door that stops someone from being promoted. A category can have doors: we have to open a door to become a professor.

We have already heard how that opening can be a battle. When women of color become professors, what then? Doors still come up. Heidi Mirza (2017, 43) describes a conversation she had at the drinks after her inaugural lecture as professor: "A white male professor leaned in to me at the celebration drinks and whispered bitterly in my ear, 'Well they are giving Chairs to anyone for anything these days.'" This "anyone" is an echo. A white male professor does not let a Brown woman in because she could be anyone. A white man professor tells a Brown woman professor that if she can be a professor, anyone can. A professor can be a building; some of us are not supposed to get in; some of us are not supposed to become one. This is how becoming a professor is a story of getting in. I think of his use of the verb *giving* ("they are giving"). Diversity is often imagined as a gift, as what we have been given, not what we have earned. And indeed, when diversity is imagined as a gift, what we have loses value: if she can be a professor, anyone can.

Diversity is often figured as an open door; perhaps that door becomes a gift: come in, come in! We are back to that nonperformative: Birds welcome! A welcome is often in a tag line: we are an equal opportunity employer; minorities welcome; underrepresented groups encouraged to apply. To reword my argument from chapter 4, a door can be closed by how a space is occupied. If that is the case, then doors can be closed by appearing to be open. Another woman of color described her department as a revolving door: women and minorities enter; perhaps they are even encouraged to enter—come in, come in—only to head right out again: whoosh, whoosh. You can be kept out by what you find out. Getting in can be how you are shown the way out.

The open door of diversity is doing something. One university transformed the "open door" into a project of attaching photographs of Black and minority ethnic staff and students to door panels across the campus. Black and minority ethnic students and staff are pictured not even as going through the door but as being on the door. An open door can be used to indicate a commitment, becoming another kind of window dressing, or perhaps we can be more literal; an open door as *door dressing*. The video accompanying the project shows the vice chancellor opening the door with a Black face on it. When you dress the door, you are not addressed by the door. The white man is again holding the door.

6.3 Diversity: how you are
shown the way out.

Perhaps when diversity is imagined as an open door, diversity becomes a door, a different way of entering the same building. The diversity
door might be a back door; to enter that door is how you are assumed to
have been given special accommodation. You might be assumed to enter
that door because you were not good enough to enter the front door. This
assumption has utility, allowing those who enter through the front door
to imagine they do so because of their own merit. The front door of a
university might as well have a sign on it: "Merit!" Doors teach us whose
entry is deemed legitimate; those who are assumed to arrive because of
their own merit arrive without debt.

However people of color arrive, we are assumed to have gone through
the diversity door. When you are assumed to have gone through the diversity door, your arrival is framed as debt. Diversity is another kind of
door deal: that door can be shut if you do not repay a debt. A debt, I suggested earlier, requires a certain kind of attitude, well captured by a disabled student as "groveling gratefulness." A debt can also be experienced
as a duty. We can recall the words, shared in chapter 4, of the postdoctoral
researcher who had been hired as part of a diversity program: "I don't

want to do something that is going to threaten a program that is supposed to diversify the faculty." We can hear what is closed by the diversity door. You can end up having to close the door on a complaint because of how you are made responsible for keeping that door open to others.

In creating an impression of an opening, an open space, hospitable, warm even, the diversity door shuts out evidence of who is shut out. We can return to the experiences of the Indigenous woman academic discussed in the previous section. She worked at a university with strong commitments to diversity. She is an Indigenous scholar working in an Indigenous studies program. Surely there is no question of her right to be there? Her testimony reveals how she has to fight at every point to be there. The doors shut on her promotion were the same doors that were shut in her department: doors of meeting rooms, common rooms, offices. She is constantly questioned by senior faculty: "My tone of voice, my mannerisms were constantly being called into question by senior faculty." She pointed in particular to "three white women who were anthropologists, who were from an older generation, and all of them British, who had parents or grandparents who migrated from Britain." These women are her colleagues; they did not treat her as a colleague. Perhaps these women are used to studying the Natives. Perhaps they are not used to having colleagues who are Native.

One of these women is the chair of the department. It is she who uses the word *inappropriate*, a word that gets under her skin, as I described in my introduction to this book. Let me share her words again: "My chair constantly uses this word, in many things that she speaks about but in particular my annual review and other meetings, she uses this word often, *inappropriate*, her qualifier, at my interactions. It causes me to put this big lens upon myself, how I am *inappropriate*, what does that mean, what does she see, how is that being defined?" How does it feel, what does it do, to be deemed inappropriate? Your own body, how you speak, how you hold yourself, how you are yourself, becomes a problem to be managed. If their eyes land on you, their eyes become a "big lens" you put on yourself. When you keep being questioned, you end up questioning yourself. She thought perhaps she spoke too loudly: "I think my voice was a little louder. Well, I had been covering up for years that I have severe hearing loss when I was a child and I couldn't get access to key resources in the States as a Native." Being hard of hearing, having to fight for what she needed as a Native woman, was how she acquired her voice. Her voice becomes wrong, too much. She explains how her experiences as a graduate student meant being used to taking up space: "I came from a department where the graduate students were all the middle, where we had an office in the center of the professors, all women of color, all diverse, proudly feminist. . . . We were very strong, and they speak to each other across the hallway; there were expletives coming out of our mouths all the time. These were strong anchors; that is where I came from, it was something I was used to." To take up space like that, to speak like that, to be comfortable, at home, like that, is to be inappropriate, too much, too strong, too anchored. If you embody diversity, you are supposed to do so quietly: do so, be so, at the edge of the room, not in the middle of the room; you are supposed to slip and slide over the ground, not claim space, not be rooted. For some to be is to be too much; perhaps you are not supposed to be there at all, or if you are supposed to be there you are supposed to keep quiet, not to question what is being done.

Doors can be shut through perception: who you are perceived as being, how you are perceived as being. You can be shut out by being registered as an intrusion, sensory or otherwise. If the diversity door appears open, the diversity door is how so much does not appear. One time, she questions how a funding decision was made. The response is extreme:

> Okay, I get it, we are talking about money and race, and how dare I, how dare I step up, how dare I be a voice, how dare I question how things are in the department, and how I dare I influence these white men. I realized this is what [was] engendering all of this aggression from these white women who were bullying me, harassing me: I am disrupting the system they have put in place; I am not being a passive Native woman.

Money and race: so often how resources are allocated is about race, race shapes who gets to do what, who gets what (and who does not). A hierarchy can be enacted in how people are expected to inhabit a space. That hierarchy has a history; a colonial history can be inherited as stereotype; she is not being what she is supposed to be, "a passive Native woman." When a hierarchy is challenged by virtue of who inhabits space, how they inhabit space, harassment follows.

The diversity door is shut when those who embody diversity question an allocation. The diversity door is shut in order to protect resources. This should not be surprising given what we have already learned: *holding the door* is about who you have to go through in order to get information, energy, and resources.[10] The *door holders* are often called *gatekeepers*. Sometimes diversity appears as a door behind which there is a room rich with resources. Consider how often projects and programs are funded under the rubric of diversity. In chapter 4, I described how a woman of color is shut out of a project we could call "diversity related." She is named in the funding application. She is a well-known and well-respected scholar in her field. Including her name gave the project a much better chance of getting funded. But when they get the funding, she is shut out: "And that is painful actually; it is unbelievably painful for me. I think that is the one thing that made me want to burn the house down out of rage." Houses are resources; they are in need of resources. A scholar who has the knowledge, knows the theory, provides the color, can be useful. It is how she is used and discarded that keeps the house standing. The project directors opened the diversity door to get the money only to shut that door when they got the money. One of the directors is not just a senior white woman; she is a descendant of colonizers: "She is high-colonial British Raj. . . . Her grandmother's gravestone is in Calcutta, and that's rare, you have to be really high up in the British Raj." I will return to the grandmother's gravestone in chapter 8. We can summarize what we have found. We can generalize that funding. *The colonizer wins the diversity award.*[11] It is not surprising she wants to burn the house down. Diversity can be how you are colonized again; what you have, what you are, is taken from you. The colonizers do not enter the diversity door. They hold the door, which is how they can open it long enough to access the knowledge (also being) of those who enter only to shut it again.

To enter the diversity door can be how you are shut out from the allocation of resources. Or perhaps we can simplify: to enter the diversity door can be how you are shut out. I am speaking to an academic; she is a biracial disabled queer woman. She calls herself "the poster diversity girl. I ticked all the boxes." I referred in chapter 1 to how she was shocked by what she encountered when she was hired by her institution: the sexism, the racism, the ableism that made her university a hostile environment. She realizes how the management has remained so white: because many academics including Indigenous academics have "disappeared." We are back to diversity as a revolving door, a story of how people get out because of what they find out when they get in. She added, "The people who disappeared were those who didn't toe the party line." The diversity door can be a disciplinary door, how you are made even more subject to norms and conventions because you are deemed not to be a subject in the same way. She does not toe the line: she notices what she is supposed to overlook; she talks about what she notices, "the corruption," the "nepotism." A "hostile complaint" is made against her, leading to a disciplinary process. As I noted in chapter 4, a complainer is often a magnet: if you complain about a hostile environment, that complaint is quickly directed back at you. When the environment is hostile, complaints can be hostile.

Many have said this to me: you can tell when your management is out to get you because they start looking for something to justify a decision that has already been made. She said, "They couldn't get me on substantive issues. . . . They couldn't get me on the policy stuff." So they conducted a financial audit and trail through all of her files. They found what they were looking for: "irregularities." And they could find those "irregularities" because of the culture of the institution: "There was an illusion that we were all friends, we are all pals. Let's not follow the official processes. There were no official commissions—if you applied for access to funds— that was all done verbally. It all sounded really good. The idea is that we didn't need to be managed; it was collectivist. Little did I know that was going to come back and bite me." That informal culture, the suspension of procedures, not leaving a paper trail, can appear friendly, as if we are all in it together. But if we are not all in it together, and we are not all in it together, the lack of formal procedure can be how they get you. You don't have to destroy paper: you can eliminate evidence of an agreement by not putting it on paper, paper she could have pointed to that would have supported her case (although, as we have learned, having evidence does not guarantee success; evidence can be blanked because it exists). They go through her files; she ends up under more and more scrutiny: "Every part of your life is trailed through."

And that that happened *to her* silences others: "People were thinking, my god, if it could happen to her." Of course, when they look at you, they don't have to look at themselves: "They didn't want to look at corruption. They didn't want to look at the white men who had years of corrupt practices, financially corrupt, corrupt in terms of sexual politics, nepotism, all these kinds of issues. It was a total closing of ranks: they didn't want to look at these kinds of issues at all. I knew I was being hung out to dry." Diversity: if you don't toe the line, you reach the end of the line. She leaves her job; her home is dispossessed; her relationship ends. She stated, "You can go from an associate dean and then in ten months to using food banks." When we are talking about the diversity door being shut, we can be talking about not having the means to live, to get by, to make do; we are talking about institutional violence, social violence, economic violence.

When you enter the diversity door, when you are deemed dependent on that door being opened, that door can be shut at any point. Doors can be shut to stop you getting in. Doors can be shut because you get in. A

Black woman academic is racially harassed and bullied by a white woman who is her head of department: "I had put down that I would like to work toward becoming a professor, and she just laughed in my face."[12] That laughter can be the sound of another door being slammed. Some of us in becoming professors become trespassers; you are being told you need permission to enter by being told you do not have permission.

I suggested earlier that perceptions can be doors: how you are perceived as being as how you are stopped from progressing. This is not to say that we are always stopped; you have to work harder to get through the doors of perception. Even announcing an expectation that you might become a professor is met with incredulity. Consider too that that laugher takes place behind closed doors. Closed doors can stop us from learning about closed doors. I think of the diversity door: nod, nod, yes, yes; *slam*. You notice the doors when they are slammed in your face. And noticing doors is also about explaining what is going on: "I think what she wanted to do was to maintain her position as the director, and I was supposed to be some pleb. You know what I mean: she had to be the boss, and I had to be the servant type of thing. That was how her particular version of white

6.4 Some of us in becoming professors become trespassers. Photo: Kim Albright/Phrenzee.

supremacy worked, so not just belittling my academic credentials and academic capabilities but also belittling me in front of the students, belittling me in front of administrators." How do you know it's about race? That's a question we often get asked. Racism is how we know it's about race; that wall, whiteness, or let's call it what it is, as she has, white supremacy, we come to know intimately as it is what keeps coming up. To have got there—a Black woman in a white institution, a lecturer, a senior lecturer, on her way to becoming a professor, she is now a professor—is to be understood as getting above your station, above yourself, ahead of yourself.

To belittle someone, to make them little, functions as a command: Be little! And that command is being sent not only to her but to those who are deemed to share the status of being subordinate: students, administrators. Racial harassment can be the effort to restore a hierarchy: how you are being told you are not where you should be, you are above where you should be, or even you are where *I* should be, you have taken *my* place. Indeed, the bullying and harassment are not only performed in front of students; they are directed at her students: "It even extended to doing really bad things like making sure one of my PhD students who was an Asian student failed at her first go at her upgrade. To spite me, that was really what it was about. The student suffered and I suffered, but I got her through it." You can bully someone by bullying their students. You can target a person by targeting those attached to that person who are more vulnerable, easier to target, to stop, to fail.

If we think of harassment as a means of slowing people down, we learn more about how academic houses are built. She shares another experience with me:

[She] told me I was going to be sharing my room with this white man. I had never met him. There was plenty of room in the building. Even the PhD students were saying, there is a PhD room here, we never use it, you can have that. And there was also a fellow's room which was never used at all right next door. She could have put him in there. I wrote back saying, I don't think it's appropriate for him to share with me; I have never met him. One day I went to work, and went downstairs to make a drink, and came back and there was a white man sitting at my desk in my chair. I have to say it in that way. It was like Goldilocks. I had never met him, didn't know who he was. I walked in the room and he looked at me as if to say, who are you, and then he proceeded to say, who are you, to the person whose room this is, who

are you, and then to cap it off, his female companion was already looking at my books, reading through them. I never invited them in. I said,
all right, it's you; let me get you a key for the fellow's room you can go
there. That very day she wrote to me: I said he can go in there. I said, I
have no wish to share with him and it's unnecessary. I do not like the
way he approached me when I came into the room, as if I was a cleaner
or somebody who should not be there at all.

You turn up, you become a stranger in your own office, you find a white
man seated in your chair; you are asked, "Who are you?" Perhaps you
are assumed to be a cleaner, there to clean their room. You turn up, you
enter your own office, and they are looking at your books, a man and his
companion, your books, reading through them. There are other rooms he
could have used; there are other rooms available to use. A Black woman
becomes a stranger, a body out of place, in her office, in the office where
she does her work. The white woman, her head of department, is telling her something: that she is the one who is holding the door; that she
decides who resides, who will be let in, who will get in. We are back to
harassment as entitlement, the right to use or to have something as the
right to house or unhouse somebody.

If diversity is a door deal, the door is opened if you are willing to be
compliant. *Compliant* and *complaint* share the same letters. A woman of
color student wrote to me, "A few times writing this, I mixed up typing
complaint with compliant and I have been reflecting on that productive
accident." A productive accident, letters that swap places, can be how a
door is closed. I think the open door might be exchanged not only for
compliance but alliance. Her supervisor is a star professor. She is also
a woman of color. This student admires her supervisor; she wanted to
work with her, to learn from her: "Her readings, critiques, analyses of
power structures, interlocking systems of oppression, race and gender,
whether aimed at literature, popular culture, or injustice in America and
internationally, were elegant, bristling, derisive, biting in their precision,
unflinching and loud."

What you critique you can still enact. Within the seminar room, her
office, the woman of color professor seems to target for abuse women
of a similar "ethnoracial background" as herself: "Her abuse took the
form of attacks on my still-forming or imperfectly articulated thoughts,
analyses, and ideas in class when other students were encouraged and
helped along, and so there was unevenly applied criticism, inconsistent,
unclear, and conflicting feedback on my writing, where she told me I had

some sort of blockage or problem that was getting in the way of being an articulate thinker and coherent writer." She does not open the door for her student, another woman of color, but shuts it on her, belittling her, criticizing her, making her feel smaller, wrong. In contrast, she praises and elevates two white students in the class: "They were the stars and darlings of the department, well-awarded, published, and conferenced, and didn't share my experiences at all, and they more or less minimized her behavior." Those who benefit from relationships with abusive people often minimize the abuse to keep the benefits (chapter 3). Could this be another diversity deal: women of color can become professors, even star professors, singled out, by identifying with the master, becoming like him, loving who he would love, targeting who he would target? Diversity as a door deal: doors might be opened to some of us as long as we are willing to shut that door right behind us. The door might be shut on those who are not willing to shut the door on others.

There are many ways the diversity door can be shut. The door can be shut to stop us becoming professors. The door can be shut so only some of us become professors. The door can be shut because some of us become professors. I am speaking to a Black woman. She had been a professor; she had been a dean. I use the past tense because she is no longer a professor, nor a dean; she was dismissed from her post. The stories we share of becoming professors need to be supplemented by stories of unbecoming professors. The case began as an administrative dispute (chapter 1). Because of her concern with procedure, because she has evidence that they did not follow their own procedures, she took the case to judicial review. She is dismissed from her post for misconduct, which was described as "disgraceful and scandalous" (these words are used in her university's charter and statutes),[13] in part because she took the case to the courts: "The scandal was that you have brought it into the public domain"; "what they are saying is you've created a scandal."[14] She also notes that there was a clause in her contract that said "you cannot bring the university into disrepute." Creating a scandal is framed as damage to the reputation of her institution. Because they could not use taking the case to the courts as evidence of bringing the university into disrepute, they have to find evidence elsewhere. They use the fact that students had complained about their examination results as evidence that she had disclosed information to students.[15] She was told she had not used internal processes. And she realized that that was what this was about: "Keep it internal means do as you are told, keep quiet, keep it very internal." In house, the master's house; to keep information inside is how the house can appear in order from the outside.

She does not back down. If you don't back down, walls come up. Even when complaints are not about sexism and racism, sexism and racism come up in what comes down. She explained, "Race and gender are always in there. I thought, this has never happened before. The first time it happens is when you have a Black woman dean." Race and gender: they are always in there, in the situations we find ourselves in, those of us who are not white, not men. You can be caught out at any point, however well you do, however far you get; remember, if you have to be "whiter than white," you have already failed to have what you are assumed to need (chapter 4). If you are not compliant, if you are defiant, they will do what they can to stop you. A slamming of the door can be lived as a perpetual threat and thus even become a state of existence. No matter how far you go, how well you do, that door can be slammed.

CONCLUSION: DISTANCE FROM COMPLAINT

From complaints about power, we learn about power. We learn what it means for some to be *holding the door* to the institution, to the profession, to categories of personhood. The human, for instance, is a history of doors. (So many have been shut out of the human.) I suggested earlier that doors can be deals. A door can be opened in return for silence. Moving up within the institution, advancing your own career, might require being silent about certain problems *as* institutional problems; moving up might depend upon keeping your distance from complaint and from the complainer. A woman of color who experienced racism, sexism, and harassment in her department talked to me about how she was "not supported" by a senior white feminist professor who was head of another department. She had hoped for help in finding a route out of a situation—she had hoped she could change departments. But the white feminist professor does not open the door; instead she said there was no room in her department: "She told me it was too difficult to move departments and that they couldn't even consider it. And then a year after I left, twelve people moved into her department." Doors can be used to harass and bully someone, to tell them the office is not theirs, the university is not theirs, that they can be lodged or dislodged at will. The same door can be used not to give room to someone who has been bullied and harassed. When the white woman does not open the door, she is using the door in the same way others have used it before.

Not supporting someone can be enough to stop someone. The woman of color left not only her department but the university: "It's easy to be radical on paper, but in reality, it's quite different. Her politics were to do with advancing her career and nothing to do with changing the landscape for women." Those who seek support in making complaints often know all about paper feminists—those who are feminist on paper but not in practice. We might call this *white liberal feminism*: when career advancement for individual women is dependent on the extent to which they show they are willing not to address institutional problems. *Silence as promotion*.

I have suggested that complaints can be sticky data; if you get associated with a complaint, it can stick (chapter 1). I then qualified my argument by suggesting it is the complainer who is sticky; not everyone who makes a complaint has the negative data of a complaint stick to them (chapter 4). I communicated informally with a woman of color academic who told me she had given her support to a white feminist colleague who had made an informal complaint about plagiarism by a senior white man. She wrote, "She decided that she cannot speak publicly about the theft of her work by him. Her openness about it previously has apparently hurt his career. She fears it is hurting hers as she still needs him to be a reference for future jobs. So, a complaint made public now becomes detached from one person—literally let go, and now it is still attached to a few others but mainly me." Her white woman colleague lets the complaint go in order to keep the door open for her own career. She understood that to speak about his theft of her work openly would be to hurt his career. If his career was hurt, hers would be too because she needs a reference from him. Yes, references can be doors. But the complaint does not go away or disappear from the public realm; it becomes stuck to her, a woman of color, who gave her support. If some people can free themselves of their own complaints, others remain stuck with them. We can even get stuck by other people's complaints.

White liberal feminism can also be this: how a white woman's career advancement is made dependent on keeping her distance from complaints and complainers. It should not be surprising that a consideration of "holding the door" ended with the problem of white liberal feminism. But white liberal feminism is not our only problem. It might be that as somebody who embodies diversity, who adds color to white institutions, you can move faster and further if you accept a door deal, if you avoid making complaints whether by using complaints procedures or what I called earlier complaint holders, or complaints folders—those words, terms, categories that make sense of what we come up against. Diversity as a door deal: you might have a door opened for you on condition you shut that door quickly behind you, if you shut the door on others like you. And *shut that door* can mean not only doing what you can to stop others from getting in but also stopping thinking of yourself as one of the others. To accept that deal is to enact distance not only from those who complain, those who refuse not to use words like *racism* or *white supremacy*, but from our own complaints, our own experiences of racism, the unresolved trauma of colonization; it is to separate ourselves from our own truths. We know some of us accept this invitation. We know why; we know how. I have shared one such story in this chapter; I know of many others. And we also know that even if you accept that deal, even if you benefit from that acceptance, even if doors are opened to you because of what you are willing to do, or willing not to do, you can still be shut out.

Holding the door is always a social as well as an institutional achievement. Those who complain, who dare to complain, become, in the words of the professor whose testimony I shared earlier, "dead wood." I shared her story, but I did not share how her story ends, at least the story of her complaint, an institutional story. She describes how, in her last post, she is bullied by a dean. When she goes to her union to talk to them about it, they tell her that hers is the sixth case of "people who had felt and had been bullied by the dean." They prepare a case: "They wrote to HR and I wrote a very long letter of grievance, and basically HR came straight back and offered me a payout with no questions asked." She has had enough by this point; a complaint biography can be a story of reaching the point of having had enough. She takes the payout; she gets out. She said, "You are just a disposable number. There is plenty more where you come from. That's a very blatant attitude, that you are just raw material and there's plenty more raw material out there, basically, and if you don't want to do it, there are plenty of people out there gagging for a job in higher education. The sort of people they drive out they just characterize as dead wood." We both laughed at the image of dead wood. I said, "Dead wood: you can drift away and the further away you drift the better." She said, "And then you get washed up." I said, "Somewhere else, on someone else's shore." Becoming dead wood: how a complainer ends up further away; another shore; another door.

A door system is a sorting system; you sort people out by shutting some people out. Closing the door is not only about who stays, who gets to stay or who is allowed to stay, and who leaves. It is about stopping certain kinds of stances, ways of questioning, forms of opposition, yes complaints, from flourishing, from acquiring roots as well as routes. In chapter 8 I will turn to how complaints become an alternative communication system. Paths that have become faint from not being used do not necessarily disappear; perhaps they only appear to disappear.

PART IV

CONCLUSIONS

If it can be difficult to know how to start the story of a complaint because it is difficult to know when a complaint starts, it can be difficult to know how to end that story because it is difficult to know when a complaint ends. The kinds of complaints I have discussed in this book do not have a point that, once reached, means we are post-complaint or after complaint. When a complaint is taken through a formal process, the end of that process—you might have received a letter, a decision, although sometimes you don't even get that, you are left hanging—is not necessarily the end of the complaint. To end the story of a complaint can be to cut it off at some arbitrary point. Perhaps the story ends when we no longer have the time or energy to keep telling it.

There are so many ways of telling the story of complaint. There are so many threads to pull from the stories I have collected. The second chapter of each part of the book thus far has had a concluding section. The titles of those conclusions tell their own story: "Sensitive Information," "Letters in the Box," and "Distance from Complaint." Before I turn to the conclusions of the book, let me to return to these concluding sections. Each offered an explanation of how complaints are contained or end up in containers. That complaints contain "sensitive information" or "sticky data" might be why they end up in containers (chapter 2). In other words, complaints are contained because of what they threaten to reveal. Some become complainers because of what they are trying to reveal. Complaints we express in our own way, in our own terms, can end up contained in the spaces in which they were made or which they were about (chapter 4). Or it might be that doors are closed on complaints, and on those who make them, in order to open the door for others. An open door can be predicated on keeping distance from complaint (chapter 6). Those who complain can end up with nowhere to go. To explain how complaints are contained is thus to explain how institutions are reproduced, how the paths that can be followed are made narrower by stopping those who are trying to question how things are going or who are trying to go a different way.

Even if a complaint is contained or those who complain end up without a path to follow, a complaint might still go somewhere. Complaints might go somewhere because of how they affect those whom they come into contact with. If you leave because of a complaint, you do not just leave the problem behind. The effort you made to deal with that problem, even if you did not seem to get anywhere, becomes part of the institution, part of its history; however hidden, it happened. It might be that the story gets out, the information you gathered gets out, either accidentally or through a deliberate action. We will hear of such accidents and actions in due course. But what can be leaked as a result of complaint is more than information. What we have to do to gather that information, the work of complaint, is even harder to contain. Complaint is an outward-facing action: it involves people, many people, some of whom do not even meet. That involvement matters.

This book ends with two concluding chapters. The first was written by members of the collective I was privileged to join, Leila Whitley, Tiffany Page, and Alice Corble, with support from Heidi Hasbrouck, Chryssa Sdrolia, and others. Not everyone who was part of our collective is named as an author, but given that writing about the work of complaint is a continuation of the work, everyone who was part of the collective has shaped the writing. It is important to them, to us, and it is important for this book that they get to tell the story, in their own terms, in their own way. I learn so much from how they describe a "we" being formed, light, even tenuous, out of differences, each person having their own story of getting to a point that is shared. If we have to combine our forces in order to get anywhere, that combination has a history, that combination has a life of its own; even telling the story can be another way of combining forces.

In chapter 8, I return to the stories I have collected for this book, which include many instances of students and academics working together to get complaints through the system. I show how those who complain often end up politicized by complaint, becoming complaint activists, pressing against organizations, using their time and resources, even wasting their time and resources, to keep complaints alive. The last section of chapter 8—perhaps it is the conclusion of the conclusion—is titled "Survival and Haunting." We can think back to, think with, the image of the complaint graveyard. Even the complaints that end up there, buried, under the ground, have gone somewhere. What has been put away can come back. To tell stories of complaint, leaky, ghostly, haunting, is to be reminded of what can be inherited from actions that did not seem to succeed. We do not always know where complaints will go.

CHAPTER SEVEN

COLLECTIVE CONCLUSIONS

by Leila Whitley, Tiffany Page, and Alice Corble,
with Heidi Hasbrouck, Chryssa Sdrolia, and others

There is no one story of how our collective came together. In part, this is because our collectivity took shape slowly, drawing on relationships and trust built over years. There is no single turning point which marked the shift from working alongside one another as peers and fellow students, toward friendship, toward collectivity. Instead, we were a collective long before we realized it.

We also do not have a single story that marks the beginning of our collective because it was forged across our different experiences. We entered our university department at different times and in different year groups. While many of us overlapped, not all of us were students at the same time. We did not even all complete the same degree program. And we did not all have the same experience of harassment and of the sexualized, undermining conditions and abuses of power that characterized the culture and teaching environment. Some of us lived within and alongside these conditions for years. For those of us who had these years, the origins of our collectivity cannot be separated from these experiences. Our collectivity formed in response to what we were faced with.

You can be faced with abuses without being able to name them, let alone complain about them. The sexualized abuses of power that structured our department happened in the open: at departmental receptions, in our weekly graduate seminars. We would be grabbed at and touched, or we would watch others be grabbed at and touched. We would feel the sticky attention turn toward us—sexual attention, when we wanted mentorship—or we would feel attention turn away from us when we wanted mentorship because we weren't where sexualized attention was directed in that moment. We would hear what was said—about sex, about our bodies—and what insinuated about who had slept with whom. Sometimes we were the ones who were implicated, and what was said was about our sexuality and our bodies; sometimes it was someone else. These abuses were implicitly condoned in the department. If everything happened in the open, the problem was that no one seemed to think there was a problem with any of it. The story of how we formed a complaint collective is also a story about the culture of a department.

There were many ways that what was happening was made sense of, and so enabled. These ways of making sense of things shifted and were remarkably flexible. There were many versions of allowance, many justifications. If what happened, happened to us, we were told, "But he's a nice person. Really, he means well. This is just how he is." If what happened, happened to others, we were told, "Maybe she likes it. Maybe she's wise to it. She's an adult. It's not really anyone else's business. If she doesn't say something, why should we?" But we *were* saying. We were saying we didn't like what was being done to us, and we were saying that it wasn't only our business—that how we were treated in the department was, for us, a departmental issue. Even if not everyone felt that way, we certainly did. And when we objected, we were told, "Think of what you'll do to the department. Think of what will happen to him. Just loosen up. Feminists: so sex-negative, so uptight. Don't overreact. Don't be so divisive."

In this climate, and for a while, it seemed like the only way to make it through the situation was by trying to resist it quietly, each of us on her own. There were many of us who were doing this. We learned to study alongside it, to quietly try to avoid the invasive reaches. We were warned in the networks of whispers passed between generations of students: warned never to let ourselves be alone with anyone known for their "long hands"; warned to bring our partners, if we had them, to events to act as buffers, to signal our unavailability. Those of us who felt able turned down invitations for tutorials over dinner, turned down tutorials on weekends at the homes of those responsible for teaching us, turned down tutorials over drinks. Working to find our way through the conditions we were given, we withdrew. But saying no meant we could not attend events hosted by our department and could not access teaching, mentorship, or guidance. So sometimes we said yes to tutorials over drinks or dinner, to supervisions in living rooms. Whether we withdrew or participated, we were caught in these conditions. The conditions we experienced were both psychological and physical abuses of power.

Our quiet ways of making do and of finding our ways through the department while living alongside harassment as an everyday practice, as the only mode in which our education might be negotiated, might not appear to be a form of complaining. The ways that we were articulating our nos, each of us on her own, but also each of us knowing that our no was not the only no, might not even appear. But for those of us who lived in this way, our complaint begins here. Our ways of surviving, of withdrawing and not participating, of trying to protect ourselves and sharing strategies with each other, were also ways of rejecting and resisting the conditions we were given. For those of us who lived in this way, our story of collectivity is impossible without these stories of saying no even as we held quiet, and even as the system of harassment made us feel alone.

We never stopped talking to each other about what was happening. Over those years, we collected each other's stories. We were each hearing and holding on to so many things that had happened to so many people. We each had different breaking points, different moments when it became too much. But those breaking points, even if experienced separately, also moved us together. We were watching what had happened—and was happening—to us, happen again, and to each other, and recognizing there was both a pattern and a system in place. When we decided we weren't going to cope anymore by avoiding it, but would try to counter it and work together against it, it wasn't about any one of us: it was about understanding it was about much more than us. We did not want future cohorts of students to be confronted with what had happened to us and to the people we knew. We knew this couldn't continue to be how things were. A breaking point can be a turning point.

Another story of our origin as a collective begins here. It begins in this turning toward each other, in this gathering together not only with one another but for one another, and for those we didn't yet know. We started having meetings. We started writing together. As we came into this work, some of us already knew one another well, and others among us hadn't met before. Some of us who came together at that moment to begin to write are the same as those of us who gathered to contribute to this piece. Some are not.

What we wrote together the first time was a report on our department that set out to document the sexualization and abuses of power that characterized the complexities of our conditions of study. Our goal in writing the report was to hold the institution responsible for what it was enabling. This meant insisting on recognizing and naming what was happening and insisting on institutional complicity in enabling it. In gathering like this, both in person and in writing, we were sharing our experiences and understandings with one another. We were coming together to articulate, differently, an understanding of what was happening around us, and of our conditions. Rather than accepting these conditions as inevitable, we were formulating together a collective position that rejected them. So much of the work we have done collectively has been about shifting how things are understood. Because many of the sexualized abuses of power that shaped our conditions of study happened out in the open, our task was not simply to point to what was happening, and not simply to reveal the presence of abuses of power. Instead, what we were faced with was a struggle to change how these abuses of power were understood, how they were made sense of, and how they were valued: a reorienting of knowledge that was normalized. What we were trying to do was challenge the acceptance of these abuses as permissible and inevitable. We were drawing our own collective conclusions.

In response, we were told we had come to the wrong conclusions. So often we had our experiences explained back to us: it was our misunderstanding that was at fault. And it was this misunderstanding that was dangerous rather than the behavior of faculty. We were told our misunderstanding would cause harm: to the department, to faculty, and to the reputation of the institution. In this way, our collective was formed around a shared desire to build an understanding of the structures of sexualized abuses of power in our department and an insistence on naming and making visible the systematic harm caused. It was also formed around a desire to support one another between and across our different positions. It was our differences that gave us the vantage point to see, together, what any one of us could not fully see alone: to see the extent of the condition we were in.

We wrote the first report both collectively and anonymously. We did not follow the path of complaint as laid out by the institution. We knew the institution had a formal complaints procedure. We had looked up their process and found that as a matter of policy the university considered faculty–student relationships a private matter. For us, this meant that, by policy, the institution actively did not want to know about abuses of power. Some of us had also tried to use the complaint process in an earlier attempt at institutional accountability. This meant we already knew complaining was ineffective and costly. We knew that if we followed the institutional path, we'd be separated from each other. We would be required to write individual, named complaints. And we knew that even if we made multiple complaints, stacking ourselves together, the complaints process was designed to keep us separate. Each complaint would be taken on its own, and each person would be on her own. Keeping us separate would be a way to cut between us. It would be a way to make less visible what we could see when we looked at it not individually but together. And we also knew that if we wrote as individuals, the institution would hand us over: it would give our named, individual complaints to those about whom we wrote. They would be invited to defend themselves. There was no accountability.

We did not trust the institution. We did not trust them to protect us, and we also did not trust them to act. We did not trust their judgment or their motivations. It was the institution, after all, that maintained our department and that systematically looked away from what happened in the open. It was the institution that imbued those who abused their power with that power, and which invested itself in and aligned itself with those it had chosen to employ. For many of us, writing the report induced a range of different fears. We weren't going to give them our names, and we were going to stand together on what we said, but it was still a risk. We held on to this action while not knowing whether the university would disclose our names. We feared that the faculty members we wrote about would retaliate. To attempt to complete our degrees while navigating the fraught power struggles that characterized the ongoing sexualization of students within the department was precarious at best. Turning down advances meant risking alienating those who held power over us. Insisting that the institution take notice of, respond to, and no longer implicitly condone this climate meant intensifying the ways we were already vulnerable.

Collectivity was a way to share the cost of complaint. Rather than each of us being on her own, we would stand together. By writing collectively, we were insisting that we be allowed to write from the perspective not only of a first-person testimonial, with all of the attendant costs for the one positioned to give such a report, but from a perspective that insisted we get to speak up for each other when it cost too much for one of us to say it alone. Writing collectively and articulating what we could see only when we looked together was also an insistence that what was happening was an environment, something happening to all of us. We were not just a collection of individuals, and those of us who were being grabbed at or groomed were not the only ones affected by the abuses of power that striated the department. Anonymity, too, was a refusal of the individual-izing logics of the complaints process. By insisting on our anonymity, we were also insisting that this was not a matter of an individual conflict; this was not a matter of one person in need of resolution with another, not a matter of a dispute between two equal parties. And we were also insist-ing that we not be required to place our full trust, and ourselves, again in institutional hands. We withheld ourselves.

The ways the institution responded to us further shaped us as a col-lective. Their own structures meant that our reporting remained largely illegible to them. Following the close of an informal inquiry after our report, they responded to us, writing that while we had given "a very clear account of generic abuse of power and inappropriate behaviors," we had not provided them with a specific complaint. Without this, we were told, the institution had "nothing specific to act against." In short, we were informed what while the institution "wanted" to act, it was our refusal of their process that prevented them from doing so. For the institution, a named individual complaint was the only way to register what we de-scribed. It was the sole mechanism for the institution to *know*, and any other means of communicating the abuses of power were refused. The structure of complaint therefore became a way of preventing the institu-tion from recognizing what was happening. The requirement of a named individual complaint was too costly a requirement for those of us who were in the midst of an ongoing situation of abuse of power, such that it was largely inaccessible. It also meant that those who lived alongside the abuses of power, and were deeply affected by them, but did not have direct experiences of harassment were left with no means to report their own experiences. In this way, the institutional refusal to "hear" a collec-tive complaint was a consolidation of the refusal to acknowledge or act in response to the situation they continued to enable.

Labor, and the cost of this labor, was again returned to us. Members of the collective met with a member of senior management, which was the only option given to us in order to receive the report of the findings of the informal inquiry. The institution expected to hand us their knowledge, the official documentation of the department, which we were to receive. Instead we decided that we would insist the university be confronted with how each of us had experienced the institution. In that meeting, which lasted many hours, individuals began to tell of their experiences of sexual harassment. In this way, the collective began a process of reorientation: to center the narrative, words, voices, emotions, and experiences of those who had studied in the department and to force the institution to account for its willful ignorance of its own workings in front of the women who had been harmed. After the meeting, the university agreed to receive anonymous complaints alongside or instead of named complaints from students.

The decision to enter into the process of writing individual complaints was, like other decisions, made in relation to one another and enabled by one another. The institution required of us first-person testimony of abuses of power. If we provided this, they indicated they would finally be willing to act. As we began, in this context, to take the risk of writing individual testimonies of our experiences, we did so because we hoped these testimonies could be used for structural change.

In what followed, we gathered around each other. Care was always prioritized over complaint work. Through our collective working, our time spent listening, we each knew each other's stories. Individuals who were able to make a complaint, did so. Those who had not felt able to report their experiences without anonymity took the risk of making these reports once anonymity was an option. Others decided to be named in their complaints. Our complaints were written to document what had happened to us, but also to create a document for those who were unable to communicate their experience. We reached out to other students who we knew had also experienced sexualized and other abuses of power. We knew that institutional communication would not reach them and that, for some, removing themselves from the university was the only way to continue studying. Switching off from the institution, turning down its violence, was a survival mechanism. It also meant that they would not hear that complaints had been made. Each individual was supported if they wanted to write a complaint, but equally supported if they did not.

Through our encounters we were learning an institutional language. Witnessing the university's reactions to our verbal and written testimonies, we realized that to be heard we had to make our experiences legible to the university. For some of us, the institution expected emotion and hurt to be expressed. For others who had different experiences, such emotional expressions were viewed as irrelevant or even detrimental to complaint. Suggesting the motivations of a person's actions, even when these were experienced by us as physical violence, was challenged. We each read these written complaints, sharing our learning on writing, commenting on language, reminding each other of what we might have forgotten or thought wasn't important, deciding on tone. There were revelations in this process of abusive behavior people had normalized, and experiences that had been buried away. We tried to write down the complaints so our evidence could not be disputed, so that our knowledge could not be refused. We described how the behaviors we detailed made us feel and their impact on our studies. These complaints often did not sound like us: we had such a narrow channel in which to describe what happened to us, what it meant, and what it did. This translation became a means by which we used the institutional language to resist the ways it sought to silence us.

How much time was spent convincing the institution of its own practices is striking. To make a complaint was to witness institutional time conflicting with the time of experiencing sexualized abuses of power. Some of us first experienced these abuses as undergraduates. They continued throughout our doctoral studies. This slow time of violence overlaid our time in higher education. It coexisted with witnessing the workings of an institution that maintained structures that intricately tied this time of violence to the progression of our studies. Each time we made movements or adjusted ourselves in order to move time forward, either to leave, to seek alternative supervisors, or to disclose what had happened to us, the institution moved to keep us in place, reminding us of the stability of violence.

GETTING THE COMPLAINT OUT

The university has never publicly acknowledged what took place. Institutional silence has been structural to their approach, and consistent across it. Even when, after years of collective labor on our part, there were moments of institutional will to, if in limited ways, address the sexualized abuse that shaped the culture of the department, there was never a public acknowledgment of what had happened and what was happening. This silence has mattered to us, as a collective. It has, in part, mattered because ignoring what was done to us, to people before us, and what we were faced with, was essential to enabling it. Our conditions were not a matter of a rogue person abusing his power, not a matter of a single individual, or even of individuals. It was a matter of a culture and a system that allowed these abuses of power to happen in the open and that normalized their occurrence. What we provided to each other, in coming together, was a space for validation that what did not feel okay to us was not, in fact, okay. We created a space to hear each other and to affirm what it meant to each of us. Our work together has been about taking that collective agreement and insisting that those who did not want to hear us, and did not want to acknowledge or recognize this, see it. We pushed, together, for a shift in the social and institutional conditions that enabled and perpetuated the sexualized abuses of power we faced.

We wanted public recognition from the institution of how we had studied because the institution was responsible. We wanted it because for so long the university had invested in denying and ignoring what was taking place. And we wanted institutional recognition because, precisely, this recognition could have been essential to shifting the narrative around these abuses that persisted in the department. Recognition would have signaled that what happened to students might have mattered to the university.

While we worked to convince the institution of their responsibility to stop perpetuating the sexualized abuses of power, we also worked to shift the conversations and understandings among our peers in the department. As with our engagements with the institution, our work was to explain both the persistence of sexualized abuses of power and that these conditions were not acceptable. Our work was about making visible what had long been condoned. We also wanted to expose the systematic nature of sexism so that we could intervene in its reproduction and institutionalization. Among the many costs of how it was left to us was the fracturing of our social world. We took the risks of talking to our peers—those with whom we'd studied and built friendships. Many of them turned away from us, blaming us for putting the department at risk and interrupting their own precarious passage through the institution. Many students were starved of support and isolated by the same structures that enabled abuses of power. In this sense, institutional culture continues to travel through its investments in normalizing logics, enveloping many more individuals than those impacted specifically by sexual harassment.

In a way, we countered institutional silence by finding other ways of communicating about what had gone on, opening up complaint. Our internal departmental listserv devolved into extended debates about how to respond to sexualized abuses of power and whether or not it mattered if some of us had been faced with this. Many of our peers insisted it did not matter, stacking against our experiences their own claim to an acceptable, positive experience. Others denied our accounts. Sometimes these debates devolved further into personal attacks, in which we were accused of using our sexuality to get ahead, in exchange for jobs and publication opportunities.

Motivated by how we saw one another targeted and attacked, we intervened collectively. We were protective of one another. We worked together to write a public statement that implored our peers to remember that just because, as we put it, "some students have not had the experiences we have had, does not make the abuses of power any less real."[1] To our memory, if this statement had some small and marginal effects, it had little impact on the dominant climate in the department. We were viewed as using institutional power against faculty.

Working collaboratively, we were increasingly aware that while our institution had allowed this to happen to us, faculty abuses were also happening in other universities. To reach others we built a website, Strategic Misogyny, to collect accounts of what students faced within and beyond our department.[2] Those involved in this project are, again, more capacious than those of us who first gathered: our collectivity has expanded in moments, incorporating others with whom we've worked and whom we've supported. In this space, we gathered first-person accounts of sexism and sexualized abuses of power, seeking to make connections and interrupt the invisibility of these abuses. If official channels wouldn't recognize our stories, and if the record of what we experienced was erased, we would create our own.

Once it became clear there would never be public acknowledgment of what had taken place, some of us worked with allies to organize a conference in late 2015 addressing sexual harassment in higher education. Again, we worked to translate our experiences, this time into the language of academia; again, we did this work because the institution refused to. The event was student-led and received, in total, £1,752 funding from the university. Six months later the university claimed our event as evidence of its commitment to addressing sexual harassment on campus.[3] On the day, very few faculty and staff members attended. And even as we hosted the conference in order to create space for the specific histories of the university, we did not name these specific histories on the day. We were too worried about the consequences of naming. Because we did not name what had happened, we felt nothing was changed by hosting the event. This was a failure that we felt acutely. After the event, one of us went to the university library and pulled all the copies of books written by one of these unnamed professors down from the shelves, and wrote inside each book that the author was responsible for sexual harassment and abuses of power. This was not an individual act: it was an attempt to voice what had happened to us, to collect these experiences and complain. We named him in his own record, in order to put his behavior on record.

Over the years actions followed ours, using and building upon this alternative archive of institutional knowledge. The books were found and photographed; a blog was established to document and ask questions of the institution's history; students organized a conference out of frustration at the responding institutional silence when they began to ask questions; and a visual campaign depicting brick walls appeared on campus.

COLLECTIVE FUTURES

If a cost of our collective work was lost relationships and a fractured social world, our collective also transformed our relationships to each other. Our friendships before we began working together allowed us to talk about what was happening and to come together out of a sense of the need to protect one another. But some of us didn't yet know each other. Some of us formed relationships by working together. And some of our friendships, even if they already existed, were entirely transformed by working together. We built intimacies; we built trust.

The boundaries of our collective have always been fluid. If there are people within the collective who have remained consistent over time, there are plenty who have come in and out. Each of us contributes what she is able when she is able. Each of us leaves room for others to both come and go, finding ways to support one another while recognizing that we may not all be able to gather at any given time. We have different strengths and abilities, different conditions shaping our lives. And the costs of the work are not the same for all of us. It is because of this collective fluidity and flexibility, and this ability to step in for one another, that we have been able to keep going.

Our collective has also not been bounded at the limits of our own relationships with each other. For all of us, the labor and support of those beyond us have also made our collective work—and survival—possible. Those who absorbed our stress and our tears, those who acted alongside us, those who became our doctoral supervisors and attended to our research and to us in careful, generous ways, and those to whom we went for nights and weekends off and who brought us back rested and fed, sustained the work we did. There were also moments when we were exhausted and when the work of complaint—and of our studies—no longer felt possible. There were times when we had exhausted all of our resources, when we resorted to sleeping on each other's couches.

Our collectivity also does not end at the bounds of those we already know—or even at the limits of those we will ever know. If our work has been done in the name of one another and enabled by our relationships to one another, it also gestures toward those who come after us. One way we think of this chapter is as a gesture to those we do not know: we are here, and we know you are there. Sharing thinking space together is a way of sharing collectivity.

Complaints have consequences. As we write this piece, we are scattered—across cities, and in some cases countries; across careers; across our lives. We are no longer students. Many of us were able to complete our degrees. This was not a given. Our collective labor, and the support we received as our collective grew, made these degrees possible. Complaint became how many of us managed to make it through when we might not have.

But not all of us were able to finish the degrees we dedicated years of our lives to. And even for those of us who did complete our programs, our degrees were, more often than not, interrupted, with years added before we finished. Studying alongside both the sexualized abuses of power that characterized the department and the slow institutional time of complaint, while taking on the labor of complaint, had costs. Our degrees often required changes in supervision after periods of having gone without; in many cases they required departmental switches; they have relied on extended debt and expiring funding deadlines; and in some cases, completing those programs became impossible. Some of these costs and complications can be traced to the sexualized abuses of power. And some of the opportunities that opened, like access to a new supervisor or a departmental transfer, became possible as a result of complaint. But complaint, too, was costly. The labor it required—the hours dedicated to writing reports, attending meetings, and negotiating and articulating together our shared understanding—happened alongside our research and teaching and other work, unrecognized. This particular iteration of the collective spent years doing this work. The absence of doctoral supervision, the prolonged trauma of what we experienced, the wearing down of making complaints, all had a huge impact on studies designed to be completed within a specified timeframe.

Even among those of us who did complete our degrees, our futures remain, largely, uncertain. Few of us work in the academic jobs for which we were trained. For many of us, there is residual anger over not having been able to study without experiencing sexualized abuses of power. There is no easy remedy that would restore what was taken from so many of us. While the story of precarity in academia is also a story of austerity, and of the international gutting of higher education, and while there is no way to know what might have been otherwise had things been otherwise, complaint too had its effects and its toll. It too made its contributions to precarity.

The story of the entrenchment of sexualized abuses of power is a story of loss. This has always been our point. When we set out as a collective with a complaint, so many responded to us by foregrounding concern for the consequences of our complaint for those who abused their power, for the department and the university, for what might be lost in relation to these people and these structures. Our own concern, instead, was for the losses that abuse constitutes for the generations of students unable to study and whose voices were lost because of how costly it became to remain.

Complaint both enabled us to remain and intensified the costs we took on. Complaint is both how some of us survived and related to how most of us are no longer part of the academy. But our hope is that our complaint might mean a shift in this loss: that what we have left behind us means that so many will not have to be lost.

Our collective work, expanding through and beyond the bounds of our collective, had consequences: things are no longer as they were in our graduate department.[4] The future of our collective labor is that, at least in our own small corner, the sexualized abuses of power were interrupted. We moved something.

CHAPTER EIGHT

COMPLAINT COLLECTIVES

In this book I have assembled a complaint collective. This book *is* a complaint collective. My task in this concluding chapter is to reflect on how complaint collectives work, how we assemble ourselves. I have collected different people's experiences of complaint, sharing with you (some of you, I expect, are complainers too) as much as I can of what has been shared with me. A collective is a collection of stories, of experiences, but also more than that, more than a collection.

I think of the first time I presented this material.[1] I was standing on a stage, and the lights were out. I could hear an audience, the sounds, the groans, sometimes laughter, but I could not see anyone. The words: they were so heavy. I was conscious of the weight of them, of the pain in them. And as I read the words that had been shared with me, knowing the words were also behind me, lit up as text, I had a strong sense, a shivering feeling, of the person who shared those words saying them to me, of you as you said them, of you being there to say them. I felt you there, all of you, because you were there, helping me withstand the pressure I felt to do the best I could, to share the words so they could be picked up, heard by others who might have been there, in that painful place, that difficult place (complaint can be a place), so your words could do something, so your words could go somewhere. And each time I have presented this work, the feeling has been the same, of you being there with me. Maybe to keep doing it, to keep saying it, that is what I needed, for you to be there with me. A complaint collective can be a feeling we have of being there for each other, with each other, because of what we have been through. We recognize each other from what we have been through; we even know each other. It can be hard to convey in writing how much that feeling matters.

A collective can be a support system, what we need, who we need, to keep a complaint going. Over the past years friends as well as strangers have expressed concern, worry even, for my welfare, because of my choice to stay close to scenes of institutional violence, the same scenes that led me to leave my post and a profession that I had loved. I too questioned myself about this: Why stay so proximate to what has been so hard, and yes, so painful? Pain can have clarity. It is clear to me *that* I have, and *how* I have, been supported by doing this work. It has helped me come to terms with what happened, to pick up the pieces of a shattered academic career (yes, I do understand that career to have ended as a direct result of my participation in a complaint), to make and to understand the connections between what happened to me and what happened to others. And that the research has supported me has also taught me; if a complaint collective is what I have assembled, a complaint collective is how I have learned. *Learned* is one of the most used words in this book for a reason.

In sharing your words, more words have been shared with me; so many people have come up to me after lectures and seminars telling me stories of complaint. A collective: we combine; how we combine. That combination can be a matter of hearing. I listened to each account and I listened again, transcribing, reflecting, thinking, feeling. And in listening to you, becoming a feminist ear, as I described in my introduction, I also put my ear to the doors of the institution (there are many reasons doors keep coming up, as I explained in part III), listening out for what is usually kept inaudible, who is made inaudible, hearing about conversations that mostly happen behind closed doors. I was able to hear the sound of institutional machinery—that clunk, clunk—from those who have tried to stop that machine from working, from those who came to understand how it works, for whom it works. When I think of the collective assembled here, I think *institutional wisdom*. I think of how much we come to know by combining our forces, our energies. I think of how much we come to know because of the difficulties we had getting through.

The difficulties we had getting through: we have been hearing how complaint means committing yourself, your time, your energy, your being, to a course of action that often leads you away from the work you want to do even if you complain in order to do the work you want to do (as many do). Trying to address an institutional problem often means

inhabiting the institution *all the more*. In chapter 1, I described how you
end up in the shadowy corners of the institution. Inhabitance can thus
involve reentry: you reenter the institution through the back door. You
find out about doors, secret doors, trapdoors: how you can be shut out,
how you can be shut in. You learn about processes, procedures, policies;
you point out what they fail to do, pointing to, pointing out; you fill in
more and more forms; forms become norms; files become futures; filing
cabinets, graves.

Even when a file or a grave is a shared destination, there are many different routes for ending up there. Complaints can be buried by a process.
Or, we might bury our own complaints if it takes too much out of us to
keep making them. A postgraduate student describes how her peers kept
expressing concern when they heard she was making a complaint. She
said that concern can "rob you of your own complexity. It reduces you to
one story, one narrative, and a victim one at that." When you have to keep
telling the story of a complaint, it can end up feeling like another way of
being dominated. A story about what happened to you can end up being
a story about what somebody else did. She adds, "It was almost like I got
muted out. I got removed from my own story as it became his story or
their story about him." Sometimes in order not to be removed from our
stories we bury them.

A burial of a story can be necessary. A burial is part of the story. To tell
the story of a burial is to unbury the story. I could write this book, pull it
together, only because complaints did not stay buried. When I think of
this book as an unburial, I think again of the arm that is still rising in the
Grimm story. In this book I have tried to catch complaints at that moment of suspension: a complaint as an arm still rising, still coming out of
the ground, not yet done, not yet beaten. To tell the story of a complaint is
how the complaint comes out from where it has been buried. The sound
of the book is not just the sound of institutional machinery—that clunk,
clunk—but the sound of the effort of coming up, of what we bring when
we bring something up; who, too, we bring up. The physical effort, you
can hear it: the wear and the tear, the groans, the moans. One academic
said she could hear herself moaning when she was telling me about the
different complaints she had made at different times. She comments, "I
am moaning now, I can feel that whining in my voice [*makes whining
sound*]." I reply, "We have plenty to moan about." We can hear it in our
own voices; we can hear it in each other's voices. We can hear it because
we feel it: the sound of how hard we keep having to push. I think of that
push as collective, a complaint collective.

We have to push harder. I am aware that if these stories have been hard to share (to share an experience that is hard is hard), this book might have been hard to read, hard on you, readers. I know some of you will have picked this book up because of experiences you have had that are hard, experiences that led you to complain, experiences of complaint. You might have had moments of recognition, painful and profound, as I did when I listened to these testimonies. It can help to share something painful, although not always, and not only. One academic said to me at the end of our dialogue, "It's really helpful talking to you. It reminds me that I am not alone." It was helpful for me to talk to you too. A complaint collective: how we remind ourselves we are not alone. We need reminders.

My hope is that this book can be a reminder: we are not alone. We sound louder when we are heard together; we are louder. In this concluding chapter, I reflect on the significance of how complaints can lead you to find out about other complaints (and thus to find others who complained). Complaint offers a fresh lens, which is also an old and weathered lens, on collectivity itself.

FROM COLLECTIVE COMPLAINTS TO COMPLAINT COLLECTIVES

To approach the question of collectivity through complaint is to approach collectivity as a practical question of how to pull a complaint together. In chapter 4, I described how a woman of color academic submitted a collective complaint about the impact of sexism and racism on the research culture of her department. She talks me through the process: "I got them to write in an email their experience of the research culture—I collated about twenty of these statements—and submitted them to the [deputy vice chancellor] at the time." The labor of collating experiences creates a single document. That document is a collective complaint. A collective complaint is how you show that the judgment that there is a problem is shared. The process was not straightforward. Even though each statement was anonymized, there were some people in her department who did not feel they could become part of it. She notes, "In that process of gathering testimonies there were at least three women in the department who felt they didn't want to contribute, they didn't want to go above the parapet, because they felt their opportunities for further employment would be affected. . . . They were all on temporary contract, or just finished their PhDs. They felt quite strongly that even though they agreed with the sentiment, they could not join in even though it was anonymous." For those who are trying to get a foot in the door, being part of a complaint collective, even anonymously, can be understood as risking too much.

A collective complaint, that is, a document pulled together by a collective, does not include all those who "agreed with the sentiment." Collectives tend to exceed the forms in which they are given. And even though the document was collective, it was received as if it originated with a single person. Yes, she was the only named person; she was the person who submitted the document. But it was still clear in the document that it was a collection of statements authored by different people from the same department. Individuation and atomization can be determined at any point in the complaint process. A response to a collective can be to treat the collective as an individual. The collectivity of complaints is often erased by how complaints are received.

To write a collective complaint requires finding a way to share experiences, one way or another way. To become a collective is to find a way. Collectivity can be how we make a complaint as well as an effect of making a complaint: collectivity as a means as well as an end. A postdoctoral researcher participated in a complaint about transphobia and bullying on a research project. The complaint was put forward after she herself had left the institution; if we leave because of a problem, a problem can be what we leave behind. She reflects on the nature of the process:

> I think the laborious part of it was trying to translate our individual and collective experience into something that institutionally made sense and [could] be recognizable as a complaint. In terms of what we did, we Skyped a lot and we emailed a lot and we swung back and forth between sharing our stories or being like, this awful thing happened and this awful thing happened and this awful thing happened, and then have to come back and work out how to put that on paper.

To create a document that can be recognized as a complaint is laborious: it requires considerable time as well as effort. You need to combine your experiences but also render that combination legible in a form that is not your own. You need to communicate with each other, swinging back and forth. I think of that swinging as teaching us how complaint as a style of communication is also a motion, a movement. And in swinging back and forth you find out about the "awful things that happened" to others; they find out about the "awful things that happened" to you.

A collective complaint can thus be a form of consciousness-raising. I suggested in chapter 4 that a complaint can begin with a feeling of structure; that feeling is shared. When we think of consciousness-raising we might think of being in a room with others reflecting on shared experiences. To understand collective complaint as consciousness-raising points to how consciousness is achieved *in the act of taking up a practical task*. The more you have to do, the more you come to recognize. You raise consciousness of a problem in the process of trying to redress that problem. Consciousness-raising here is not about a space of withdrawal and reflection but a scene of action. A collective complaint is made possible, acquiring the status of a document, because of how many are willing to take up that task. If complaint can be understood as a phenomenology of the institution, complaint is a *practical phenomenology* (Ahmed 2012, 174–80). We come to know how institutions work from the practical effort of making a complaint about how they work.

A complaint collective can be how we gather more information about what is going on. There is an intimacy between how much we come to know and how we work together. I spoke to one professor who had supported students who made a complaint about sexual misconduct and sexual harassment by a lecturer in the department who had justified his behavior as "a perk of the job" (chapter 5). She describes the process: "A student, a young student, came and said to me that this guy had seduced her basically. And then in conversation with another woman she found out he had done the same to her. And then it snowballed, and then we found out there were ten women. He was just going through one woman after another after another after another." I think of snowballing, how complaints can bring more complaints about, *watch us roll*, how a complaint can acquire momentum because of how much there is to pick up.[2] You find out more; you find out there were more ("another after another after another"). The more who have been harassed, the more there are to participate in a complaint about harassment, although we have also learned that not everyone who has been harassed can or will participate in a complaint about it.

Complaint collectives can be how more information is released. A number of people I spoke to talked about how they read stories in newspapers about sexual harassment at universities, how they were affected by that, moved by that. Those stories are themselves products of collective labor. It is not just that these stories are shared, but they can help others to keep their complaints going. One lecturer described reading a story in the *Guardian*: "I became a little bit less tired, less afraid of dealing with this." We can be picked up by feeling less: less tired, less afraid.

Complaint collectives can also be created as an effect of how information is released. In chapter 5, I described how a group of three women made a complaint about sexual harassment they had experienced as undergraduates. How did the collective end up being formed so much later? These women had stayed in touch; they were in contact on Facebook. And a story broke about sexual harassment in the university where they had been undergraduates. One woman posts a link to the story with the comment "No surprises there." Another responds, "Some things don't change." A story about harassment in the present can open the door to the past; it can lead to a discussion about the harassment that happened previously. The comments on the Facebook post led to further conversation: "We kind of disclosed everything to each other, what had happened." They meet up in person. As one of the women explains, "So we arranged to meet up, we wanted to meet up anyway. I hadn't seen her [since] we left college. And so we did, and she then made me aware that our other friend had this sort of experience. And between us, it turned out that between us we had knowledge and firsthand experience of harassment and/or assault from five male members of staff within one department." The more has been suppressed, the more there is to come out. But something has to happen to initiate this process. A story about a present-day case of sexual harassment can be a trigger to a series of conversations that might not otherwise have happened. #MeToo as a movement can be understood in these terms: how the release of a story can trigger a process of further releasing: the *too* points to *you*; the point of the *too* is *you*. Also note the significance of the time: a complaint in the present is how past experiences are shared that were not complained about when they happened. I will return to the timely nature of communication in due course.

These acts of disclosure led to the creation of a collective of three women. Perhaps they were a four-women collective; their friend who had taken her own life was part of it, was part of the complaint, even if they did not make it then, even if they only made it now, when she was no longer with them. They got in touch with the university, and together they submit a formal grievance: "It was exhausting and there were three of us doing it collectively, sharing out the emotional load, supporting each other. I was doing quite a lot of the emails and things, then, when I was flagging a bit, [another woman] took that on, and [the third woman] was in the background bolstering and supporting." I have talked throughout this book of the exhaustion of the complaint process—it can feel like the point of the process is to exhaust those who enter it. Complaint collectives are formed *given* this exhaustion. What a given. By working together, you share the load. You give each other support. And each of you can do the work that is attuned to the skills you have, coming to the foreground or being in the background, depending on what is being asked of you.

In another example, four women postgraduates worked together on a complaint that began with an incident I shared in this book: one of the women turned up to a postgraduate retreat only to find that sexist jokes had become routine (chapter 3). When she did not participate in those jokes by going along with them, laughter as going along, she became the target. She submits an informal complaint; she speaks to the head of department. She also began to talk to other students: "A group of us began to connect up, and we found out there was a much richer history of [this student] acting inappropriately toward women." Sharing notes is how you recognize that an incident, an event, a one-off, has a longer history. It was because they combined their resources that they became aware of this history; that the problem was a structure as a well as an event. But, as I explored in part II of this book, the more you challenge structures, the more you come up against them. Another student who was part of the collective describes, "I think there's this assumption that when you put in a complaint in an academic setting everyone is very convivial, but actually things were being said that were being passed back to us, that there was a real physical aggressive threat that these men were starting to build up, and things had been said like, we might get a brick through our window or we might get our hand pounded in iron." When violence against those who complain escalates, that violence is often hidden by assumptions of conviviality or by the closed doors of confidentiality. The more people participate in a complaint, the more people are likely to be targeted. Threats of violence toward an *us* ("our window," "our hand") are also being "passed back to" an *us*. To share the situation of being the target of violence can be part of the work of a complaint collective. In other words, a collective can be what you need for violence to be *witnessed* by others. A collective can be what you need to *withstand* this violence. The more force applied to stop a complaint from being made, the more you need more, more people, more complainers, to witness and withstand that force.

My own experience of being part of a complaint collective was of withstanding, of working together to support each other through a process that made it difficult to keep standing or to keep the complaint going. As I noted in my introduction to this book, I joined a complaint collective that had been created by students. You have heard, in chapter 7, from some of those who were involved in that collective, what they did, how they worked, what they learned. Once formed, a collective can become a support system, holding each person up; when weight is distributed more, each person carries less. In the same academic year that I began working with this complaint collective, another complaint collective was formed by master's students to put forward a complaint about harassment and bullying from a lecturer in the same department. A complaint collective can lead to the creation of other complaint collectives. You end up with a collective of complaint collectives. The work of these collectives became the work of our new center, the Centre for Feminist Research. That center from the beginning was filled by complaint, the work of it, the charge of it, the feeling; yes, negation can be quite a sensation. It was filled with a sense of urgency of the task at hand.

When a complaint is shared, you can also widen the range of activities undertaken. Together we conducted a curriculum review, analyzing how sexism and racism were built into the materials being taught. We organized conferences in which our task was to work *on* the institution, such as the inaugural conference of the center, which was on the topic of sexism (yes, that word can carry a complaint), which took place in 2014. We read feminist work together, and we were picked up by what those books picked up. The center, housing complaint collectives, felt like a pocket within the institution in which we could breathe. We needed that pocket in order to fight the institution; we needed that pocket to survive the institution.

If complaint collectives are formed to keep a complaint going, complaint collectives can keep us going. Long after a collective complaint is submitted, after what follows, all that follows (we don't always know what follows), those relationships you have with each other can be what you take with you, wherever you go. Sometimes the relationships built through complaint can become conduits of pain, reminders of pain, triggers. It can sometimes be too much to be proximate to those with whom you shared such shattering experiences. I think of one senior researcher whose complaint about harassment and bullying led her to leave a post she had loved. She was invited by another woman involved in that complaint to meet up. When she is deciding whether to go, disturbed even by the difficulty of the decision, her husband says to her, "This is like veterans' reunions." She explains, "Whenever you meet, you go back and you talk about the past and how it is haunting all of you. So, for my own protection, I needed distance, because we would invariably go back and it would upset me. It would destabilize me. It would pull me back. I need to put all my energy in rebuilding everything they destroyed: self-esteem, self-belief, self-worth." I will return to how we can be haunted by complaints, how a "we" can be haunted. Sometimes rebuilding a life, rebuilding yourself, makes it hard to meet those who shared the experience that destroyed the life you had, the self you had. This is not to say those relationships we make through complaint do not matter: not meeting up can be how they matter, just as meeting up can be too.

I think of the different ways we meet each other. In a way, the work we already do, as feminists, is the work of a complaint collective, which is not to say that is all there is to say about the work we do. A woman of color researcher describes to me the importance of that collection to her: "Almost every woman of color I have shared this with has some story like this. Documenting how endemic it is, *adding to that collection*, it's an important part of the process. The uselessness of the bureaucratic machine. It is more enraging to me that people won't know that happened. At least I know that more people know. I know at least that other women of color in particular can benefit from it, it is building that archive." To share our complaints, to share our stories of making complaints, is to become part of a collective as well as a collection. It is a way of documenting something, a way of showing as well as knowing. Another woman of color academic described her complaint as "a very Do it Yourself model." A complaint archive is also a DIY archive. Adding our stories to a collection is how we do it ourselves, how we become part of a building, create a shelter, so that we have somewhere to go, somewhere to be.

COMPLAINT ACTIVISM

Many of the stories I have collected in this book seem to be stories of working very hard not to get very far. We learn from what we fail to achieve. The complainer knows how much work goes into things staying the same. Being involved in a complaint can thus be a politicizing process in a similar way to participating in a protest or demonstration. It can be violence that brings you to the protest, the violence of the police, for instance. But in protesting against violence, you witness that violence all the more—the violence of the police, the violence of the media which misrepresents the violence of the police as caused by the protestors—you learn how violence is directed, against whom violence is directed. You come to learn how violence against those who challenge violence is how structures are maintained. You come to realize that some are more readily targeted. A formal complaint can lead you in a direction similar to a protest: you come to witness the violence of the status quo when you challenge the violence of the status quo; you come to realize the politics of who gets identified as the origin of the complaint. When you make a complaint, you might not necessarily begin by thinking of yourself as part of a movement nor as a critic of the institution, let alone as trying "to dismantle the master's house," to evoke the title of Audre Lorde's important essay. But that is where many who make complaints end up. There is hope in this trajectory.

Making complaints can lead some to become complaint activists. I first thought of the term *complaint activism* when I was talking to a disabled woman about the complaints she had made as a student. She needed to make a formal complaint in order to be able to study part time, to have the time she needed to be able to do the work. I drew on her testimony especially in chapter 4; she taught us how you can be heard as complaining if you do not display the right attitude as a disabled person, how you have to show "groveling gratefulness" in order not to be "a pain in the ass." She told me not only about her experiences of making a complaint at her former university but how she took what she learned *out*, onto the streets. Becoming a complainer at her university led to her becoming a complainer wherever she went: "I have started doing this activism using the law and in particular the part of the Equality Act (2010) that only applies to disability regarding reasonable adjustments." She made use of the law, however limited, as a tool to try to press organizations to become accessible, to become compliant with existing legislation. If complaints can lead you to learn how institutions work, how policies work, what they do and do not do, you can take that knowledge with you. I noted in chapter 6 how a complaint can leave a blank space in a cv, but really it could be claimed as a transferable skill. Even if you can't claim those skills, you can still make use of them.

Her activism was probably well described by what she said her former university perceived her to be: "a complete pain in the ass." She was indeed described in local media as trying to ruin small businesses because of demanding they be accessible to her as a wheelchair user, a demand she should not have to make. From her I learned how complaints about institutions can be used to press against them. You are making noise; you are making demands on their time; you are requiring them to do work (even the work of covering over a problem is work) and to use up their resources. A complaint can be a way of *occupying their time*. You complain again and again about inaccessible rooms and buildings; yes, you are saying it because they are doing it, but it does not mean it is not worth saying it; we just need more to say it as well as to say it more. Perhaps they hope you will stop saying it. You keep saying it: even if you don't have much hope that they will stop doing it; you don't want their hope you will stop to stop you. If the complainer is irritating, complaint activism might involve being willing to be an irritant, an institutional killjoy.

To be an institutional killjoy, a killjoy at work, you need to work with others. Complaint activism can lead to forming new kinds of collectives. She began working with a group of disabled activists, to use compliance with the law as a method for putting organizations under pressure to be as accessible as they claim to be. Complaint activists can thus also be understood as *complaint supporters*; you not only work with each other, but in working together, in pooling your resources, you are also more able to give advice and practical support to those who are making complaints.

This kind of complaint activism has a long history. Beverley Bryan, Stella Dadzie, and Suzanne Scafe ([1985] 2008) in the Black British feminist classic text *The Heart of the Race* quote from a Black woman talking about the work of her activist group in the 1970s. She refers to how they gave support to a Black mother "in making a complaint against the police" (158). She expands: "We picketed the local Police Station and called in the local press. Then we got involved in a People's Enquiry, gathering information and evidence on the courts, the police, our housing situation, employment and education practices—everything which affected the Black community in our area. A lot of Black people came along to give evidence on how they had been dealt with by the local police and we helped to compile a report" (159). Supporting a complaint can be about how you make a complaint more public and visible, using pickets and the press, as well as how you collect the evidence needed to compile reports. To make a complaint against an institution is how you gather more evidence of its violence.

We can turn our own experience of institutional violence into a shared resource for others. Complaint activism can point to how an experience of making a complaint within an institution can lead outward or elsewhere. I also think of The 1752 Group, which was set up by some of the students I had worked with on the inquiries.[3] They describe themselves as a lobby group: they lobby for institutional change, specifically to deal with staff–student sexual misconduct. To lobby around this specific issue is also to lobby against inequalities of many kinds. That a complainer within an institution can become an interinstitutional lobbyist is another hopeful trajectory. In reflecting on the work of the group, Tiffany Page, Anna Bull, and Emma Chapman (2019, 1318) describe how the "work of complaint can sometimes extend into activism to change the processes within an institution when these are shown not to work." To experience failed processes can lead to the activism of changing processes, which is a "slow activism":

> Our approach as a group has been to balance, often somewhat precariously, the need for fast visibility with the slowing down of the ensuing rush to propose solutions and "fix the problem." Nowhere in the world are there adequate solutions to address this issue, and while there is immediate need, this demand for change has to be tempered with understandings of institutional speed as well as the fixity of institutional processes: Once a solution is put in place, regardless of its appropriateness and capacity to address the problem, it becomes very difficult to modify or change it. For example, institutions that have implemented particular campaigns and solutions (often accompanied by high-profile launches) to address sexual violence on campus may then refuse to engage with critique of their program or to invest further. The presence of an "institutional solution," in this way, can have the impact of *closing down* discussion. (1317)

It is important to work slowly, given how solutions become problems; ways of saying we have done something can be how we don't do something. To be a complaint activist is to work on new policies and procedures as a way of opening up rather than closing down difficult discussions (chapter 1). You have to slow the work down in order to resist how institutions use the work we do, our own work, as solutions.

Complaints can be understood as among the many "tools at our disposal" as we press for organizational change (Page, Bull, and Chapman 2019, 1320). To press for change is to press against organizations. When thinking about press and pressure, we might recall how much pressure we are put under not to make complaints (chapter 2). The fact that there is so much pressure not to complain tells us something about what complaints can do, or at least what they are perceived as having the capacity to do. Even when complaints are handled in house, that they are framed by organizations as potentially damaging teaches us that complaints can do more than keep that house in order. We can seek to make complaints fulfill the potential they are perceived as having. If to modify an existing arrangement, a way of doing things, is deemed damaging, to be a complaint activist is to be willing to cause damage. To be a complaint activist is to refuse to be warned away from complaint by tired stories about tired processes. To be a complaint activist is to be willing to go through the motions, to be there, in the wear and tear, for as long as it takes.

Many who participate in formal complaints develop strong critiques of institutional power, which is another way of thinking about how we can be politicized through complaint. Carolyn M. West (2010) offers an important account of how she recovered from an experience of making a complaint about sexual harassment by a professor in her department. A recovery can be in resistance. She describes how she drew on her Black feminist foremothers, such as Ida B. Wells, "who used journalism and activism in the classroom as her weapons against racial bigotry and sexism" (186). Complaint can be a Black feminist lineage. West notes: "I now consider it my life's work to articulate how living at the intersection of multiple forms of oppression influences Black women's experiences with the violence in their lives" (186). West inspires us to think of how making complaints against those who abuse the power given to them by virtue of position can be part of a journey into activism. The work of complaint can lead you to find your "life's work."

Politicization also occurs through the kinds of labor that making a complaint requires, including the communicative labor I described in chapter 1, how you have to talk to many different people within the organization from staff in Human Resources to unions. I spoke to a retired academic about her complaint history; she gave me her history in different chapters, each chapter corresponding to her experiences at the three different universities in which she had been employed (chapter 6). She conveyed to me how being a person who had complained, being a complainer, mattered to her: "I took a huge risk by complaining and fighting and not accepting what they had done to me." She continued, "I bloody decided to fight them, and I've seen so many people who don't and I've seen so many people crushed in many ways because they haven't gone to the union, they haven't gone to access-to-work; they'd just been so isolated that they just get crushed. . . . There's no way I was going to let them do that to me."[4] A complaint is a way of *not being crushed*. You are fighting, and you are talking to other people who are involved in fighting. A fight can be about gathering resources. She suggested, "You've got to pull in as many resources as you can." Complaints do not just lead you into the secret chambers of the institution, along the narrow corridors of power, as I suggested earlier. They can also lead you to form new partnerships both within institutions and beyond them.

When complaints are made in order to fight the institution, complaints are made costly by the institution. This book has certainly been about the costs of complaint. Power works by making it costly to challenge how power works. Complaint collectives can be how we share some of these costs. To return to the testimony of the retired academic, the tragedy for her was not so much the cost of fighting the institution as the cost of not fighting the institution: "For me the tragedy was that I have seen so many other colleagues go under because they've been too scared to fight that fight. And I completely understand why they have been." It might be fear that stops people from fighting that fight. But whatever stops people from fighting that fight, an effect of some being stopped is that there are fewer people fighting that fight. She added, "It's really hard because people are so overworked and don't have the time to defend themselves or campaign about everything." From complaint we learn about the costs of *not* complaining. Those costs include, of course, the costs of leaving problems unaddressed. These problems—such as harassment—can lead some to leave, "to go under." Even though her complaints led her to leave, she left having fought for what she would have needed in order to stay.

Complaint activism might describe a stance or a style, a willingness to fight back, to fight for more, whatever the costs, whether or not you get through. Not getting through does not mean not getting somewhere. This also means that getting somewhere is not always about getting through. Complaint activism is a way of thinking about what we get from complaint even when we do not get through. To complain is also to create a record. Remember: you have to record what you do not want to reproduce. If you record what you do not want to reproduce, that record exists even if what is reproduced is still reproduced. Yes, a record can end up in a file. But the record is also what you retain: you can take it with you wherever you go. A complaint becomes a companion, a noisy companion. One lecturer who made a complaint about bullying at her former institution told me,

> I believe in complaining, even when it's a bad outcome, just creating that record of what happened. I am glad that it exists for me, and that if any questions are raised I have it. I did lodge a grievance, I had a go, I did try. And for the record: that matters to me. It matters to me not that I tried to seek justice, because I don't really believe the process can deliver that, but just to have some accountability and explanation in the hope of institutional change, which was I think all I was asking for in the end.

A record can be what matters to the one who assembles it; a record can be a reminder that you made an effort, that you had a go, even if that effort did not lead to institutional change.

To be a complaint activist is not necessarily to enter a process believing it can deliver an end such as justice. Complaint activism does not come from an optimism in the law or in complaints procedures; if anything, complaint activism comes *out* of the knowledge of institutional violence that comes *from* making complaints. I noted earlier that there is hope in the trajectory of becoming a complaint activist. The hope of this trajectory is not tied to success. Complaint activism comes from an experience of institutional failures of many kinds. One student said, "You know the process is broken, but still, you know you must do it, because if you don't, more falls to the wayside. So, it's like a painful repetitive cycle where you do what you know is right, knowing it may not make a difference at that time, but you always hope, you always have that hope, that maybe because I did this, it paves the way for something else." Complaint activism involves the willingness to make use of complaints procedures even though you know "the process is broken" and you are likely to enter "a painful repetitive cycle," which you can recognize because you have already been through it. You have hope because even if a complaint does not make a difference at the time you make it, it could still "pave the way for something else." I think of how paving can become pavement, how possibility can be preparing the ground. The hope of complaint could be thought of as a *weary hope*, not agentic, bright, forward, and thrusting, but a hope that is close to the ground, even below the ground, slow, low, below; a hope born from what is worn.

Even going through an exhausting of processes can have creative potential. Yes, we can be in a state of exhaustion because of that process. But complaints, even formal ones, slow and tedious ones, long and drawn out, can be creative. Consider how feminist artists have made use of complaint, or how feminist art can be complaint. The Guerrilla Girls, for instance, had an exhibition called *Complaints Department*, in which individuals and organizations were invited to post "about art, culture, politics, the environment, or any other issue they care about." They also ran office hours where you could share your complaints "face to face."[5] You can turn what might be assumed to be a mundane administrative practice into an art project. The direction of travel goes both ways. Those who make complaints, who enter that department, the Complaint Department (though of course making formal complaints often means entering many departments), can turn what they do—it might seem tedious, it might seem dull, all those papers—into art. Or perhaps there is no turning involved; perhaps there is an art in the mundane, to the mundane.

I noted in my introduction to this book that to express can mean to press something out. So much complaint activism is about finding other ways to express complaints. You can fill spaces with complaints or turn spaces into complaints. One group of students organized a grievance fest, in which people were invited to share their complaints with others.[6] You can turn a body into a complaint. I think of Emma Sulkowicz's *Mattress Performance (Carry That Weight)*, in which she carried a mattress around campus to call attention to the campus sexual assaults, including her own rape by another student in 2012.[7] A complaint can be shown as weight: what some have to carry around with them.

I have learned so much from the creativity of student-led complaint activism. A queer feminist student shared a written testimony about their activism. They described their work to make violence more visible as the work of complaint: "We complained through posters that there is gendered discrimination. We performed complaint through spoken word poem recital." A complaint can be a poster, a performance, a recital. They took on a role as student representative on an internal committee that dealt with complaints. To be on the complaints committee is to learn whose complaints get uptake, whose complaints get shut down. They described the systems for dealing with complaint as "institutional mechanisms built for complaints by the powerful." They worked to give support to complainants who were not supported by those mechanisms.

The complaints committee can be one place where you do the work of complaint. The classroom is another place. A professor made problematic statements about "fat women" and "people who can't give birth." When they challenged the professor, they were asked to leave the class but stood their ground. This student had a complaint to make, but before they could make it, the professor complained about them: "Before I could complain, he complained. The complaint was addressed behind closed doors with other professors." We have learned to listen to the doors. They have something to tell us. One of the professors said, "The department is my family," and the student was made to apologize. Yes, a complainer can become the wayward child, the one who refuses to love, or to love in the right way, the institution or those who embody it. They become, in their words, "a nuisance for the admin." To let complaints out—all that negativity, what a nuisance—is to become a *complaint magnet*. Willingly, willfully, you make complaints knowing that they will come right back at you. In the final year of their studies, they "did not have the energy to continue to be complained about," although they continued complaining informally in communications with others. And so, they turned their complaints into a dissertation project.

So many turns, so many complaints, so many projects. Complaint activism is not simply about using formal complaints procedures to press against institutions, although it involves that. It is also about taking complaints out, making complaints across different sites: the walls, the committees, the classrooms, the dissertations. Complaints can be expressed queerly, coming out all over the place. Complaints can be sneaky as well as leaky.

LIFTING THE LID

To make a complaint is to assemble materials: documents, policies, letters. There have been so many letters referenced in this book: those written by complainers, those written to complainers. Even when the materials end up buried, becoming files, housed in cabinets, they still provide evidence that somebody tried to address a problem. These materials matter wherever they end up. Where they end up also matters. Complaint activism turns the filing cabinet into a political object par excellence. The filing cabinet is another site for complaint.

The filing cabinet may be thought of as an institutional closet; complaints are buried here because of what they can reveal. I am using the

8.1 A political object, an institutional closet.

word *closet* to evoke a queer history: to be in the closet is to keep something secret, being gay, say: *that* stigma, *that* source of shame. But there are other histories evoked by closets; so many skeletons are buried here. To complain can cause quite a rattle. In chapter 3, I explored how to complain is to come out, to bring the violence out so that it can be faced. The filing cabinet is a function as well as an object: you have to file something because of what would come out if it came out. It can take work to bring out what has been filed away; I am calling this work *complaint activism*.

So many histories are lodged in filing cabinets, those institutional closets. I think of one utilitarian philosopher who said that a scholar could find out more about India, that British colony, from "his closet in England" than from using his eyes and ears in India.[8] One could speculate about the utility of "his closet," what he might be putting there, what other histories are being held there. Consider colonial archives, all the papers that are held. We know that some of the most revealing papers in the colonial archives—and by *revealing*, I mean revealing of colonial violence—were destroyed by the colonizers.[9] It can be telling, which papers are not preserved. Universities too are colonial archives. Universities do not only house papers and other materials deemed useful for scholars, so well described by Edward Said (1978) as Orientalism; many were funded by empire; they are spoils of empire. Perhaps what spoils empire, spoils an idea of empire, empire as gift, is kept a secret or destroyed.

If some histories are hard to tell because the papers have been destroyed, we can sometimes give a history of a destruction. Destruction can be an instruction. I described in chapter 1 how one woman shared with me her complaint file that included papers she was told to destroy. We can, as I noted then, refuse the instructions. When papers are destroyed, we find other ways of coming out with it; we find other ways of telling the histories the papers would have preserved. It might be that the effort to stop a complaint in the present is an attempt to keep the lid on history. One postgraduate student reported, "The scale of the response was so extreme, in a way, compared to what we were complaining about. Now on reflection I guess it was because there were hundreds of complaints they had suppressed that they did not want to have a lid lifted on it." To complain is to lift a lid; the more complaints are suppressed (to suppress is to restrain and restrict as well as to keep something secret), the more spills out. It can be explosive: what comes out. Even what or who has been binned or buried can acquire a life. The acquisition of life is not always immediate or even obvious.

When complaints end up in files, we don't always know where they went before they got there. One student who wrote to me about making a complaint about a sexual assault by a lecturer (her story was the second door story in chapter 5) describes what happened to her complaint as a mystery:

Who knows where my papers went and who took it into consideration? It is still a mystery, since I was not at all informed by any means. During those times, listening to many different stories of harassment, rape and abuse under institutions, I was consoling myself by saying that "ok, you already knew that your case wouldn't have resulted well, so you did what you did." I kept thinking like this for a few years until two research assistants from my alma mater informed me that my ex-department changed the teacher of that course right after my case was heard. They told me that my complaint became an influence on many in the faculty, it stirred discussions and uneasiness. Then a bit later, another researcher told me that after me, new and new official complaints started being submitted [by those] who had been harassed by this person. I don't know how true it is. To be honest I never had the will to go through that bureaucratic system to confirm it. But even to hear it gave me hope.

Even though you don't know where your papers go, you hear something because they went somewhere. When the door is shut on your complaint, when you are shown the back of the door, that complaint can still cause trouble later, stir things up, discussions, make things uneasy, make things difficult.

Complaints can stir things up. Complaints can stir up other complaints. Let's return to the disabled student whose work inspired the term *complaint activist*. She was not getting anywhere with her complaint about the failure of her university to make reasonable adjustments. She had a particularly difficult meeting; a meeting can be when you feel that wall coming down. After the meeting, a file suddenly appeared: "A load of documents turned up on the students' union fax machine, and we don't know where they came from. They were historical documents about students who had to leave." The documents included a handwritten letter to a human rights charity by a former student who had cancer and who was trying to get the university to let her finish her degree part time.

How did this file appear? Why did it appear? She speculates, "It came from somewhere in the university. We have no idea where it came from. My best theory is that someone in admin cared about it for some personal reason, like they are disabled, their kid is disabled, and decided to carry [out] their own little bit of direct action." The release of a file can be direct action. If someone from the administration put the file there, they did so because they wanted the student to know of this history but were not supposed to pass that file on to the student. The support she received from administrators often required acts of subversion: "Lots of people in the disability support service are diversity workers, and lots of them are disabled and were really personally supportive but weren't allowed to be publicly supportive. They would say things to me like 'I can't give you any advice on this but I know somebody who used this lawyer' or 'Can't give you any advice on this but have you checked the statutory code on education.'" Administrators gave advice to her by telling her they were not allowed to give her advice. In chapter 5, I described how some people who appear supportive in public, by standing up and committing to new policies, withdraw that support behind closed doors. The reverse can also be true: some people who are not supportive in public, because they are required to toe an institutional line, give their support secretly, behind closed doors.

I think of the word *secretary*, which derives from *secret*; the secretary as the keeper of secrets. It should not be surprising that a secretary becomes a saboteur; those who do administration, institutional housework, know about stuff, know where to find stuff, know what to do to get stuff out. Complaint activism can be a way of thinking about what it takes, the different actions that have to happen, for that stuff to get out. Complaints can be politicizing not only for those who make them but also for those who deal with them; even those who file complaints away can be touched in unexpected ways.

The hands that release the letter touch the hand that wrote it. I think of the student who wrote that letter by hand. We can't know, we won't know, what happened to her. But that she wrote the letter mattered. We can make the letter matter; a complaint can be a hand stretched out from the past. If the student I spoke to hadn't made her complaint, that file would have stayed put, the letter too: dusty, buried. Somebody else still had to pull the file out, to send the materials to a place she would find them, possibly a secretary who had been at that difficult meeting. Many have to meet to pull something out, to pull something off.

You can meet in an action without meeting in person. A collective can thus be created without ever meeting in person; over time, in time, a complaint, whether made or not, filed or not, can be a meeting point. A postgraduate student makes a complaint about bullying and harassment by her supervisors. She receives a letter in her post box: "I got a secret letter in my mailbox saying that they had heard I was having a difficult time with [them] and that there was a history of women leaving the department bullied by them. And there were two personal emails. I contacted them both." If she had not made her complaint, she would not have known about others before her who had made a complaint. Sometimes we don't know about someone because of what they went through. She finds out about them because her complaint was how they found out about her. A secret letter can be how we are put in touch with a history, a history of those who went through what we are going through.

I think of another student who made a complaint about bullying and gender-based harassment. She told me about a woman who had complained before she did: "There was a woman who had filed a complaint and she was outcast . . . , no one goes near her." We have heard so many of these stories, how those who complain are turned into outcasts, made into the origin of their own misfortune. Making a complaint can be how we acquire skepticism toward stories told about complainers, stories that are rarely told from the complainer's point of view. She said, "People told me the story. It is so difficult to get my head around because at the time I was so willing to go along with it. And now there I am, recognizing that if I were to move forward, I would likely be experiencing some of the same things she did." "And now there I am": she came to see through it, a story she had been told that she had been willing to go along with, about a woman who had complained, who had "filed a complaint," who "no one goes near." She came to see through that story because she recognized that to go through a complaint would be to go through some of the same things she did, that woman who had become an outcast. If a story can be inherited as distance ("no one goes near her"), a complaint gives you proximity, an unwilled proximity, to those who have been cast out.

Complaint can offer a transgenerational intimacy, to go back, to go over, as to go toward. She realizes it was "the system that almost pulls some of us apart." The *almost* is hopeful: we can pull together. Pulling together can be risky. "To associate with her," she admits, would be "to go off the deep end." Sometimes we take the risk; we don't let ourselves be pulled apart by the system. We take a leap, we "go off the deep end." That is what forming a complaint collective can do: those who are cast out can pull together, leap into the unknown.

A leap can be a leak. Earlier in this book I noted how feminism is often treated as infection, as what causes a complaint to spread. When complaints happen behind closed doors, doors are used to stop a complaint from spreading. The work of getting a complaint out thus requires finding ways to enable what has been contained to spread. What is represented as an organic process is often dependent on political work. Consider one of the actions mentioned in chapter 7. After a public event about sexual harassment in which so much remained unsaid, one member of the collective went to the library and scribbled their complaints into books written by one of the academics who had been the subject of the inquiries. Later, another student found those books in the library, took photos of the scribbles, and shared the photos on a blog. That's what it took for some of the professors to be named. The communications between these students, separated by time but not place, occurred through a complaint expressed as graffiti in a book. When a formal complaint leads to a burial, that graffiti becomes legible. Complaints require other lines of communication to be passed on, to be passed down.

The riskier it is to speak out, to put a name to a complaint, the more inventive we need to become. When we are blocked by following the official paths, we create our own pathways, ways of communicating, whisper networks, unofficial ways, old ways, of passing information down a line.[10] I think of another group of students who, after going through the proper complaint procedures, watched a professor who harassed them get away with it. They wrote down what they knew and turned their letters into leaflets that they shared with other students. Faculty from the department called their action "vigilantism" and damaging because of the failure to follow due process.[11] But this direct action was necessary because of the failure of due process. They could take the matter into their own hands because they had made formal complaints, they had the materials, the receipts, the letters, because of what they had been through. If direct action is often necessary because of the failure of a formal process, it is also made possible by that process. This is why I do not understand formal complaints as a separate sphere of action to that of direct action.

If we have to find ways to get our complaints out because of how they have been contained, the containers are part of the story. We too can be containers. But however well we contain a complaint, we might reach a point when we can no longer contain it. We might be in the middle of a meeting, and a complaint comes out, spills out, like that *eehhhhh*. Or sometimes, to get the information out, we get out. Resignation letters too are part of the story: how we leak complaints from containers, whether filing cabinets or our own bodies or both. When I made the reasons for my resignation public, I shared information—not very much, but enough—that there had been these inquiries. I became a leak: drip,

drip. In chapter 4, I noted how organizations respond in the mode of damage limitation, treating information as mess. The more you share, the more they mop. While that experience of being met with a mop was frustrating—more than that, enraging—I know now that *that* was not what mattered. Posting a letter about my resignation did something else, which was far more important: it helped other people to find me, the complainers. We are quite an army, those of us who have made complaints within institutions that led us to confront institutions head on, which then led us to leave.[12]

A mop can be a bit like a door, a clue that something is up. There is hope here: to mop something up is to reveal there is something to mop up. There is hope here: they cannot mop it all up. A leap can be a leak. A leak can be a lead. By becoming a leak, I became easier to find; people came to me with their complaints. *That we find each other through complaint is a finding.* This finding is not so much a finding from the research but what led me to it; it is how I could do it. As I noted in my introduction to this book, my resignation letter, at least the version I shared in public, was how many I spoke to found me. Posting that letter was how I became part of a collective, a complaint collective; we are assembled before you.

To resign can be how you get the letters out. Even complaints that do not seem to get anywhere can lead us to each other. One lecturer who left the academy after her complaint did not get anywhere (it was she who likened complaint to a little bird scratching away at something) turned her resignation letter into a performance: "I wrote a two-page letter and it was really important to me to put everything in there that I felt so that it was down on paper. And then I asked for a meeting with the dean. I kind of read the letter out in a performative kind of way just to have some kind of event." We find ways to make our letters matter. I think of her action, in that room, expressing her complaint. I think of the experience this lecturer had shared with me, of how a doctor tried to get her to sign his version of what she said, how she had to refuse to let him express her complaint (chapter 4). To perform her complaint, to express it, was to counter a history of being denied that expression.

You can do so much and still want to do more. She wanted to express more, to express herself in more places, to express herself all over the place. She wanted to put that letter on the wall: "I just thought, I am not the kind of person who would put my resignation letter on the wall, but I just wonder what it is that made me feel that I am not that kind of person because inside I am that kind of person. I just couldn't quite get it out." Perhaps that is what complaints are about: how we help each other to get it out. What you put down, down on paper, everything in there, others can pick up. We don't always know when. We don't always know how.

Perhaps that is why letters keep mattering, because of the doors they might yet open. Another lecturer whom I communicated with informally described what she found in writing her resignation letter: "I found it was powerful to write the final resignation complaint letter addressed to no one (that is, without any 'To' or 'Dear') and refer to everyone by their name (rather than 'you'). I think it alarmed my manager that the letter could land anywhere. Also, how cathartic that final letter is! Whenever I have doubts, I can read it over and remind myself what happened and why I left." To write a resignation letter can be to share your reasons for leaving. We read what we write to remind ourselves of what happened. We become reminders. Her letter contained information; she named names. The letter didn't use *you* to conceal *who*. It did not narrow its audience by addressing someone. In not being addressed to someone, the letter could be received by anyone. What we leave behind can be alarming. That letter, it "could land anywhere."

We don't know what *may* happen when we create a record of what *did* happen. We don't know what *will* happen to that record. It "could land anywhere." It is a hope, a promise, and also, perhaps, a threat. I suggested earlier that even when our complaints end up in filing cabinets, we take them with us. I also noted that we don't always know where complaints go, before they are filed. But even when complaints end up in filing cabinets, they can get out; we can get them out. Filing cabinets are temporary shelters. The more letters written, the more letters to leak. This is how complaints can be a queer method. In chapter 1, I shared a picture of what a complaint can feel like (figure 8.2).

So many letters, so many lines: it is such a mess, a tangle. What if we were to consider this mess as a queer map of an organization? Queer maps are useful because they tell us where to go to find queer places, places that come and go, providing temporary shelters (gay bars can be our nests), where we won't be, as it were, displaced by the letters in the box. If queer maps are useful, they are also created by use. Those lines tell us where we have been, what we found, who we found, by going that way, by not following the official paths we are told would have opened the door or eased our progression. A complaint can leave a trail, however faint. I think of other queer maps. Paul Harfleet, for instance, turned his experience of homophobic violence into an art project, planting pansies where acts of violence and abuse had taken place.[13] Perhaps a complaint is *what we plant*, a new growth of some kind that marks the site of violence.

8.2 A queer map.

The site of violence is the site of protesting that violence, saying *no* to that violence. That complaints are made is how we come to know something happened there: *no* as a tale, as trail.

No as a trail, *no* as a tale: who knows then who will find you because you expressed that *no*, because even if it took getting out, you got it out. Sometimes leaving a trail is a deliberate action. Sometimes it is not. In chapter 4, I shared the testimony of an Indigenous student who made an informal complaint about white supremacy in her classroom. A white professor read out her complaint in the class she complained about. Her complaint, it seemed, ended up in the classroom; a classroom can be a filing cabinet, another container. However much the complaint was contained, it stuck to her. She became, in her own terms, "a monster," an "Indigenous feminist monster," and is now completing her PhD off campus. She said that "an unexpected little gift" was how other students could come to her: "They know you are out there and they can reach out to you." She uses that expression twice, "an unexpected little gift." A complaint gives you something back because of how you can be reached. Even when our complaints lead us to leave, we leave something of ourselves behind by complaining. Complaints in pointing back can also point forward, to

8.3 A complaint as writing on the wall.

those who come after, who can receive something from you because of what you tried to do, even though you did not get through, even though all you seemed to do was scratch the surface.

Yes, those scratches, we are back to those scratches.

They seemed at first to show the limits of what we could accomplish (chapter 1). They can also be what we leave behind. A complaint as writing on the wall, a complaint as how we get those letters on the wall. What appears as scratch and scribble—that scramble of letters, remember that sound, *eehhhhh*—can be testimony. We can hear a *no* in a scramble, spillage as speech. In saying *no*, we keep a history alive. The letters can tell a story: *no*, we did not let go; we did not let it go. Sometimes to hold on is to pass a complaint on.

SURVIVAL AND HAUNTING

If a complaint can be how we keep a history alive, a complaint can be how we survive a history. I think of Audre Lorde's words (1978, 31): "Some of us were never meant to survive." For some of us, survival can be politically ambitious. It can require us to be inventive. It can require we chip away at those walls, however much they keep finding those chips on our shoulders. Audre Lorde (1984, 112) also suggests that "those of us who stand outside the circle of this society's definition of acceptable women" know that survival "*is not an academic skill.*" Those of us who are outside the circle but inside the academy might also know that surviving the academy is *"not an academic skill."*

Transforming institutions can be necessary if we are to survive them. But we still need to survive the institutions we are trying to transform. In chapter 6, I shared fragments from a testimony by an Indigenous woman academic. She told me how she could hardly manage to get to campus after a sustained campaign of bullying and harassment from white faculty, including a concerted effort by a senior manager to sabotage her tenure case as well as the tenure cases of other Indigenous academics. When you are harassed and bullied, when doors are closed, nay, slammed, making it hard to get anywhere, it is history you are up against, thrown up against. She did try to make a formal complaint only to be blanked (chapter 2). Blanking can be how we come up against that history, a violent history, how some complaints are made to disappear, how some are made to disappear. Perhaps sometimes to refuse *that* history, you might refuse to complain or you might to try to pass through the institution by passing out of the figure of the complainer (chapter 4). She suggests, "It is possible I learned very early that in order to keep my job and to have a stable income—I was so privileged and lucky to have a job in one of these institutions—that I better just keep my mouth shut, and learn how to avoid these encounters, and to protect myself, and to keep quiet about it." Many find that surviving institutions requires trying to avoid "these encounters" by being silent or keeping quiet about "these encounters." Not to be silent can feel like turning yourself into a target again. No wonder some refuse to refuse to be silent—if your family, your people, have been targeted, you might lie low, be quiet, doing what you can to survive.

Doing what you can to survive: to survive certain histories can require not expressing complaints in the usual places, not filling in forms, not sharing in public what you think or feel about a given situation. There are different ways of saying *no* and of doing *no*. Recall that a complaint can also mean the cause of a protest or outcry. Survival can be how you say *no*, how you protest a world that expects your disappearance or demands your disappearance. Survival can be a complaint. Some of the actions that might seem to be about "not complaining" can be oblique complaints, complaints that are not quite expressed or fully expressed, complaints that are below the surface, quiet complaints, hidden complaints, underground complaints, queer complaints.

A complaint can be what you have to do to go on. But you still have to work out what you can take on. She went on by taking them on:

I took everything off my door, my posters, my activism, my pamphlets. I smudged everything all around the building. I knew I was going to war; I did a war ritual in our tradition. I pulled down the curtain. I pulled on a mask. My people, we have a mask. . . . And I never opened my door for a year. I just let it be a crack. And only my students could come in. I would not let a single person come in to my office who I had not already invited there for a whole year.

Closing a door can be a survival strategy; she closes the door to the institution by withdrawing herself, her commitments, from it. She still does her work; she still teaches her students. She uses the door to shut out what she can, who she can. She takes herself off the door; she depersonalizes it. And she pulls down those blinds and she pulls on a mask, the mask of her people, connecting her fight to the battles that came before, because, quite frankly, for her, this is a war.

If doors are shut on complaints, a shut door can be a complaint. A shut door can be how we work *on* the institution; who knows what we might be plotting behind the door. Or a shut door can be how we say *no* to the institution, how we withdraw ourselves as well as our labor from it. To withdraw *from* can still be to work *on*. Withdrawal becomes a political action given the demand for access and upon whom that demands falls, how some have to make themselves available to others. Angela Mae Kupenda (2007) reflects on how, as a Black woman, she is expected to keep her door open. A white administrator emails her in frustration that she was not revealing more about herself. He says, " 'You must trust us more if you want to succeed here: there are no spooks behind that door!' " (20).[14] An open door can be used as a warning and thus also a threat: she is being told that if she does not open the door, to open the door as to trust them more, she will not succeed. She refuses to be told. She is telling the truth. She does not open that door, there are ghosts behind it: "To tell the truth, ghosts *have* haunted me: the ghosts of Jim Crow; the goblin of slavery-like, white, presumed superiority; and ghouls of sexism, racism, and classism just will not leave me alone" (Kupenda 2007, 20). Sometimes, to be haunted by a history can require we use doors to shut it out.

You might close a door because of what is still. You might open a door because of what is still. Let me return to the complaint testimony shared by an Indigenous academic. Early on in her testimony, she evokes another door, a door she says she has yet to open too widely: "There is a genealogy of experience, a genealogy of consciousness in my body that is now at this stage traumatized beyond the capacity to go to the university. There's a legacy, a genealogy, and I haven't really opened that door too widely as I have been so focused on my experience in the last seven years." To be traumatized is to hold a history in a body; you can be easily shattered. There is only so much you can take on because there is only so much you can take in. In chapter 3, I used the expression "the door of consciousness" to describe how we sometimes shut violence out, perhaps because it is too difficult to deal with, perhaps to hold on to something we fear losing, perhaps so we can focus or function. We can inherit closed doors. In other words, a trauma can be inherited by being made inaccessible, all that happened that was too hard, too painful, to share or reveal. Decolonial feminist work, Black feminist work, feminist of color work is often about opening these doors, the door to what came before, colonial as well as patriarchal histories, harassment as the hardening of *that* history, a history of who gets to do what, who gets to be what, who is deemed entitled to whom. To open these doors, the door to what came before, is to account for what is still. When complaints take us back, they take us back further *still*. Christina Sharpe (2016, 18–20) attends to the word *still*; she thinks *still* with Black poets Dionne Brand and NourbeSe Philip, crafting dialogues out of what is still. Sharpe shows how to live "in the wake" of slavery is to live with what is still.

When we open the door to what came before, we open the door to more doors. Doors, then, can be how we remember what is still. Dionne Brand (2001) offers a map of the Door of No Return at the House of Slaves, a museum to the Atlantic Slave Trade. The Door of No Return is a *memorial door*, a door that remembers the exit point for millions of Africans. For Brand, the door is "real and metaphoric" (18). She writes, "I have not visited the Door of No Return, but by relying on random shards of history and unwritten memoir of descendants of those who passed through it, including me, I am constructing a map of the region, paying attention to faces, to the unknowable, to unintended acts of returning, to impressions of doorways" (19). Those descended from those who cannot return, return to that door. The door of no return "was the door of a million exits multiplied. It is a door many of us wish never existed. It is a door which makes the word *door* impossible and dangerous, cunning and disagreeable" (19). A door can be saturated by history; a history is what you can hear when you hear the word *door*. Brand approaches the Door of No Return as consciousness, as haunting: "Black experience in any modern city or town in the Americas is a haunting. One enters a room and history follows; one enters a room and history precedes" (25).

Doorways become places you visit in accounting for a history that haunts the present. Doorways leave or make impressions ("impressions of doorways"). Joan Anim-Addo (1998) evokes "another doorway" in asking how Black women might enter the museums of history differently, by noticing who does not appear here, how Black women do not appear here, seeing differently, relating differently to, all that is held here.[15] "Another doorway" becomes, in Anim-Addo's hands, a poem. Her "another doorway" has a "missing sign," "Welcome here we women," a sign that points to how women are here, busy, pounding maize, concocting relishes, cooking dishes. Her "another doorway" has "an alternative sign," a sign that also points to how women are here, leaving gifts of food for those who are journeying, who are burying their dead. Her poem "Another Doorway" asks "where the bodies?" and promises "to follow, follow" the bodies that are not here, that have been taken, stolen (95).

To follow the many who are missing is to find many doorways. Audre Lorde in her poem "A Litany for Survival" also evokes doorways: "For those of us who live at the shoreline, standing upon the constant edges of decision, crucial and alone, for those of us who cannot indulge the passing dreams of choice, who love in doorways coming and going in the hours between dawns" (1978, 31). Lorde addresses "those of us," those of us who live and love on the edges of social experiences, in doorways, shadows, those of us who fall like shadows fall, the fallen, those of us for whom coming into full view would be dangerous. Not coming into full view might be how some survive. To stay alive can be another view, another way of coming and going. Saidiya Hartman (2019, 18, 22) evokes Lorde in giving an intimate history of Black girls, of their wayward loves and lives; she describes how Black girls "love in doorways" and "peered out of doorways."

A doorway can be a viewing point. A doorway can be a meeting place. Living and loving in doorways: rather than scurrying through, some stop; some linger, at the borders, in the shadows, on the edges. A doorway can be a space around a door or an empty space where a door would be. I hear Lorde knocking on a door, telling us something's up. In an interview with Adrienne Rich, Lorde (1981) describes her fascination with a poem by Walter de La Mare, "The Listener." She had been telling a story about finding old books, used books, in a library in Harlem, books that were in "the worst condition." How I love how she finds those books! And not just them; she finds a poem there too, this poem, "A Listener," a poem about a traveler who rides a horse up to the door of an apparently empty house. Lorde describes the poem:

He knocks at the door and nobody answers. "'Is there anybody there?'
he said." That poem imprinted itself on me. And finally, he's beating
down the door and nobody answers, and he has a feeling that there
really is somebody in there. And then he turns his horse and he says,
"'Tell them I came, and nobody answered. That I kept my word,'" I
used to recite that poem to myself all the time. It was one of my favor-
ites. And if you'd asked me, what is it about, I don't think I could have
told you. But this was the first cause of my own writing, my need to
say things I couldn't say otherwise when I couldn't find other poems
to serve. (715)

It is important to follow Lorde, to go where she goes. When we are fas-
cinated by something, we do not always know why. What captures your
attention, causing you to write, to express yourself, might not have the
crispness or the edges of an about. Lorde keeps reciting the poem. I think
of how "it imprinted" on her. An imprint: the print of a poem on a person.
There is a door in that poem; it too leaves a print. Knocking on the door
can be the sound of an imprint. The point is not in the answer, whether
someone answers, but in the knock; the knock is the action. Remember:
you can meet in an action without meeting in person. To keep your word
is to keep turning up, to find new forms of expression, ways of saying
what you otherwise could not say.

Ways of saying otherwise, hearing otherwise. You might be knocking
on the door of consciousness; remember, that door can be an inheritance,
trying to hear something, to admit what has been shut out, the violence
that is passed down by being made inaccessible. Or, you might be knocking on the door of the master's house because you know that house is
haunted. Knocking is hard. Knocking can be how we learn that the door
of consciousness, how violence is shut out, can be the same door shut by
institutions to keep violence in. And so, the data of complaint, our data,
our truths, ends up under lock and key. To knock on *that* door, to make
that sound—not "Knock, knock, who is there?" but "Knock, knock, I am
here"—is how you are haunted by the house; you do not make it your
possession, you are possessed by it.

You are possessed by it. You have a feeling someone is there. Feelings
can be in the room. Someone is there. To complain is to keep knocking
on *that* door, hoping to create an impression, to cause a disturbance, to
disturb someone who is there: the spirits who linger there because of the
violence that has not been dealt with. Avery Gordon ([1997] 2008, xvi)
describes haunting as "an animated state in which a repressed or unre-

solved social violence is making itself known, sometimes very directly, sometimes more obliquely." With reference to the work of Luisa Valenzuela and Toni Morrison, Gordon suggests haunting can be used to describe "those singular and yet repetitive instances when home becomes unfamiliar, when your bearings on the world lose direction, when the over-and-done-with comes alive, when what's been in your blind field comes into view" (xvi). The complaint graveyard: complaints that appear over and done with, buried, beneath the ground, come alive; they come back. Complaints raise the blind; what goes down, comes up. We see what has been kept *out of view*, the institutional view.

There are ghosts because of what is not gone, and who too, because of who is not gone. To receive complaints is to have your own complaint history. Perhaps it was because I received complaints as a child of empire—Pakistan, England, Australia; a family history as a colonial history—that I could hear them, the ghosts. We bring the ghosts into the room; we can hear them because they come with us. In chapter 6, I shared a testimony from a woman of color academic who was shut out of a project on diversity directed by a white woman who was a direct descendant of the colonizers. There was a gravestone in that story; let me share it again: "This woman is high-colonial British Raj. . . . Her grandmother's gravestone is in Calcutta, and that's rare. You have to be really high up in the British Raj."

A gravestone can be a reminder of hierarchy, an enactment of history. We are that history; it lives with us, through us. She added,

We have to go back to understand what is happening, the colonial history of Britain, how we are still refusing to have a dialogue about South Asian and East Asian histories, because the relatives are still alive, the descendants are still alive, and *reparations* is a dirty word for these people; it means having to confront their wealth, the filth of their wealth, having to confront the genocide that took place that resulted in millions of Indians being killed, the profits they are living off.

We have to go back; we keep going back. They refuse to go back, a colonial history living on, in and through the wealth of descendants, those for whom going back, dealing with that level of violence, that many dead, that much death, would mean giving up wealth.

There cannot *not* be ghosts in these testimonies—ghosts, graveyards, hauntings—because we are dealing with what has not been dealt with. Perhaps we are the ghosts, Brown and Black peoples in white institutions, Indigenous peoples in settler colonial institutions, reminders of a history they refuse to give up. Perhaps we are the ghosts, but we too are haunted by them, by what is not gone, by what goes on. That history, the violence of that history, is embedded in the very fabric of institutions, universities: the walls, the narrow corridors, the windows with blinds that come down, the doors with locks on them. That history, the violence of that history is also manifest as attitude: who is higher, lower, who is more, less; in material relations, in expectations of service and servitude that are so often realized in who is required to do what.

In chapter 6, I shared fragments of a testimony by a Black woman academic who was on her way to becoming a professor; she is now a professor. She described how she was treated by a white woman: "She had to be the boss, and I had to be the servant type of thing." A boss, a master: a history can be kept alive in an expectation of servitude. For her, a Black woman, to become a professor did not stop her from being treated as a servant. *Workloads are history lessons*, a history of who is freed by whom is required to take the load, to take more of the load. To complain can be to refuse this history, to refuse to be of service to it, to serve it up, to be served up. You have to be vigilant, to keep watch. She also said, "In order to survive in a hostile environment like that, a toxic one, where you are more than marginal, you have to do this work of institutional analysis all the time. They are going to do this, and I have to do that, and then I do this, and they do that: you know what I mean? It's constant, this watchfulness that you have to have in order to protect yourself from being really knocked." You knock on the door; you can be knocked by the door. That work, watching out, being watchful, on your toes, what's next, what comes next, protecting yourself from being "really knocked," is the work of institutional analysis, the work of theory; it is the work of survival, the work of complaint.

It can be hard: to be taunted, to be haunted. We can be haunted by what we hear, just as we can be haunted in the room where we hear it. We can return to Angela Mae Kupenda's (2012, 27) consideration of the "spooks behind the door." She shows how the spooks follow her from behind the door into the room because they are already in the room: "They are present and dwell in our lives and structures and institutions, in a society that pretends that racism, sexism and all the other -isms do not exist." Kupenda suggests the "ghosts will fade" only when they are faced (27). We can turn to Gail Lewis (2019, 419), who observes, "*Racism* has absolutely haunted me. I think that was because of the ways it was in the front room, and class wound has haunted me as well." Racism, class, how we come to embody the violence of a history, a body as room, a body in the front room, to be in that room as to face up to that history. A room, a house, even the air, can be occupied by history. Aileen Moreton-Robinson (2015, 81) describes how Indigenous sovereignty "continues in the presence of Indigenous people and their land, haunting the house that Jack built, shaking its foundations, rattling the picket fence." That rattling is the sound of disturbance on the edges of the house that Jack built, the house of whiteness, the master's house. The refusal of Indigenous people to disappear can shake the foundations. Eve Tuck and C. Ree (2013, 647) suggest that "decolonization must mean attending to ghosts, and arresting widespread denial of the violence done to them." To deny something is to refuse to admit its truth. To complain is to admit the truth of violence. To complain is to let the ghosts in.

To be haunted is to be hit by an inheritance. No wonder doors matter so much. Behind closed doors, that is where complaints are often found, so that is where you will find us, too, those of us for whom the house was not built, what we bring with us, who we bring with us, the worlds that would not be here if some of us were not here; the data we hold, our bodies, our memories; the more we have to spill, the tighter the hold. We knock on the door from behind the door, to complain as to knock on the doors of history. To knock on the doors of history is to inhabit the present even more, all the more; to breathe it in. No walls, no doors are solid enough to stop the ghosts from entering. The complaints in the graveyard can come back to haunt institutions. We can come back to haunt institutions. It is a promise.

I shared the image of a complaint graveyard with one person that had been shared with me by another. A dialogue is possible when we collect tales, leave trails. She said:

> You have to think about the impact of doing this. Because having yet another complaint, it means that you give more credibility to the one who comes after you. When you talk about haunting, you are talking about the size of the graveyard. And I think this is important. Because when you have one tombstone, one lonely little ghost, it doesn't actually have any effect; you can have a nice cute little cemetery outside your window, but when you start having a massive one, common graveyards and so on, it becomes something else; it becomes much harder to manage.

We can and do form complaint collectives. We can and do become harder to manage. But we do not always assemble at the same time or in the same place. You might feel like a lonely little ghost right now. Your complaint might seem to have evaporated like steam: puff, puff. But your complaint can still be picked up and amplified by others. You might not be able to hear it now; it might not have happened yet. Even complaints you do not make can be picked up. After all, complaints we do not make, we store. That store is another complaint collective. Unmade complaints might end up in the complaint graveyard, too, little ghosts, less lonely for getting there, less lonely for being there. I think of little ghosts and I hear little birds, "little birds scratching away at something."

Little ghosts, little birds, a common graveyard, a queer nest. If a complaint leads to death, institutional death, to complain is to give support to life: you plant something in saying *no*, by saying *no*, the twists and turns of new growth. To make a nest possible, to make it possible to nest, you have to stop what usually happens from happening; you have to stop the letters being posted, from piling up, from taking up space. The work of making possible is the work of complaint. You can't always tell, you don't always know, what a complaint makes possible. But from complaint we learn how possibility is not plucked out of thin air. Possibility comes

8.4 "Little birds scratching away at something."

from intimacy with what has thickened over time. You might be chipping away at the old block, those structures, that wall, that barrier, and all you seem to have done is scratched the surface. That scratching is learning. We learn *how* structures stay up from how they are justified. Remember: the more we complain, the more they have to justify (chapter 3). Also, the more we question how things are, the more we know how things are: institutionalism fatalism; history as inheritance; reader, I inherited him.[16] And you know what; we know what. Arguments can stop working. Justifications can become tired. The inevitable turns out to be avoidable.

We cannot always perceive the weakening of structures until they collapse. When structures begin to collapse, the impact of past efforts becomes tangible. Complaints can participate in the weakening of structures without that impact being tangible. Impact is a slow inheritance. This book is about *that* inheritance, complaint as inheritance. Each complaint gathers more, however slowly, however long it takes, to gather as a gathering of momentum, no, no, no, no, *eehhhhh*, the sounds of refusal. To say *no*, to scramble the letters—they don't pile up, they don't make sense—is to fight against something, what is tight, what is narrow, to create room for something else, somebody else: to weaken is to loosen; to loosen is to open. There you are, doing what you do, little ghosts, little birds, scratching away at something, trying to make room, to create a nest, from what has been left behind, from what has been left scattered.

A complaint can open the door to those who came before.

NOTES

INTRODUCTION

1. The piece is titled "It Is Not like Asian Ladies to Answer Back" and is included in *Writing Black Britain: An Interdisciplinary Anthology* (2000). See also Wilson ([1978] 2018).

2. In this short description is a clue as to how a secretary can become a saboteur. See chapter 8 for discussion.

3. This definition is derived from the Merriam Webster dictionary, accessed December 2, 2020, https://www.merriam-webster.com/dictionary/complaint.

4. Please see in this volume chapter 7 by Whitley et al. They describe how, when they submitted individual complaints, they did so by working collectively. We can resist the demands of the institution to take form in a certain way by appearing to take form in a certain way.

5. #Complaintasfeministpedagogy became my Twitter hashtag for the project. Please feel free to use it to share your complaints!

6. I decided to research complaint about six months before I resigned on December 11, 2015. I wrote in a Facebook post, "I am thinking after my project on 'the uses of use' I want to write a book called *Complaint*. Just the one word. And I want to do some more empirical research by talking to those who have made complaints about harassment and bullying within the workplace. I think there is so much to learn from what happens to those who complain and what happens to a complaint."

7. Most of the people I spoke to are, like me, based in the UK. My discussion of policy frameworks and complaints procedures is in this context. Given that those I communicated with mainly approached me and given I did not delimit my study by location, I have also communicated with people from outside of the UK. I have received written and oral testimonies from students and academics based in Turkey, Portugal, India, Australia, Lithuania, the US, and Canada. However, this research is not a comparative study. I made the decision not to locate the data although I have not removed references to national

location from the data. There are many differences in how complaints are handled across national contexts as well as within them. I also didn't want to clutter or cramp the text by adding too many identifiers. I tend to introduce the material primarily with reference to the person's academic position at the time of a complaint (whether, say, they are a student or early career researcher). I follow how people identify themselves (so, for instance, if someone talks about an experience they had as a woman of color or as a lesbian, I will introduce them as a woman of color or as a lesbian).

8. My website included a page for the project as well as an email address (complaintstudy@gmail.com). That page and email will remain live for as long as I am.

9. Initially I did not intend to conduct interviews with administrators, although I had done so for my project on diversity, just because I wanted to focus on the experiences of those who make complaints. However, one administrator based in the UK asked to speak to me, and her testimony was immensely rich and valuable (see chapter 1). I have had many informal conversations with administrators, some of which are referred to in the chapters that follow. In addition, two people I spoke to had experience of administering as well as making complaints and shared valuable insights acquired from occupying different positions in the complaints process. One of these people gave me one of the best descriptions of best practice for how to receive complaints as an administrator. She said, "The way I would walk them through that process, my own version of it, of course, I tend to be very empathetic, a listener, what you're doing, I guess. I listen[ed] to the story first and then made a decision. Some of those turned into formal complaints, some of them did not. I always let the person choose. I never felt it was my place, especially having filed complaints and knowing the repercussions of what happens, I never wanted to push people into doing something or not doing something."

10. This is the second major study I have conducted using social science methods. I am by training a humanities scholar, and I have no doubt this shows in how I am making use of the data—with my close attention to words, sounds, figures, and images. Scholars working at the intersection of Black British feminism and cultural studies have influenced my methodology; I think especially of work by Avtar Brah (1996), Yasmin Gunaratnam (2003), and Gail Lewis (2000). This work recognizes, in Gunaratnam's terms, that "social discourses are enmeshed in lived experience and institutional and social power relations that have emotional, material and embodied consequences for individuals and for groups" (7). My approach is also influenced by my sustained engagement with the phenomenological tradition, which has shaped scholarship in the humanities as well as social sciences.

11. I always specify when quotes are from an informal communication (such as an email sent to me or a conversation). If not, the quote will be from spoken or written testimony.

12. My previous empirical study of diversity in higher education institutions had been funded. We ended up constrained by what the funders wanted from the research: they wanted to use the research to tell a story of how well the sector was doing in promoting race equality. We refused to tell that story, because that was not what we found. Our report was too much of a complaint—they even said we had focused "too much" on racism. They did not publish our report, which now circulates only unofficially. So I arrived at this project well aware that doing the work of institutional critique, or institutional complaint, can be, will be, constrained when that work is resourced by institutions.

13. I created my own consent form, which was sent to each participant along with a project description before the interview. I also talked to each person about the recording and how I would make use of the stories they shared.

14. I am referring to the first door story in chapter 5.

15. Please see the powerful description in chapter 1 from a woman professor who made a complaint about bullying by her head of department. She talked about how, when you make a complaint, you fear what is going to come through the door.

16. I became interested in testimony as a cultural form early on in my academic career, when I was based in women's studies at Lancaster. Please see the special issue "Testimonial Cultures" (Ahmed and Stacey 2001), which I coedited with Jackie Stacey, based on contributions to a conference held at the Institute for Women's Studies in 2000, Testimonial Cultures and Feminist Agendas. In this book I am especially interested in whose testimony is rendered incredible. See also Leigh Gilmour's (2016, 1) important account of testimony and witnessing, which considers how "judgment falls unequally on women who bear witness."

17. With thanks to Sarah Franklin for this formulation.

18. I return to how listening to these testimonies affected me in the opening to chapter 8. When I think "affected," I think learning. It is impossible for me to separate what I learned from this study from how I was affected by the stories I share.

19. The sense of complaint being in the present matters so much in the telling of these stories. For this reason, I have chosen mainly to use the present tense in writing about the experiences shared with me even though these experiences are in the past. At times, I will shift between tenses in order to convey the quality of the experience being narrated. I am aware this might be an unsettling experience for readers.

20. See chapter 8 for a discussion of how complaint activism turns the filing cabinet into a political object.

21. I considered giving those I spoke to pseudonyms and presenting each story more fully, but it did not feel right as a way of presenting the material. My aim is to reflect on complaint collectively, so I think of each quote as a fragment of a collective story as much as an individual story. In some instances, I connect different fragments of the same individual story when connecting

the fragments allowed me to show something I would not otherwise be able to show. See my chapter 8 on how complaint provides an "old and weathered lens" on collectivity.

22. Most interviews took around ninety minutes. The longest, which was an in-person interview, took just under three hours.

23. My emphasis on the affective nature of complaint connects with Lauren Berlant's (2008) consideration of female complaint. Berlant describes complaint as "a way of archiving experience and turning experience into evidence and evidence into argument and argument into convention and convention into cliché, clichés so powerful they can hold a person her entire life" (227). My discussion is more about feminist than female complaint. (I shared a post titled "Feminist Complaint" on my blog in 2014, well before I decided to conduct the research.) Feminist complaint can also "hold a person her entire life," although perhaps less through convention and cliché. With thanks to Lauren Berlant for the inspiration of her work. See also Green (2017) and Washick (2020) for discussions of feminist complaint that draw on Berlant's approach to female complaint. While I do not situate this book in relation to academic work on the literary genre of complaint, the question of feeling connects my concerns with more literary ones. Just consider this description of complaint as a literary genre: "The complaint is a literary genre based on seemingly interminable lamenting (in contrast to elegy, which, after pointing out sorrow, aims at putting it in its place, mourning and then moving on). When a poet writes a complaint, he or she uses the poem to prolong the experience of loss, not, like the elegist, to frame the loss and put it into perspective" (Mikics 2010, 67). A complaint is often framed as the failure to get over loss or as holding on to loss, a complaint as how some are deemed stuck on being negative.

24. In *What's the Use? On the Uses of Use* (2019) I explore exclamation marks, first by considering how they can be overused, then by considering how they become warnings, and finally by reflecting on how diversity workers are often heard as exclamation points.

25. The root is *plāk*, Indo-European, meaning "strike."

26. Definition from Online Etymology Dictionary, accessed November 16, 2020, https://www.etymonline.com/word/express#etymonline_v_14105.

27. I will explore in chapter 4 how unbecoming complainers becomes a project for those exhausted by complaint.

28. Chapter 2 discusses the kinds of conversations people have in the early and informal stage of a complaint process, which I describe as "institutional," as they are conversations with people with an official role in the complaint process. Chapter 3 considers the conversations people have when deciding whether to make complaints with friends and peers. I learn so much from hearing about these different conversations together.

29. Although I use the idea of complaint biography as a way of *not* reducing complaints to formal complaints, most of the data in this book comes from those who made or considered making formal complaints. Academic studies of

formal complaints are scattered across different fields. One of the best-known studies of a complaint system is of complaints against the police (Maguire and Corbett 1991). There is a more extensive qualitative literature on the experiences of complaint (from the point of view of the complainant) in health and medicine than in other sectors. See, for example, Mulcahy (2003). The scoping project on existing research on complaint funded by the UK's Health and Care Professions Council has many additional sources for complaints in health and medicine and can be downloaded from their website, accessed July 21, 2020, https://www.hcpc-uk.org/resources/. There is not much qualitative research into people's experience of making complaints within universities, although there are a number of first-person accounts of making complaints. Anna Bull and Rachel Rye (2018) conducted a study of student complaints about staff sexual misconduct in the UK, drawing on interviews with students. Valerie Sulfaro and Rebecca Gill (2020) offer some practical guidance on filing formal complaints on sexual harassment using Title IX, drawing on their own experiences of sexual harassment in the academy. Carolyn West (2010) writes compellingly of her own experience of making a complaint about sexual harassment. She reflects specifically on how Black women experience racialized sexual harassment. Jennifer Doyle (2015) offers a feminist analysis of what complaints do (and how complaints can lead to countercomplaints), which begins with her own experience of filing a complaint against a student via her university's Title IV office. Julia H. Chang (2020) offers a very powerful description of what happened (or did not happen) when she filed a complaint about racism and gives helpful advice on "things to be mindful of" (267–68). See also Enakshi Dua's (2009) important research into antiracist policies in Canadian universities, which is based on interviews with antiracist practitioners, some of whom had responsibility for handling grievances and complaints. She discusses how and why complaints about racism do not go forward despite commitments to race equality at the level of policy.

30. Quote is from Andrea Garcia Giribet, "Tarana Burke: The Woman behind Me Too," Amnesty International, August 21, 2018, https://www.amnesty.org/en/latest/education/2018/08/tarana-burke-me-too/. That #MeToo went viral when it was popularized by a white woman about sexual harassment in the entertainment industry might have something to tell us about whose complaints get "taken up." See chapter 4 for a discussion of "take up" and Alison Phipps (2020) for a critique of how mainstream white feminism took up the hashtag #MeToo with more stress on the Me than the Too. For reflections on sexual violence in the academy that take #MeToo as a reference point, see the essays collected by Karuna Chandrashekar, Kimberly Lacroix, and Sabah Siddiqui (2018) and by Laura A. Gray-Rosendale (2020).

31. I noted earlier that this book is not about *all* or *any* complaints. This book is also *not* about *all* or *any* complaints made within universities. I do not consider complaints that relate to the quality of teaching or course provision. Having said this, I show how complaints about harassment can be managed

and filtered by being treated as if they are complaints about the quality of teaching or course provision (chapter 5). I also do not deal with complaints relating to administrative processes, such as examinations. Having said this, my book includes an example of how a disagreement about examination regulations ended up in a disciplinary action (chapter 1). It can be hard to untangle what happens to complaints made within universities from relations of structural inequality and power. Given that this book is about complaints made *at* the university, and is thus *on* the university, it could also be situated in relation to the field of critical university studies. Although I have not positioned my work in relation to this field, I very much appreciate learning from Tseen Khoo, James Burford, Emily Henderson, Helena Liu, and Z. Nicolazzo (2020) about some of the connections.

32. I think of the following texts by Black feminists and feminists of color as offering the companionship of the counterinstitutional: Alexander (2006), Bilge (2020b), Essed (1996), Hampton (2020), Kamaloni (2019), Mirza (2017), Mohanty (2003), Sian (2019), Smith (2010), Tate (2017), and Wekker (2016).

33. *Diversity work* is work because of what diversity can be used not to do. In *Living a Feminist Life* (2017), I use *diversity work* in two senses: the work we do to transform institutions by opening them up to those who have been excluded; and the work we do when we do not quite inhabit the norms of an institution. These two senses often meet in a body: those who do not quite inhabit the norms of an institution are often given the task of transforming these norms. In chapter 4 of this book, I explore *complaint as diversity work*: the work we do when we are not accommodated; the work we do in order to be accommodated. This way of approaching diversity work has also been shaped by listening to disabled academics and students talk about the work of securing reasonable adjustments and making complaints about ableism and inaccessibility.

34. McClintock is challenging Laura Kipnis's critique of student activism around sexual violence in the US context. Her critique of the critique is such a sharp description of so much student-led activism around sexual violence at universities in the US and beyond. With thanks to Anne McClintock for the inspiration of her work. See also Rentschler (2018) for a discussion of the innovative nature of student activism around sexual violence.

35. I am writing this introduction in June 2020, as Black Lives Matter protests in response to the police's murder of George Floyd on May 25 promise to change the landscape of the universities. Decisions have been made to remove statues and to rename buildings with relative speed after years of resistance to student-led protests and demands. It is important to think of these earlier struggles as the enabling condition for what is happening now. See the final few paragraphs of chapter 8 for a discussion of complaint as slow inheritance.

36. See Olufemi et al. (2019) for a powerful collection of essays about the experiences of Black women and women of color at elite universities. This

collection could itself be read as a form of complaint activism. See also Olufemi (2020) for an important new articulation of a radical Black feminism.

37. Davis (2016, 19) also suggests that "behind the concept of intersectionality is a rich history of struggle." With thanks to Angela Y. Davis for teaching me to appreciate how concepts come out of activism and into academia rather than the other way around. I have tried to keep her insistence in mind when writing about complaint: when complaints are part of an effort to modify the world, those who make them come to know the world differently.

38. With thanks to Kimberlé Crenshaw for her important work. Intersectionality is one of *many* vital contributions of Black feminism. See Holland (2012) and Nash (2018) on the importance of not reducing Black feminism to intersectionality. For a critique of how intersectionality can be "whitened," which is especially convincing in its analysis of what happens to intersectionality when it travels into European gender studies, see Bilge (2013). I find intersectionality a profoundly useful way of understanding the complexity of social experience because of how intersectionality enables us to show how people's relation to one social category is affected by their relation to other social categories. A useful elaboration of how intersectionality can be used to challenge "additive models" is offered by Brewer (1993). For a cartographic approach to intersectionality, see Brah (1996). For an elaboration of how intersectionality can be understood as a "bottom-up method" rather than originating top down from the work of a single theorist, see Phoenix and Bauer (2012). For a discussion of the significance of intersectionality for qualitative research informed by grounded theory, see Cuádraz and Uttal (1999). Although I am primarily approaching intersectionality as a method, I appreciate Collins and Bilge's (2016, 37) suggestion that "intersectionality is more than a research method, it is a tool for empowering people." The lenses we use to show and make sense of the complexity of social worlds can be research methods as well as tools for empowerment.

39. In chapter 6, I explore how, when Black women and women of color raise issues other than sexism or racism (Black women and women of color do have other issues!), sexism and racism can still shape what happens. For a wonderful collection of essays on Black women and women of color "surviving and thriving in British academia," see Gabriel and Tate (2017).

ONE. MIND THE GAP!

1. I have used the concept of nonperformativity in different ways over the years. The term first came to my mind during a discussion at an event on racism and the university that took place in 2002. It was during the time in which universities were writing racial equality policies and statements as a result of changes to legislation. *Nonperformative* seemed to capture how saying something was not doing something. I first made use of the term in a written publication to make sense of how declarative speech acts are used in critical

whiteness studies (Ahmed 2004). In *On Being Included*, I defined the term more precisely as speech acts that do not bring into effect what they name (Ahmed 2012, 113; see also Ahmed 2017). This definition was borrowing the terms of Judith Butler's (1993, 2) definition of performativity as how discourse produces "the effect it names." More recently, I defined nonperformativity in relation to use: nonperformative policies come into existence without coming into use (Ahmed 2019). As I am completing this book in the summer of 2020 there has been an intensification of what I would call nonperformative statements by universities as well as other organizations and institutions. These statements are in fact more typically called performative statements (with performativity being used to imply empty performances). These statements take the form of commitments to Black Lives Matter that have been authored and shared after the protests against the police murder of George Floyd on May 25, 2020. My thesis of nonperformativity would not lead me to call for organizations to stop making such statements (though I would understand why some might make such a call, given that many organizations making statements of commitment remain hostile environments for Black people). My argument is more of an explanation of how such statements do not do what they say they do. We can still make use of such statements to do things, for instance, by pointing out the failure to follow them.

2. In chapter 3, I will explore a different version of a complaint file: a complaint file as where you put all the complaints you do not make.

3. I return to the experiences that led her to complain in more detail in chapter 4, in the section titled "Complaint and Misfitting."

4. I will return to her testimony, and the significance of the use of the word *scandal*, in the final section of chapter 6.

5. Another academic also described how making a complaint, in her case about workloads and the failure to make reasonable accommodations, led her to realize how deals were being made: "You realize when you have a conversation it is not the same for everybody. The deals are being done behind closed doors."

6. I will return to how complaints procedures can be understood as "the master's tools" a few times in this book, although that is not my primary way of approaching complaints. In chapter 4, with reference to Audre Lorde's (1984) essay, I turn to how complaints teach us about "the master's house." In chapter 5, I explore how the understanding of complaints as "the master's tools" can itself be used to try to dissuade people from making complaints (and can thus be a way of reproducing problematic forms of behavior). In chapter 8, I consider how complaint activists make use of complaints procedures to push against institutions in part by occupying their time. When the master's tools are repurposed, they can be queer tools. One of the most powerful descriptions of how complaints can be the master's tools is offered by Julia H. Chang (2020), who details how the investigation that followed the complaint she filed about racism was handled in such a way that she could not even know whether there

had been an investigation. She concludes, "This is what happens when you attempt to dismantle the master's house with the master's tools!" (265).

7. See the section "Not Being Promoted" in chapter 6 for a fuller discussion of his complaint.

8. For an important critique of that statement by Anna Bull, Tiffany Page, and Leila Whitley, see "Statement," Sexual Harassment in Higher Education, December 2, 2015, https://shhegoldsmiths.wordpress.com/statement/.

9. I was reminded of my own experience writing a race equality policy. We crafted a policy that made use of critical vocabularies, naming whiteness as an institutional problem, for instance. The Equality Challenge Unit ranked the policy as "excellent." At a meeting with university lecturers the vice chancellor, with the letter in his hand, congratulated the university for being excellent at racial equality. A document that documents racism becomes usable as a measure of good performance.

10. For a fuller elaboration of the connection between uses of diversity and complaints procedures, see my chapter "Use and the University," in *What's the Use? On the Uses of Use* (2019). See also Nicola Rollack (2018) for a discussion of diversity as a "gestural politics," as well as Rinaldo Walcott (2019) for a critique of the use of the language of diversity (as well as equity and antiracism). I develop the critique of diversity in the section "A Hostile Environment" in chapter 4 and the section "The Diversity Door" in chapter 6.

11. In chapter 8, I discuss how policy work can be part of what I am calling "complaint activism." I am thinking especially of the work done by The 1752 Group. Putting pressure on organizations to change policies and procedures, *if done publicly and collectively*, can be about creating a different culture around complaint.

12. Included in the documents sent to her was a defense of how the organization had handled the case on the grounds that it had "adhered" to its plan and that the investigation "had been in line with our disciplinary policy and procedure." Having read the documentation, I would disagree with their self-assessment. But I would also say that the injustice in their handling of the case was not simply about the failure to follow procedures. *Injustices can be procedural*: you can follow procedures and still make unjust decisions because those decisions are predicated on judgments that might exercise the norms and values that the complainer is trying to contest. See chapter 5 for how impartial reporting can involve, for example, sympathetic identification with harassers.

13. For a discussion of what was problematic about this policy, see my post "Resignation Is a Feminist Issue," *Feminist Killjoys*, August 27, 2016, https://feministkilljoys.com/2016/08/27/resignation-is-a-feminist-issue/.

14. That sentence was standard and appeared in a number of university policies in the UK. It is only after immense pressure from groups like The 1752 Group that this sentence has largely disappeared from policies. (As I write this note, I found two universities or colleges that still have this sentence in policies available online.) I should add that the activist work that leads to policy

amendment, so often led by students and precarious staff, tends to disappear from view once policies are amended; policies then are quickly transformed into institutional gifts and as expressive of an organization's commitments.

15. My wording is deliberately cautious as policies can be treated as if they are expressive of values in problematic ways. If an organization responds to a complaint about racism by saying, "We value diversity," the expression of values is used to counter a lived experience of racism. If an organization responds to a complaint about sexual harassment by saying they do not tolerate sexual harassment, that statement is used to counter a lived experience of sexual harassment.

16. This is very important. Too many appeals to procedures or due process are made as if having clear procedures or following due process would guarantee justice or fairness. The most important complaint activism comes from those who have followed procedures only to learn how procedures can be used to bury complaints. To fight for better procedures might require giving up any conviction that procedures are neutral or that they will be the solution. See also the section on complaint activism from chapter 8 on how using formal complaints procedures can be a form of direct action.

17. Athena SWAN is a framework to support and transform gender equality in higher education. The data in this section comes from academics working in British universities. However, the Athena SWAN framework is used by many different countries. For further information, see "Athena Swan Charter," Advance HE, accessed November 7, 2020, https://www.advance-he.ac.uk/equality -charters/athena-swan-charter.

18. For good feminist critiques of Athena SWAN that draw on qualitative research, see Nash et al. (2020) and Pierce and Tzanakou (2018).

19. Kalwant Bhopal and Holly Henderson (2019) suggest that the Race Equality Charter in the UK needs to be attached to compensation in order to be effective in the same way as Athena SWAN. While I agree with their argument that gender equality is taken more seriously than racial equality, I would note that if racial equality is treated in the same way as gender equality, it too would enable only certain kinds of race work—the more positive and marketable kinds. See also Bhopal and Pitkin (2020) for an important discussion of how new equality policies can enact inequalities, as well my earlier discussion of equality in relation to performance culture in chapter 5 of *On Being Included* (2012).

20. This was a familiar position. As a feminist of color, many of my experiences of being a feminist killjoy are of killing feminist joy, for instance, by pointing out racism in so much feminist politics or by identifying the whiteness of so many feminist spaces. See the introduction to chapter 4.

TWO. ON BEING STOPPED

1. In chapter 6, I will explore how warnings not to complain can be considered part of a cluster of activities we call "career advice."

2. *Sticky data* is a term used in marketing to describe how online communication can leave a virtual fingerprint. For example, when consumers use the same email address, they give companies information that is then used to anticipate the interests of that consumer. For a description of the commercial value of sticky data, see Phil Davis, "What Is Sticky Data and Why Do I Need It?," Towerdata, July 9, 2015, https://www.towerdata.com/blog/what-is-sticky-data-and-why-do-i-need-it. A warning about complaint is often telling someone that if they complain, it will stick to them, and if it sticks to them, they will get stuck. I will return to how complaints "stick" to some people, as a story of how some people become complainers (a becoming that is not reducible to whether or not someone makes a complaint), in the section "Becoming/Unbecoming Complainers" in chapter 4, and then again in the concluding section of chapter 6.

3. In *Living a Feminist Life* (2017), I talked about *gender fatalism* along similar lines: the statement "Boys will be boys" can function as prediction and expectation.

4. I had a number of experiences of what I am calling qualified support. One time a feminist colleague said she supported me in making a public disclosure that there had been these inquiries, but that she was *concerned* about the effect on the college's reputation. The qualification of that support was an articulation of a concern as well as a warning (not to act in a way that would be damaging to the college's reputation).

5. In chapter 4, I return to the significance of this expression "rocking the boat" in relation to institutional passing.

6. See the section "Nonreproductive Labor" in chapter 4 for an example of a trans student who was threatened with dismissal for disclosing that the university had threatened them with dismissal.

7. Complaints Procedure, accessed November 23, 2020, https://www.york.ac.uk/about/departments/support-and-admin/sas/complaints/.

8. Not everyone I spoke to who felt encouraged by the initial response to their complaint talked about nodding. The reason I am titling this section "Nods" is that nodding is how a yes is *communicated*. I learned from nods how the creation of an impression of being sympathetic is what matters, not necessarily the content of what is being said.

9. Something can be treated as contagious without being contagious. When a complaint is treated as contagious, however, so much follows. I made a similar argument about unhappiness in *The Promise of Happiness* (2010): the idea that you can catch unhappiness from others can be how distance from others is justified as necessary for the preservation of happiness.

10. Of course, sometimes we need to create spaces to vent our frustrations because of how much we are required to contain ourselves. We might need to vent in order not to explode because frankly we have work to do and it is hard to work and explode at the same time. We let it out so we can get about. See the section "Coming Out" in chapter 3 for a related discussion.

11. Of course, not everyone would be encouraged by being told their complaints are not the first complaints. Another student took a complaint about harassment from her course tutor to the director of her program. The director responded by saying, "I hear a lot of these complaints every year," in an intonation that almost implied a yawn, as if to say: Heard that before, *been there, done that*. The student asked in response, "If you hear them every year, why is it continuing?" A question can be cutting, exposing the failure of logic.

12. The erasure or deletion of a complaint through a formal process can be related to other kinds of erasures and deletions. See my discussion of collegiality and the erasure of complaint in chapter 5.

13. Leila Whitley (2020) considers, for instance, how being on a temporary contract can mean you do not have the time you need to make a complaint. Temporariness can be how complaints become inaccessible, which also means that temporariness makes people more vulnerable to harassment.

14. The Office of the Independent Adjudicator for Higher Education is an independent body set up to review student complaints at higher education providers in England and Wales. Their remit is rather narrow: they are not concerned with the content of complaints, but rather with whether student complaints have been handled fairly or properly. See their website, https://www.oiahe.org.uk/.

15. The journalist David Batty wrote, "Only when Prof Sara Ahmed, who resigned from her post at the university in the summer of 2016, blew the whistle did the scandal emerge." David Batty, "UK Universities Must Break Their Silence around Harassment and Bullying," *Guardian*, April 18, 2019, https://www.theguardian.com/commentisfree/2019/apr/18/uk-universities-silence-harassment-bullying-gagging-orders-staff.

PART II   INTRODUCTION

1. I am using *intentionality* in the phenomenological sense. For further discussion of "orientations toward objects," see chapter 1 of *Queer Phenomenology* (Ahmed 2006).

2. For work on queer time/queer temporality, see also Freeman (2010); Halberstam (2005, 2011); McCallum and Tuhkanen (2011).

THREE. IN THE THICK OF IT

1. In my book, *On Being Included* (2012), I considered how a diversity practitioner, who identified as a feminist, disidentified herself from the previous equity office by using the figure of the feminazi (as if to say, I am not that). I return in chapter 5 to how the figure of the feminazi is exercised as part of the repertoire of antifeminism, used to dismiss complaints as a feminist plot.

2. I will return to the labor of pointing out how syllabi are occupied as nonreproductive labor in chapter 4.

3. I will return to the question of scale in a different way in chapter 5, reflecting on how routine it becomes to make things smaller than they are, such that any attention to them is framed as making them bigger than they are or need be.

4. In her case, she started a formal complaint process: she spoke to her supervisor, head of department, and the Title IX office. From the Title IX office she received a fatalistic warning (see chapter 2). But she decided not to complete the formal complaint process, as she did not want her complaint to become "a note in his file."

5. For a discussion of snap, see my chapter "Feminist Snap" in *Living a Feminist Life* (2017) as well as my conclusion, "Queer Use," in *What's the Use? On the Uses of Use* (2019).

6. In chapter 4, I consider laughing as a form of institutional passing. I also deepen my analysis of how and when the figure of the complainer appears.

7. Given that harassment can be the effort to stop the identification of harassment, it is important we do not assume the absence of identification as the absence of harassment. The implications of this point are far reaching, especially for policies on sexual harassment. Most policies define sexual harassment as "unwelcome" or "unwanted" sexual advances. We can immediately see a problem: some behavior will not be identified as sexual harassment *because* of the nature of sexual harassment. This is why it has been politically important to introduce "sexual misconduct" to indicate a wide range of behaviors that are problematic in themselves and not because someone has identified them as problematic. Even if we use sexual misconduct in this way, it remains important not to assume that sexual harassment does not exist because it has not been identified. We need to explain how abuses of power take place by making it hard to identify behaviors as unwanted or unwelcome in the first place. If we use the term *sexual misconduct* to indicate a wider range of problematic behaviors, it is important we don't accept or assume the official definition of sexual harassment by narrowing it to unwanted or unwelcome sexual advances. It is my own view that *sexual harassment* remains a better description of many of the behaviors that now tend to be named as sexual misconduct, even if we need to use the term *sexual misconduct* for strategic reasons. *Sexual harassment* helps to describe the nature of so much of the behavior (how it works slowly to wear people down); the role of power relations as well as a wider environment in enabling that behavior (sexual harassment as the creation of a hostile environment); and how stopping complaints about that behavior is an effect of that behavior (harassment stops complaints about harassment).

8. See also chapter 6 for more discussion of back doors in relation to diversity policies.

9. One of the hardest parts of my own experience was dealing with rumors, which became more vicious after I left my post. It is hard to challenge rumors without giving them the attention they need to flourish. You have to try to find a way to live with them in part by understanding where they come from. It is

convenient to pathologize those who initiate or support a complaint especially if that complaint implicates in some way a person or an institution in which others are invested.

10. In my data I have many examples of control over the narrative of complaint. In another instance, a professor returned to the department where she did her MA to give a research seminar. She had made an informal complaint after being assaulted by a lecturer in that department. (Hers is the first "door" story in chapter 5.) She described what happened after she gave her talk: "Afterwards I was just chatting with some staff, and he was notorious, they all knew what he was like, and I said to the now head of department, you do realize I made a complaint about him when I was a student here, and he says, oh no, that's not how he tells it. He says that you pursued him and that he had to rebuff you. . . . So that was a second blow, in a way. I thought, so who else has he been saying this to?" That the person who harassed or assaulted you can misrepresent what happened is experienced as a second blow, a repetition of the violence. And note that the control of the narrative can be achieved despite what everyone knows ("he was notorious, they all knew what he was like"). For more examples of controlling the narrative, see chapter 5.

11. Distance from complaint can also be understood as the effort to unbecome the complainer. See chapter 4 for a discussion of unbecoming complainers. See the concluding section of chapter 6 for a related discussion of how some try to distance themselves from complaint in order to progress more quickly within organizations.

12. I will return to how the complainer is judged as cutting themself off from the collective in chapter 5.

13. I will return in chapter 5 to how the support given to the students who harassed other students has a familial dynamic, as well as how "not taking sides" is a way of siding with the harassers.

14. There are many ways that definitions can function as institutional blinds. I spoke to a student informally about an inquiry into sexual harassment that involved a number of academics from the same department. An administrator had told her that they had received only one complaint about sexual harassment. I realized how the administrator could say that (without lying, although I have no doubt there are many lies circulating as official discourse). She could say that only because she had defined sexual harassment as sexual assault and only one student had reported a sexual assault. In fact, the university had received multiple complaints about sexual harassment understood as hostile environment. Complaints about sexual harassment can be shut down by a restriction in the meaning or definition of sexual harassment. See also my discussion in chapter 5 of institutional doors that are used to shut violence in. Also note that policies can operate as blinds: we can return to my discussion in chapter 1 of how policies on conflict of interest used the sentence "The College does not wish to prevent, or even necessarily be aware of, liaisons between staff and students and it relies upon the integrity of both parties to ensure that

abuses of power do not occur." The policy pulls the blind down by making explicit what the college does not want to know or see.

15. I will return to how the complainer becomes a stranger in chapter 4.

16. This is also true for the term *transphobia*: I have come across countless instances where the use of the term *transphobia* is identified as an attempt to restrict the freedom of some people to act in a certain way. (Many transphobic utterances are given theoretical justification.) Misgendering is often justified as freedom of speech both in classroom settings and beyond. When some gender critical academics say that "out of politeness" they respect the pronouns of their students, they are implying they are free to do so or not to do so. They are in fact not free not to do so; they are required to do so under existing equality law. The guidance to the Equality Law 2010 by the Equality and Human Rights Commission includes deliberate misgendering as an example of harassment of persons with the "protected characteristic" of gender reassignment. See "Gender Reassignment Discrimination," Equality and Human Rights Commission, accessed November 19, 2020, https://www.equalityhumanrights.com/en/advice-and-guidance/gender-reassignment-discrimination. Also, using theory to justify misgendering (I can call you *he* because my theories mean I don't recognize you as *she*) is no less harassment than it would be without said justification: your theory does not exempt you from the requirement to act in a certain way. One has a sense here of the political stakes of the attack on "gender theory."

17. In this book I share a number of examples of how people relate the way they complained to being working class or having a working-class background. However, as I will show in chapter 4, the figure of the complainer is often evoked as a member of a privileged class. *We are learning who disappears from complaint in the production of that figure.* The following texts consider the experiences of working-class academics and students: Benoit, Olson, and Johnson (2019); Binns (2019); Reay (2018). See also my discussion of how the figure of the complainer as privileged is put to work in chapter 6.

FOUR. OCCUPIED

1. For a discussion of how universities are structured around the assumption of an able body, see Jay Dolmage (2017). See also the important blog written by disabled postgraduate students, *PhDisabled*, accessed July 28, 2020, https://phdisabled.wordpress.com/.

2. Online Etymology Dictionary, accessed January 29, 2021, https://www.etymonline.com/word/harass#etymonline_v_6153.

3. Definition available at Lexico, accessed November 16, 2020, https://www.lexico.com/definition/complaint.

4. See the formative work of Beverley Skeggs (1995, 1997, 2004) on working-class subjectivity that addresses the question of entitlement, as well as Valerie Hey (2003) on the position of working-class feminist academics, which discusses how class is lived as a relocation.

5. I have so much more data on harassment and bullying experienced by senior women managers than I am able to share. Women senior managers encounter what one feminist academic described as "breathtaking sexism." As lesbian and queer women, we often receive horror reactions when we take on senior roles, as if to say, "What are you? Who do you think you are?" As Black women and women of color, we often have to deal with so much abusive behavior when we take on senior roles. See Lynn Fujiwara's (2020) institutional autoethnography of white fragility, in which she reflects on what happened when she, as an Asian American woman, was appointed departmental head. She wrote, "I do not expect the degradation and marginalisation I experienced at the college administrative level, or the cost of not remaining complicit" (113). She did make formal complaints about some of the communications she received from an "accusatory administrator," but "nothing was addressed" (114). See chapter 6 for further discussion of the relationship between racial harassment and hierarchy.

6. Officially organizations will present themselves as gay- or queer-friendly, but this does not mean they are not experienced as hostile environments for lesbians and other queer academics and students. This "does not mean" covers so much. See Yvette Taylor (2018) for an important discussion of how she "navigates the emotional landscape" of the university. Taylor describes the difficulty of receiving official mail about happy welcoming diversity while experiencing the university as an environment that is hard to fit into as a working-class lesbian academic (66–67).

7. This is very much the case for complaints about racism. It is not just that when you use the word *racism* you are heard as complaining. Using the word *racism* is heard as making something about race. If you use the word *racism* you are likely to be complained about, including for being racist. See Fiona Nicoll (2004a) on how "calling someone racist" is treated as an accusation that takes the place of racism, as well as Alana Lentin's (2020) chapter on "not racism" for a discussion of how racism is performed by the denial of racism. See also my discussion of how categories like racism and sexism are treated as strangers, as impositions from the outside made by outsiders, which restrict the free speech of insiders, in the section "Complaint and Escalation," chapter 3.

8. I know of a number of instances when feminists (in particular feminists of color) in becoming leaders are positioned as pushing their own agendas (for example, by initiating new commitments such as decolonizing the curriculum). The mainstream or status quo does not need to be pushed to be maintained. That agenda is often framed as identity: as if you are pushing *that* because of who you are, pushing *that* as pushing yourself forward. We can learn to be skeptical about who is framed as a bully. However, as I will explore in chapter 6, it does not follow that those who are minorities do not abuse the power they come to have. Many of the systems in place are in effect systems for rewarding abusive behavior. Trying to untangle how power is operating in

this or that instance often requires what I would call *complaint literacy*, a way of being able to read, often between the lines, case materials as well as local or situational knowledge. I will return to how bullying can be enacted by using institutional resources such as complaints procedures, reviews, evaluation, and mediation in chapter 5.

9. We need to take care when we talk about cases of complaints procedures being misused as tools for bullying and harassment because many (even most) people respond to complaints made against them by arguing that complaints procedures are misused. I certainly have evidence of the misuse of complaints procedures. But I also have evidence of the "misuse of the misuse of complaints," when people try to deflect attention from their own abuses of power by pathologizing the complainer as suffering from a will to power.

10. She won the case because she had a case: the university had failed to meet its equality and dignity at work commitments. As I discussed in chapter 1, having evidence of the failure of policy does not guarantee the success of an action. There are good reasons she needed an expert to make the case on her behalf.

11. I do know of instances where informal complaints of this kind have been investigated, which means a formal complaints process is triggered. However, even when a formal process is not triggered, these kinds of informal complaints can create a hostile environment. See Patricia Williams (1991, 32) for some examples of complaints made against her because of how she was teaching law as a Black feminist. See also my discussion of hostile complaints in the final section of this chapter.

12. It is tricky to work out who becomes a complainer given this nonreducibility. A complainer seems to be the one who is demanding something that the many or most do not want; that is, there is a connection between who becomes a complainer and what counters a hegemony. But are there not hegemonic complainers? Let's take the meme/figure of Karen, now used to evoke the privileged white woman as complainer. If Karen is complaining, would we not say that Karen's complaints are more likely to be heard? And if so, then is Karen not also evidence that whether complaints are heard or not heard is a simple measure of who is making them? My own view is that, yes, Karen is likely to be heard, but she is likely to be heard because she is *not* heard as complaining by those she addresses. Let's say Karen calls the police because people of color are enjoying themselves in the local park. The point here is that Karen might be received well (by the police) because her call not only is *not* heard as complaining but is heard as being the action of a responsible citizen; she is called upon (by the police) to make that call. This is, after all, how Neighborhood Watch works: the good citizen is supposed to report anything (anyone) suspicious to the police. In fact, *that* Karen becomes a figure, nameable as a hegemonic complainer, is itself dependent on a counterhegemonic action: we make use of her to show how hegemony works by *not* identifying certain forms of action as complaining. If we make use of Karen as a figure of the hegemonic complainer as part of a

counterhegemonic strategy (which is not what I have chosen to do, but it could be done), we would still need to keep in mind how this figure can be used for other purposes. See my analysis in chapter 5 of how the complainer is treated as a manager. Another instance would be how, in the UK, some gender critical academics represent trans students who complain about transphobia as hegemonic complainers who are stifling their freedom of expression. My research has taught me that trans students have legitimate grounds for complaint and are in fact often not supported by the system in doing so. The figure of the hegemonic complainer can be used to conceal so much because hegemony often works by inflating the power of those who challenge it. It is given what the figure of the hegemonic complainer is routinely used to do that I do not use this figure in *Complaint!*

13. Of course, not all acts of complaining will be heard as disrespectful of a legacy. We might even be directed to complain about some things, the weather for instance, because those complaints can be shared. Complaining can sometimes offer a weak form of social bonding. We might be directed toward complaining about some things as a way of being directed away from making other kinds of complaints, perhaps those complaints that are disrespectful of a legacy, complaints that snap that bond. This book is an exploration of snappy, not happy, complaints.

14. For important critiques of how the hostile environment became a national policy on immigration, see Gentleman (2019); Goodfellow (2019). Hostile environment provides a way of connecting institutional racism and everyday racism. For a discussion of racism within universities, which draws on interviews with racially marked academics, focusing on the everydayness of the institutional, see Sian (2019). See also Essed's (1991) classic account of everyday racism, which shows the intertwining of micro and macro dimensions.

15. Being used to symbolize diversity is also about being digested by the university or having what they can use extracted from your body or work. See Sirma Bilge (2020b, 319) for a discussion of how the "neoliberal white university" makes an "array of minority thought projects desirable as extractable resources." Following Bilge, we can consider diversity as being "at the table" but "on the menu."

16. For the risks of decolonizing becoming (like diversity) a "tick-box," see Adebisi (2020), or on how decolonizing (unlike diversity) requires "to commit to dismantling the Master's House," see Qureshi (2019, 213). On the risks of decolonizing being treated as a metaphor, see Tuck and Yang (2012). To critique how the decolonial can be a colonizing tool is to point in a different direction. Zoe Todd (2016), for instance, offers a powerful critique of how white theorists take up Indigenous ideas without citing Indigenous scholars as well as how those theorists then get taken up as originating those ideas. Todd's work provides us with the tools to examine how decolonizing disciplines or theories, if performed in the same old ways by the same old subjects, operates as another colonizing method. These tools are the same tools that enable us to do the work

of decolonizing differently, in a way that comes from rather than erases Indigenous, Black, and anticolonial knowledges. For more tools, see also the second edition of Linda Tuhiawi Smith's path-breaking *Decolonizing Methodologies*, where she reflects on her "most quoted" sentence: "The word itself, 'research,' is probably one of the dirtiest words in the Indigenous world's vocabulary" (2012 [1999], ix). See also Sylvia Tamale's important book, *Decolonization and Afro-Feminism* (2020). Tamale argues that "the imperial machinery never eases its stranglehold over the world and knowledge production and distribution" (2). Tamale offers an alternative vision of what decolonizing means: "For the colonized, decolonization of the mind is really about returning to the annals of history to find ourselves, to become fluent in our cultural knowledge systems, to cultivate critical consciousness, and to reclaim our humanity" (2). For collections of essays on "dismantling race in higher education," see Arday and Mirza (2018), and on "decolonizing the university," see Bhambra, Gebrial, and Nişancıoğlu (2018).

17. Consider bell hooks's (2000, 56) description: "A group of white feminist activists who do not know one another may be present at a meeting to discuss feminist theory. They may feel they are bonded on the basis of shared womanhood, but the atmosphere will noticeably change when a woman of color enters the room. The white women will become tense, no longer relaxed, no longer celebratory." A woman of color just has to arrive to get in the way of an occupation of space. We learn how whiteness is occupying from those who get in the way. An arrival can be registered as complaint. So, yes, we learn about occupation from those deemed complainers.

18. For a discussion of transphobic and homophobic bullying at universities, see Rivers (2016). For a collection on the experiences of trans people in universities, see Beemyn (2019). See Nicolazzo (2016) for a powerful set of reflections on how trans students navigate the university. With thanks to Z. Nicolazzo for killjoy solidarity.

19. See Gayle Salamon's (2018) critical phenomenology of transphobia for an account of how trans people are judged as inciting the violence against them, with reference to the case of the murder of Latisha King.

20. Another racism story, another bus story. I think of the testimony of a woman of color researcher who described how the university used her face and research as "coercive diversity." She described what happened when she shared an experience of racism with a senior academic: "I had experienced an extremely racist altercation on my commute home from campus (I was called 'skanky Hindu,' 'skindoo,' effing Hindu, etc. by a white couple on a bus). I shared this with the graduate head. I wanted the department to know I was deeply affected by this incident and was having trouble coping. I was completely ignored other than him responding with a white savior narrative about how he stopped a racist altercation once in the 1970s." She was not making a complaint but telling the graduate head about what happened because of how it affected her, her well-being. But even then, you encounter the wall, the wall of

whiteness, how some cannot hear about the problem of racism because of how much they have invested in themselves as being the solution to that problem ("the white savior narrative").

21. This expression "I could live with myself" or "I couldn't live with myself" came up a few times in my testimonies. A postgraduate student made a complaint about the conduct of her supervisor: "A lot of people are: Why you are doing this? You are at risk or do you want the moral ground. For me it might sound dramatic, but it is simply true: I couldn't live with myself." Note the negative: not to complain would be not being able to "live with myself." A decision whether to complain is also a judgment about what you can live with; it becomes a way of expressing not simply your values and commitments but the values and commitments you could not give up with giving up on yourself.

22. Franklin's (2015) essay on sexism as a means of reproduction is an object lesson on complaint. She reflects back on an essay she wrote as a student that offered a feminist critique of Durkheim. The essay was read by Professor P as complaint. That reading was enacted by the outrage of the marker, who in scrawling all over the essay in red ink turned it into "a bloody document." Complaints could be thought of as bloody documents, the red ink as blood, text as flesh and body. Franklin's essay was first read out loud—maybe I could even say *expressed*—at the conference on sexism that took place at the Centre for Feminist Research in 2015. It was cathartic to have the "bloody document" right in front of us, to see the machinery, to hear it too, how it works.

23. This is another clear instance of how a complaint, or being heard as making a complaint, leads to an escalation of the violence the complaint is about.

24. Mary Daly (1978, 15) defines the hag as "an intractable person, especially: a woman reluctant to yield to wooing." You become a hag by not yielding, whether to sexual advances or other kinds of advances. This student did make a formal complaint after the completion of her MA. See chapter 6 for a discussion of what happened and how her complaint "closed the door" on doing a PhD.

25. The rumors that were spread about me during the inquiries included that I wanted the jobs of the men who were under investigation, that I wanted their center for myself, and that I was in relationships with students in the center. The implication is that you complain because you want what they have, that a complaint is a will to power. See the section "The Complainer as Manager" in chapter 5 for a development of this argument.

26. I will return to the significance of complaint collectives in chapter 8, with specific reference to what she had to do to create the document.

27. See Roderick Ferguson (2017, 26) for an important analysis of how the "visions for social and institutional transformation" offered by student activists are reduced to "expressions of personal grievance." See also Ferguson's (2012) earlier critique of how the demands of political movements were appropriated and neutralized by institutions.

28. See also my discussion of doors and progression in chapter 6. I am suggesting here that doors opened to some complaints are the same doors opened to some people.

29. See Chelsea Bond's powerful description of the academy, including Indigenous studies, as the dispossession of Indigenous peoples: "The academy as an apparatus of the colonial project has always been committed to the task of dispossession via knowledge production, and having witnessed the violence of the Indigenising curricular agendas within recent years, I know too well how it functions to dispossess us from knowing even ourselves—you see, dispossession is more than the stuff of land" (in Mukandi and Bond 2019, 262).

30. For an important discussion of white tears, see Hamad (2019).

PART III   INTRODUCTION

1. In my book *The Promise of Happiness* (2010), I discussed the sequel to this film, *If These Walls Could Talk, 2* (2000, directed by Jane Anderson, Martha Coolidge, and Anne Heche), in a discussion of happy/unhappy queers. In my reading of the sequel, I did make specific reference to the walls, while referring back to another depiction of walls in Radclyffe Hall's ([1928] 1982) *The Well of Loneliness*. I wrote then, "The walls, if they could talk, would tell the story. Indeed, reflecting back on *The Well*, we might note the significance of 'the walls' as a motif: the walls create spaces; they mark the edge between what is inside and out. The walls contain things by holding up; they bear the weight of residence. In *The Well*, the walls contain misery, and the revolution of the ending involves bringing them down. In this film, the walls are container devices, but 'what' they contain depends on the passing of time; shaped by the comings and goings of different bodies. Inside the house, we are occupied. Things happen" (Ahmed 2010, 107).

2. With thanks to artist Rachel Whiteread for her piece *Double-Doors*, which is on the front cover of this book, and to Aimee Harrison for her design. *Double-Doors* is described as follows: "Look carefully—this work is more complicated than it seems. These are not doors; instead, they capture the space created by doors. Whiteread made plaster casts of both sides of two doors, then assembled the casts back to back. The finished work combines the spaces on either side of a threshold—fusing entrance and exit into one solid form. The pale doors suggest the ambiguous emotions attached to coming and going and, in the way they resemble funerary slabs, maybe even the fleeting passage of life" (Museum of Fine Arts, Boston, accessed February 12, 2021, https://collections.mfa.org/objects/516136). My own practice in writing about complaint echos Whiteread's techniques. I too am working around doors (whether we think of what is around doors in spatial or temporal terms), trying to bring out what they conceal. To listen to doors is to hear about comings and goings, entries and exits, lives and deaths.

1. There are seven references to doors in her testimony, which include references to actual doors to convey something about the nature of the institution, the use of the expression *behind closed doors*, as well as references to closed doors to describe the nature of the process and procedure. It is important to add that the doors are there because of what she herself noticed. It is not just that I, as a writer or researcher, am noticing what is in the testimonies I have gathered. Rather, those who are talking to me about their complaint experience are noticing things and reflecting upon what they notice. *Noticing* is part of the complaint experience; I am sharing what we notice.

2. The data I will be sharing in this chapter relates specifically to complaints about harassment or bullying.

3. Many experiences of sexual harassment by (cis het) academic men have been shared with me by lesbian and queer women. Being understood to have withdrawn from intimate sexual relations with men can increase vulnerability to sexual harassment and sexual assault. See the report by Green and Wong (2015) that suggests that LGBT students are more at risk of sexual assault on campus.

4. Sometimes it is unclear why some people are protected and others not. In another instance, a female professor made a complaint about bullying from her head of department. The complaint was collective; a number of staff from the same department participated in it. But the university protected him. She could not understand why; he was not a star professor. She said, "It was not even for the good of the organization. It was not even good strategic management. If I could see the purpose, and think I could see why they did that, I can see the benefit. . . . But they have lost all their readers, professors for the REF [Research Excellence Framework]. . . . So they have lost what they had. I couldn't see what the point was." My own sense from listening to multiple stories is that protection usually follows reputation and status, but it does not always do so. It can also be shaped by who uses their weight more (for example, by threatening to sue for defamation or by threatening to make a countercomplaint).

5. Protection is thus also about damage limitation; see the final section of this chapter.

6. In the UK there have been a number of articles in the mainstream press about the "epidemic" levels of harassment at universities. An example of such a story is David Batty, Sally Wheale, and Caroline Bannock, "Sexual Harassment at 'Epidemic Levels' in UK Universities," *Guardian*, March 5, 2017, https://www.theguardian.com/education/2017/mar/05/students-staff-uk-universities-sexual-harassment-epidemic. For academic research on sexual harassment in universities, see Bacchi (1998); Brant and Too (1994); Dziech and Hawkins (2011); Paludi (1990); Whitley and Page (2005).

7. I had two interviews: the first with the woman whose testimony I opened this chapter with, the second with two women.

8. Century Dictionary, cited by Online Etymology Dictionary, accessed November 19, 2020, https://www.etymonline.com/word/conduct#etymonline _v_17339.

9. In chapter 6, I will show how those who abuse power given to them by virtue of position often represent themselves as open doors (as opening the door for others). In other words, power over others is achieved by creating an impression of debt.

10. I will return in chapter 8 to the significance of how complaints lead you to find out about earlier complaints.

11. We learned from door story 3 that in some instances stopping a complaint about racism (by stopping a complaint about harassment and bullying) can also be a PR exercise.

12. I should add here that being concerned for the effects of complaint on the person or persons who are the objects of complaint is another reason some people do not make complaints or do so with great reluctance. As I noted in chapter 4, most people who complain about harassment or bullying do so because they want the behavior to stop—they do not necessarily want the person to be disciplined, to lose their position, post, or status. What complaint teaches us is *what it takes to stop* some forms of conduct. It is sometimes impossible to stop some forms of conduct: you come up against the history of how it is enabled, history as a wall, without removing persons, posts, or even programs. Such removals remain, however, rare. When persons are removed from their post, usually after a long and sustained struggle, this tends to happen behind closed doors, leading to the relocation of the problem to another program. Many people who witness how their informal complaints about harassment and bullying are treated (including by those who are the objects of complaint) come to a fuller appreciation of how the system works and who benefits from that system. A woman professor I spoke to informally said, "By the end I just wanted to put a flame to the whole thing." See chapter 8 for how the complaints process can be politicizing.

13. We need to remember that physical and sexual assault can also be characterized as a form of expression (for example, as blunt speech or as a direct style of management). This is how, when someone uses force against another or is physically violent, they can still say, "I didn't mean anything" or "It didn't mean anything."

14. We can refer back to my suggestion in chapter 1 that complaints procedures are "the master's tools"; if they are developed "in house," they are designed to keep the house in order. That critique of what procedures do can be used to justify not following procedures.

15. Complaints can be used to discipline academics for their minority views or status, as I discussed in chapter 4, whether by students, academics, or management. Passing depends on being near a possibility to succeed. What I am suggesting is that the possibility that complaints procedures can be misused can be misused. In my study I have uncovered as many examples of

the "misuse of the misuse of complaint" as I have of "the misuse of complaint" (if not more). *Neoliberalism* is used to imply the misuse of complaint because that term is convincing not only as an explanation of wider processes but as a critique of those processes.

16. I am suggesting that some critiques of neoliberalism can be used to mask or disguise an abuse of power and can thus in effect be part of a conservative regime. See also the section "Utility and Policy" from *What's the Use?* (Ahmed 2019) for a related discussion of how some critiques of neoliberalism take the form of reactions to universities being opened up to nontraditional subjects and students. Please note I am not saying that we do not need critiques of neoliberalism in universities and beyond. Feminist critiques of neoliberalism, which show how neoliberalism is a landscape in which we do diversity and equality work, are especially useful. See the edited collections by Palko, Wagman, and Sapra (2020) and Taylor and Lahad (2018). For a critique of the "imperial university" that relates questions of neoliberalism to militarization and the policing of dissent and protest, see the collection by Chatterjee and Maira (2014). See Pereira (2017) for a feminist critique of the performative university. See Phipps (2018) for a discussion of how addressing the problem of sexual violence in universities is shaped by neoliberal concerns with market and reputation.

17. I am not denying that there are neoliberal versions of feminism. (In the next section, I will describe how neoliberal feminism can operate within universities as a way of avoiding proximity to complaint and to complainers.) Rather, I am suggesting that when feminism as such is treated as neoliberal, feminist complaints about sexual harassment and gender inequality can be dismissed under the guise of a radical or progressive politics.

18. In chapter 2, I noted how power can be the power to suspend the usual procedures. The suspension of the procedures can also be justified as a form of resistance or a refusal to comply with the demands of management. Some of these procedures, such as record keeping and systems for monitoring student progress, are how problems would routinely be identified. A number of people who made complaints about harassment or bullying spoke to me about how the problem was exacerbated by a lack of concern for formal procedure and an "informality" in how decisions were made. For an example of how informality can be weaponized, see the section "The Diversity Door" in chapter 6.

19. Some students relayed to me that they were called "carceral feminists" for making complaints about harassment. This misuse of the term *carceral feminist* to describe anyone who supports or enters a formal complaint process implies that to make a formal complaint is to become a prison guard not only to police but to punish. In one case, a serial harasser left his post after multiple complaints from students about sexual harassment. His supporters not only represented the complainers as carceral feminists but implied that the students should have used restorative justice instead. They implied that students could have just talked to him and talked him out of behaving that way. Of course,

students had tried to address the problem informally; formal complaints are usually the last resort for a reason. The professor concerned still did not (and still does not) recognize anything wrong with his behavior. Sometimes the solutions offered reveal the failure to recognize the nature of the problem. What is revealing (and very difficult) is how the solutions offered can be wrapped up in critical feminist language.

20. I am not trying to dismiss the seriousness of sexist speech. In chapter 3, I discussed how sexist speech can be a way of occupying space and can include threats of violence directed to those who are not compliant. The point is rather that sexist speech is framed as light and is also often attached to freedom (sexist speech as free speech). Complaints about harassment or misconduct are turned into complaints about sexist speech in order to make light of those complaints and in order to position those complaints as restrictions on free speech.

21. For a very good account of how working-class and unionized women changed the meaning of sexual harassment to include hostile environment, see Baker (2008, 67–81).

22. By *sharing information*, I mean they distributed leaflets to incoming students. The information took the form of warning those students about the conduct of the professor. The case was eventually reopened, and the professor has since left his post. I will return to how some complainers are disciplined for "taking the matter into their own hands" in chapter 8.

23. In other words, by using that term, loaded with history, they position this professor as if he was a Black man (he was a non-Black person of color) to position the complaint as an extreme act of violence, as murder. I should add that the term *lynching* can also be used in problematic ways when claims of sexual harassment are brought against Black men. See Kimberlé Crenshaw's (1993) important critique of how Clarence Thomas used the term "high-tech lynching" to describe the hearings in response to Anita Hill's complaints about sexual harassment. Crenshaw states, "Thomas's move to drape himself in a history of black male repression was particularly effective in an all-white male Senate, whose members could not muster the moral authority to challenge Thomas's sensationalist characterization" (416). Crenshaw points out that the lynching metaphor worked powerfully as "cases involving sexual accusations against black men have stood as hallmarks of racial injustice" (417). In contrast, "the names and faces of black women whose bodies also bore the scars of racial oppression are lost to history" (418). We need to learn from how an accusation by a Black woman of harassment by a Black man can be made into a symptom of racial repression.

24. For a discussion of the performativity (and nonperformativity) of apologies as speech acts, see the chapter "Shame before Others" in *The Cultural Politics of Emotion* (Ahmed 2004).

25. The use of reconciliation as a governing strategy by organizations is not unrelated to the use of reconciliation by settler colonial nation-states.

Reconciliation can be the demand that Indigenous peoples reconcile them-selves *to* the situation of occupation as well as with the colonizer (see Nicoll 2004b). The use of reconciliation in the settler colonial context can imply, as Glen Sean Coulthard (2004) has noted, that the task for Native peoples is to overcome "negative feelings" in the promotion of harmony. He writes, "It is frequently inferred by proponents of political reconciliation that restoring these relationships requires that individuals and groups work to overcome the debilitating pain, anger, and resentment that frequently persist in being injured or harmed by a real or perceived injustice" (107).

26. Maybe if I had kept Audre Lorde's lessons closer to mind, I would have thought of feminism's relation to the institution differently. As I pointed out in my introduction to chapter 4, Lorde (1984, 112) explains that dismantling work "is only threatening to those women who still define the master's house as their only source of support."

27. I will return to secret support in a different way in chapter 8, showing how sometimes keeping support behind closed doors can be necessary given one's position with the organization.

SIX. HOLDING THE DOOR

1. I gave details from this student's testimony in part II of the book: it was she who took a while to get her "no" out (chapter 3) and was verbally harassed when she said she was interested in the questions of gender and race (chap-ter 4). She had many other encounters with the professor in which she was "insulted, undermined, threatened."

2. The data in this section is drawn from PhD students or students in MA programs.

3. If we turn this around, we have a story about promise and rewards: the less you complain, the more opportunities you will receive.

4. To listen to complaint is to build a theory of how power is held or concentrated even when it seems to be dispersed or through seeming to be dispersed. Complaints teach us about doors, and doors teach us about power. Institutional power (which is also about who holds power within an institu-tion) is power over others. Coercion is not only about repression or stopping something (the use of fear, threats, and warnings) but also about production or enabling something (the use of happiness, promises, and rewards).

5. Some students I worked with expressed concern for me to me. This con-cern was not so much about the impact of supporting their complaint on my career progression (I was already a professor) but on my well-being. One stu-dent wrote, "We're all concerned that your office has become something of an emergency drop-in centre for women in various states of crisis. I hope you're alright." I am still moved by her hope. In the end, I think so many complaint collectives work out of and as concern for each other, hope that we are all right. See also chapter 8 for a discussion of complaint collectives.

6. Considering power as "holding the door" allows us to show how power can operate through rather than against will. When there is an asymmetry of power, being willing or saying yes might feel like a requirement. For example, you might feel you cannot afford not to be willing to have sex with your lecturer if your access to resources is made dependent upon him. This is why the distinction between sexual misconduct and sexual harassment becomes blurred. In fact, much sexual harassment does not appear as sexual harassment because of the assumption that "being willing" means not being coerced. In one case, an academic was accused of sexual misconduct by a number of students. I communicated informally with an administrator about this case. She told me that he said to her that he "only did it with students who were willing." I also communicated with one of the students who put forward that complaint. She described his behavior thus: "During that time I was a subject of and witness to X's frequent abuses of power, including his use of alcohol and drugs to coax otherwise unwilling women into bed." Those who abuse the power given to them by virtue of position can protect themselves from seeing what they are doing. The perception that students were willing is how conduct is justified or made justifiable.

7. This is a clue as to what is not in my data given that we don't tend to notice doors that are open or what enables us to enter. Privilege can be what does not appear in the stories. We have to take care in how we acknowledge this given how many complainers are dismissed as privileged (chapter 4). It is also worth acknowledging that many who complain do so because they are stopped, or many are stopped because they complain. Many of the people I spoke with also spoke of their privileges (including privileges relating to gender, sexuality, ability, race, class, and citizenship status). I think of a trans student I spoke to whose complaint led to a countercomplaint, which put them at risk of losing their funding and position. (See the final section of chapter 4 for discussion of their situation.) They said, "In a way it is good they picked on me and not anyone else involved in writing that statement because the TERFs [trans-exclusionary radical feminists] don't really care about trans-masculine people. I have got British citizenship so I am not going to be deported if this goes wrong. I don't have that much to lose." They did have a lot to lose—a post, a position, funding, not to mention the potential effects on physical and mental health and well-being—but they were still conscious that with a different gender presentation or citizenship status they would have so much more to lose or have been so much more at risk.

8. A senior lecturer talked to me informally about what happened when she became director of postgraduate studies in her department. She ended up supporting students who had put in a collective complaint about sexual harassment by a professor in her department. She described how all these "vulnerable women" started coming to her office. She told me how she came to realize he had access to their files. He picked out students who had documented mental health issues as well as students who were from working-class backgrounds and had financial difficulties. When vulnerability is filed, those files can be used.

9. I will return to her testimony in my concluding chapter to discuss some of her tactics to avoid brutalization. These include using the institution's doors to shut the institution out.

10. Thinking about doors in relation to resources is another way of thinking about how some become *conductors*. In other words, to know who can open the door is to learn how information, energy, and resources travel (see chapter 5).

11. Much funding for projects that address in some way the experiences of peoples colonized by European powers goes to the beneficiaries of the colonial system. These projects might be named under the following categories: postcolonial, race and ethnicity, diversity, diaspora, migration, multiculturalism, and so on. "The colonizer wins the diversity award" helps identify an important problem. My research has uncovered many cases of violence against minoritized people on projects that were supposedly addressing violence against minoritized people. Another example is a major funded project on trans people's lives in which the project directors were routinely transphobic. One of the researchers on the project described it: "The PI [principle investigator] would disclose the HIV status of some of the participants; she would deliberately misgender academics associated with the project; she would laugh at people's gender presentation." Let me understate the problem. The people who get the funding are the people who are good at getting funding (who use the right terms, fill in the forms in the right way, know the right people, etc.), rather than the people who should be getting funding because of their knowledge or expertise. That much we do know. The people who are good at getting funding for diversity-related projects are often the same people who not only reproduce colonial, racist, sexist, cissexist, and heterosexist regimes *but who benefit from that reproduction*. That's the diversity door: *slammed right there*. Furthermore, when diversity is funded, the research also has to be channeled in a certain direction. I have been told informally of Black academics not getting funding because they do not do diversity in the right way (according to those who evaluate the merits of applications and allocate resources, typically white academics).

12. For important discussions of racial harassment experienced by Black women and women of color in universities in the UK, see Bhopal (2015) and Rollack (2019).

13. This definition of misconduct appears in the charters or statutes of many UK universities: "conduct of an immoral, scandalous or disgraceful nature incompatible with the duties of the office or employment." The most well-known use of this definition of misconduct in a dismissal of an academic is a case of sexual misconduct. That the same definition can be used to dismiss a Black woman dean who entered into a dispute about an administrative process should be a cause of protest.

14. I also created a scandal by bringing the fact there had been inquiries into sexual harassment at my university into the public domain. I did so in the form of a resignation letter. Perhaps if I hadn't resigned but had still brought

that information into the public domain, they would or could have dismissed me. With reference to the previous note, I could add here that a disclosure about an inquiry into sexual or academic misconduct if brought into the public domain could be grounds for dismissal. It thus becomes technically possible to dismiss the person who discloses information about sexual misconduct and not dismiss the person found to be guilty of sexual misconduct. A technical possibility could also be described as ideology: the damage caused by the disclosure of sexual misconduct is often taken more seriously than the damage caused by sexual misconduct (see also chapter 5 on damage limitation). Some UK universities do have protection for whistle-blowers, for those who bring information about misconduct into the public domain, but many do not. Reflecting back, I can now see that my own action of disclosing information about what happened at my former institution was understood by some of my former colleagues as more "disgraceful and scandalous" than the conduct of the professors and lecturers accused of sexual misconduct.

15. In fact, it turned out that only two students had complained (and one of those complaints was about how she as a Black woman professor had been treated). But the university in response to those two complaints communicated with all students, leading to the dispute about marks becoming more general knowledge. In other words, the university created the leak they then used as evidence that she had caused a scandal.

SEVEN. COLLECTIVE CONCLUSIONS

1. Goldsmiths Feminist Voices, February 11, 2014. While the Goldsmiths Feminist Voices website is still available, the post is no longer accessible.

2. Strategic Misogyny, accessed December 6, 2020, https://strategicmisogyny .wordpress.com/.

3. Sexual Harassment in Higher Education, December 2, 2015, https:// shhegoldsmiths.wordpress.com/statement/.

4. Our complaint had many consequences. If things are no longer as they were, part of how that was brought about was by dissolving our graduate department. One method employed by institutions, including universities, for moving on is to erase the site in which violence took place; a method for deleting institutional history. Again, we see how complaints lead to closures, and how closure can also be a form of loss. Our collective work, expanding through and beyond the bounds of our collective, intended to create a record: to say that what happened mattered.

EIGHT. COMPLAINT COLLECTIVES

1. I am referring here to my lecture "On Complaint" presented at the Wheeler Centre, Melbourne, on October 28, 2018. I had presented material from the project before, but this was the first time I presented a lecture based

entirely on the testimonies I had collected. Previously I had shared the material with the scaffolding drawn from my project on the uses of use (Ahmed 2019). It made a difference to present complaint as complaint; without the scaffolding, I was much more exposed.

2. "Watch us roll" is the last sentence of my book *Living a Feminist Life* (2017). I am showing here what I intended to pick up by that sentence.

3. The website for The 1752 Group is https://1752group.com/.

4. This academic described the union as providing key resources that enabled her to fight the institution. Her account contrasts with that of an academic who experienced the union as being too close to, and siding with, management (see chapter 2). I received many more contrasting accounts of the role of unions in handling complaints. Some people had positive experiences with their union not only because of the support they received from them but because the union helped them to understand how their own complaint or grievance related to wider institutional politics. Others described their union as unsupportive, sometimes because the union was too aligned with management, sometimes because union representatives were friends or colleagues with harassers/bullies and worked to protect them, and sometimes because the culture within the union seemed to be the same culture that the complaint was about (one participant described her union as having a "macho culture"). We need a much fuller account of the role of unions in handling complaints made at universities than I was able to provide in this study.

5. See "Complaints Department Operated by Guerrilla Girls," Tate, accessed July 2, 2020, https://www.tate.org.uk/whats-on/tate-modern/tate-exchange /workshop/complaints-department.

6. The Facebook page for Grievance Fest is https://www.facebook.com /events/uc-davis-memorial-union-quad/grievance-fest/2210672555867283/.

7. Lauren Gambino, "Columbia University Student Carries Rape Protest Mattress to Graduation," *Guardian*, May 19, 2015, https://www.theguardian .com/us-news/2015/may/19/columbia-university-emma-sulkowicz-mattress -graduation.

8. For a longer discussion of utilitarianism and empire, see Ahmed (2019). This is a quote from James Mill ([1818] 1997, 74), who wrote many volumes of books about India without visiting India.

9. For a report on the destruction of papers in Britain's colonial archives, see Ian Cobain, Owen Bowcott, and Richard Norton-Taylor, "Britain Destroyed Records of Colonial Crimes," *Guardian*, April 17, 2012, https://www .theguardian.com/uk/2012/apr/18/britain-destroyed-records-colonial-crimes.

10. *Whisper networks* is a term used to convey how women privately shared with each other information about harassers and harassment. Even if sharing information happened in private (privacy can be about safety), whisper networks can also be understood as creating a feminist public. New technologies have enabled these networks to become public in a different way because of how information can be made public (in the form of lists of harassers in

different sectors, for example). On the implications of whisper networks and other informal channels for communicating complaints used in the #MeToo movement for the development of better formal complaints procedures, see Turkheimer (2019). For discussion of how whisper networks went public in the #MeToo movement, see Brunner and Partlow-Lefevre (2020).

11. I also reference this case in chapter 5, where I discuss how their action was described as a lynching.

12. For important discussions on what experiences of leaving posts or the academy have to teach us about the academy, see De La Cruz, Hayes, and Sapra (2020) and Dutt-Ballerstadt (2020).

13. The website for the Pansy Project is http://www.thepansyproject.com /about. See also the Queering the Map project, accessed June 8, 2020, https:// www.queeringthemap.com/. With thanks to Paul Harfleet and Lucas LaRo- chelle for creative inspirations.

14. For an excellent discussion of this article, see Bilge (2020a). With thanks to Sirma Bilge for her work and inspiration.

15. Joan Anim-Addo (1998) uses this motif of "another doorway" in an article about how Black women, as members of the Caribbean Women Writer's Alliance (cwwa), "undertook a rewriting of the museum experience so as to insert a hitherto largely absent presence, that of the Black woman, into the museum context" (93). As a group they organized workshops at Horniman, their local museum in South East London. One of these workshops was led by the Canadian writer and poet M. NourbeSe Philip, whom Anim-Addo cites with care in her piece. Those doorways become a Black feminist connection across time and space, a diasporic connection. Anim-Addo explains the use of the doorway motif as follows: "The original line of thinking was cognisant of doorposts signifying home where women are to be found even if nowhere else, despite the refusal on the part of collectors, exhibitors, or curators to render such presence visible" (94). She explains that the poem was inspired by carved wooden door panels from southeastern Nigeria and are "believed to have come from a Yakü elder or chief" (104). The story of how the door panels got into the museum (like so many stories of objects in museums) is an imperial story: they were collected and donated by a British anthropologist and Africanist and his wife. The poem was included in an anthology edited by Anim-Addo also titled *Another Doorway* (1999). With thanks to Joan Anim-Addo for the inspiration of her work and for helping to create a space for Black feminism in the British academy and beyond.

16. "Reader, I inherited him" is a play on the famous sentence from *Jane Eyre*, "Reader, I married him," as well as an allusion to how a vice chancellor justified keeping the name of a eugenicist on a building by saying, "My only defense is I inherited him." For a discussion of the latter speech act, see Ahmed (2019, ch. 4).

REFERENCES

Adebisi, Foluke. 2020. "Decolonization Is Not about Ticking a Box: It Must Disrupt." *Critical Legal Thinking*, March 12. https://criticallegalthinking.com/2020/03/12/decolonisation-is-not-about-ticking-a-box/.

Ahmed, Sara. 2000. *Strange Encounters: Embodied Others in Post-Coloniality*. London: Routledge.

Ahmed, Sara. 2004. "Declarations of Whiteness: The Non-Performativity of Anti-Racism." *borderlands* 3, no. 2: n.p.

Ahmed, Sara. 2006. *Queer Phenomenology: Orientations, Objects, Others*. Durham, NC: Duke University Press.

Ahmed, Sara. 2010. *The Promise of Happiness*. Durham, NC: Duke University Press.

Ahmed, Sara. 2012. *On Being Included: Racism and Diversity in Institutional Life*. Durham, NC: Duke University Press.

Ahmed, Sara. 2014. *Willful Subjects*. Durham, NC: Duke University Press.

Ahmed, Sara. 2017. *Living a Feminist Life*. Durham, NC: Duke University Press.

Ahmed, Sara. 2019. *What's the Use? On the Uses of Use*. Durham, NC: Duke University Press.

Ahmed, Sara, and Jackie Stacey. 2001. "Testimonial Cultures." *Cultural Values* 5, no. 1. https://doi.org/10.1080/14797580109367217.

Alexander, M. Jacqui. 2006. *Pedagogies of Crossing: Meditations on Feminism, Sexual Politics, Memory, and the Sacred*. Durham, NC: Duke University Press.

Anim-Addo, Joan. 1998. "Another Doorway: Black Women Writing the Museum Experience." *Journal of Museum Ethnography*, no. 10: 94–104.

Anim-Addo, Joan, ed. 1999. *Another Doorway: Visible inside the Museum*. London: Mango.

Arday, Jason, and Heidi Mirza, eds. 2018. *Dismantling Race in Higher Education: Racism, Whiteness and Decolonising the Academy*. London: Palgrave.

Bacchi, Carol. 1998. "Changing the Harassment Agenda." In *Gender and Institutions: Welfare, Work and Citizenship*, edited by Moira Gatens and Alison Mackinnon, 75–89. Cambridge: Cambridge University Press.

Baker, Carrie N. 2008. *The Women's Movement against Sexual Harassment.* Cambridge: Cambridge University Press.

Beemyn, Genny, ed. 2019. *Trans People in Higher Education.* Albany: State University of New York Press.

Benoit, Anne C., Joann S. Olson, and Carrie Johnson, eds. 2019. *Leaps of Faith: Stories from Working-Class Scholars.* Charlotte, NC: Information Age.

Berlant, Lauren. 2008. *The Female Complaint: The Unfinished Business of Sentimentality in American Culture.* Durham, NC: Duke University Press.

Bhambra, Gurminder K., Dalia Gebrial, and Kerem Nişancıoğlu, eds. 2018. *Decolonizing the University.* London: Pluto.

Bhopal, Kalwant. 2015. *The Experience of Black and Minority Ethnic Academics.* London: Routledge.

Bhopal, Kalwant, and Holly Henderson. 2019. "Gender versus Race: Competing Inequalities in Higher Education in the UK." *Educational Review*, August 1. https://www.tandfonline.com/doi/full/10.1080/00131911.2019.1642305.

Bhopal, Kalwant, and Clare Pitkin. 2020. "'Same Old Story, Just a Different Policy': Race and Policy Making in Higher Education in the UK." *Race, Ethnicity and Education* 23, no. 4: n.p.

Bilge, Sirma. 2013. "Saving Intersectionality from Feminist Intersectionality Studies." *Du Bois Review: Social Science Research on Race* 10, no. 2: 405–24.

Bilge, Sirma. 2020a. "The Fungibility of Intersectionality: An Afropessimist Reading." *Ethnic and Racial Studies*, March 23. https://www.tandfonline.com/doi/abs/10.1080/01419870.2020.1740289.

Bilge, Sirma. 2020b. "We've Joined the Table but We're Still on the Menu: Click-baiting Diversity in Today's University." In *Routledge Handbook of Contemporary Racisms*, edited by John Solomos, 317–31. London: Routledge.

Binns, Carole. 2019. *Experiences of Academics from a Working-Class Heritage.* Cambridge: Cambridge University Press.

Brah, Avtar. 1996. *Cartographies of Diaspora: Contesting Identities.* London: Routledge.

Brand, Dionne. 2001. *The Map to the Door of No Return.* Toronto: Vintage Canada.

Brant, Clare, and Yun Lee Too, eds. 1994. *Rethinking Sexual Harassment.* London: Sage.

Brewer, Rose M. 1993. "Theorizing Race, Class and Gender: The New Scholarship of Black Feminist Intellectuals and Black Women's Labor." In *Theorizing Black Feminisms: The Visionary Pragmatism of Black Women*, edited by Stanlie Myrise James and Abena P. A. Busia, 13–30. London: Routledge.

Brunner, Elizabeth, and Sarah Partlow-Lefevre. 2020. "#Metoo as Networked Collective: Examining Consciousness-Raising on Wild Public Networks." *Communication and Critical/Cultural Studies* 17, no. 2. https://doi.org/10.1080/14791420.2020.1750043.

Bryan, Beverley, Stella Dadzie, and Suzanne Scafe. (1985) 2018. *Heart of the Race: Black Women's Lives in Britain.* 2nd edition. London: Verso.

Bull, Anna, and Rachel Rye. 2018. "Silencing Students: Institutional Responses to Staff Sexual Misconduct in Higher Education." *1752*, September. https://1752group.com/sexual-misconduct-research-silencing-students/.

Butler, Judith. 1993. *Bodies That Matter: On the Discursive Limits of "Sex."* London: Routledge.

Cary, Lorene. 1991. *Black Ice.* New York: Random House.

Chandrashekar, Karuna, Kimberly Lacroix, and Sabah Siddiqui, eds. 2018. "Sex and Power in the Academy." Special issue, *Annual Review of Critical Psychology* 15.

Chang, Julia H. 2020. "Spectacular Bodies: Racism, Pregnancy, and the Code of Silence in Academe." In *Presumed Incompetent II: Race, Class, Power, and Resistance of Women in Academia*, edited by Yolande Flores Niemann, Gabriella Gutiérrz y Muhs, and Carmen G. González, 259–68. Logan: Utah State University Press.

Chatterjee, Piya, and Sunaina Maira, eds. 2014. *The Imperial University: Academic Repression and Scholarly Dissent.* Minneapolis: University of Minnesota Press.

Collins, Patricia Hill. (1990) 2000. *Black Feminist Thought: Knowledge, Consciousness and the Politics of Empowerment.* London: Routledge.

Collins, Patricia Hill, and Sirma Bilge. 2016. *Intersectionality: Key Concepts.* Cambridge: Polity.

Coulthard, Glen Sean. 2004. *Red Skins, White Masks: Rejecting the Colonial Politics of Recognition.* Minneapolis: University of Minnesota Press.

Crenshaw, Kimberlé. 1989. "Demarginalizing the Intersection of Race and Sex: A Black Feminist Politics of Antidiscrimination Doctrine, Feminist Theory and Anti-Racist Politics." *University of Chicago Legal Forum*, 139–67.

Crenshaw, Kimberlé. 1993. "Whose Story Is It Anyway? Feminist and Anti-Racist Appropriations of Anita Hill." In *Race-ing Justice, Engendering Power: Essays on Anita Hill, Clarence Thomas and the Construction of Social Reality*, edited by Toni Morrison, 402–40. London: Chatto and Windus.

Cuádraz, Gloria Holguín, and Lynet Uttal. 1999. "Intersectionality and In-Depth Interviews: Methodological Strategies for Analysing Race, Class and Gender." *Race, Gender and Class Journal* 6, no. 3: 156–58.

Daly, Mary. 1978. *Gynecology: The Metaethics of Radical Feminism.* Boston: Beacon.

Davis, Angela Y. 2016. *Freedom Is a Constant Struggle.* Chicago: Haymarket Books.

De La Cruz, Sonia, Nini Hayes, and Sonalini Sapra. 2020. "Labouring in Line with Our Values: Lessons Learned in the Struggle to Unionize." In *Feminist Responses to the Neoliberalisation of the University: From Surviving to Thriving*, edited by Abby Palko, Jamie Sachman, and Sonalini Sapra, 85–110. London: Lexington Books.

Dolmage, Jay. 2017. *Academic Ableism: Disability and Higher Education*. Ann Arbor: University of Michigan Press.

Douglas, Mary. (1966) 1994. *Purity and Danger: An Analysis of the Concepts of Pollution and Taboo*. London: Routledge.

Doyle, Jennifer. 2015. *Campus Sex, Campus Security*. Cambridge, MA: MIT Press.

Dua, Enakshi. 2009. "On the Effectiveness of Anti-Racist Politics at Canadian Universities." In *Racism in the Canadian University: Demanding Social Justice, Inclusion and Equity*, edited by Francis Henry and Carol Taylor, 160–96. Toronto: University of Toronto Press.

Dutt-Ballerstadt, Reshmi. 2020. "In Our Own Words: Institutional Betrayals." *Inside Higher Ed*, March 6. https://www.insidehighered.com/advice/2020/03/06/underrepresented-faculty-members-share-real-reasons-they-have-left-various.

Dziech, Billie Wright, and Michael W. Hawkins, eds. 2011. *Sexual Harassment and Higher Education: Reflections and New Perspectives*. New York: Routledge.

Essed, Philomena. 1991. *Understanding Everyday Racism: An Interdisciplinary Theory*. London: Sage.

Essed, Philomena. 1996. *Diversity: Gender, Color, and Culture*. Translated by Rita Gircour. Amherst: University of Massachusetts Press.

Felman, Shoshana. 1992. "Education and Crisis, or the Vicissitudes of Teaching." In Shoshana Felman and Dori Laub, *Testimony: Crises of Witnessing in Literature, Psychoanalysis, and History*, 1–26. New York: Routledge.

Ferguson, Roderick A. 2012. *The Reorder of Things: The University and Its Pedagogies of Minority Difference*. Minneapolis: University of Minnesota Press.

Ferguson, Roderick A. 2017. *We Demand: The University and Student Protests*. Oakland: University of California Press.

Fleming, Crystal. 2018. *How to Be Less Stupid about Race*. Boston: Beacon.

Frankenberg, Ruth, and Lata Mani. 1993. "Crosscurrents, Crosstalk: Race, 'Post-Coloniality' and the Politics of Location." *Cultural Studies* 7, no. 2: 292–310.

Franklin, Sarah. 2015. "Sexism as a Means of Reproduction." *New Formations* 86: 14–33.

Freeman, Elizabeth. 2010. *Time Binds: Queer Temporalities, Queer Histories*. Durham, NC: Duke University Press.

Freire, Paulo. (1970) 2000. *Pedagogy of the Oppressed*. Translated by Myra Bergman Ramos. New York: Continuum.

Frye, Marilyn. 1983. *The Politics of Reality: Essays in Feminist Theory*. Trumansburg, NY: Crossing.

Fujiwara, Lynn. 2020. "Racial Harm in a Predominantly White Liberal University: An Institutional Autoethnography of White Fragility." In *Presumed Incompetent II: Race, Class, Power, and Resistance of Women in Academia*, edited by Yolande Flores Niemann, Gabriella Gutiérrz y Muhs, and Carmen G. González, 101–16. Logan: Utah State University Press.

Gabriel, Deborah, and Shirley Anne Tate, eds. 2017. *Inside the Ivory Tower: Narratives of Women of Colour Surviving and Thriving in British Academia*. London: IOE Press.

Garland-Thomson, Rosemarie. 2011. "Misfits: A Feminist Materialist Disability Concept." *Hypatia: A Journal of Feminist Philosophy* 26, no. 3: 591–609.

Garland-Thomson, Rosemarie. 2014. "The Story of My Work: How I Became Disabled." *Disability Studies Quarterly* 34, no. 2: n.p.

Gentleman, Amelia. 2019. *The Windrush Betrayal: Exposing the Hostile Environment*. London: Guardian Faber.

Gilmour, Leigh. 2016. *Tainted Witness: Why We Doubt What Women Say about Their Lives*. New York: Columbia University Press.

Goodfellow, Maya. 2019. *The Hostile Environment: How Immigrants Become Scapegoats*. London: Verso.

Gordon, Avery. (1997) 2008. *Ghostly Matters: Haunting and the Sociological Imagination*. 2nd edition. Minneapolis: University of Minnesota Press.

Gray-Rosendale, Laura A., ed. 2020. *Me Too, Feminist Theory and Surviving Sexual Violence in the Academy*. London: Lexington Books.

Green, Adrienne, and Alia Wong. 2015. "LGBT Students and Campus Sexual Assault." *Atlantic*, September 22. https://www.theatlantic.com/education /archive/2015/09/campus-sexual-assault-lgbt-students/406684/.

Green, Barbara. 2017. *Feminist Periodicals and Daily Life: Women and Modernity in British Culture*. London: Macmillan.

Grimm, Jacob, and Wilhelm Grimm. 1884. *Household Tales*, vol. 2. Translated by Margaret Hunt. London: George Bell.

Grogan, Erin. 2020. "Chronology." In *Cambridge Companion to Queer Studies*, edited by Siobhan Sommerville, xv–xxiv. Cambridge: Cambridge University Press.

Gumbs, Alexis Pauline. 2016. *Spill: Scenes of Black Feminist Fugitivity*. Durham, NC: Duke University Press.

Gunaratnam, Yasmin. 2003. *Researching "Race" and Ethnicity: Methods, Knowledge and Power*. London: Sage.

Halberstam, Jack. 2005. *In a Queer Time and Space*. Durham, NC: Duke University Press.

Halberstam, Jack. 2011. *The Queer Art of Failure*. Durham, NC: Duke University Press.

Hall, Radclyffe. (1928) 1982. *The Well of Loneliness*. London: Virago.

Hamad, Ruby. 2019. *White Tears, Brown Scars: How White Feminism Betrays Women of Colour.* Melbourne: Melbourne University Press.

Hampton, Rosalind. 2020. *Black Racialization and Resistance in an Elite University.* Toronto: University of Toronto Press.

Hamraie, Aimi. 2017. *Building Access: Universal Design and the Politics of Disability.* Minneapolis: University of Minnesota Press.

Hartman, Saidiya. 2019. *Wayward Lives, Beautiful Experiments: Intimate Histories of Social Upheaval.* London: Serpent's Tail.

Hey, Valerie. 2003. "Joining the Club? Academic and Working-Class Femininities." *Gender and Education* 15, no. 3. https://www.tandfonline.com/doi/abs/10.1080/09540250303863.

Holland, Sharon Patricia. 2012. *The Erotic Life of Racism.* Durham, NC: Duke University Press.

hooks, bell. 2000. *Feminist Theory: From Margin to Centre.* London: Pluto.

Inckle, Kay. 2018. "Unreasonable Adjustments: The Additional Unpaid Labour of Academics with Disabilities." *Disability and Society* 33, no. 8: 1372–76.

Joseph-Salisbury, Remi. 2019. "Institutionalised Whiteness, Racial Microaggressions and Black Bodies Out of Place in Higher Education." *Whiteness and Education* 4, no. 1. https://www.tandfonline.com/doi/full/10.1080/23793406.2019.1620629.

Kamaloni, Sunshine. 2019. *Understanding Racism in a Post-Racial World: Visible Invisibilities.* London: Palgrave Macmillan.

Khoo, Tseen, James Burford, Emily Henderson, Helena Liu, and Z. Nicolazzo. 2020. "Not Getting Over It: The Impact of Sara Ahmed's Work in the Field of Critical University Studies." *Journal of Intercultural Studies* (December). https://www.tandfonline.com/doi/full/10.1080/07256868.2020.1859209.

Kupenda, Angela Mae. 2007. "Facing Down the Spooks." In *Presumed Incompetent: The Intersections of Race and Class for Women in Academia,* edited by Gabriella Gutiérrez y Muhs, Yolanda Flores Niemann, Camren G. González, and Angela P. Harris, 20–28. Boulder: University Press of Colorado.

Lentin, Alana 2020. *Why Race Still Matters.* Cambridge: Polity.

Lewis, Gail. 2000. *"Race," Gender, Social Welfare: Encounters in a Postcolonial Society.* Cambridge: Polity.

Lewis, Gail. 2019. "'Where Might We Go If We Dare': Moving beyond the 'Thick, Suffocating Fog of Whiteness' in Feminism." Interview with Clare Hemmings. *Feminist Theory* 20, no. 4: 405–21.

Lorde, Audre. 1978. *The Black Unicorn.* New York: Norton.

Lorde, Audre. 1981. "Interview with Adrienne Rich." *Signs* 6, no. 4: 713–16.

Lorde, Audre. 1984. *Sister Outsider: Essays and Speeches.* Trumansburg, NY: Crossing.

Lorde, Audre. 1988. *A Burst of Light: Essays.* Ithaca, NY: Firebrand Books.

Love, Heather. 2007. *Feeling Backward: Loss and the Politics of Queer History.* Cambridge, MA: Harvard University Press.

Maguire, Mike, and Clare Corbett. 1991. *A Study of the Police Complaints System.* London: HMSO.

McCallum, E. L., and Mikko Tuhkanen, eds. 2011. *Queer Times, Queer Becomings.* Albany: State University of New York Press.

McClintock, Anne. 2017. "Who's Afraid of Title IX?" *Jacobin*, October 24. https://www.jacobinmag.com/2017/10/title-ix-betsy-devos-doe-colleges-assault-dear-colleague.

Mikics, David. 2010. *A New Handbook of Literary Terms.* New Haven, CT: Yale University Press.

Mill, James. (1818) 1997. *History of British India.* London: Routledge.

Mirza, Heidi. 2017. "'One in a Million': A Journey of a Post-Colonial Woman of Colour in the White Academy." In *Inside the Ivory Tower: Narratives of Women of Colour Surviving and Thriving in British Academia*, edited by Deborah Gabriel and Shirley Anne Tate, 39–53. London: IOE Press.

Mohanty, Chandra Talpade. 2003. *Feminism without Borders: Decolonizing Theory, Practicing Solidarity.* Durham, NC: Duke University Press.

Moreton-Robinson, Aileen. 2015. *The White Possessive: Property, Power, and Indigenous Sovereignty.* Minneapolis: University of Minnesota Press.

Mukandi, Bryan, and Chelsea Bond. 2019. "'Good in the Hood' or 'Burn It Down'? Reconciling Black Presence in the Academy." *Journal of Intercultural Studies* 40, no. 2: 254–68.

Mulcahy, Linda. 2003. *Disputing Doctors: The Socio-Legal Framework for Complaints.* Maidenhead, UK: Open University Press.

Nash, Jennifer C. 2018. *Black Feminism Reimagined: After Intersectionality.* Durham, NC: Duke University Press.

Nash, Meredith, Ruby Grant, Li-Min Lee, Ariadna Martiniz-Marrades, and Tania Winzenberg. 2020. "An Exploration of Perceptions of Gender Equity among SAGE Athena SWAN Self-Assessment Team Members in a Regional Australian University." *Higher Education and Development*, March 23. https://www.tandfonline.com/doi/full/10.1080/07294360.2020.1737657.

Nicolazzo, Z. 2016. *Trans* in College: Transgender Students' Strategies for Navigating Campus.* Sterling, VA: Stylus.

Nicoll, Fiona. 2004a. "'Are You Calling Me a Racist?': Teaching Critical Whiteness Theory in Indigenous Sovereignty." *borderlands* 3, no. 2: n.p.

Nicoll, Fiona. 2004b. "Reconciliation in and out of Perspective: White Knowing, Seeing, Curating and Being at Home in and against Indigenous Sovereignty." In *Whitening Race: Essays in Social and Cultural Criticism*, edited by Aileen Moreton-Robinson, 17–31. Canberra: Aboriginal Studies Press.

Olufemi, Lola. 2020. *Feminism Interrupted: Disrupting Power.* London: Pluto.

Olufemi, Lola, Odelia Younge, Waithera Sebatindira, and Suhaiymah Manzoor-Khan, eds. 2019. *A Fly Girl's Guide to University: Being a Woman of Colour at Cambridge and Other Institutions of Power and Elitism.* Birmingham, UK: Verve Poetry Press.

Page, Tiffany, Anna Bull, and Emma Chapman. 2019. "Making Power Visible: 'Slow Activism' to Address Staff Misconduct in Higher Education." *Violence against Women* 5, no. 11: 1309–30.

Palko, Abby, Jamie Wagman, and Sonalini Sapra, eds. 2020. *Feminist Responses to the Neoliberalisation of the University: From Surviving to Thriving.* London: Lexington Books.

Paludi, Michele Antoinette, ed. 1990. *Sexual Harassment at College Campuses: Abusing the Ivory Power.* Albany: State University of New York Press.

Pereira, Maria Do Mar. 2017. *Power, Knowledge and Feminist Scholarship: An Ethnography of Academia.* London: Routledge.

Phipps, Alison. 2018. "Reckoning Up: Sexual Harassment and Violence in the Neoliberal University." *Gender and Education,* June 6. https://www.tandfonline.com/doi/full/10.1080/09540253.2018.1482413.

Phipps, Alison. 2020. *Me, Not You: The Trouble with Mainstream Feminism.* Manchester: Manchester University Press.

Phoenix, Ann, and Elaine Bauer. 2012. "Psychosocial Intersections: Contextualising the Accounts of Adults Who Grew Up in Visibly Ethnically Different Households." *European Journal of Women's Studies,* November 30. https://journals.sagepub.com/doi/10.1177/1350506812455994.

Pierce, Ruth, and Charikleia Tzanakou. 2018. "Moderate Feminism within or against the Neoliberal University? The Example of Athena SWAN." *Gender, Work and Organization* 26, no. 8: 1190–211.

Price, Margaret. 2011. *Mad at School: Rhetorics of Mental Disability and Academic Life.* Ann Arbor: University of Michigan Press.

Puwar, Nirmal. 2004. *Space Invaders: Race, Gender and Bodies Out of Place.* Oxford: Berg.

Qureshi, Sadiah. 2019. "A Manifesto for Survival." In *To Exist Is to Resist: Black Feminism in Europe,* edited by Akwugo Emejulu and Francesca Sobande, 205–18. London: Pluto.

Reay, Diane. 2018. "Working-Class Educational Transitions to University: The Limits of Success." *European Journal of Education,* September 24. https://onlinelibrary.wiley.com/doi/abs/10.1111/ejed.12298.

Rentschler, Carrie. 2018. "#Metoo and Student Activism against Sexual Violence." *Communication, Culture and Critique* 11, no. 3: 503–7.

Rivers, Ian. 2016. "Homophobic and Transphobic Bullying at Universities." In *Bullying among University Students: Cross-National Perspectives,* edited by Helen Cowie and Carrie Anne Myers, 48–60. Oxford: Routledge.

Rollack, Nicola. 2018. "The Heart of Whiteness: Racial Gesture Politics, Equity, Higher Education." In *Dismantling Race in Higher Education,* edited by Jason Arday and Heidi Mirza, 313–30. London: Palgrave Macmillan.

Rollack, Nicola. 2019. *Staying Power: The Career Experiences and Strategies of UK Black Female Professors*. UCU Report. https://nicolarollock.com/black-female-profs.

Said, Edward. 1978. *Orientalism*. London: Routledge.

Salamon, Gayle. 2018. *The Life and Death of Latisha King: A Critical Phenomenology of Transphobia*. New York: New York University Press.

Sedgwick, Eve Kosofsky. 1985. *Between Men: Literature and Homosocial Desire*. New York: Columbia University Press.

Sharpe, Christina. 2016. *In the Wake: On Blackness and Being*. Durham, NC: Duke University Press.

Sian, Katy. 2019. *Navigating Institutional Racism in British Universities*. London: Palgrave Macmillan.

Skeggs, Beverley. 1995. "Women's Studies in the 1990s: Entitlement Cultures and Institutional Constraints." *Women's Studies International Forum* 18, no. 4: 475–85.

Skeggs, Beverley. 1997. *Formations of Class and Gender: Becoming Respectable*. London: Sage.

Skeggs, Beverley. 2004. *Class, Self, Culture*. London: Routledge.

Smith, Linda Tuhiawi. (1999) 2012. *Decolonizing Methodologies: Research and Indigenous Peoples*. London: Zed.

Smith, Malinda. 2010. "Gender, Whiteness, and 'Other Others' in the Academy." In *States of Race: Critical Race Feminism for the 21st Century*, edited by Sherene Razack, Malinda Smith, and Sunera Thobani, 23–35. Toronto: Between the Lines.

Sulfaro, Valerie A., and Rebecca Gill. 2020. "Title IX: Help or Hindrance?" In *Me Too, Political Science*, edited by Nadia Brown, 204–27. Oxford: Routledge.

Swan, Elaine. 2010. "Commodity Diversity: Smiling Faces as a Strategy of Containment." *Organization* 17, no. 1: 77–100.

Tamale, Sylvia. 2020. *Decolonization and Afro-Feminism*. Ottawa: Daraju.

Tate, Shirley Anne. 2017. "How Do You Feel? 'Well-Being' as a Deracinated Strategic Goal in UK Universities." In *Inside the Ivory Tower: Narratives of Women of Colour Surviving and Thriving in British Academia*, edited by Deborah Gabriel and Shirley Anne Tate, 54–66. London: IOE Press.

Taylor, Yvette. 2018. "Navigating the Emotional Landscapes of Academia: Queer Encounters." In *Feeling Academic in the Neoliberal University*, edited by Yvette Taylor and Kinneret Lahad, 61–86. London: Palgrave Macmillan.

Taylor, Yvette, and Kinneret Lahad, eds. 2018. *Feeling Academic in the Neoliberal University*. London: Palgrave Macmillan.

Thompson, Meaghan. 2019. "Digital Activism and Story Telling: Exploring the Radical Potential of the #MeToo Movement." In *Resistance in Pop Culture and Contemporary Culture*, edited by Leisa Clark, Amanda Firestone, and Mary Pharr, 21–32. Jefferson, NC: McFarland.

Todd, Zoe. 2016. "An Indigenous Feminist's Take on the Ontological Turn: 'Ontology' Is Just Another Word for Colonialism." *Journal of Historical Sociology* 29, no. 1: 4–22.

Tuck, Eve, and C. Ree. 2013. "A Glossary of Haunting." In *A Handbook of Auto-Ethnography*, edited by Stacey Holman Jones, Tony E. Adams, and Carolyn Ellis, 639–58. Walnut Creek, CA: Left Coast.

Tuck, Eve, and Kayne Wayne Yang. 2012. "Decolonization Is Not a Metaphor." *Decolonization: Indigeneity, Education and Society* 1, no. 1: 1–40.

Turkheimer, Deborah. 2019. "Unofficial Reporting in the #MeToo Era." *University of Chicago Legal Forum*, article 10. https://chicagounbound.uchicago.edu/uclf/vol2019/iss1/10.

Walcott, Rinaldo. 2019. "The End of Diversity." *Public Culture* 31, no. 2: 393–418.

Washick, Bonnie. 2020. "Complaint and the World-Building Politics of Feminist Moderation." *Signs* 45, no. 3: 555–80.

Wekker, Gloria. 2016. *White Innocence: Paradoxes of Colonialism and Race.* Durham, NC: Duke University Press.

West, Carolyn M. 2010. "Resistance as Recovery: Winning a Sexual Harassment Complaint." In *African Americans Doing Feminism: Putting Theory into Everyday Practice*, edited by Aaronette M. White, 175–88. New York: State University of New York Press.

Whitley, Leila. 2020. "How Contingent Faculty Contracts Contribute to Sexual Violence on Campus." Gender Policy Report, University of Minnesota, June 16. https://genderpolicyreport.umn.edu/how-contingent-faculty-contracts-contribute-to-sexual-violence-on-campus/.

Whitley, Leila. Forthcoming. "The Displacement of Harm." *Signs.*

Whitley, Leila, and Tiffany Page. 2015. "Sexism at the Centre: Locating the Problem of Sexual Harassment." *New Formations* 86: 34–53.

Williams, Patricia. 1991. *The Alchemy of Race and Rights.* Cambridge, MA: Harvard University Press.

Wilson, Amrit. (1976) 2000. "It Is Not like Asian Ladies to Answer Back." In *Writing Black Britain: An Interdisciplinary Anthology 1948–1988*, edited by James Proctor, 184–92. Manchester: Manchester University Press.

Wilson, Amrit. (1978) 2018. *Finding a Voice: Asian Women in Britain.* Cantley, Québec: Daraja.

Yergeau, Melanie. 2017. *Authoring Autism: On Rhetoric and Neurological Queerness.* Durham, NC: Duke University Press.

INDEX

175–219, 318n5, 333n12; and the occupa-
tion of space, 137–39, 149, 172, 338n11;
power and the holding of, 220–56,
333n9, 336n4, 337nn6–7; work on,
331n2, 332n1, 338n10, 341n15
Double-Doors (Whiteread), 331n2
Douglas, Mary, 213
Doyle, Jennifer, 168, 314n29
Dua, Enakshi, 314n29
Durkheim, Émile, 330n22

emotional labor, 200, 228, 234–35
Equality Act of 2010 (UK), 50, 59, 169,
284
Equality and Human Rights Commis-
sion, 325n16
Equality Law (UK), 325n16
erasure, 89, 93, 171, 206–7, 232, 247.
See also blanking; silence and silencing
Essed, Philomena, 22

fatalism, 73–76, 199, 233, 310, 321n3, 323n4
Felman, Shoshana, 13
feminism: the association between
complaint and, 117, 225, 262, 283, 295,
314n23; Black, 1–4, 23, 139, 287, 303,
317n38, 341n15; and the feminist ear,
3–9, 17, 23; and feminist killjoys, 1, 67,
116, 195, 205, 320n20; and institutions,
217–18, 336n26; liberal white, 254,
315n30, 329n17; and neoliberalism,
334nn16–17; and the occupation of
space, 139, 326n8; and the stopping of
complaints, 63–68, 74, 104–5, 109–12,
204–9, 334n19; vilification of, 131–32,
150–51, 167, 198–99, 206, 215, 322n1.
See also gender; sexism
files: complainers as, 108, 117–18, 147–48,
152; and the disappearance and stopping of complaints, 73, 84, 90–96, 184,
248, 276, 293; and the emergence of
complaints, 291–99; and institutional
mechanics, 33–40, 44, 211, 337n8; and
the storage of complaint, 15, 20, 298
Fleming, Crystal, 162
Floyd, George, 316n35, 317n1
formal complaints, 4, 19–21, 102, 340n10;
backlash against, 143–44, 159, 202, 226,

334n19; and collectivity and complaint
activism, 280–89, 296; as damage control, 213–16; and institutional doors,
223–26, 241; and institutional mechanics, 5, 27, 30–40, 43–64, 203, 265–66;
reaching, 104, 128–30, 164, 168, 187,
312n9, 327n11; stopping, 71–72, 75–78,
85, 88–96, 125, 183–84, 196, 301, 323n4.
See also complaints
Frankenberg, Ruth, 221
Franklin, Sarah, 165, 171, 330n22
Freire, Paulo, 148
Frye, Marilyn, 168
Fujiwara, Lynn, 326n5

gaps, 28–67, 70–71, 92, 112, 115
Garcia Giribet, Andrea, 315n30
Garland-Thomson, Rosemarie, 140
gender, 4, 147, 239–40, 303–7, 314n23,
320n19, 321n3, 337n7. *See also* femi-
nism; sexism; transphobia
gender studies, 225–26
Gill, Rebecca, 314n29
Gilmour, Leigh, 313n16
Gordon, Avery, 305–6
Gorris, Marleen, 4
graveyards, 37, 208, 259, 276, 306–9.
See also burying
Grogan, Erin, 101
grooming, 112, 191–93, 214, 266.
See also sexual assault, harassment,
and misconduct
Guardian (periodical), 279
Guerrilla Girls, 289
Gumbs, Alexis Pauline, 18
Gunaratnam, Yasmin, 312n10

hag figure, 166–67, 330n24
Halls, Radclyffe, 331n1
Hampton, Rosalind, 22
Hamraie, Aimi, 175
harassment, 113–16, 142, 154, 235, 323n7,
325n16; and collectivity, 263, 279–80,
340n10; and countercomplaints, 129–30,
150, 168–70, 327n9, 335n20; cultures of,
7, 115, 122–23, 191–201, 213–15, 262–69;
doors and institutional violence and,
183–219, 242; and the emergence

Lorde, Audre, 50, 139, 177, 217, 284, 300, 304–5, 336n26
Love, Heather, 101

Mani, Lata, 221, 242
Manzoor-Khan, Suhaiymah, 23
master's tools metaphor, 50, 139, 177, 253, 284, 305, 318n6, 333n14, 336n26
"Master's Tools Will Never Dismantle the Master's House, The" (Lorde), 139
Mattress Performance (Carry That Weight) (Sulkowicz), 290
May, Theresa, 154
McClintock, Anne, 23, 316n34
#MeToo movement, 22, 191, 206, 280, 315n30, 340n10
Mill, James, 340n8
Mirza, Heidi, 22, 156, 243
misfitting, 140–47, 158. *See also* ableism
Mohanty, Chandra Talpade, 22
Moreton-Robinson, Aileen, 308
Morrison, Toni, 306

NDAS. *See* nondisclosure agreements
neoliberalism, 202–4, 333–34nn15–17
nods, 79–86, 186, 249, 321n8. *See also* nonperformativity; performativity
nondisclosure agreements (NDAS), 10, 15, 99. *See also* silence and silencing
nonperformativity, 30, 317n1; and blanking and nodding, 80, 85, 186; and diversity, 171, 317n1; policies and procedures and, 28–30, 47–48, 52, 56, 65, 68, 153–54. *See also* nods; performativity
nonreproductive labor, 163–72, 225

occupation of space and time, 137–74, 194–95, 211–12, 245–46, 284, 308, 329n17
Office of the Independent Adjudicator for Higher Education, 95, 322n14
Olufemi, Lola, 23
On Being Included (Ahmed), 27, 52, 59, 87, 317n1, 322n1

Page, Tiffany, 23, 26, 110, 147, 258, 261–73, 285
performativity, 84–86, 199, 317n1, 319n9. *See also* nods; nonperformativity

phenomenology of the institution, complaint as, 19, 41, 279
Philip, M. NourbeSe, 303, 341n15
Phipps, Alison, 315n30
politicization through complaint. *See* complaints
positive duty, 59–68, 86, 98–99, 143, 198
positive profiles, 113, 186, 206, 229. *See also* collegiality
power, 169, 287, 333n9; and complaint, 17, 24–25, 125, 202, 327n12, 336n4; and doors, 177, 220–56, 333n9, 336n4, 337nn6–7; and institutional mechanics, 7, 44–49, 326n8
precarity: in academia, 265, 269, 273; diversity and equity work and, 62, 157; situations of, 94–95, 106, 112–14, 229; and use in warnings, 73, 77, 222
privilege, 48–49, 146, 207, 234, 337n7
Promise of Happiness, The, 321n9, 331n1
promises, 225, 233, 336n3
promotions, 232–42, 253

qualified support, 74–75, 321n4
queerness: and coming out, 119, 291–92; and complaints, 101, 291, 298–301, 309; and diversity, 62, 66; and institutions, 43–44, 52, 326n6; and maps, 298–99; and misfitting, 158; and sexual assault and harassment, 182–83, 332n3; and temporality, 101, 322n2; and use, 137, 318n6
queer use, 137, 318n6
Question of Silence, A (film), 4, 87

Race Equality Charter (UK), 320n19
race studies, 151, 225–26
racism: and anti-Indigenous discrimination, 154–55, 172–73, 240–42, 245–47, 328n16; and doors, 176–77, 221, 240–55, 302; and feminism, 139, 254, 320n20, 329n17; and haunting, 303–8; and hearing and dismissal of complaint, 1–3, 16, 65, 79, 315n30, 327n12; and hostile environments, 154–62, 172–73, 317n1, 328n14; institutional complicity with, 23, 190, 200–201, 313n12, 319n9, 328n16, 329n20; and intersectionality,

CPSIA information can be obtained
at www.ICGtesting.com
Printed in the USA
LVHW012248030921
696896LV00002B/3

9 781478 017714